NIXON'S SUPER-SECRETARIES

Joseph V. Hughes Jr. and Holly O. Hughes Series on the Presidency and Leadership

James P. Pfiffner, General Editor

A list of all titles in this series is available at the end of the book.

NIXON'S SUPER-SECRETARIES

The Last Grand Presidential Reorganization Effort

Mordecai Lee

TEXAS A&M UNIVERSITY PRESS : COLLEGE STATION

Copyright © 2010 by Mordecai Lee
Manufactured in the United States of America
All rights reserved
First edition

This paper meets the requirements of
ANSI/NISO, Z39.48-1992
(Permanence of Paper).
Binding materials have been
chosen for durability.

LIBRARY OF CONGRESS CATALOGING-IN-PUBLICATION DATA

Lee, Mordecai, 1948–
Nixon's super-secretaries : the last grand presidential reorganization effort /
Mordecai Lee. — 1st ed.
p. cm. — (Joseph V. Hughes Jr. and Holly O. Hughes series on the presidency
and leadership)
Includes bibliographical references and index.
ISBN-13: 978-1-60344-179-7 (cloth : alk. paper)
ISBN-10: 1-60344-179-4 (cloth : alk. paper)
1. United States—Politics and government—1969–1974.
2. Presidents—United States—Staff—History—20th century.   3. Executive
departments—United States—Reorganization—History—20th century.
4. Cabinet officers—United States—History—20th century.   5. Executive power—
United States—History—20th century. 6. Nixon, Richard M. (Richard Milhous),
1913–1994.   7. Weinberger, Caspar W.   8. Lynn, James T., 1927–
9. Butz, Earl L. (Earl Lauer), 1909–2008.   I. Title.   II. Series: Joseph V. Hughes, Jr.,
and Holly O. Hughes series in the presidency and leadership studies.
E855.L44   2010
973.924—dc22
2010002448

In memory of my grandparents,

Sam and Frieda Levy and Shimen and Rose Kamesar.

Like so many Jewish Americans,

I am descended from immigrants

who were born in Eastern Europe

and came to the United States early

in the twentieth century,

hoping for a better life.

I know how proud of this book

they would have been

and that they would, yet again,

have thanked America

for the unparalleled opportunities

it gave them and their progeny.

CONTENTS

List of Figures   viii

List of Major Abbreviations   ix

Preface   xi

CHAPTERS

1. Introduction   1
2. Planning, November 1972–January 1973   27
3. Launch, January–February 1973   54
4. In Operation, January–April 1973   77
5. Counsellor for Human Resources Caspar Weinberger:
     The Super-Secretary as Assistant President   107
6. Counsellor for Community Development James Lynn:
     The Super-Secretary as Presidential Coordinator   133
7. Counsellor for Natural Resources Earl Butz:
     The Dutiful and Passive Super-Secretary   156
8. Demise, April–May 1973   180
9. Legacy and Significance   196

Notes   211

Bibliography   255

Index   261

LIST OF FIGURES

1. White House organization chart prepared for Nixon's second term,   59
2. President Nixon meeting with his counsellors,   81
3. Joint appearance of the counsellors on *Meet the Press*,   87

MAJOR ABBREVIATIONS

AP: Associated Press (news wire service)

BCA: Better Communities Act (title the Nixon administration used for legislation creating a special revenue sharing program to replace several categorical grants in the area of community development)

CD: community development

DC: Domestic Council (unit in EOP)

DCD: Department of Community Development (proposed)

DOD: Department of Defense

DOT: Department of Transportation

EOP: Executive Office of the President

FY: fiscal year (At the time of the events recounted here, a fiscal year began on July 1 and ended on June 30; FY1974, for example extended from July 1, 1973, to June 30, 1974.)

HEW: Department of Health, Education, and Welfare

HR: human resources (In current usage, the term denotes personnel management. However, the Nixon administration used the term to mean the human potential of citizens, such as could be achieved by improving their health, education, and welfare.)

HUD: Department of Housing and Urban Development

MD/LoC: Manuscript Division, Library of Congress, Washington, D.C.

NPL: Nixon Presidential Library (At the time of the archival research for this project, all of President Nixon's papers were at the National Archives II site in College Park, Maryland. After the completion of the field research, the collection was gradually moved to the Nixon Presidential Library in Yorba Linda, California.)

NR: natural resources

OEO: Office of Economic Opportunity (War on Poverty agency, a unit in EOP)

OEOB: Old Executive Office Building (Originally called the State-War-Navy Building, it is now known as the Eisenhower Executive Office Building, part of the White House complex.)

OMB: Office of Management and Budget (a unit in EOP, known as the
   Bureau of the Budget [BOB] from 1921 to 1970)
SMOF: Staff Member and Office Files
UPI: United Press International (news wire service)
USDA: U.S. Department of Agriculture
WHCF: White House Central Files
WHSF: White House Special Files

PREFACE

Sometimes, in life, one is just plain lucky. In late 1972, I had moved from Syracuse University to Washington, D.C., to conduct research for my dissertation and serve as a guest scholar at the Brookings Institution. I was interested in President Nixon's first-term effort to limit public relations (PR) in federal agencies (and a concomitant budgetary effort in Congress to do the same in the DOD). I was still unpacking when the president made a dramatic announcement on January 5, 1973. For his second term, he was going to reorganize the domestic side of the federal government, ignoring the fact that Congress had refused to approve his legislative proposals to do so during his first term. Now reelected by a wide margin and with an expansive view of presidential powers vis-à-vis Congress, Nixon was reorganizing the domestic bureaucracy *administratively*. He appointed three Cabinet secretaries to serve simultaneously as "counsellors to the president" for human resources, community development, and natural resources. He gave them offices in the White House complex and authorized them to oversee all federal activities in their respective domains.

The media immediately dubbed these officials "super-secretaries." As a doctoral candidate in public administration, I knew this move was big. One could not be a graduate student in those days without being inculcated in the academic dogma of FDR's Brownlow Committee reorganization in 1937. The news coverage of Nixon's bold act was, for a change, commensurate with the importance of the event, at least from my perspective. I felt lucky to be there as it was happening, to be reading the *Washington Post* every morning. (Sometimes, during the unraveling of the Watergate cover-up in 1973, late in the evening I'd walk a few blocks down Connecticut Avenue to the Mayflower Hotel to buy an early edition of the next day's *Post*. There was usually a small group of regulars milling around waiting for the paper to be delivered. Always standing apart was a man who looked vaguely familiar. Once the Senate Watergate Committee began its televised hearings, I finally recognized James McCord, one of the Watergate burglars.) The extensive news coverage of Nixon's reorganization meant that public administration was getting its fifteen minutes of fame. But then, as is inherent in the roving and restless spotlight of news coverage, the subject of the reorganization disappeared as fast as it arose. Instead, the super-secretaries sank out of sight as they settled in to the daily grind of governing—an eye-glazingly boring subject for the media.

I was electrified by Nixon's reorganization action and very curious about it but was already committed to studying a different aspect of his presidency for my dissertation. In another stroke of luck, a colleague at Brookings, Dan Mazmanian, was interested in natural resource policy and especially curious about how Nixon's plans would affect that policy area. So, while spending most of my time on my dissertation, we wrote an analysis of Nixon's revived plan to create a Department of Energy and Natural Resources, and we included a brief review of the recently terminated "counsellors to the president" project. Unfortunately, it was not published, although we did publish a different piece.[1]

I was also lucky to find myself walking past the office suites of Nixon's three super-secretaries nearly every day. That made Dan's and my project, and my broader interest in reorganization, all the more tangible and concrete. I had been fortunate to be granted full access to all of the Office of Management and Budget (OMB) files on Nixon's anti-PR effort by Joe Laitin, OMB's public information officer (and a legendary government spokesman then and later). Joe's only condition was that I not publish anything until enough time had passed that none of the individuals who were cooperating with me would suffer any political embarrassment. I kept my word and waited until 1997.[2]

So, for several months in early 1973, I reported daily to the entrance to the Old Executive Office Building (OEOB, now the Eisenhower Building) on Pennsylvania Avenue. The guard from the White House police would carefully cross-check my identity with the list of permitted visitors called in that day by those with offices in the building. When he found that Laitin's office had called in my name, he then assigned me a visitor badge. No examinations of briefcases, no metal detectors, no walk through security screening. Also, no escorts were required. I would walk alone to Joe's office on the second floor of OEOB to read and copy the files. Security was so lax that sometimes at the end of the day I borrowed some of the thicker files and took them back to Brookings to take advantage of the then-novel feature of a copier having a high-speed feeder. I returned the original documents to the OMB files the next morning. My briefcase was never checked on my way out or in.

Sometimes, I needed a break from the drudgery of hours of reading and copying the files in Laitin's office. When that happened, I would often walk a few circuits around the square corridor of the building, usually on the second floor, sometimes on others. I also had other occasions to walk through OEOB's high-prestige first floor for dissertation-related interviews with Neal Ball, deputy press secretary; William Safire, special assistant to the president; Herbert Klein, communications director; and Margita White, Klein's assistant. My research also entailed interviews with several lower-ranking OMB staffers on the less prestigious higher floors. While walking the corridors of the OEOB, I was fascinated as I recognized the nameplates on the office doors of the three super-secretaries and a few times fleetingly saw those famous—at least to me—personages. It was intriguing and exciting to be so close to such an interesting public administration topic. However, Joe cautioned me not to do too much wandering around the building, especially when the president was using his hideaway office on OEOB's first floor. When he was there, Joe said, the Secret Service aggressively patrolled the corridors of the building and stopped anyone who was not where they were supposed to be. Thanks to Joe's warning, I was careful and that never happened to me.

That oblique proximity to the counsellors, as well as Dan's and my unpublished paper, left a lingering curiosity about the super-secretary reorganization even though, due to Watergate, Nixon revoked it in May 1973. The short life of the project seemed to justify its quick disappearance from the news and from the writings of academic observers. After all, it lasted less than half a year. But, I kept wondering, it was a major reorganization, so how did it go? Surely there was some modest record of the activities of the super-secretaries that could answer that question. Thirty-five years later, the time seemed right for a historical study. Again, I was lucky. One of the super-secretaries, James Lynn, was still alive and agreed to a telephone interview. He was a terrific raconteur. I was able to locate and interview at least one staffer from each of the three counsellors' offices as well as all three associate directors of the Domestic Council who were assigned to work with their counterpart counsellor. I am indebted to all the people who talked to me or helped locate other key people to interview. These former public servants bear the perpetual burden of being contacted by researchers interested in arcane details about often brief chapters of their extensive careers, seeking in-depth information about the historical roles they had played in events that had happened decades earlier. All the people I was in contact with bore this burden with patience and good humor. They were exceedingly helpful.

Another bit of luck was that almost all the relevant archival records were now open. I greatly benefited from documents at the Nixon Presidential Library, Ford Presidential Library, and Library of Congress. Caspar Weinberger's executors, Caspar Weinberger Jr. and William H. Taft IV, granted me access to his then-closed papers; Julia Vadala Taft shared her personal files; Angela Parker provided research assistance at the Ford Library; and James Reichley permitted me to quote from the transcript of his 1977 interview with Fred Malek, now in the collection of the Ford Library. My thanks to all of them. The only documents I could not access were Lynn's papers at the Nixon Library, which are closed to researchers until at least 2015.[3] However, Lynn told me that the documents from his counsellor service probably filled only about half of a standard archival box and were mostly drafts of policy memos for two or three of the major issues he worked on. Lack of access to these did not seem problematic because I found related documents in other places.

While oral histories and archival documents are primary sources, they need to be treated carefully when reconstructing events. I have tried my best to present a balanced narrative based on the sources available. However, others could perhaps interpret the record differently or may, in the future, have additional sources that contribute to a different telling of the story.

I'm pleased to acknowledge the help of scores of other information professionals for their cheerful and diligent attention. While it is impossible to name all of them, special thanks go to Rod Ross at the National Archives' Center for Legislative Archives; Betsy Moon at the U.S. Senate Library; Leigh Dorsey and her staff at Golda Meir Library, University of Wisconsin–Milwaukee; and Nancy Mulhern, the Wisconsin Historical Society's government documents librarian. I also benefited from the collections of the Milwaukee Public Library's downtown branch, Marquette University's Law Library, University of Wisconsin–Madison's Memorial Library, as well as two high school libraries, Waukesha West and Nicolet, which subscribed to some ProQuest Historical newspapers that other libraries did not. My program associate, Andrea Zweifel, once again demonstrated her phenomenal proofreading skills.

By its nature, history involves selection, choice, interpretation and judgment. So, besides giving the usual disclaimer about being solely responsible for any mistakes, I have an especially strong caveat in this case. All historical interpretations provided here are mine alone and should not be associated in any way with the participants in these events who graciously and frankly talked with me about their experiences or shared material they possessed or controlled. History is never done. If journalism is the first draft of history, and the second version of Nixon's super-secretaries was Richard Nathan's sinister recounting in *The Plot That Failed: Nixon and the Administrative Presidency* (1975), then this inquiry might perhaps be counted as the third. I hope it will not be the last.

NIXON'S SUPER-SECRETARIES

1

INTRODUCTION

Even before his reelection in November 1972, President Richard Nixon began planning to accomplish in his second term what he had been unable to do during the first. One item was to reorganize the domestic side of the federal government. When it came to his interest in a grand reorganization of the executive branch, Nixon was no presidential outlier. He was following a reflexive behavior exhibited by almost all of the presidents who had preceded him in the twentieth century. In late 1972 rumors began to spread that Nixon had ambitious plans for a major reorganization in preparation for his second term. Two journalists tried to place the president's effort in the context of contemporary political history. Robert Toth of the *Los Angeles Times* reminded readers that "for at least 35 years, reorganization commissions have been created to tell the President how to do his job better. Now, once again, a President wants to reform the government to make it more efficient and more responsive to his direction." Nixon's prospects? Jack Rosenthal of the *New York Times* observed that "other Administrations have sought to harness the mixed allegiances of the vast department bureaucracies, answerable in fact to Congress and their own special constituencies as well as the White House. For the most part, all these efforts have produced is exasperation."[1] Notwithstanding their pessimism, Nixon went ahead with his second-term reorganization. This is a historical study of what happened. Were the reporters right or wrong?

FAILING AT GRAND REORGANIZATION
IN THE FIRST TERM

Like so many of his twentieth-century predecessors, President Nixon thought the federal executive branch needed to be reorganized. In 1969, at the beginning of his first term, he created a council headed by California businessman Roy Ash to study the structure and management of government. Among the recommendations it made in 1970, the Ash Council called for a macro-reorganization of federal domestic programs into four super-departments based on fundamental *purposes* of government. Similar to the grand reorganization developed in the preceding term by President Lyndon Johnson's Heineman Task Force (but never submitted to Congress), the Ash Council's proposal would create departments for human resources, community development, natural resources, and economic affairs. The council suggested three reasons for such broad entities. First, their breadth would reduce the need for interdepartmental coordination. Second, the president's span of control would be reduced to a reasonable number of direct reports. Third, the scope of the departments would reduce the ability of a single special interest group to capture its policy-making apparatus. Nixon agreed, wanting to improve the management of the bureaucracy as well as to make it more accountable and responsive to him. For him, this was an instance when politics and governance were in harmony.[2]

In his State of the Union address in January 1971 Nixon listed reorganization as one of the six goals he was setting for the national agenda. Two months later, he released more details in a message to Congress on reorganization. Disappearing into the four super-departments would be seven Cabinet departments (in alphabetical order): Agriculture; Commerce; Health, Education, and Welfare; Housing and Urban Development; Interior; Labor; and Transportation. Independent agencies that would be wholly subsumed into the super-departments included the Small Business Administration, Railroad Retirement Board, Water Resources Council, and the Federal Mediation and Conciliation Service. Portions of the Army Corps of Engineers, NASA, Atomic Energy Commission, National Science Foundation, and the Office of Economic Opportunity would, too. As an indication of the importance he attached to the subject, on the day he sent his reorganization message to Congress Nixon made a rare appearance in the White House Press Room to express his support. The next day, Nixon invited Representative Chet Holifield (D-Calif.), chair of the House Government Operations Committee, to accompany him on an Air Force One flight to California so that he could lobby him on reorganization. Eventually, Holifield—who had spoken negatively about Nixon's grand reorganization earlier—held hearings on the proposals, as did the Senate Government Operations Committee, but neither committee took formal action on any of the four bills that year.[3]

In March 1972 the president reiterated his request in another message to Congress, this one dedicated solely to reorganization. The major change between his 1971 and 1972 proposals was dropping the Department of Agriculture (USDA) from the proposed Department of Natural Resources. Farmers wanted their own department and Nixon wanted their support in his 1972 reelection campaign. Again, Congress acted on none of the four proposals in early 1972. Finally, in May the House Government Operations Committee recommended the Department of Community Development (DCD) bill by a bipartisan vote of 26 to 8. But then the bill was held by the Rules Committee and not scheduled for a floor vote. By midsummer a reporter concluded that "the far-reaching Nixon plans for governmental reorganization have skidded almost into oblivion."[4]

Nixon was not giving up, however. The administration kept pushing for the House and then the Senate to pass the DCD bill during the summer floor session or in the short (pre-election) fall session. All summer Nixon continued listing reorganization on his short list of subjects the Democratic-majority Congress had not yet acted on, hinting at a campaign theme similar to Harry Truman's successful denunciations of a "do-nothing Congress" in 1948. Senator Mike Mansfield (D-Mont.), the usually mild-mannered majority leader, responded vehemently: "The President asked for pie in the sky, a huge reorganization, which was impossible to consider in toto, certainly impossible to consider in one Congress. . . . Beyond the rhetoric, I have detected little interest by the administration in pushing even its own party members on this matter. Indeed, I have detected little genuine interest from any quarter inside the government or out." Mansfield's statement accurately captured the politics of reorganization bills. There was no substantial political or policy constituency on Capitol Hill or in public opinion *for* such bills. Politics usually trumps policy in Washington, but in this case there was not much to trump. House leaders would not give Nixon a major legislative win in a campaign year. They never sent the DCD bill to the House floor for a vote in 1972.[5]

To Nixon, the failure of Congress to pass his grand reorganization plan during his first term confirmed everything he already thought about the federal bureaucracy. Here was an entrenched and beyond-reach institution that was committed to spending, policies, and priorities with which he disagreed. He viewed it as being in league with a (seemingly permanent) Democratic-majority Congress and special interest groups that benefited from federal programs. Nixon perceived the federal government to be a thick and virtually impermeable machinery geared to liberal values, increased domestic spending, and an ever-expanding role for the federal government in American society. From his perspective, the bureaucracy and its allies in Congress were indeed the enemy, and in many ways his assessment was accurate. First, with a civil service system, most federal employees were immune to political pressures. Second, the expansions of the role of the federal government as a result of the New Deal and Great Society programs were embodied in agencies whose raison d'être was to implement those programs. Third, the "iron triangle" of congressional committee, special interest groups, and agencies created a powerful and virtually impenetrable network of political power. Nixon believed these trends diminished the power of a conservative president. So, besides the traditional good government and managerial arguments for a grand reorganization, Nixon also supported it as a way to break the back of the bureaucracy.

President Nixon was determined to get control over the bureaucracy in his second term, one way or another. In a rare interview (at the Republican National Convention), his top domestic aide, John Ehrlichman, made it clear that reorganization would be a priority. According to the interviewer, "Reform is a thankless job, however, and that is all the more reason Ehrlichman sees it as a fitting objective of a second-term President." Nixon came out swinging. Besides unilateral reorganization, his multipronged strategy included impounding congressional appropriations with which he disagreed, imposing spending limits, governing by veto, issuing a budget proposal for FY1974 that would reduce the scope of federal operations, naming loyal first-term White House staffers to senior positions in the departments and agencies for the second term, exercising greater discipline over decision making in the executive branch, strengthening the role of the Office of Management and Budget, and asserting a broad doctrine of executive privilege.[6]

OVERVIEW OF NIXON'S SECOND-TERM REORGANIZATION

On January 5, 1973, the president dramatically announced at a breakfast for congressional leaders that he was going ahead with some of his reorganization proposals from his first term, but this time he was implementing them unilaterally by exercising his inherent presidential powers. He was reorganizing *administratively*. No advance congressional consent would be required, no laws would need to be changed, and no reorganization plans would be subject to a legislative veto under the Reorganization Act powers Congress had routinely delegated to presidents since the Herbert Hoover administration. Nixon thus rendered Congress's powers moot. This was a de facto reorganization that the legislative branch could not stop. In one bold move Nixon was doing what almost every president since Warren Harding had been proposing to Congress and that Congress had been rejecting.

The new reorganization plan, largely designed by Ehrlichman, created three domestic super-departments. Nixon designated the secretaries of three Cabinet departments to serve simultaneously as "counsellors to the president," with offices in the White House complex and sweeping powers to oversee the bureaucracy. The secretaries headed the three existing Cabinet departments that would form the core of the three domestic super-departments Nixon had proposed to Congress in his first term. He named Caspar Weinberger, secretary-designate of the Department of Health, Education, and Welfare (HEW), as counsellor to the president for human resources; James Lynn, secretary-designate of the Department Housing and Urban Development (HUD), as counsellor to the president for community development; and Earl Butz, secretary of the Department of Agriculture, as counsellor to the president for natural resources. The media quickly began referring to them as super-secretaries.[7]

The three counsellors served from Nixon's January announcement until an equally abrupt presidential decision to terminate their work five months later. At a Cabinet meeting convened on short notice on May 10, 1973, Nixon disbanded the reorganization effort, a move that was deeply intertwined with the unraveling of the Watergate cover-up. Ehrlichman and the powerful White House chief of staff, H. R. Haldeman, had resigned the previous week when it became publicly apparent that there had been criminal activity related to the cover-up. Haldeman's successor, Alexander Haig, viewed the super-secretaries as an Ehrlichman project that no one else in the White House really cared about. The president, while having been authentically supportive of the counsellor structure, was now preoccupied with a different and much more important goal: political survival. Also, Haig was looking for initiatives to jump-start the administration's second term and undo the image of a president isolated from the rest of his official family, including the Cabinet. The White House was in such operational chaos at that point that no one gave the three counsellors advance notice of the announcement that Nixon would make at the Cabinet meeting. They found out when everyone else did, during the meeting. So ended Nixon's grand reorganization.

Since then, no president has proposed a structural reorganization of large swaths of the executive branch. Instead, Nixon's successors largely focused on expanding the Cabinet by adding more departments one at a time or on making nonstructural managerial reforms. Similarly, since the brief reign of the super-secretaries, Congress has become increasingly reluctant to delegate any lesser reorganization powers to presidents; it finally allowed the Reorganization Act to expire altogether in 1984. After that, no president has even asked Congress to renew it.

Is the super-secretary initiative worth a detailed historical study? After all, it lasted less than half a year. It is the argument of this book that Nixon's super-secretary project was the last grand presidential reorganization effort and that it influenced the historical arc of developments relating to federal reorganization, including both presidential initiatives and congressional responses. This argument is generally contrary to the extant historical, academic, and biographical literature, which has given the super-secretaries little attention or focused on the work of a single author who presented the initiative in a negative light. To make the case for its having a discernible and creditable role in presidential, congressional, and public administration history, there must be more than a mere presentation of the historical record of what happened before and after. There is also a predicate obligation to provide a more comprehensive historical narrative of Nixon's reorganization based on original and primary sources. Such a detailed recounting has not been published before. What did the super-secretaries actually *do*? How did they operate? Did they appear to be integral to the White House governance or peripheral to it? Did they make a difference in the policy process or not? Did they seem to be accomplishing what Nixon and Ehrlichman hoped they would or not? Were they merely a new layer of bureaucracy and paperwork or a constructive factor in program coordination and policy planning? Such baseline information has largely been absent from the scholarly historical record published to date.

My hope is that this historical inquiry will appeal to readers interested in history, public administration, political science, and related fields. The goal is to provide more detailed information about Nixon's super-secretary reorganization than heretofore available. Scholars will then be in a better position to make more textured, informed, and independent judgments about the reorganization's role and relative significance in American governmental history. I assume that some will end up disagreeing with my premise that Nixon's effort was the last in the twentieth-century political tradition of grand presidential reorganization efforts. Even if that is so, this narrative may, nonetheless, have value for anyone considering the super-secretaries in the context of larger questions and bodies of knowledge in political science and public administration.

While this study is structured as a historical inquiry, the subject straddles the confluence of several streams of academic foci besides history, including presidential studies, congressional studies, bureaucratic politics, interinstitutional politics, organizational design and reform, separation of powers, public law, and American political development. Ranging beyond an exclusively public sector focus, this inquiry may also be relevant to such fields as management theory and organization theory. Those fields seek to develop pan-sectoral and generic bodies of knowledge that are valid for understanding the management of organizations, irrespective of their placement in the business, governmental, or nonprofit (or nongovernmental [NGO]) sectors. Similarly, the emerging field of management history may find this study to be relevant to the historical arc of modern management.

PRESIDENTIAL REORGANIZATION PATTERNS

Plans for grand reorganizations of the federal government were much in vogue in the first seven decades of the twentieth century. Whether emanating from presidents, public administration professors, or "good government" reformers, the desire to impose rationality on the illogical and confusing structure of the federal government was a strong and widely accepted impulse. There seemed to be a broad consensus that *something* needed to be done. Generally, these reorganization plans involved a wholesale restructuring of the executive branch that would create a seemingly logical and orderly pattern of Cabinet departments. Large departments, each generally based on a broad common function or purpose, would be the basic building block of the federal executive branch. These grand reorganization plans then proposed moving from the far corners of the sprawling government and into super-departments all federal activities according to their function. Out of disorder would come order and, implicitly, good government and cost savings. This quintessential American optimism about the value and benefits of reorganization was a powerful siren call through many presidencies of the twentieth century. A seemingly perpetual cottage industry generated dozens of proposals, each attempting in one bold move to clear the cluttered federal slate and rewrite it with logic and rationality. The manipulation of extensive organization charts, with boxes being moved hither and yon, became a long-running Washington parlor game.

The standard list of modern presidential reorganization commissions usually begins with Theodore Roosevelt's Keep Commission (1905–1909). However, he directed it to focus on management improvements that did not require congressional approval, which had the effect of limiting the commission's involvement in structural reorganization. Suggestions from presidents for congressional action on plans for a major structural reorganization of the federal executive branch began with William Taft's Commission on Economy and Efficiency (1910–1913) and included Harding's Joint Committee on Reorganization (1921–1924), Franklin Roosevelt's Brownlow Committee (1936–1937), Truman's First Hoover Commission (1947–1949), Dwight Eisenhower's Second Hoover Commission (1953–1959), Johnson's Price and Heineman task forces (1964, 1966–1967) and Nixon's Ash Council (1969–1970).[8]

Then, after Nixon, there was a distinct break with this historical pattern. According to Peri Arnold in the 1990s, "Comprehensive reorganization planning ended badly for presidents in the 1970's. . . . After the 1970's, reorganization planning appears less attractive and less necessary for a president than it did during the 1950's and 1960's." Similarly, scholars writing in 2002 saw the end of grand presidential reorganizations with Nixon, concluding that "the idea of super agencies threatened too many vested interest [*sic*] to gain much political traction. . . . The seventy-five year trend toward consolidating power in the White House had run its course." The first elected president after Nixon, Jimmy Carter, campaigned in 1976 on the need to reorganize the federal government in the same way he had reorganized Georgia state government. He claimed he had "abolished" 278 of the 300 agencies in the state's executive branch. This statement was disingenuous because he had actually merged them into larger super-agencies and thus had not significantly reduced the size of the bureaucracy. But during his presidential term (1977–1981) Carter never convened a reorganization commission and never submitted a grand reorganization to Congress. President Ronald Reagan established the Grace Commission, but it did not focus on structural reorganization. Clinton's National Performance Review emphasized the need for managerial improvements, not structural reorganization. George W. Bush, the first president with a master's in business administration, did not pursue a structural reorganization of the bulk of the executive branch.[9]

During these post-Nixon presidencies, there were structural changes in the federal executive branch, but none involved a major reshuffling of multiple departments. They were one-organization reorganizations or, at most, one-subject reorganizations. The Cabinet-level reorganizations after Nixon *expanded* the number of departments, usually by elevating subdepartmental entities or independent agencies to full-fledged department status. These were not comprehensive reorganizations like those put forward by Nixon and his predecessors. Most reflected a kind of Cabinet inflation. Carter, with Congress's approval, created a new Department of Energy by merging several non-Cabinet agencies. He also stripped the Department of Health, Education, and Welfare of its education component, creating the Department of Education and renaming the original entity the Department of Health and Human Services. (Reagan wanted to eliminate the Department of Education, but Congress never gave it serious consideration.) Reagan signed legislation expanding the Cabinet by refashioning the Veterans Administration as the Department of Veterans Affairs. George W. Bush signed a law creating the Department of Homeland Security. While this creation was the most substantial of the post-Nixon restructurings, it involved only gathering subentities from many existing departments into one new department, but no departments were eliminated and no major offices were shifted *into* existing departments. Similarly, Bush and Congress statutorily reorganized the intelligence agencies, but without a major change in the existing structural landscape, instead adding a new director of national intelligence to oversee the preexisting apparatus.

CONGRESSIONAL REORGANIZATION PATTERNS

A second historical pattern regarding reorganization can be seen in congressional decision making. Beginning in 1932, Congress created an alternate venue for presidents to pursue reorganization. The traditional approach was of presidents submitting to Congress legislative proposals that would change the statutes governing the structure of the executive branch. In response to the frantic desire to cut spending in the Great Depression, in 1932 Congress gave President Hoover the power to pursue major reorganization through a procedure other than legislation. The Economy Act of 1932 authorized presidents to reorganize the federal executive branch by executive order, subject to a legislative veto within sixty days. The executive order would go into effect unless at least one house passed a resolution disallowing it.

Congress continued these delegations of authority to all presidents between Hoover and Nixon. These delegations came to be called Reorganization Acts, for the serial laws passed by Congress. Generally, these acts gave the president the power to submit a reorganization plan to Congress if it did not conflict with existing statutes. Then, if Congress did not disapprove the plan within two to three months, it would go into effect. From 1933 to 1935, Franklin Roosevelt was given powers similar to those Hoover had possessed. In 1939 (following the blowout in 1937 regarding the Brownlow Committee's grand reorganization plan), Congress passed a Reorganization Act, using that title for first time. It expired in 1941. Subsequent Reorganization Acts passed in 1945 and 1949 for Truman; in 1953, 1955, and 1957 for Eisenhower; in 1961 for Kennedy; in 1965 for Johnson; and in 1969 and 1971 for Nixon. The 1971 act was set to expire in April 1973, precisely at the time of the events recounted here. Then, breaking with the past, Congress did not routinely renew the act as it had done so consistently since 1945 and with some gaps since 1932.[10]

President Gerald Ford asked for a four-year renewal and did not get it. The first time Congress passed a Reorganization Act after Nixon's expired in 1973 was in 1977, for Carter. However, this version contained more restrictions and constraints on a president's reorganization powers than the standard template that had first been used in the Hoover administration. The 1977 Reorganization Act expired in 1981. In 1984, Congress passed another Reorganization Act, as requested by President Reagan. It limited the life of the law to the shortest time frame yet—only until the end of the calendar year. Also, due to the Supreme Court's *Chedda* decision (1983), the legislative veto feature that had been integral to all the reorganization delegations of authority to presidents was deleted in the 1984 act. Instead, a presidential reorganization plan would need to be affirmatively approved by votes of both houses of Congress within ninety days. It was little different from trying to pass a law. Reagan never used the act to propose a reorganization.[11]

Again, here was a distinct historical pattern before and after Nixon, this time regarding congressional delegation of across-the-board reorganization authority to presidents. From Hoover to Nixon, and especially from Truman to Nixon, Congress routinely passed Reorganization Acts that gave presidents reorganization powers subject to legislative veto. There were only brief lapses in such powers from 1945 to 1973. After Nixon, the renewals were less frequent, the lapses longer, the delegated reorganization authority more limited and constrained, and the durations of the acts shorter. The support within Congress for passing any more across-the-board Reorganization Acts had petered out.[12]

Another historical pattern of congressional behavior related to its reaction to grand reorganization proposals often generated presidential commissions that required major statutory changes and, therefore, could not be implemented by a Reorganization Act plan. The first came from Taft's Commission on Economy and Efficiency, which Congress did not adopt. Subsequent ones were developed under President Harding, including a comprehensive proposal from then-Commerce Secretary Herbert Hoover that was also not adopted. As lame duck president, Hoover tried again and failed. Roosevelt did not propose any sweeping structural reorganizations until he was reelected in 1936. His Brownlow Committee plan for a major reorganization was rejected by Congress after a battle royal in 1937. (In 1939, under the new Reorganization Act, Roosevelt was able to obtain congressional assent for some important but less-than-grand structural reorganizations.) Truman appointed former president Hoover to recommend reforms of the federal government, as did Eisenhower. Again, while some of the more modest proposals were permitted by Congress, grander and more sweeping ones were not. In his State of the Union address in 1967, President Johnson proposed merging the Departments of Labor and Commerce. Congress did not approve it. His Heineman Task Force plan for a major reorganization was never submitted to Congress. In 1971, like his predecessors, Nixon asked Congress to pass four bills for a grand departmental reorganization of the domestic side of the executive branch, largely following the recommendations of the Ash Council. None was enacted. A fixed pattern of a political pas de deux seems to be apparent from this recounting of grand reorganization proposals, of presidents proposing and Congress disposing—negatively. Little stuff was acceptable, but not the big stuff.

THE GIVEN NARRATIVE

What should we make of the historical patterns of presidential behavior toward grand reorganization before and after Nixon, along with Congress's behavior regarding the Reorganization Acts before and after Nixon? In both cases, the arc of developments changed after Nixon. Until Nixon's administration, presidents routinely proposed grand reorganizations. After his presidency, no one did. Until Nixon, Congress routinely passed Reorganization Acts giving presidents the power to propose medium-level reorganizations. After Nixon, fewer and fewer such acts were passed until, finally, they vanished. It seems a reasonable inference that at least part of the explanation for the break in these two historical trends is related to Nixon. As noted earlier, this book's fundamental argument is that a key factor in these two parallel pivots in historical trends was the grand domestic reorganization Nixon began in 1973 without congressional approval. The dramatic change in practice suggests that the super-secretary experiment soured post-Nixon presidents on grand reorganizations and, at the other end of Pennsylvania Avenue, soured Congress on delegating any reorganization powers to presidents. Nixon not only broke with precedent but also shattered the mold. This observation is not meant to assert that the counsellor plan was the only explanation for the change in historical trends or even the single most important one. But, certainly, that reorganization was more significant than history has generally accorded, particularly given that Nixon's super-secretaries have been of little interest to historians and academicians up to now.

The most specific and detailed description and discussion of Nixon's super-secretary reorganization was Richard Nathan's *The Plot That Failed* (1975). The title expressed his view that Nixon's agenda to assert control over the federal executive branch was revolutionary, out of the mainstream consensus, dangerous, and nefarious. The section relating to super-secretaries was brief and based on generally available public information, mostly newspaper coverage. Nathan published an expanded (and equally influential) book eight years later called *The Administrative Presidency* but with no additional sources on the super-secretaries.[13]

Despite the thinness of his sources, Nathan has frequently been cited in many subsequent references to the super-secretary idea in the context of overall assessments of Nixon's record or of the contemporary presidency. He became *the* source for information about the super-secretaries.[14] Other references to the super-secretaries, not citing Nathan, were equally skimpy in details and in original research based on primary sources. This relatively common approach suggested, explicitly or implicitly, that the super-secretary scheme existed for too brief a time to merit a more detailed analysis.[15] The memoirs of several senior officials in the Nixon administration addressed the theme that the super-secretary experiment was doomed to inevitable failure because the incumbents, concurrently serving as secretaries of departments, could not be viewed as neutral policy makers when the interests of their home departments conflicted with those of other entities within their jurisdiction. Alan Dean, who had worked on reorganization at OMB, went further. He wrote that by May 1973 the super-secretary project had *already* proven itself "unsuccessful" and it was thus abandoned.[16]

Besides these Nixon-historical, presidency-oriented, or autobiographical references, a modicum of discussion about Nixon's reorganization proposals (whether his 1971–1972 legislative initiative or his 1973 super-secretary executive fiat) can be found in public administration scholars' writings. Most of it has been negative. One of the few exceptions is the work of Aaron Wildavsky, who neutrally commented on the (failed) Nixon reorganization as having potential implications for restructuring the internal budgeting and decision-making process at OMB if such a reorganization were revived by a future president. Neutrally, Kenneth Meier and John Bohte examined the "span of control" principle underlying the counsellors and tested it for empirical validity.[17] Otherwise, the literature was decidedly critical. In a consistently crabby tone, contemporaneous and post-hoc appraisals predominantly focused on what was wrong with the idea, why it would not work, or what had not been included in the proposals but should have.[18] For example, Harvey Mansfield observed that "if you have a handful of super-secretaries, then the President will have to find some way to bypass those super-secretaries to get information and critique of departmental positions that a secretary may want to screen."[19]

This concert of negativity is odd. Public administration scholarship once had a hagiographic attitude toward reorganization, beginning with the emergence of the field during the Progressive Era and even more strongly during FDR's presidency. With little to no dissent, scholars approved of the Brownlow Committee's work, endorsing its recommendations for a strong presidency that would give the chief executive administrative tools to manage the executive branch and pursue reorganization as one tool with which to rationalize the federal government. Therefore, the negative slant toward Nixon's proposals can be explained as either covert partisanship by a Democratic-leaning professoriate or a merit-based and gradually emerging post-Brownlow skepticism toward strong presidents and reorganization as an effective tool for improved management. Sidney Milkis flagged this possible partisan double standard, noting the similarities of Nixon's super-secretaries to "the strategy of pursuing policy goals through administrative capacities that had been created for the most part by Democratic presidents." Robert Gilmour charitably tried to reconcile this formerly-pro-now-anti trend in the literature by suggesting that two contradictory orthodoxies had emerged in public administration. One continued favoring reorganization, especially with an effort to strengthen presidential management of the executive branch by shifting the mission of organizations from a client-based structure to a function-based one. The second approach he labeled the "'new orthodoxy' of skepticism," which always found fault and weaknesses in pending reorganization proposals.[20] In terms of non-Nixon-specific literature in public administration about super-departments, Herbert Emmerich had been the leading figure in public administration on issues of reorganization. In a posthumously published book in 1971 (i.e., before Nixon's counsellor effort), Emmerich explicitly stated that "the creation of 'super cabinet' officials is inadvisable." However, he was skimpy on the rationale for his position, stating only that it "somehow do[es] not sound natural in the American environment" and that a president should not "abdicate any major component of his responsibility and authority." These are hardly persuasive arguments, being quite empty of substance.[21]

Hence, Nixon's super-secretary experiment has been largely dismissed in the published historical, biographical, memoir, and academic record due to pragmatic reasons ("lasted too briefly"), normative ones ("a bad idea"), or analytic explanations ("fatally flawed"). Also, the historical conclusions have depended too heavily on a single source (Nathan's accounting). This academic brush-off created a very narrow bottleneck for potentially disparate historical interpretation. Nathan's narrative practically compels a proscribing or dismissive retrospective conclusion, and the relatively broad negative consensus about the super-secretaries may be one of the reasons why no major research based on primary sources has been undertaken. Challenging this conventional wisdom, this project examines Nixon's method of governing through administrative, rather than statutory, domestic super-departments. It seeks to investigate *de novo* and from primary sources the record of the super-secretaries. The goal is to review in detail the activities they engaged in and then to develop some tentative conclusions—based on the archival and other primary historical evidence rather than preconceived explanations—whether Nixon's innovation was important or not and whether it worked as desired or not.

REVISING THE NARRATIVE

What Nixon did with his 1973 reorganization was to break the mold of the past and bring his grand reorganization *into effect*. He acted, not just proposed. From the point of view of Washington culture, Nixon had violated the ossified duet of presidents proposing and Congress rejecting. Washington was suddenly all aflutter over this breach of etiquette, with extreme rhetoric being thrown at Nixon's action. It was a "plot" and a "revolution" that was a threat to the Constitution, if not the "American way of life." Yet, from a different perspective, all Nixon did was to break with the inaction of the past and actually *do* something. A record of the operations of this grand reorganization surely is worth examining so that it can be integrated into the extant reorganization literature.

Similarly, the given narrative is that Nixon's 1973 reorganization was motivated by a nefarious goal of increasing his personal power over the bureaucracy. Sometimes the subtext of these criticisms suggests the possibility of anti-Nixon partisan and political value judgments about both his first- and second-term reorganization plans. Any effort at reexamining the 1973 reorganization needs to disregard such coloring. Instead, the focus needs to be on the sources in the literature that deal with presidential power in more institutional and historical contexts. For example, William

West and Terry Moe have observed that modern presidents often seek to centralize control within the White House. These centralization efforts are somewhat inexorable and reflexive for presidents seeking to pursue their policy goals. This would place Nixon's super-secretaries in the mainstream of such historical trends. Consequently, Nixon's 1973 reorganization would deserve to be reexamined with less of a negative characterization than has been presented by some sources in the literature. This inquiry seeks to examine the super-secretaries as a historical example of this apparent secular presidential trend of trying to centralize power in the White House.[22]

A generic centralization of presidential power still needs to be handled with greater nuance, however. In his memoirs, Ehrlichman claimed that the super-secretary initiative was misunderstood, that it actually had a centripetal motive. Reacting to the memoirs of White House communications director Herbert Klein, Ehrlichman wrote, "Herb Klein and others have written some perfect silliness about these reorganization attempts. In fact, the proposals were efforts to strengthen the Cabinet, which was enmeshed in an archaic organization. Our proposals would have had the effect of *decentralizing* much of the decision-making in the Executive Branch."[23]

This claim could be discounted as an ex post facto rationalization. However, Ehrlichman gains credibility from two academic observers who published their interpretations before his memoir. Thomas Cronin's immediate reaction to Nixon's announcement of the super-secretaries in January 1973 was that it was "a step in the right direction." This new setup would reverse the historical trend of the "swelling of the presidency" by strengthening the Cabinet with consolidated portfolios, and "a small number of strengthened Cabinet officers with closer ties to the President would resolve those conflicts instead" of White House staff. Writing three years after the super-secretaries (and six years before Ehrlichman), Ronald Moe suggested the same interpretation. Moe, a longtime observer of federal reorganization, wrote that the super-secretaries were Nixon's *reaction* to the failures of centralizing power over domestic issues in the White House in the first term when he had built up a Domestic Council staff to serve as his counterbureaucracy. "As the 1972 election approached, however, the president concluded that the liabilities of relying on the White House and Domestic Council staffs for policy implementation outweighed any benefits," Moe wrote, adding that the principal cause of Nixon's "disaffection with the counter-bureaucracy approach was that it forced the

White House to become increasingly involved in routine decisions." The super-secretaries, argued Moe, were a more refined effort at balancing centralization and decentralization impulses. They embodied "President Nixon's attempt to promote presidential influence and direction over the bureaucracy, while simultaneously *decreasing* the size and power of the executive office."[24]

Besides its intrinsic yet unappreciated historical value, the 1973 reorganization is also an interesting sidebar to Watergate. In the given narrative, the events of the unraveling of the Watergate cover-up (especially Ehrlichman's resignation) compelled Nixon to cancel the super-secretary scheme. Other than that, though, the 1973 reorganization was viewed as wholly separate from Watergate. This casual generalization, too, is subject to some challenge. In her revisionist biography of Nixon, Joan Hoff suggests that, at the very least, the coincidental Watergate context of the reorganization "generated unwarranted criticism and suspicion about its intent." From that perspective, reorganization was simply a victim of unlucky timing. The political system did not judge it on its merits or even the politics of it but simply connected it to an unrelated event that dominated and contaminated it.[25]

Haldeman went much further. He saw reorganization and Watergate as inextricably intertwined. In his memoir (admittedly, a source that needs to be treated with caution), he saw an explicit link between the super-secretaries and Watergate. He wrote that the Washington establishment used Watergate to prevent the reorganization from having its intended impact: "*Reorganization is the secret story of Watergate.* That reorganization in the winter of 1972—very little known to the American public—eventually spurred into action against Nixon the great power blocs in Washington. All of them saw danger as the hated Nixon moved more and more to control the Executive Branch from the White House, as he was constitutionally mandated to do. What they feared was real. Nixon genuinely meant to take the reins of government in hand."[26] In Haldeman's view, the investigation of the Watergate break-in was used by Nixon's opponents to derail his powerful grasp of the reins of government. Watergate was a fortuitous opportunity used by adherents of a left-of-center ideology to prevent the success of Nixon's right-of-center political philosophy. Even if not motivated by left-right ideology, Haldeman's interpretation saw this as a donnybrook between the revolutionary changes that Nixon sought and the broad coalition that benefited from the Washington status quo. In the opposite corner, he saw Congress, the bureaucracy, the Democratic

Party, special interest groups (who benefited from federal spending they had significant influence over), the East Coast elite, and the national news media. From this perspective, Nixon's super-secretary reorganization had bashed a political beehive out of its stasis. The reaction to it, under the guise of fighting Watergate, was the status quo seeking to rebalance itself by any means necessary to protect power and privileges.

Indirectly confirming Haldeman, a staff writer for the *New Yorker* captured the defeated atmosphere on Capitol Hill in March 1973. At that time, congressional Democrats had a fatalistic sense that Nixon's reorganization and other efforts (such as impoundment) to gain control of the bureaucracy and subjugate Congress were a fait accompli, that his alleged abuses of powers were unstoppable—barring some major, unforeseen development that could derail him: "The President's drive *to take over the federal government* was going well. By the end of March, those legislators who were worried about the possibility of a collapse of the Constitutional system were in a state of near-hopelessness. It seemed that the President would have his will, and Congress could not stop him; as for the public, it was uninterested in Constitutional matters."[27] Stripped of the apocalyptic tone, the description was accurate. Nixon's landslide reelection in 1972 led to his decision to use his (implied or inherent) presidential powers more aggressively vis-à-vis the hostile Democratic-majority Congress and, from his perspective, an equally recalcitrant bureaucracy that always found ways to avoid implementing his decisions. For Nixon, the election was tantamount to a national plebiscite that he had won handily. This victory suggested to him a broad endorsement of his agenda for his second term and that Congress would be contravening this national will should it try to block implementation of his program.

The worst fears of congressional Democrats in the spring of 1973 were indeed being discussed within the White House. For example, Ehrlichman saw a role for the super-secretaries in helping overturn the traditional relationship between Congress and the president. In April 1973, Special Assistant to the President W. Richard Howard proposed that the administration turn the tables on Congress by holding public hearings and "call[ing] Senators and Congressmen to testify on their legislative positions and votes." This move would have upended the traditional relationship between the two constitutional branches, often summarized by the mantra that "the president proposes and the Congress disposes." Howard's idea was to reverse the situation, with Congress proposing and the president disposing. Implicitly, the president would no longer be coequal to Congress; rather, Congress would be a supplicant to the president. Ehrlichman thought Howard's idea was "first rate." He wanted the super-secretaries to play a central and public role in implementing Howard's proposal. As presidential appointees, they were already coordinating large swaths of federal policy by having jurisdiction over multiple Cabinet departments. Ehrlichman suggested that the super-secretaries should be the ones to hold those hearings. It would be to these super-secretaries that legislators should bow to and plead for their special favors and pet projects.[28] (Further details on the interaction between Watergate-related developments and the super-secretaries are presented chronologically in subsequent chapters.)

A final and lesser reason for developing this alternative narrative is that in the extant sources some errors regarding important details have been accepted as accurate. Ehrlichman's memoirs incorrectly state that the effort was based on an *executive order* that Nixon had signed. This is a surprising misstatement given Ehrlichman's central role in the re-organization (the three super-secretaries were to report to him) and his profession as a lawyer. James Reichley and Richard Pious also state that the super-secretaries were created by executive order, but their mistakes were published before the publication of Ehrlichman's reminiscences. Hence, the two scholars were not merely repeating Ehrlichman's error. As recently as 2004, Alan Dean repeated the same error. Rather than an execu-tive order, the legal basis of the super-secretaries was an administratively confidential memorandum that was never publicly released. Flagging this mistake is more than mere pedantry. Executive orders have a legal status and are considered authoritative unless in contradiction to a statute (or the Constitution). Secret in-house memos, even if the house is the White House, carry no such formal legal weight.[29]

THREE SUPER-SECRETARIES—OR FOUR?

In preparation for his second term, Nixon made two important announce-ments. In early December 1972, via a press release, Nixon appointed the five most senior White House staffers in the second term, dubbed the "Big Five" by the media.[30] Then, on January 5, 1973, he hosted a breakfast for congressional leaders to announce to them his appointment of the next tier of his new administration: three counsellors to the president to oversee human resources, community development, and natural resources. His second announcement related to matters that were of much more direct interest to Congress, due to its power over the statutory structure of the government and the congressional approval needed for any official reorganizations of the federal executive branch. Nixon told them he was appointing three Cabinet secretaries to serve simultaneously as counsellors to the president as an internal administrative reorganization of federal domestic activities. The sequence of the announcements and the differences in the venue and form of the appointments help convey the important differences between the five assistants to the president and the three counsellors.

The Big Five would each have the title of assistant to the president. (There were other members of the White House staff with the title of assistant to the president, but they were not viewed as equivalent to these five.) Three of the five were continuing in their roles from the first term: Haldeman as chief of staff, Ehrlichman as domestic policy advisor, and Henry Kissinger as foreign affairs advisor (who formally headed the staff of the White House National Security Council). In addition, Treasury Secretary George Shultz (who was continuing in that position from the first term) would now simultaneously serve as assistant to the president for economic policy. Formally, his new presidential role would essentially involve chairing the new Cabinet-level Council on Economic Policy. The final member of the Big Five would be incoming OMB director Ash, who would also be assistant to the president for management. Of the five, three were in "two-hatted" situations. Shultz was the only one who was also secretary of a department (and therefore subject to Senate confirmation for that position), while Kissinger and Ash headed smaller presidential agencies. While slightly different from previous White House structures, the appointment of the five was, nonetheless, relatively traditional for a president's inner circle and highest ranking aides.

Haldeman and Ehrlichman, continuing in their roles with a single set of responsibilities, had "one-hatted" roles. Two others, Kissinger and Ash, were "two-hatted" but with few additional responsibilities. As new assistants to the president, their second title did not add much to the traditional functions they and their predecessors had performed. They were not Cabinet secretaries and were not subject to Senate confirmation. (Later OMB directors were subject to confirmation.) In the first Nixon term, OMB directors acquired a second office (in addition to their primary office in OEOB, near OMB staff), and it was located in the West

Wing of the White House. Kissinger's only office, the one reserved for the national security advisor, was already in the White House. So, Ash's and Kissinger's additional duties as assistants to the president did not bring them significantly closer to the president physically (if power is measured by proximity) nor did they involve any major new responsibilities. Both men were already senior advisors to the president due to their positions, regardless of having a second title as assistant to the president. The head of OMB/BOB was automatically an advisor to the president on budgeting issues, which inherently also related to management matters. Similarly, the head of the National Security Council was already a senior advisor to the president on foreign affairs and military matters. Especially for Kissinger, the second title was a distinction without a difference. Rather, it was a kind of booby prize. He had expected to become secretary of state in the second term, but the incumbent, William Rogers, refused to go with the rest of the Cabinet members not being retained by Nixon. Rogers did not want to be associated with Nixon's housecleaning. He would resign later, when it did not look like he was being forced out. Nixon was unable to insist that he go because Rogers was someone with whom he "had a long-standing relationship."[31] Kissinger was disappointed and had to wait until later in 1973 to become secretary of state.

Of the Big Five assistants to the president, the most similar to the three counsellors was Treasury Secretary Shultz. He was like them in that he headed a Cabinet department but now had also formally received a second hat as a White House appointee, with a small staff in the White House complex and with responsibilities for a policy area broader than that of his department's jurisdiction. His domain was roughly that of the super-department of economic affairs that had been part of the Ash Council's reorganization proposal in 1971. Shultz's super-secretary role was also similar to that of the counsellors in that his personal style and his self-definition of the position greatly affected how he operated. In his case, Shultz liked to operate in an extremely informal way, almost solely through a daily morning meeting of all the relevant working-level officials (as opposed to principals) involved in economic matters. (See next section for a discussion of how the three counsellors defined their respective roles.) Finally, like the other three, Shultz's work was mostly executed by task forces and ad hoc groupings rather than through meetings of the Cabinet-level principals.

But the differences are greater than the similarities. First, the difference in titles was more than mere semantics. Shultz reported directly to the president and was the coequal of the other four assistants to the president. In contrast, the three counsellors were in the next tier of the administration, functionally reporting to Ehrlichman, who was one of Shultz's peers. Second, Shultz's role was not significantly out of the ordinary because treasury secretaries had often been the administration's lead person on all economic policy. In that respect, Nixon was merely shifting his treasury secretary's role from de facto to de jure. Shultz wrote in 1998 that each person who followed him in his Cabinet position "continues to take the lead on economic issues." By contrast, the counsellor structure was unprecedented. Third, Shultz identified what he felt was a crucial difference between his work and that of the three counsellors, one that emanated from differences between his area of economic policy and the three domestic policy areas of the counsellors. Economic policy issues, he wrote, "were not closely tied to the welfare of large departmental bureaucracies or of well-organized clientele groups. International trade issues and price controls, for example, were not so deeply enmeshed in the traditional departmental and congressional mechanisms of the advocacy system as were many of the subsidy, grant-in-aid, and regulatory issues faced by the counsellors." So, Shultz himself did not see his two-hatted appointment as the equivalent of the three counsellor positions. Fourth, Shultz was given only one professional staffer for his super-departmental responsibilities, while the three counsellors were given budgets for three to four professional staffers.[32]

The modest academic literature on the 1973 reorganization has been split as to whether the events of the first half of 1973 resulted in Nixon appointing three or four super-secretaries. Harold Seidman differentiated between the three counsellors and Shultz's role. Similarly (in reverse chronological order), Bradley Patterson, Terry Moe, Carl Tubbesing, and Moshe Shani focused on three rather than four.[33] On the other hand, scholars such as Andrew Rudalevige, Robert Mason, Stephen Hess, Melvin Small, and Sidney Milkis counted four super-secretaries.[34] Without a broad consensus in the literature, the issue permits taking either side. In this inquiry, the focus will be on the three counsellors, not the four super-secretaries. First, as reviewed above, Shultz himself did not view his work as similar to that of the counsellors. Second, the archival record shows frequent contacts and meetings between the three counsellors and the staffs while very little with Shultz, hinting that he was not a bird of the same feather or, shifting metaphors, in the same orbit. Third, from the perspective of valid comparisons, Shultz's situation was not identical to that of the three counsellors. The benefit of focusing only on the three is their having the *identical* status, powers, and staffing. This allows for directly comparing and contrasting their activities and records. So the focus here will be on an in-depth examination of the day-to-day work of the three counsellors. Still, the similarities between Shultz's two-hatted role and that of the counsellors are close enough to merit a summative historical comparison (chapter 9).

The nomenclature "counsellor," spelled with the double el, deserves a brief explanation. In common American parlance, "counsel" means a lawyer. However, since the 1940s the State Department has had a senior official at the assistant secretary level called and spelled "counselor," with the meaning of senior advisor.[35] In 1969, Nixon created a new rank of senior presidential assistant called and spelled "counsellor." According to speechwriter Ray Price, this title signified "ministers-without-portfolio in the Cabinet." A *de novo* American dictionary published in 1966 explained the double-el usage as "esp[ecially] Brit[ish]." It could be that Nixon, himself a lawyer, wanted a title that clearly differentiated legal from policy work. It could also be that he felt the British spelling was more distinguished and implied a more elevated position.[36] Newspapers, however, seemed determined to "correct" Nixon's odd spelling. Virtually all journalistic references spelled the title as "counselor," presumably based on newsroom stylebooks. However, occasionally, the administration's preferred spelling slipped through in the *New York Times, Washington Post,* and *Christian Science Monitor.* This inquiry uses the spelling Nixon favored.[37]

At the beginning of Nixon's presidency, there was only one counsellor, Arthur Burns, who was assigned broad responsibility for domestic policy. Given Nixon's keen interest in foreign policy, Burns could have emerged as a kind of assistant president for domestic affairs. However, the professorial Burns was not interested in that. He was more interested in an advisory role ("staff," in management jargon) than in directly managing the domestic bureaucracy ("line").[38] The senior status of a counsellor was confirmed when the White House determined that in formal protocol counsellors outranked assistants to the president, such as Kissinger and Haldeman.[39]

When Burns took over as chair of the Federal Reserve, Nixon named Daniel Moynihan, domestic affairs assistant (and later a Democratic senator from New York), to replace him as counsellor. Nixon began using the counsellor title as a way station for people he was "kicking upstairs." When Robert Finch proved unable to manage HEW to the president's satisfaction, Nixon appointed him counsellor, as he did with Robert Mayo, who was ousted as budget director.[40] Neither stayed very long. After serving as head of the Office of Economic Opportunity, Donald Rumsfeld, a former congressional representative from Illinois, was also appointed counsellor.[41] To criticism that women were not given important positions in his administration, in late 1972, Nixon named Anne Armstrong counsellor with Cabinet rank and a grab bag of duties.[42] In mid-1973, after disbanding the super-secretaries and making another try at shaking off Watergate, Nixon appointed Melvin Laird, his first-term defense secretary, to be a counsellor for domestic affairs.[43] So, while the title had formal prestige through its protocol ranking, it sometimes conveyed a significant and important role and at other times was almost an honorific.

THREE COUNSELLORS, THREE HISTORICAL EXEMPLARS

History is best presented in chronological order. In some respects, this is merely a natural aspect of storytelling, of letting the audience experience the story as it unfolds. For example, the actions of the major actors in this narrative were based on what they knew at that time and what they were trying to accomplish. They did not know that the counsellorships would be suddenly aborted. Hence, conveying their actions in the context of unfolding events permits a more full-throated telling of the story as it happened and from a ground-level perspective. This approach also permits glimpses into what might have transpired had the super-secretaries lasted longer. Therefore, the book is entirely in sequential order, except when the story covers the simultaneous activities of each counsellor during the period of "normalcy." Those chapters have similar structures, facilitating a comparison of each counsellor's activities with those of his two counterparts.

As historical luck would have it, the three personalities and management styles that these individuals brought to their jobs greatly affected their performance. The position was so unprecedented that there were no templates to follow, no administrative, policy, or political furrows to guide one's work. The job was what one made of it, and the three counsellors did exactly that. These different personalities and management styles present three very different scenarios of how Nixon's experiment could have played out had it lasted longer. In a sense, these are three distinct test cases of how a presidential appointee who was responsible for more than one Cabinet department could operationalize the job. The order of the chapters discussing the individual activities of the three counsellors was chosen to reflect the extensiveness (or limitations) of the self-definition that each member of the trio assumed about his role: Weinberger, embodying the broadest scope of the position, Lynn in the middle range, and Butz as the least active. Weinberger acted like he had been appointed assistant president, Lynn viewed himself as a presidential coordinator, and Butz was a dutiful but unenergetic counsellor.

Caspar Weinberger was a very well organized person who liked structure, details, meetings, and memos. He wanted his office to operate as *he* believed the president wanted. In other words, he wanted to be in charge. He was a hands-on manager and truly wanted to be a super-secretary, directing multiple federal departments and agencies. He would be, in effect, the assistant president for human resources. His record is recounted in chapter 5. However, given Weinberger's expansive and precedent-setting behavior, his activities sometimes were a synecdoche for the entire counsellor project. Therefore, for some aspects of his work, such as reporting to the president and relationships with OMB, Weinberger's performance is discussed in the chapter on the overall work of the counsellors (chapter 4), rather than in the chapter devoted solely to Weinberger's counsellorship (chapter 5).

James Lynn was a conscientious member of the president's political team. He wanted to be a team player from the White House perspective. Coming from the Commerce Department, where he had been general counsel and then undersecretary, Lynn was a novice to community development, but he had faith in his ability to master new policy areas. In a sense, he represented the underlying philosophy of generalist public administration. A person with generic managerial talents was expected to be able to oversee just about any policy portfolio. Lynn's service as counsellor embodied one of the descriptors generally used by the White House for this project, namely, to be a *coordinator* for the president. (Lynn's subsequent role as OMB director for President Ford was a continuation of that career track as a generalist senior government manager.) Chapter 6 recounts Lynn's counsellorship.

Earl Butz assumed his counsellorship when he was at an age when some people begin thinking about retirement (or had already retired). In 1973, he was sixty-three, whereas Weinberger was fifty-five and Lynn, forty-six. He had no particular interest in nonagricultural matters, was less ambitious about obtaining any new powers in the administration, and was more passive in his managerial approach to the job. But the president had asked him to do something, and he, dutifully, agreed. He was to be a passive and reactive counsellor (chapter 7).

2

PLANNING, NOVEMBER 1972–
JANUARY 1973

On Tuesday, November 7, 1972, President Nixon was reelected, defeating the Democratic nominee, Senator George McGovern of South Dakota. In political terms, it was a landslide. Nixon received 61 percent of the popular vote and carried forty-nine states, losing only Massachusetts and the District of Columbia. Of 538 Electoral College votes (270 needed to win), he received 520. Nixon believed this overwhelming victory was more than a personal win; it was also an explicit endorsement of the policies he had promoted during his first term and that had not been enacted due to powerful political forces that opposed him. Using a poker analogy, he indicated that he had been blocked during his first term by "'all four aces' in Washington: Congress, the bureaucracy, the media, and the lawyers and lobbyists." Nixon was determined to use his victory to accomplish what he had not been able to do in his first term. "He needed more *control*."[1] Then, he'd be able to get his way notwithstanding the resistance of those four aces of Washington power.

PRE-ELECTION PREPARATIONS FOR REORGANIZATION

The morning after the election, Nixon asked for the resignations of all Cabinet secretaries, all White House staffers, and all members of the sub-cabinet. (The latter category consists of positions for which the president nominates candidates subject to Senate confirmation, such as assistant secretaries, deputy secretaries, undersecretaries, and general counsels.) The memo distributed by Haldeman explained that the reason for the requested resignation letters was "to give the President a free hand to strengthen the *structure* of the government as he begins his second term." This was a hint of the contemplated reorganization that would address personnel appointments, organizational structures, responsibilities, reporting lines, and coordination. Nixon then left for a post-election stay at his Florida vacation home in Key Biscayne to mull over the decisions he needed to make by the beginning of his second term.[2]

However, in-house planning for the reorganization was already well under way before the election and overlapped with the Watergate cover-up. On September 15, 1972, White House legal counsel John Dean had his first extensive meeting with the president to brief him on the Watergate cover-up. It took place in the Oval Office, and Haldeman was also present. Earlier that day, federal prosecutors had indicted the seven Watergate burglars, but no one else. It was as though the break-in had been immaculately conceived. It looked like the cover-up was working. According to Stanley Kutler, "This fateful meeting gives lie to Nixon's later claims that he never met John Dean until late February 1973. Dean, the cover-up's chief field officer, reports to the man on top." But they did not discuss only Watergate that day. Nixon smoothly segued from discussing the cover-up to another important subject that was on his mind that day, "my long-term determination to restructure the bureaucracy in Washington." Haldeman wrote that Nixon talked that day about "the sprawling Federal bureaucracy [that] had to be streamlined and brought under control. . . . And so, on September 15, 1972, less than seven weeks before he was reelected, Nixon pondered the reorganization that was to take place."[3]

Following up on that meeting, Haldeman then asked Assistant to the President Peter Flanigan (who also served as executive director of the White House Council on International Economic Policy) to prepare a draft memo to the president outlining a reorganization plan. He had likely turned to Flanigan because of his previous career as a Wall Street investment banker. In that private sector role, Flanigan had observed the senior management of some of the largest and most prestigious businesses in the United States. Haldeman specifically asked Flanigan to confer with Roy Ash, who had headed the Ash Council during Nixon's first term. That council had proposed the reorganization of the domestic executive branch into super-departments based on function. Ash was now expected to become OMB director (the post Caspar Weinberger occupied at the time) in the second term. Oddly, given that background, Ash had little to say to Flanigan and had not been planning on submitting anything to the president on the subject of reorganization.[4] (The reasons for this apparent disinterest became clear a few months later.)

Flanigan proposed retaining the Cabinet's composition (with its size possibly shrinking if any of the Ash Council reorganization proposals were adopted by Congress) but radically redefining the Cabinet's work and orientation. A major problem, he suggested, was that Cabinet secretaries had their offices in their departments and came to the White House only for specific meetings: "This physical separation tends, however, to create in the Secretaries a Departmental point of view, rather than a Presidential view. This Departmental loyalty often results in conflicts between the Departments and the White House, or between individual Departments, which must be arbitrated at the White House. Instead of being an Executive Committee under the President for the management of the Executive Branch, the Secretaries tend to become a group of semi-independent 'barons' with whom the President deals at arm's length through his White House Staff."[5] He suggested using a corporate model based on the structures of large conglomerates. In corporate practice, a CEO would run the organization through an executive committee that consisted of vice presidents who headed major corporate units. They had their offices down the hall from the CEO, so that all could be in touch easily and frequently. This physical proximity also helped build and maintain a team-based orientation that viewed the corporation from a centralized perspective. They were all working to accomplish the goals set by the CEO. They were *his* men.[6]

Flanigan wanted the Cabinet secretaries to adopt the same mentality and for each of them to spend the majority of his time at an office in the Old Executive Office Building (OEOB), part of the White House complex.[7] Not only would they be across the alley from the White House proper, but because in his first term Nixon had set up a "hideaway" office in OEOB, where he preferred to work rather than in the Oval Office, the Cabinet officers would be down the hall from the president, just like in corporate conglomerates. As a result of this physical proximity and frequent contact, "the Secretaries would then become the President's Executive Committee, each with the primary responsibility for dealing with his own Department. Each would have the Presidential point of view as his Assistants now do, and thus would represent the President's interests to the Departments rather than the Department's interests to the President."[8]

In Flanigan's plan, departments would be run on a day-to-day basis by the deputy secretary or undersecretary. The secretary would be in touch with the deputy secretary to ensure that the president's agenda was being implemented and to handle issues that could not be resolved within the department. Finally, Flanigan emphasized that Cabinet secretaries could no longer be appointed for political reasons, for reasons of geographical or ethnic balance, or to please special interest groups. Instead, they must be men who were good managers, who could be good public spokesmen for the administration, and, most importantly, were men with whom the president was comfortable working. If all this was accomplished, then "the President would have much tighter control of the Executive Branch, a greater degree of management support, and a substantial reduction in Executive Branch friction." It was a bold plan to structure government more like a business. Flanigan's memo ended up being very influential, with much of his thinking embedded in the final reorganization plan Nixon announced on January 5, 1973.[9]

APPROVING THE CONCEPT AND THE MEN

On Thursday, November 9, two days after the election, the *Washington Evening Star* published an interview that Nixon had given its reporter a few days before the election but with the condition that it not be published until after the election. The president's overview of his plans for the second term explicitly included reorganization. "We have had very little success in getting action on our reorganization plans," he said. Therefore, "I intend to accomplish it, as much as I can, through action at the executive level unless and until the Congress acts." It was a clear statement of his plans—a grand reorganization of the federal executive branch through executive action alone. According to the *New York Times*, Nixon's "immediate goal was to find some means of translating his wishes and policies more effectively to the operating departments."[10]

Reorganization became the running theme of the news coverage during the entire interregnum. Headlines from November 1972 included such examples as "Nixon Holds Talks on Reorganization," "Nixon Confers with Cabinet Aides on Reorganization," and "Nixon Goes to Camp David to Work on Reorganization."[11] However, as used by the media, the term *reorganization* gradually became a shorthand reference that covered not only structural reorganization but also a panoply of personnel and other changes he was planning for the White House, the Executive Office of the President, the Cabinet, and the subcabinet.

The press reporting was generally accurate about what was going on behind the scenes. Detailed in-house plans for the executive-based reorganization were being finalized quickly. November 14 (exactly one week after the election) was a key day in the development of the plan. First, OMB director Caspar Weinberger submitted a proposal to the president for the reorganization. (As the president's central management agency, OMB had for the previous two years been the lead agency in designing, drafting, and advocating for the legislative reorganization proposals Nixon had submitted to Congress.) Weinberger, who at this point did not know what role (if any) the president had in mind for him in the second term, suggested grouping related Cabinet departments and independent agencies into four or five clusters. Each cluster would be overseen by a presidential appointee with the title of executive vice president or assistant to the president: "These officers would *not* have day-to-day administrative duties, but rather would coordinate the activities of those departments and agencies placed under him. . . . Together they would give the President the ability to secure more rapid execution of Presidential decisions and policy throughout the government, since each would be free of detailed administrative duties or of the task of 'running' an agency." Weinberger wrote that when he had been finance director to California governor Ronald Reagan, he had proposed something similar, that Reagan had indeed pursued it using his administrative powers, that it had worked well, and that, consequently, two years later the state legislature had given statutory sanction to the super-department reorganization.[12]

Also on November 14, Walter Minnick, an attorney within Ehrlichman's White House domain, shuttled up to Camp David (where Nixon was ensconced after his post-election vacation in Florida) with a detailed draft of a reorganization plan that had been prepared based on Ehrlichman's guidance.[13] Later that day, with the packet from Minnick, Ehrlichman and Haldeman had a "long" meeting with the president to go over the administrative reorganization they were proposing. Nixon "bought the concept."[14] Essentially, there would be three senior aides to the president for substantive policy (i.e., excluding Haldeman's chief of staff role). One would be responsible for foreign affairs, one for economic issues, and the third—Ehrlichman—for domestic policy. Under Ehrlichman there would be three senior officials, each responsible for a functional area of federal domestic activities. Per the Ash Council, their rubrics would be human resources, community development, and natural resources.[15] (The Justice Department would remain outside these arrangements.)

After their November 14 meeting with the president, Haldeman and Ehrlichman met with John Dean to discuss the latest developments in the Watergate cover-up. Ehrlichman was in a euphoric mood, delighted that his approach to domestic reorganization had been approved by the president. According to Dean, Ehrlichman "was riding high and was totally absorbed in the reorganization," with little interest in spending time on Watergate minutiae. In Dean's (unstated) opinion, the plan would make Ehrlichman "in effect, chief executive of domestic affairs, because Nixon did not interest himself much in such matters and ordinarily deferred to Ehrlichman's judgment." When asked about the impact and scope of the plan, he said to Dean somewhat enigmatically, "I think it will make the birds sing." Dean, aware of Minnick's legal work on the reorganization and protective of his own prerogatives as the president's legal counsel, claimed that there could be some legal issues about a reorganization that was not authorized by Congress and that he (Dean) must be included in the planning and the preparation of the official documents. Ehrlichman unenthusiastically assented, not particularly happy to add another person who could put his thumbprint on Ehrlichman's plan.[16]

Even though Nixon had approved the reorganization concept in principle on November 14, it was still only a concept. At this stage, many of the details still needed to be determined. For example, a contemporaneous staff paper summarizing the thinking at that point and highlighting issues that were unresolved referred to the officers as "Executive Secretaries" and discussed whether they were line or staff. In other words, were they directly responsible for running the agencies under their bailiwicks or were they merely advisors to the president? Was the president delegating his decision-making and policy-making powers to them or was he merely asking them for advice on what he should do?[17]

Other subjects were raised in a list titled "Open Questions" that was attached to the concept paper. Haldeman answered some, skipping others. To the question of whether the Interior Department should be assigned to the economics area or to that of domestic policy, he wrote, "Probably so—but gets too big." Would the Cabinet be abolished? "No." Would there be councils for the three domestic areas? "Yes." The key open question was, "What is the legality of the Executive Secretaries directing the Departments?" Haldeman wrote, "No prob[lem]—deleg[ation] by P[resident]."[18]

Haldeman and Ehrlichman quickly finalized some of the details that needed to be determined for the process to proceed. The officers would be called counsellors, they would have *line* responsibilities over the departments in their domain, and they would simultaneously serve as the secretary of the department that would be the core of the administratively reorganized super-department. They were expected to assume that the deputy or undersecretary would run the department on a day-to-day basis. The counsellors were to avoid getting enmeshed in the *management* of their home departments. Instead, they were to focus on developing and implementing White House policy, whether for their individual departments or for their larger counsellor domains. Given these responsibilities, they would be spending large portions of their time at their offices in the White House complex, not at their departmental offices. The last structural issue that Haldeman and Ehrlichman worked out was that one of the counsellors' levers of power would be to chair a White House council whose members would be the secretaries and agency heads in their super-departmental domain.

In terms of personnel, Ehrlichman recommended who would fill the three counsellor offices that would be reporting to him. Caspar Weinberger, with a reputation as a budget cutter, would become HEW secretary and counsellor for human resources (HR), with the special mandate to cut domestic programs and spending. James Lynn, undersecretary of commerce, would become HUD secretary and counsellor for community development (CD). Earl Butz, secretary of agriculture, would be one of the few secretaries to be kept from the first term and would be counsellor for natural resources (NR). Haldeman and the president agreed to those recommendations. They were ready to start informing people of their assignments.

Before they could do that, a leak to the *Washington Star* ruined Nixon's secrecy about one aspect of the reorganization. On Sunday, November 19, 1972, the *Star* ran a front-page story that Nixon was planning to implement his 1971 reorganization of Cabinet departments through the maximal use of his powers and would not seek congressional approval, as he had done in the first term. The story was based on information from "one source close to the reorganization."[19]

Nixon was livid. *Another* leak. During the first term, he had wanted total control of news management and wanted even more for the second. The president quickly reached for the telephone to complain to his senior staff about the story and asked that the source be ferreted out. "Go to the limits of the law," he told his press secretary, Ron Ziegler, and then Haldeman, to find the source of the leak. It is "no excuse that this is exactly what we're gonna do. It's a question of when we say it, in the right context," he told Haldeman.[20] With his passion for secrecy and control, Nixon had an intrinsic disdain for leaks, but he was on target in believing that early leaks of the reorganization plan would allow more time for opponents to oppose it, more time for legislators to raise questions about the legality and constitutionality of his plan, more time for negative stories, more time for individuals to lobby him to protect specific programs and agencies. It would be policy death by a thousand paper cuts. He wanted a PR plan that would announce the reorganization in one swift move and as a fait accompli. Still, the story was accurate. He had given up on getting any major reorganization through Congress and wanted to do it by executive fiat. From now on, whenever the administration would soothingly reassure Congress that changes planned and implemented were merely in anticipation of reorganization plans to be submitted to Congress, they were engaging in political double-talk.

Nixon's next call was to aide Charles Colson. Besides complaining about the leak, he also made a few comments reflecting his thinking about the rationale for the reorganization. They talked about what secretaryship to offer Peter J. Brennan, a union official from the building trades who had supported Nixon's reelection, even though most organized labor was Democratic. Nixon said that offering him HUD would not be a good idea because we're "gonna make that a super thing, [including] basically shut down" the Model Cities program. However inarticulately, he had effectively conveyed how the counsellor plan would downgrade HUD. Later in the conversation, he and Colson were talking about the exercise of political power. Nixon said that the "best thing we['re] doing is getting this goddam government reorganized." He complained that "these Cabinet people sit on their ass" and don't forcefully try to help the president—whether in the exercise of power or in reelection campaigns.[21] Again, it was a frank statement of the downgrading of rank-and-file Cabinet officers that would be accomplished through the super-secretary proposal.

With the in-house details worked out by Ehrlichman and Haldeman, Nixon was ready on November 20 to begin seeing at Camp David the men he would name for the second-term Cabinet and the ones he did not want to remain but felt he had to tell in person (such as Secretary of State Rogers). Weinberger recalled his helicopter flight to Camp David. Not knowing in advance what Nixon's decision would be for him, he joked with a fellow passenger that if they saw a trap door on the floor of the helicopter, they would know what Nixon's decision was.[22]

Haldeman and Ehrlichman had carefully prepared a detailed four-part questionnaire that potential nominees for Cabinet secretary or heads of the independent agencies would have to fill out—with the "correct" answers if they hoped to fill the position. The questionnaire dealt with the entire scope of the reorganization. The first section focused on the role of the counsellors (and the assistants to the president), who would be responsible, on behalf of the president, for *policy*. Second, OMB would be renamed the Office of Executive Management and would be in charge of overseeing the *management* and implementation by the departments of policies set by the president. The third section of the questionnaire required the appointee to agree that the White House would directly appoint and oversee the four subcabinet positions in the department that were viewed as key levers of power: assistant secretaries for public affairs and for congressional relations, the general counsel (who was at the same hierarchical level as assistant secretaries), and the officer in charge of personnel management. The final part of the questionnaire dealt with miscellaneous issues related to the modus operandi for the second term, such as responsibility for leaked documents, limits on use of government aircraft for secretarial travel, and a conflict of interest policy.

The first section of the questionnaire, dealing with the role of the counsellors vis-à-vis Cabinet secretaries, contained ten statements that nominees would have to agree to in advance. Some of the questions were:

> 1. It is the President's policy that insofar as possible all interdepartmental and inter agency issues should be resolved by the Counsellors and not the White House. . . .
> 3. A Cabinet Secretary should not be encouraged to anticipate either free access or frequent consultation with the President. Rather, his views will be transmitted to the President either in writing or via a principal secretary [i.e., counsellor] or Assistant [to the president] depending on the nature of the matter.
> 4. Cabinet secretaries will be requested to delegate to Counsellors substantial authority concerning the operation of their Departments. This delegation will be express and precise and, in each case, will be made in advance. . . .

8. Cabinet meetings will be rare. Cabinet officers will be expected to act in concert with their colleagues in policy groups and policy councils [the latter chaired by counsellors]. . . .

10. The Secretary agrees to submit to the appropriate Counsellor all Congressional testimony and public statements for clearance prior to release.[23]

It was an audacious and sweeping reorganization, essentially giving the three counsellors (and the assistant to the president for domestic affairs, Ehrlichman, to whom *they* reported) extensive power over the other secretaries and agency heads within their domains.

One of the items in the fourth part of the questionnaire applied especially to the counsellors, even though it was applicable to all secretaries-designate. It directed that, "in the case of the Counsellor particularly, and to a lesser extent in other departments, the Under Secretaries or Deputy Secretaries will play increasingly important roles. Cabinet Secretaries will be expected to vest in their Number Two men broad capacity to operate and manage the Department."[24] Nixon, Haldeman, and Ehrlichman wanted to be sure that the counsellors would not try to serve as de facto secretaries, only as de jure ones.

At the meetings with Butz, Lynn, and Weinberger, Nixon was explicit about his wishes. Nixon said to Butz that the counsellor for natural resources could just as easily go to the secretary of interior as to the head of USDA, since both departments were deeply involved in natural resource issues. However, Nixon said he selected Butz because Butz was "tougher, more ruthless [and] will do what needs to be done. [I] Hope you're a bastard." In general, Nixon said, he wanted "creative thinking at [the] top level." Butz agreed to all of the conditions outlined in the questionnaire and in the meeting, but he apparently did not *really* absorb the message: later in the meeting he advocated more frequent and regularly scheduled Cabinet meetings, perhaps every two weeks. He wanted to reduce the feeling that secretaries were being isolated from the president and that Cabinet meetings were usually called on short notice largely to serve as stage props for presidential news making. This was precisely the opposite direction that Nixon wanted to go. After Butz left the room, Nixon told Ehrlichman and Haldeman to have Cabinet meetings "perhaps" once a month, probably less, certainly not more frequently than that.[25]

Lynn told Nixon he welcomed the appointment, that it would be a "challenge" and that he had a "clean [i.e., open] mind" regarding the policy issues. Nixon told Lynn not to be like George Romney, the outgoing HUD secretary who, in Nixon's opinion, had "pandered" to blacks. He said to Ehrlichman that Lynn should "flush Model Cities & G[rea]t soc[iety]" programs. "It's failed," he said. He wanted programs that truly led to community development.[26] Weinberger had been hoping for DOD, but Nixon had decided to send HEW Secretary Elliot Richardson there. In Nixon's logic, Weinberger was good at cutting spending, so he belonged at HEW. Richardson was viewed as the opposite. He was good at spending money. Therefore, he should be at the Pentagon, where Nixon wanted to increase military spending in the cold war arms race with the Soviet Union.[27]

The first detailed public hint of what was to come resulted from a White House leak to friendly columnists Rowland Evans and Robert Novak. In their column on November 22, 1972, they wrote that "masterbureaucrats would be given jurisdictions inside the White House roughly paralleling the 1971 reorganization [plan], with responsibilities cutting across existing departments and agencies." They said that the Domestic Council would be abolished because its jurisdiction was too broad. It would be replaced by more "manageable units," councils each chaired by these masterbureaucrats for their policy areas. The goal of the reorganization was "a federal bureaucracy responsive to Mr. Nixon." But to prove that they were not stooges of the Nixon White House, Evans and Novak two days later ran a column about the potential problems Nixon's reorganization would have on Capitol Hill, with both majority Democrats and minority Republicans, because legislators from both parties felt frozen out of what was happening at Camp David.[28]

On November 27, five days after the initial Evans and Novak column about masterbureaucrats, Nixon briefed the press and hinted at what was to come. The White House staff has "rather grown like Topsy.... It is now time to reverse that growth to do a more effective job, by bringing the Cabinet members into closer contact with the White House." He wanted to take the power that was assigned to the president and "have that power given to and delegated to, where it possibly can, to responsible members of the Administration team in the Cabinet."[29]

CREATING THE STRUCTURE

In-house planning continued apace in December. Dean prepared a packet of legal documents to be used to establish the counsellor system. He envisioned a broader system of counsellors reporting to their respective assistant to the president not just in domestic affairs but also for economic affairs and for a combination of national defense and foreign affairs. Each counsellor would also head a "Group," comprising the secretaries and agency heads in the counsellor's domain, who would advise him. Dean's key recommendation was that the counsellor system be established by issuing an executive order to be signed by the president. An executive order, while not having the full force of law, would still have a strong legal status. Especially since the FDR administration, executive orders had been used by presidents to create binding and authoritative policies that they imposed on the executive branch, with Congress playing no role (short of passing a law that negated or superseded the executive order). Executive orders were promulgated by issuance in the *Federal Register*, were codified into an ongoing integrated code (like laws or formal regulations), and were recognized as having some official and authoritative force by the courts.[30] The recommendation to base the reorganization on an executive order was an important detail. Dean wanted the counsellors (and the assistants to the president they reported to) to have maximum legal standing short of congressional enactment of a reorganization bill or plan. His packet of documents included a nine-page draft executive order.[31]

The draft legal documents also included an addendum discussing the options for the legal status of the counsellors. Dean outlined three options. First, while they would physically be in OEOB, organizationally they could be wholly outside the president's official inner "family," thus giving them equal status to the Cabinet secretaries not affected by the reorganization, such as the attorney general. However, a drawback to this was that the counsellors would have little perceived status over other Cabinet secretaries. A second option was that they could be a new organizational entity within the Executive Office of the President (EOP), placing them on par with such presidential agencies as OMB and DC, but this would go against Nixon's already proclaimed policy of simplifying EOP. In the third option, they could be appointees within the White House Office. In that case, they would have "greatest status," clearly outranking the rank-

and-file Cabinet secretaries. However, based on the practice during the first term, counsellors outranked assistants to the president in protocol, the opposite of the decision already made—that counsellors would report *to* assistants to the president. Also, Dean noted, as appointees within the White House Office, they could invoke the controversial legal doctrine of executive privilege and decline to testify before Congress.[32]

Other hands were also at work on the plan. Roy Ash, the incoming OMB director (and concurrently to be one of the Big Five, with the title of assistant to the president for management), contributed a draft presidential statement outlining the rationale for the changes. He was careful to predicate the administrative reorganization as a first step to a statutory reorganization, hoping the link would strengthen the legitimacy of Nixon's actions. However, Ash had heard informally that Haldeman and Ehrlichman were leaning away from any request for legislation. Ash was not quite sure how strongly he wanted to disagree with them but wanted to make the point nonetheless. For example, he was concerned about what the legal status of any of the counsellors would be before a formal reorganization bill would be submitted to Congress. And what if the administration eventually decided to submit the CD and HR reorganization proposals but not the NR one? Would that automatically delegitimize the continued operations of the NR counsellor? Finally, if Congress approved one or two of the super-departments, would the counsellor for the unapproved super-department have to be terminated? Therefore, Ash proposed several different ways for handling this legal issue in the draft presidential statement. Options were "in preparation for (in anticipation of) (pending) actual reorganization restructuring."[33] Ash was trying to prepare for all eventualities.

Yet, privately, Ash did not support the proposal. He felt it was a misrepresentation to claim that the counsellor system would be a partial implementation of the Ash Council's recommendations for super-departments. In particular, he felt that it was untenable that a counsellor concurrently serve as the secretary of the principal department forming the core of the counsellor's domain. What if, he wondered, there was a dispute between a Cabinet department within the counsellor's area of responsibility and the counsellor's own department? And what if the counsellor resolved the conflict in favor of his own department? Wouldn't that smack of a lack of objectivity, a lack of fairness? Therefore, he believed that the counsellor concept that Ehrlichman had pressed for was fatally flawed. However, Ash did not believe that this topic was one that merited a line in the sand. One must pick and choose one's fights, he knew. "I wasn't going to dig in my heels in my first week in office," he stated. "So, I went along with it."[34]

Mark Alger, OMB's assistant director in charge of the agency's general government division, had overall responsibility for government-wide reorganization issues. Therefore, he began preparing a document about the counsellor system. One issue he addressed in the document was how to pin down precisely which federal activities would fall under, for example, the HR domain. (With Weinberger still officially the head of OMB, presumably this list was prepared partly at Weinberger's behest.) Of a list of fourteen affected agencies, only half would be wholly under the HR counsellor, and all of them were independent agencies, including the Veterans Administration and some small agencies such as the Special Action Office for Drug Abuse Prevention (the "drug czar," a presidential office in EOP), the National Foundation for the Arts and Humanities, and the Railroad Retirement Board. Of six Cabinet agencies, *none* would be wholly under the HR counsellor, not even all of HEW, of which the counsellor would also be secretary. According to OMB, two HEW programs, library construction and the National Institute for Occupational Safety and Health, did not belong under the rubric of human resources. Parts of other departments that would fall under Weinberger's purview would come from Labor, Interior, HUD (which was the principal agency of the CD counsellor), Commerce, and USDA (the principal agency of the NR counsellor). Not even all of the Office of Economic Opportunity (OEO, which was LBJ's War on Poverty agency), an agency presumably focused solely on poverty issues, would be under Weinberger.[35] It was an indication of both the complexity of what Nixon was trying to accomplish and the reasons why Congress had been so resistant to grand reorganizations, namely, that grand reorganizations would affect the structure and jurisdictions of House and Senate committees. None of the powerful committee chairs wanted to give up any power.

Another unresolved issue was the precise title for Secretary Butz's counsellorship. While many of the early planning documents used the term "natural resources," two others suggested "energy and natural resources." This reflected a prescient and early recognition of the importance that energy policy issues would play in the mid-1970s.[36]

Stronger public indications of the reorganization to come occurred throughout December 1972. Early in the month the White House announced that George Shultz would continue to serve as treasury secretary and that Roy Ash would head OMB. When Ziegler made the Shultz an-

nouncement to the media, he said that Shultz would simultaneously serve
as assistant to the president and "will be the focal point and the overall
coordinator of the entire economic policy decision-making process."
Shultz briefly met with the media after Ziegler's announcement and said
that "I will also have an office in the White House and a very small staff
to help me in carrying out the duties" he was given as policy coordinator,
duties that were separate from his treasury secretaryship.[37] The next day,
Ziegler announced Ash's concurrent appointments as OMB director and
assistant to the president for management: "This dual role parallels somewhat the new role that we announced for Secretary Shultz yesterday."[38]
These appointments were models that the counsellors would follow, of
holding two offices, one to run an agency and one in the White House
complex, except that they were one rung down and reported to Ehrlichman, who was one of the Big Five assistants to the president, in his case,
for domestic affairs.

Other public announcements in mid-December gave further hints of
the new structure. In an effort to set an example when the administration
imposed a freeze on federal hiring, Shultz announced that Nixon would
also be making "very substantial reductions" in the staffing of the White
House and of EOP.[39] Also, the Domestic Council was undergoing change.
Its staff would no longer be headed by Ehrlichman but by Kenneth Cole.[40]
The first step in the streamlining of the EOP was the signing of an executive order abolishing the Office of Intergovernmental Relations (chaired
by Vice President Agnew) and transferring its functions to the Domestic
Council.[41]

Behind closed doors, the planning for the reorganization focused on
determining some of the important details that were still outstanding. Ash
again raised with Haldeman and Ehrlichman the question of whether the
administration would seek super-department legislation at the same time
it established the counsellor system. Reflecting the president's tough post-
election view of Congress, the two had reached the "tentative conclusion"
that the counsellor reorganization would go ahead without the administration *ever* seeking formal super-department legislation from Congress.
"Who needs them [Congress]?" was the attitude permeating the White
House from Nixon on down. Ash was even more concerned than his November draft presidential statement on the reorganization had suggested.
He thought a request for legislation *must* be part of the whole package, thus
echoing Dean's earlier stated concern of the need to establish a legal basis
for the administrative change. Ash used just about any reason he could

think of to make his case. Not requesting legislation would undercut the goodwill built up with Representative Chet Holifield (D-Calif.), chair of the House Government Operations Committee, who had supported the DCD legislation that year. Furthermore, not introducing reorganization legislation would permit the administration's enemies to say that the 1971 reorganization legislation request had not been a serious one, that bypassing Congress on the issue could trigger counterproductive events, and that criticism of the counsellor structure while legislation was pending would permit the president to say that he "must manage in the best possible way pending legislation."[42]

Staff Secretary Bruce Kehrli (essentially the business manager of the White House) had the thankless job of trying to figure out how to shoehorn the counsellors into the prime real estate of OEOB, which was second in prestige only to the West Wing of the White House. The size of each counsellor's staff would greatly affect the amount of office space he needed to find for them. Given the difficulty of clearing three office suites in OEOB, Kehrli suggested to his boss, Haldeman, that "we should start with a limit of two assistants—knowing that the Counsellors will seek more."[43] But Haldeman and Ehrlichman were firm that the maximum funding by the White House would be three professional assistants plus clerical support staff.

Kehrli was given another planning parameter about office allocation (probably by Ehrlichman). To promote a close working relationship between each counsellor and the associate director of the Domestic Council for the same policy area, Kehrli assigned them side-by-side offices. They would be separated by only a door.[44] The disadvantage of the arrangement was that this physically separated the associate directors from their boss, DC director Cole. But the advantages outweighed the disadvantages. The physical proximity would make it easier for the counsellors to work very closely with the (reduced) Domestic Council staff. Counsellors and DC could then more easily develop hand-in-glove cooperation rather than jockeying against each other. This arrangement might mean it would be hard to differentiate the work of the Domestic Council staff from that of the counsellors, but that was fine by Ehrlichman. All reported to him, so the better the integration of their work, the easier it would be for him to carry out his supervisory responsibilities for domestic policy.

Kehrli was just scratching the surface of all the issues that would have to be settled regarding this unprecedented White House entity. A few days later, he wanted guidance from Haldeman on the salary arrangements for the counsellors and their staffs. Would they be paid from presidential salary funds? Would the positions be allocated from White House slots? Kehrli recommended that wherever possible, the counsellors' staff be detailed (i.e., lent out) by the home departments of the counsellors. The White House would then reimburse the departments from its general contingency expenses fund (which was not a salary account). In that way neither the slots nor the salaries would appear on any formal accounting of White House staffing. Given the president's announced intention of cutting White House and EOP staff, this was a sleight of hand to "implement" the reduction. Kehrli also noted that the requirement of detailing staff might be an internal brake on counsellors trying to build up the size of their White House staffs since that would come at the expense of their home departments.[45]

Another important decision signaling the power of the counsellors and their proximity to the president related to stationery. The stationery that counsellors would be using simply said "The White House," which was in contrast, for example, to the powerful OMB, which used letterhead identifying it as part of the Executive Office of the President. This detail meant that counsellors were within the White House Office, part of the inner White House, not in EOP as part of an outer presidential ring. It was a signal that Washington insiders would pick up on. The counsellors were representing the president; giving them White House stationery was one way to give the experiment a better chance to succeed. If counsellors were viewed as speaking for the White House, then they had a better chance of prevailing in all manner of bureaucratic combat.

Weinberger continued to try to influence the planning process so that counsellors' roles would be as expansive as possible. Under his direction (since Weinberger was still OMB director), Alger finalized a comprehensive memo to Ehrlichman, trying to spell out the specific responsibilities and operations of the counsellors' offices. Alger now proposed that the counsellors play a role in the budgets, personnel, legislation, program evaluation, management information, and policy communication of all the programs in their respective domains. Alger also recommended that to prevent counsellors from becoming advocates of their home departments, they would not have a role in the submission of their departments' budget requests to OMB. In general, Alger was conceptualizing a strong counsellor system, a de facto secretary of the super-department, practically as it would be if Congress passed the reorganization legislation. This concept reflected Weinberger's views. As for staffing, Alger suggested that each counsellor have about half a dozen professional staffers and slightly fewer secretaries. He concluded his memo with a discussion of the power that counsellors should exercise over their "subordinates"—a word implying total managerial control. Recognizing the touchiness of the subject with those "subordinates," Alger wrote, "Nothing need be put in writing, at least initially."[46]

However, after Alger submitted the memo, Weinberger raised a major problem about it, to the point of wanting Alger to withdraw the report and revise it. Apparently, Weinberger objected to Alger's discussion of the relationship between the counsellor's job and concurrent duties as departmental secretary. According to Alger's original memo, "His ability to perform the more important job of Counsellor will depend on how successfully he can delegate to his Under Secretary responsibility for management of his department. Clearly the Secretary must rely on the Under Secretary to do much of the day-to-day managing of the Department."[47]

Weinberger had no such intention for HEW, even though that arrangement was what Nixon and Ehrlichman wanted. Alger scurried to retrieve his memo from Walter Minnick, Ehrlichman's aide, and explained his problem to Tod Hullin, Ehrlichman's personal assistant. But Hullin reported back that Ehrlichman "felt very strongly on the necessity" of having the undersecretary run the counsellor's home department on a day-to-day basis and that the counsellor was "to remain as aloof as possible from staff supervision in his department." It was a fait accompli. At that point, Alger could not withdraw and revise the memo to Weinberger's satisfaction; doing so would only draw more attention to the issue. He reported back to Weinberger (his boss until Ash took over), "In light of this reflection of Ehrlichman's views, I thought it a bit awkward to make the change."[48]

Alger's draft served as the in-house planning document for the counsellor system. Changes in it from its original version on December 18 to a near-final version on December 29 embodied the evolution of the concept. First, Ehrlichman made some significant changes that reflected the additional details he had settled on. For example, each counsellor would be permitted only three professional staff members, and they would be paid from the home department's appropriation. Counsellors would be part of EOP, not the White House Office. The grouping of departmental secretaries and agency heads within each counsellor's domain would be a permanent committee of the Domestic Council, which meant that Ehrlichman was closely meshing two areas of his responsibility, the counsellors and the Domestic Council. Both would have to work closely together and could not function well unless they successfully developed a smooth, cooperative relationship. He strengthened the discussion of the role of the counsellor vis-à-vis serving simultaneously as Cabinet secretary. Alger had characterized the counsellor role as "more important" than the secretary role. Ehrlichman changed the wording to "extremely important."[49]

When Alger received Ehrlichman's version of December 29, he was in an even more awkward situation than he had been in mid-December, when Weinberger had asked him to withdraw his memo to Ehrlichman of December 19. By now, Ash was increasingly Alger's de facto boss, he was in active disagreement with Alger's de jure boss about the scope of the counsellors' operations, and Ehrlichman had signed off on a few changes Ash wanted to strengthen OMB vis-à-vis the counsellors. The best Alger could do vis-à-vis Weinberger was slip him a copy of Ehrlichman's version on January 3, but with a plaintive request that "I trust you will keep the source confidential."[50] In the Nixon White House one did not openly oppose Ehrlichman or one's incoming boss, both of whom were assistants to the president. Counsellors were lower on the food chain.

While there were still some details that had not been resolved, by the new year the major decisions about the counsellor plan had been locked in. The plans were for the president to brief the congressional leadership at a breakfast meeting on Friday, January 5, 1973, and then Ehrlichman would brief the White House press corps in the afternoon.

Given the specificity of details being worked out and documents being finalized, increasingly larger numbers of officials—both in- and out-of-house—needed to be involved. For example, on December 14, Nixon met with Senate Minority Leader Hugh Scott (R-Pa.) to talk about "the reorganization of the executive branch for the second term."[51] By late December word was leaking all over Washington, whether from pro-administration sources or otherwise. This reorganization was going to be *big*. But no one knew for sure the precise details. Evans and Novak ran a column about Nixon's plan for a "small supercabinet." They correctly named Weinberger, Lynn, and Butz, their domains, and that they would operate out of the White House. Also, in its last issue of 1972, *US News & World Report* discussed Nixon's upcoming multifaceted plans to assume more control over the bureaucracy. The magazine had clearly benefited from a friendly leak. (As a somewhat conservative weekly, *US News* was favored by the administration over *Newsweek,* which was perceived as more liberal.) The magazine correctly reported that there would be "supervisory officers" in a "super-Cabinet." A quote from "a high administration official" (probably Ehrlichman) about the rationale for these appointments was dead on: "One of the problems in the past has been that Cabinet officers tend to forget that the President is responsible for policy. They begin to build their own constituencies. For too many years, things have been done—not the way the White House wants—but the way the bureaucracy wants them. This is going to change."[52]

Somewhat inaccurately, both stories included Shultz in the list of individuals tapped to be "supervisory officers." To be precise, he was an assistant to the president for economic affairs, Ehrlichman's peer, while the counsellors would report to Ehrlichman. The *New York Times* printed a news analysis referring to the upcoming appointees as "supersecretaries." Playing catch-up, on Christmas Eve, the *Washington Post* ran a front-page story about the emergence of these related initiatives to take control of the executive branch, including the president's apparent plan to implement his 1971 departmental reorganization proposal "through his appointive power."[53]

In reaction to the press coverage, Senator Sam Ervin (D-N.C.), incoming chair of the Senate Government Operations Committee (which had jurisdiction over statutory reorganizations and Reorganization Act plans that were subject to legislative veto), quickly wrote Nixon, asserting that "the organization and structure of the Executive Branch is a matter of major concern to the Congress under the Constitution." He was careful not to say that the plans being discussed in the media would be a *violation* of the Constitution. Nonetheless, he requested that he be informed, in writing, of the administration's plans for and eventual actions, including— somewhat ominously—"the authority for such actions." Ervin received a noncommittal response the next day from the White House's congressional liaison office, stating merely that they would be sure "your letter is called to the attention of the President at the earliest opportunity." It was bluntly dismissive.[54]

At that time, Ervin was an obscure senator (serving since 1954) about to assume, for the first time, the chair of a standing (although low-prestige) committee. Only a few months later, he rose to prominence as chair of the Senate's special committee investigating Watergate. John Dean has suggested that perhaps Ervin's dogged leadership of the Senate Watergate Committee a few months later may have been partly caused by Ervin's reaction to the super-secretary project. Ervin's later aggressive behavior could have been based on a *substantive* reaction—was the president disregarding the Constitution?—and/or could have been *procedurally* driven—was an administrative reorganization marginalizing Ervin's newfound power as chair of the Government Operations Committee?[55] If Dean's speculation has some validity, that puts Ervin's vigorous and persistent leadership of the Senate Watergate Committee in 1973 in a slightly different light than the given Watergate narrative. In his memoirs about Watergate, Ervin did not explicitly link the super-secretary reorganization with his subsequent Watergate Committee role. However, he noted his disapproval of what he viewed as the administration's attempts in 1972 to politicize the bureaucracy to assist in the president's reelection. He condemned the fact that "they deemed the departments and agencies of the federal government to be the political playthings of the Nixon administration rather than impartial instruments for serving the people."[56] Indeed, the original plans of the Senate Watergate Committee were to hold a second round of public hearings in the fall of 1973 on several topics not directly related to the Watergate break-in, including Nixon's alleged politicization of the IRS, but those plans were eventually canceled.[57] This provides a mildly possible confirmation of Dean's speculation, along these lines: Unhappy about the politicization of the bureaucracy in the 1972 campaign, Ervin writes the president in December 1972 because he fears even more of such efforts if the administrative reorganization were to go into effect without a congressional role. Thus, the perception that the president was ignoring his letter and proceeding with the super-secretary plan is one factor in his decision in early 1973 to accept the chair of the Senate Watergate Committee and then to direct the committee's investigation in a vigorous way.

FINAL IN-HOUSE DETAILS

The new year started with three business days to go before the unveiling of the reorganization, and much staff work still needed to be done behind the scenes. On Tuesday, January 2, Dean submitted his final packet of documents for launching the counsellor project to Ash, Ehrlichman, and Haldeman (diplomatically listing them in alphabetical order).[58] He was trying to pull together all the serial decisions about the concept that had been resolved in the round robin of meetings and memos between and among Haldeman, Ehrlichman, Ash, Malek, Weinberger, and Alger, as well as their lesser staffs, such as Higby, Kehrli, and Hullin. But the final plans particularly reflected Dean's own thinking. Dean continued to feel strongly that Nixon's organizational plans needed to be presented as an integral whole. For example, the reorganization of the duties of the senior White House staff, the elimination of several units of EOP (to keep the president's promise of reducing the number of entities in EOP and cutting its staffing), and the counsellors and reorganization legislation were interrelated and should be implemented at the same time. Therefore, he prepared final drafts of two executive orders, plus a formal reorganization plan, for submission to Congress, along with three presidential memoranda.

In particular, Dean stressed that the counsellors, who were to be placed in EOP, should not be depicted in official documents as part of a *reorganization*. That word was fraught with legal meaning, he felt, and could trigger accusations of violating the president's reorganization powers, since counsellors' powers were not going to be promulgated through a reorganization plan submitted to Congress. Dean emphasized that the counsellor program should be described as merely an internal administrative arrangement for the president to use in exercising his constitutional role as chief executive. To further protect Nixon, Dean again stressed that, concurrent with the internal management decision establishing the counsellor structure, the administration must simultaneously announce that it would seek reorganization legislation similar to its first-term proposals. Then, counsellors could be depicted as "in no way intended as a usurpation of Congressional power, but instead the design and start of a framework for an entirely new Executive Branch structure that can only be completed by Congress." Further, in that context, the counsellors could innocently "be described as partially experimental, and a useful tool to illustrate to the Congress that structural reorganization is desirable."[59] Dean was acting as a good presidential lawyer should, with an overlay of political sensitivity as well as attention to the legalities.

The presidential memorandum that Dean had drafted regarding the counsellors assigned them broad responsibilities. They would, "to the extent permitted by law, serve as the focal point and coordinator for policies, programs and activities" in their functional areas.[60] Furthermore,

> The head of each executive department and agency with functions described in this memorandum and subordinates, where appropriate, should consult with and seek the timely advice of the Assistants to the President and the Counsellors to the President with respect

to policy, program, and budget decisions; and communications, key appointments, and other matters in conformity with the intent and purpose of this memorandum.

Initial consultations on the details of implementation should be arranged as soon as mutually convenient.[61]

With the deadline for the January 5 launch nearing, Wednesday and Thursday (January 3 and 4) were a flurry of last-minute activity. Ehrlichman returned to his office from a Christmas vacation (and delayed post-election rest) in Idaho on Wednesday morning and plunged into a series of meetings relating to domestic policy, the reorganization, and Watergate.[62] Presidential speechwriter Ray Price chimed in then and suggested to Ehrlichman and Haldeman that the new positions not be called counsellors because that term would lead to confusion regarding the other White House counsellors Nixon had established in his first term, who were generally considered "members-without-portfolio in the Cabinet." These new officers would be wholly different from that. How about calling them "coordinators"? Haldeman wrote a curt response on Price's memo: "I disagree. H."[63]

On Thursday morning (January 4), Ehrlichman had a catered breakfast with the three counsellors in one of the private dining rooms in the West Wing.[64] He wanted to be sure they understood his conception of their jobs, regardless of the rapidly changing iterations of the uncompleted paperwork. Ehrlichman was still in the midst of revising Dean's key document, the draft presidential memorandum outlining the roles and responsibilities of the counsellors, as was Ash.[65] Meanwhile, Ash wrote the president for guidance on what, if any, legislative initiatives OMB should prepare regarding the super-departments.[66] This was an important detail not only because of Dean's recommendation but also because it would likely come up at the congressional briefing the next morning.

Also that day the new head of the Domestic Council, Kenneth Cole, submitted an extensive memorandum to the president summarizing the administration's policy positions on the broad gamut of upcoming domestic policy initiatives. Cole started his memo by trying to mesh the substance of the administration's policy positions with the upcoming management reorganization: "Your second term domestic policy begins with one fundamental and practical premise—the role and structure of government must change if it is successfully to meet the complex domestic problems of the 1970's. . . . The necessary change in the structure and role of government can perhaps best be analyzed in terms of a positive, compassionate set of policy principles, all of which share your basic objective of closing the gap between the promise and performance of government."[67] But the memo also indirectly brought to the fore a different question. If the three counsellors covered the waterfront of domestic policy (exclusive of economic policy), then what exactly was the role of the Domestic Council and staff? This would need to be worked out. With Cole and the three counsellors all reporting to Ehrlichman, he would insist they figure out a cooperative relationship.

Ehrlichman and Haldeman met with the president for two hours on Thursday afternoon for a final discussion of the next day's announcement.[68] One of the last items that needed to be decided was the subject of Ash's memo. Nixon approved submitting legislation to Congress for a Department of Community Development (DCD) and the Department of Natural Resources (DNR).[69] The first had gotten the farthest in the preceding Congress, and the latter appeared to have some support in the Senate. So the three together made a pragmatic political decision that would reinforce the legitimacy of the counsellor initiative. Also, the preparatory materials for the congressional breakfast were careful to avoid using the word *reorganization.* Instead, the listed title of the topic was "Redirecting Executive Branch Management."[70] Dean's advice on both matters had been accepted, at least for the time being.

DIVIDING THE PIE

Dean's memo included three appendices that provided a specific and detailed listing of the jurisdictions of the three counsellors. In some cases, he listed the major component parts of a department—such as bureaus, administrations, and services—that were being assigned to a counsellor. At other times, the detail went as deep as the branch of a division of a service or even down to a specific program deep in the bowels of the bureaucracy. (A listing of the entities assigned to each counsellor is included in the respective chapter on each counsellor, that is, chapters 5, 6, and 7.)

The planning principle for the counsellor effort had been that the three counsellor-secretaries' traditional Cabinet departments would comprise the central building block for their counsellorship responsibilities. However, it is significant that in *no* case did any of the three have counsellorship oversight over the entirety of their own Cabinet departments. Rather, some portions of their Cabinet departments were subject to oversight by other counsellors. Parts of Butz's USDA were under the jurisdiction of the CD and HR counsellors. A small portion of Weinberger's HEW was assigned to the CD counsellor. Similarly, a small portion of HUD was under the oversight of the HR counsellor.

So, theoretically, Butz as NR counsellor had only partial oversight of his own Cabinet department, with elements of it under the jurisdiction of *both* of the other counsellors. For some USDA programs, *Secretary* Butz reported to Weinberger. For others, he reported to Lynn. The home departments of the other two counsellors were divided, though not as significantly as USDA. HEW reported largely to its secretary, the HR counsellor, but a small part reported to Lynn. Conversely, Lynn as HUD secretary was mostly under his own counsellorship, but for one program Lynn reported to Weinberger.

From the perspective of other major domestic Cabinet departments and agencies besides the counsellors' home departments (USDA, HEW, and HUD), the picture was equally complex. No domestic Cabinet department was exclusively under the jurisdiction of a single counsellor. Like USDA, the Department of Commerce reported to all three. Major parts of the Department of Transportation were overseen by the CD counsellor, but a small part was under the NR counsellor. Similarly, the Interior Department was predominantly under the NR counsellor, but portions of it were assigned to the HR counsellor. The Office of Economic Opportunity was split between the domains of the CD and HR counsellors.

Finally, some departments and agencies had portions of their activities within the counsellorship initiative while other parts of their programs were not under any of the three counsellors. In most cases, their other noncounsellor activities were subject to the guidance of Treasury Secretary Shultz in his capacity as assistant to the president for economic affairs or to Kissinger as the fifth of the Big Five assistants to the president, for foreign affairs.[71] Such dual reporting, partly to a counsellor (or two or three of them) and partly to Shultz's domain, was the case for the Department of Labor, DOT, Commerce, and the Small Business Administration. Even more confusingly, parts of the home departments of two of the three counsellors also reported to Shultz. Some activities of USDA and HEW were Shultz's economic responsibilities. International activities were in Kissinger's purview.

So, theoretically, USDA Secretary Butz not only reported to himself as counsellor, as well as to Weinberger and Lynn, but also to Shultz and to Kissinger for international agricultural matters. Similarly, Weinberger as HEW secretary not only reported to his own counsellor office and to Counsellor Lynn, but also to Shultz. It was very complicated. It *was* logical as well, but, realistically, such complexity bred operational difficulties, perhaps insurmountable considering the already built-in inertia of the federal bureaucratic apparatus.

In an effort to reduce the complexity, Ehrlichman indicated that a Cabinet secretary himself (as opposed to lower-echelon officials) would report to a counsellor-secretary only when the bulk of a department was within the counsellor's jurisdiction, such as the secretary of interior vis-à-vis the NR counsellor. When smaller chunks of a department were assigned to a counsellor, then the secretary of that department was not the "principal" who reported to and worked with the counsellor. Rather, the principal would be the head of that particular departmental subunit. So, for example, with Commerce's National Oceanic and Atmospheric Administration (NOAA) assigned to the NR counsellor, that meant the principal working with the NR counsellor would not be the commerce secretary but NOAA's administrator.

In part, the complex and confusing nature of these assignments was a prima facie argument by Nixon of the need for congressionally approved reorganization as well as a justification for his "interim" administrative arrangement. The structure of the federal executive branch that had accreted over a century of congressional and presidential decisions was jerry built to the extreme. This point would surely be obvious, the thinking went, from the lines on an organizational chart of the federal executive branch. If the executive branch was to operate efficiently and effectively, then similar programs should all be located within the same organizational entity. There was a need for clarity and for tidy tables of organization.

However, from the practical point of view of the day-to-day work of the counsellors, the situation was much more difficult. First, none had a "clean" responsibility for the entirety of his *own* department. Second, they sometimes shared jurisdictions regarding departments other than their own. So, for example, all three had some of the Commerce Department's subunits assigned to their oversight. Third, as a collectivity, the three had power over only portions of some Cabinet departments, with other portions of those departments or independent agencies outside the scope of the counsellorship project. This meant that secretaries and agency heads, with one foot in the new set-up and one foot out, might find it difficult to operate in a divided situation. The counsellor plan was a (temporary) jury-rigged solution to a (permanent) jerry-built problem. So, while the complexity of the counsellorships' responsibilities was a visible demonstration of the need for statutory reorganization in the *future,* the same complexity could contribute to difficulties for the counsellors as they operationalized their duties on a day-to-day basis in the *present.*

3

LAUNCH, JANUARY-FEBRUARY 1973

President Nixon invited legislators to breakfast at the White House on Friday, January 5, 1973. It would be his first bipartisan congressional session since the election, and as far as the legislators knew, it was to be a briefing about wage and price controls and would probably include some discussion of the Viet Nam peace talks and Christmas-time bombing of North Viet Nam. They did not know that one of the items on the agenda would be the super-secretary proposal. By making the reorganization one of the topics of the briefing, Nixon was signaling its importance to him, although he was springing it on his audience as a surprise. That tactic set the tone the president wanted for his second term. The president was saying, "This is important to me" and "Here's what I plan to do whether you like it or not." What he was about to announce was a far-reaching and dramatic challenge to the status quo. If he succeeded, Washington would never be the same.

PUBLIC UNVEILING

A relatively large number of legislators (about thirty) were invited to the breakfast. While leadership meetings tended to be limited to the House Speaker and Senate majority leader (both Democrats) and the House and Senate minority leaders, this event was for a much larger bipartisan delegation of senior legislators on the standing committees that would be involved in the main items on the agenda: renewal of the president's anti-inflation price controls and reorganization. About two dozen attended, including Representative Chet Holifield (D-Calif.), chair of the House Government Operations Committee, and Representative Frank Horton (R-N.Y.), ranking minority party member of the committee. The two also headed the subcommittee that handled reorganization legislation. Senators attending included Charles Percy (R-Ill.), ranking minority member of the Government Operations Committee, and Jacob Javits (R-N.Y.), ranking minority member of the Government Operations Subcommittee that had jurisdiction over reorganizations. Both had supported the 1971–1972 grand reorganization bills. The breakfast was held in the State Dining Room, with the tables arranged in the shape of an E. Sitting at Nixon's right was House Speaker Carl Albert (D-Okla.), and on his left was Representative Gerald Ford (R-Mich.), House minority leader. At the front table were Senate Majority Leader Mike Mansfield (D-Mont.), Minority Leader Hugh Scott (R-Pa.), and Vice President Spiro Agnew.[1]

The president's handwritten notes in preparation for the meeting were reminders to him to emphasize that, parallel to the *administrative* changes he was making through the new counsellor setup, there was also the *statutory* reorganization, for which "we shall submit plans to you." In addition, he wanted to emphasize that the counsellor format was part of a larger initiative on his part. "I have reorganized [the] executive branch" through this and several other related initiatives, he noted. However, this was not an effort to expand the White House, because he planned to "reduce by ½" the size of the EOP staff.[2] Nixon stayed on message during his introductory comments. According to a transcript, he briefly explained his administrative reorganization, arguing that it only affected reporting relationships within the executive branch. However, he said he was planning on submitting to Congress formal reorganization proposals, similar to what he had submitted in his first term. He would "carry out the effect of whatever the Congress' will happens to be," but whatever the reaction, he was moving ahead with his plans. The president described the basis of the plan as "what I have called a one-window operation." By that he meant that "there will be one individual selected from the Cabinet who will be responsible in that area to the President, and who will also be available to testify before the Congress."[3]

Then Ehrlichman provided a more detailed briefing in the form of a slide show titled "Redirecting Executive Branch Management," which carefully avoided the term *reorganization*. He also had a slide titled "Improving Communications with Departments and Agencies," suggesting that the new structure was merely a change in lines of communications, not in power.[4] His oral briefing reinforced the messages of the slides. He said the changes were "a new direction in management" but not a reorganization "under the technical meaning of the term." Indeed, the changes "can be thought of as an interim step" toward a congressionally approved reorganization. Ehrlichman colorfully described the executive branch as "a sausage with two ends, one end touched by the Congress and the other end touched by the President." He emphasized that the appointment of the three counsellors related only to the president's end of the sausage, not Congress's. In other words, not only did the changes not require congressional approval but they also did not change reporting relationships from departments and agencies to Congress and did not require Congress to reconfigure the jurisdictions of its standing committees. Representative John Anderson (R-Ill.) interjected a question about the relationship of the Domestic Council to the new counsellor system. Ehrlichman said it would be "diminished considerably," by about 60 percent, and that its main function would be to house the three standing committees of the principals assigned to each of the three counsellors.[5] Ehrlichman's slides outlined the jurisdictions of the three counsellors, but only by policy area. He did not list any specific department, agency, or bureau by name, partly because of the fluidity of the planning, no final list having yet been approved. However, in part, Ehrlichman would have known that the legislators at the breakfast (and the rest of their confreres on Capitol Hill) would immediately check to see the fate of their pet agency and, probably, complain about it. A vague list finessed that issue, at least on this day.

Holifield and Horton expressed general support, but Senators Javits and Percy wondered if, as members of the White House staff, the counsellors would invoke executive privilege and refuse to testify before Congress even though they were concurrently serving as Cabinet secretaries who had been confirmed by the Senate. Nixon and Ehrlichman said that executive privilege would be invoked only about confidential advice to the president, not about lesser subjects. For example, at that time the OMB director was a direct presidential appointee and thus not subject to Senate confirmation. Nonetheless, as OMB directors during the first term Shultz and then Weinberger had testified at congressional hearings on general subjects not relating to their advice to the president. Representative William Widnall (R-N.J.) asked about the counsellors' reporting relationships. According to one of Ehrlichman's slides, the three counsellors would report to Ehrlichman, who, in turn, would report to the president. Nixon misleadingly answered that the counsellors would "have direct access to the President."[6]

But Widnall had it right. One of the reasons for the reorganization in the first place was that Nixon wanted to make Ehrlichman the de facto assistant president for domestic affairs.

According to historian Stephen Ambrose, "the atmosphere was cold" and Nixon's unilateral reorganization was "an announcement that went down badly."[7] However, that conclusion is not obvious from the transcript of the conversation. Ambrose's only cited reference for that characterization was the transcript of the session that was prepared by the White House press secretary's staff, the same one examined by this author. At a press briefing later that day, Ehrlichman accurately summarized the congressional meeting, saying that "there were no negative comments."[8] A comparison of the Nixon transcript to the transcript of President Roosevelt's briefing of the congressional leadership on the Brownlow Committee's reorganization recommendations in 1937 seems comparable: questions, clarifications, and cautions, but no outright rejections, refusals, or denunciations.[9]

As the members of Congress left, they were given a copy of the formal presidential statement on the reorganization, which would be released publicly that afternoon. When he was leaving, Representative Holifield asked Ehrlichman for a copy of his slide show. Careful to avoid bruising any egos (and especially since Holifield had supported DCD), Ehrlichman's aide made sure the packet was dispatched that day.[10]

The formal presidential statement released that day was a blockbuster. (Significantly, it was not a message to Congress.) Nixon described the failure of his first-term reorganization proposals before Congress and the need for reform. Given the lack of action, the statement read, "I am therefore today taking the first of a series of steps aimed at increasing the management effectiveness of both the Cabinet and the White House Staff, by reordering the timeworn and, in many cases, obsolete relationships among top staff and line officials to the full extent of my legal authority to do so." The president's statement largely conformed to the dogmas of public administration that had prevailed since the Brownlow Committee. There was a need to reorganize and rationalize the executive branch so that its structure would conform to functions. The growth in the executive branch "has resulted in more officials reporting directly to the President than any one man can work with regularly on a personal basis." EOP had evolved away from its original conception as a staff function to the presidency and had taken on some line responsibilities. A president needed a support structure so that he "can devote his time and attention to overall policy formation and direction."[11]

Nixon's statement described the new White House structure as having five assistants to the president serving as the senior staffers: Haldeman for White House administration, Ehrlichman for domestic policy, Kissinger for foreign affairs, Shultz for economic policy (concurrent with being secretary of the treasury), and Ash for executive management (simultaneously serving as OMB director). Then, there would be three counsellors for domestic affairs: HEW Secretary-Designate Weinberger for human resources, HUD Secretary-Designate Lynn for community development, and USDA Secretary Butz for natural resources. Each counsellor would have an office in OEOB and would chair a committee of the Domestic Council, with the membership of the department and agency heads within their domains. The counsellor system would partly replace the Domestic Council, which was being reduced in size by about half. The three counsellors would "bring about better operational coordination and more unified policy development" in their functional areas. In particular, they were expected "to resolve with their colleagues at the Secretarial level many interdepartmental issues which have heretofore required arbitration by the President or his staff."[12]

Several assertions in the presidential statement were so misleading as to verge on being false. Nixon stated that the counsellors and other Cabinet secretaries of domestic departments would not only work with Ehrlichman "but will continue to work directly with me on important policy matters," which was flatly contradicted by the loyalty oaths that all prospective appointees had to sign at Camp David. The president also claimed that the "Cabinet as a whole will continue to function." That, too, was the opposite of the Camp David questionnaire. Finally, Nixon said that EOP was being reduced by half, but that was being accomplished largely by transferring some of its entities, such as the Office of Emergency Preparedness, outside the EOP framework.

United Press International (UPI) quickly ran a story summarizing the presidential statement and did so in time for the deadlines of evening newspapers (then still a major part of the newspaper business). "Irked by Congressional inaction" on his first-term reorganization proposals, the lead read, "President Nixon today went ahead with the proposal anyway." The three counsellors would have "super-bureaucrat" status, akin to Shultz's powers in the economic policy area, as had been announced previously.[13]

In midafternoon, using the same slides, Ehrlichman briefed the White House press corps. With his skills at turning a phrase, he described a

Reorganization: New Lines of Authority

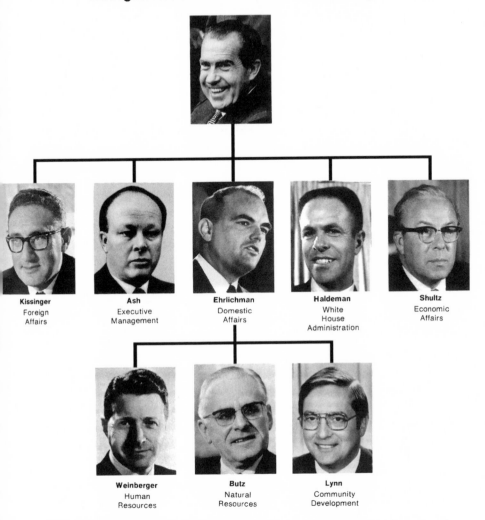

Figure 1. Organization chart of the second term of the Nixon White House, as announced on January 5, 1973. Congressional Quarterly 31:2 (January 13, 1973): 37. Reprinted by permission of Congressional Quarterly, Inc.

counsellor's role as being the "'hey, wait a minute guy' in the White House" who would make sure that policy decisions crossing departmental lines involved all related agencies.[14] The "wait a minute" role had previously been performed by the Domestic Council, the secretary to the Cabinet, and even the president, he said. Now, for matters wholly within any counsellor's domain, they would be dealt with at the counsellor level. Referring to the UPI article, he said the story was inaccurate because the counsellor structure could not be viewed as a full substitute for legislation creating the super-departments. Using the president's powers, the counsellors' work "only involves policy. It does not involve budget. It does not involve management. It does not involve personnel control in the ultimate sense, things of that kind. And those are the elixir[s] which are involved in the magic of the reorganization statutes and of course we don't come anywhere close to those. So, this isn't even half a loaf."[15]

Ehrlichman made two other points that had not come out at the congressional breakfast. First, it was simplistic to view the counsellors as proof of Nixon's centralization of power into the White House. "This is, in effect, forcing down out of the White House to the Cabinet Members themselves, off the President's desk, onto the Counsellors' desks, these policy development issues," he said, proceeding to argue vehemently that the counsellor structure was a *de*-centralization initiative, rather than a presidential power grab. Given that the counsellors would have only two or three staffers, on major policy areas "the work has got to be done in the constituent Departments and agencies. That is the genius of this. We think we will get a good work product," Ehrlichman noted. During the press conference, he twice characterized the initiative as an "experiment," suggesting that fine-tuning and revisions might come with experience, and major changes would certainly come if and when the super-department legislation were approved.[16]

Right after the briefing, Ehrlichman met one-on-one with Eugene Risher, the UPI reporter whose story he had criticized at the press briefing. Having already used the stick of public criticism, Ehrlichman then used a carrot to obtain the spin he wanted for the coverage of the reorganization. He gave Risher an "exclusive" interview about Nixon's management style, a subject closely related to the reorganization, to be used in stories before the inauguration. Risher quoted Ehrlichman as saying that the president "is a better manager now. . . . He delegates better and husbands his time better." Reciprocating, Risher's post-briefing filing, updating his earlier story, no longer referred to Nixon being "irked by Congressional inaction." Instead, he softened the wording to "sidestepping a reluctant Congress."[17]

FIRST REACTIONS

Press coverage the next day reflected the significance of the announcement. In a front-page story, the *New York Times* reported that the three "super-Secretaries" were "expected to enhance Mr. Nixon's efforts to get a firmer control on the bureaucracy."[18] However, it incorrectly reported that the action was based on an executive order, confusing the term with "executive action." The *Washington Post* also rated the announcement front-page news, reporting that Nixon had "moved to shake up and streamline the sprawling federal bureaucracy along functional lines" by creating a "functional 'super-Cabinet' closely following" his 1971 request for legislation.[19]

The first test of the initiative would be congressional reaction. Nixon, Ehrlichman, and Dean had hoped to soften the reaction by emphasizing that an *administrative* reorganization did not overlap congressional prerogatives (or committee structure) and by linking the executive changes with forthcoming legislative proposals. Further, the breakfast briefing for a large and bipartisan delegation of congressional leadership was intended to show the executive branch's institutional respect for the legislative branch. According to a White House reporter, "By acting on his own in a direction Congress had refused to go, Nixon may now draw criticism that he is usurping the authority of lawmakers. The President sought to avoid bruised feelings by explaining his plan to key legislators over breakfast at the White House before he announced it."[20] His was a very modest form of consultation, but it still occurred *before* any public announcement of the initiative. In fact, the attendees were given the presidential statement that was embargoed for release until that afternoon. This emphasized the "before" nature of the congressional consultation and also, slyly, gave attendees a chance to leak the news a few hours before its public release, something many legislators crave doing.

The *New York Times* noted that after the legislators left the breakfast, "there was no immediate protest from Congressional leaders."[21] The only protests came later from two second-tier senators. Senator Abraham Ribicoff (D-Conn.) was chair of the Government Operations Committee's Subcommittee on Reorganization, Research, and International Organizations. On the floor of the Senate the day after Nixon's announcement, Ribicoff denounced the president's unilateral action, raised five concerns about the reorganization, and summed up by saying, "We must also determine whether this plan poses any threat to the rights and responsibilities of Congress and if so, what legislation is necessary to protect them." Therefore, "to explore these and other issues the Government Operations Committee should hold prompt hearings on this reorganization." Ribicoff's grandstanding is evident from his own subsequent behavior. As chair of the subcommittee with jurisdiction over reorganizations, he could have called a hearing of his subcommittee to explore the ramifications of Nixon's super-secretary project. He never did.[22] Two days later, Senate Majority Whip Robert Byrd (D-W.Va.) criticized the plan in a television interview. He said that Nixon was "going about it in the wrong way. I think this is a terrible mistake." Byrd said that congressional action on the nominations of Weinberger as HEW secretary and Lynn as HUD secretary would provide an opportunity to explore the reorganization. He said that the Senate would "possibly consider refusing the nominations if it is not satisfied with their testimony."[23] Hence, he was defining confirmation as a referendum on the reorganization. In terms of public reactions from Capitol Hill, that was about it.

Editorially, the reaction was equally modest. The subheadline in the *Bennington (Vt.) Banner* called Nixon's announcement "a tricky maneuver," invoking the moniker of "Tricky Dick" that political opponents used to describe Nixon throughout his career.[24] The *New York Times* editorialized that it was skeptical the reorganization would work (comparing it to Mayor John Lindsay's similar initiative) and viewing the president's action "as an act of defiance" against Congress.[25] The *Washington Post* was mildly supportive, suggesting in an editorial that the reorganization "could be salutary" but adding perceptively that "for the counsellors to gain any significant authority—that is, for the change to work—they would have to be seen and known to have authority."[26] Ernest Furgurson was a Washington-based political columnist for the *Baltimore Sun,* with his columns syndicated nationally. He opined that putting Secretary of Agriculture Butz over the Department of Interior was "in the nature of appointing the fox sheriff of the chicken coop." He called the appointment "a felony against America's natural resources."[27] But, again, that was about it.

Perhaps government reorganization was too "inside baseball" to be of much interest to reporters, editorial writers, and columnists—and the politicians who lived off their attentions. These topics could be eye-glazingly boring. Ehrlichman accepted an invitation to be the guest on NBC's *Meet the Press* on January 7, 1973, just two days after the congressional breakfast.

The White House considered its longtime moderator, Lawrence Spivak, to be a (closet) conservative who was willing to give the administration a fair platform to express its views. But none of the reporters asked Ehrlichman about the new counsellors.[28] Clearly, with his January 5 congressional breakfast and public statement Nixon had signified that this reorganization was important, but this type of bureaucratic activity rarely attracted much attention or interest from the public at large or the news media. It just did not have political sex appeal. Nixon was pushing the counsellor structure not for good press or for popular favor but on the basis of his conception of presidential power.

THE CENTRAL ROLE OF THE COUNSELLOR IN THE GRAND REORGANIZATION

The day after the congressional breakfast, Ehrlichman's personal aide, Tod Hullin, sent to the three counsellors a packet of information about their new positions. Some were public materials, such as the presidential statement that had been released on Friday and the transcript of Ehrlichman's press briefing on Friday afternoon. However, one of the documents was new. Hullin's cover memo carefully pointed out that this document was "highly sensitive and is for *YOUR EYES ONLY*. It should not be staffed or reproduced." The document was a memo entitled "The Role of the Counsellors." Reflecting the sensitivity of its contents, the memo listed neither its author (it was not "from" anyone) nor the date that it was issued. Nor was it signed. It was a fugitive document.[29]

In some respects, it is unclear why the White House considered this six-page memo so sensitive. It was merely a job description for the counsellors. However, some of the contents would have been discordant to the understated and reassuring tone used on January 5 to keep Congress quiescent. Ehrlichman could easily envision that the details in the document would trigger major alarm bells on Capitol Hill. Also, the Nixon White House preferred secretiveness as a method of operation and as a management tool. The "eyes only" status of the memo would have reflected that standard operating procedure.[30]

Besides the secrecy attached to the memo, it is noteworthy that the document was not an executive order, as had been recommended by Dean, but was instead a plain White House memo. Such a method of appointment and assignment of power carried little, if any, legal weight. This meant that the three counsellors had no formal status in any official sense beyond the public statements made by the president, which seems odd, given the importance that Nixon and Ehrlichman attached to the counsellor project in their January 5 announcement and briefings. Interviewed thirty-four years later, Dean provided an interpretation that rings true.[31] The entire counsellor effort was an attempt to bypass Congress. Dean speculated that by not issuing an executive order or giving the counsellors any formal legal status, Congress and other opponents of Nixon's reorganization would have no legal "peg" on which to base a challenge. They could not claim, for example, that the executive order was illegal or that it violated a statute or impinged on Congress's constitutional powers. Similarly, lacking any formally promulgated presidential document, the counsellors project could not be challenged in court either. Nixon and Ehrlichman probably chose to act that way because they preferred a more behind-the-scenes and secretive method of allocating power. They believed that they "shouldn't have to" do anything more than what they already did. They were in charge, and this was how they wanted to play it, Congress be damned.

The content of the memo is certainly breathtaking in the vision it spelled out for the counsellors. These were to be more than conduits, advisors, and coordinators, as was so soothingly stated the day before to congressional leaders and the press. Instead, counsellors were to oversee the departments and agencies within their jurisdiction with the goal of ensuring that the president's agenda was being carried out. There is no doubt from the tone of the memo that the counsellors were, indeed, super-secretaries of their functional domains. One of Nixon's primary goals for the second term was to assume control over all executive branch activities. He wanted to run the government, not ride herd over a semi-sovereign bureaucracy. The counsellors would be part of the imposition of that agenda. This move was a presidential reorganization reflecting Nixon's doctrine about the power of the presidency, sometimes referred to as a plebiscitary presidency because he asserted that his actions were implicitly ratified by his overwhelming reelection. It also reflected his barely hidden disdain of Congress, especially a Democratic-majority Congress. Here was a grand reorganization of the president, by the president, and for the president.

Of the three counsellor roles enumerated in the memo, two echoed the public briefings. First, counsellors were intended to reduce the number of direct reports to the president, and, second, they were to coordinate departments and agencies on common matters. Their third role focused on what was unstated on January 5: the counsellors were to accomplish "increased responsiveness of departments and agencies to Presidential policy decisions." To do that, "it is essential that each Counsellor be able to provide policy direction to agencies under his responsibility." As necessary, counsellors should work with OMB "to *assure* that such direction is followed." Part of the goal of accomplishing bureaucratic responsiveness to the president was in the area of policy development. For those activities, counsellors were to be the ones who develop policy initiatives, not merely pass the line initiatives up from the bureaucracy. Then, once the president approved these policy initiatives, the counsellor's job was to "disseminate and *enforce* Presidential policy." All federal activities within a counsellor's jurisdiction were to function under the counsellors' "policy *direction.*"[32]

These were significant statements about power, especially given the turf wars that could be expected to occur between the vestigial Domestic Council (policy development, theoretically the "what" of government) and OMB (policy implementation, purportedly the "how" of management). In the reality of the federal government, there were no clear distinctions between policy development and implementation, as these two concepts, treated as separate in academic practice, were largely intermingled in the day-to-day reality of managing the federal government. For example, is changing an existing policy an activity of policy development or implementation? From this perspective, one of the most significant aspects of the "Role of the Counsellors" memo was that it clearly enunciated that counsellors had power over incoming matters for the president's attention (policy development) and outgoing matters, which were effectively presidential decisions (policy implementation). The counsellors were there to run the entire gamut of functions of the domestic bureaucracy. In this context, when Ehrlichman used the term "policy guidance" at the briefings on January 5, he was using an overarching term for both.[33] A counsellor might give pre-hoc policy guidance to the president (actually to Ehrlichman) about a decision to be made. Conversely, a counsellor would be giving post-hoc policy guidance to agencies about what the president wanted them to do.

While the memo cautioned counsellors not to become enmeshed in minor issues, it also explicitly addressed the bureaucracy's possible use of the tactic of deliberately deeming a major policy statement to be a minor one, which would not require pre-consultation with the counsellor. Counsellors were to be careful that "policy views contrary to Administration posture do not go unreviewed because he [a junior official] determines they are not sufficiently important."[34] Another caution in the memo related to the extralegal powers being assigned to the counsellor. While the counsellor's legal power to "accomplish the performance of presidential objectives" in his own department was clear, he had no formal statutory basis for providing policy direction to other departments, agencies, and programs. In those situations, the memo indicated to the counsellor that "his understanding with these officials must be made very clear."[35] The tone was ominous. As far as the White House was concerned, those outside-the-department officials must be made to acknowledge and accept the counsellor's role in ensuring the implementation of the president's policies.

The scope of activities for the counsellors was to be across the board, involving virtually every important management tool that a president could summon. Counsellors were expected to engage in program evaluation; receive and analyze management information reports; be given early warning of major problems; be involved in budget planning decisions (but without impinging on OMB's traditional role); participate in selection of senior management personnel and, generally, decisions on staffing levels for each program in their domain; be the lead person on major legislative proposals (both in the development stage and the public advocacy stage); and review in advance all major public communications by agencies, whether speeches, congressional testimony, or news events.

The detailed directive in the memo relating to agency appointments is indicative of the breadth of involvement the counsellor was expected to have for all these enumerated management functions. For all agencies and programs within the counsellor's purview (not just his home department), the counsellor was to work with the White House personnel office on all "key appointments, assignments and promotions that can be expected to impact on the Department's ability to carry out Presidential policy." How deep should this counsellor involvement in personnel decisions go? The memo was careful not to state any explicit cut-off, "because agency organizational structures vary." At the very least, the counsellor should be involved in all personnel decisions relating to "executive level positions and many super grades."[36]

Nonetheless, the memo tried to walk a fine line between the policy control exercised by these super-secretaries and day-to-day management of the bureaucracy. Nixon wanted them in charge of the larger issues, those involving major policy. He did not want them to get enmeshed in the daily crises than can engulf a manager: "Because the Counsellor's role is not that of a Departmental manager, the department or agency head will continue to provide *management support* to areas under the Counsellor's *policy direction.*"[37] So, just as the counsellor was expected to delegate the routine details of managing his own department to the undersecretary, counsellors were to similarly involve themselves only at the policy level in issues relating to other departments and agencies within their purview. Distinguishing between the two categories was easier said than done.

Drawing the line between policy and day-to-day management might have been hard to describe, but the memo successfully drew the line indirectly when it discussed the staffing that a counsellor would be permitted to have. A large staff would invariably lead to detailed involvement in running the bureaucracy, while a small staff would necessitate a more limited policy involvement. According to the memo, the counsellor could have only three professional staffers (i.e., excluding secretarial assistants) in his OEOB office and another two to seven elsewhere (presumably in secretarial roles). However, besides direct staff, the memo envisioned close cooperation between counsellors and relevant OMB and DC staff. The memo tried to walk a delicate line between turf issues over which Ash and Cole had struggled, those regarding the power and scope of the counsellors, while still conveying the message that all three entities needed to work cooperatively to enact the president's agenda. The institutionalized presidency was being harnessed to ensure that they were all pulling in the same direction and would present a united front when dealing with the bureaucracy.

Counsellors were also to coordinate closely with other parts of the White House besides DC and OMB. The memo stated that counsellors must include in their staff a legislative liaison, who would closely coordinate all legislation-related work with the president's congressional relations office. Similarly, the memo specified that one of the counsellor's staffers be a public information officer, to coordinate the publicity-related work of the counsellor with counterpart activities in the White House and the bureaucracy. Hence, the memo called for a close and interlocking effort at controlling policy in the executive branch through a tightening of the presidential role in all aspects of public administration: policy making, legislative proposals, congressional testimony, public statements, budgeting, policy evaluation, personnel matters, and management information systems.

The last part of the memo provided specific guidance on the formal structure that would underpin the counsellor's policy oversight. Each counsellor would establish a committee of the Cabinet secretaries and agency heads in his domain. Organizationally, it would be a committee of the Domestic Council. This was a way to closely integrate the work of the (downsized) DC and the counsellors. Also, the Domestic Council itself, consisting of Cabinet secretaries and agency heads, provided the ideal precedent and template for the work of the counsellors. While much work would be done by subordinates, the formal power relationship was between the counsellors and the principals who sat on their committees. This organizational structure made clear that Cabinet secretaries and agency heads reported to counsellors, not to the president. They were one rung below the counsellors, and the Domestic Council committee structure was a vivid reminder of that. The memo directed the counsellors to "establish as soon as possible the reporting channels and operating procedures" for their domains by quickly convening a meeting of their DC committees because "departmental and agency personnel need to know at the outset both the kinds of problems about which each Counsellor expects to be consulted and how these consultations are to be initiated."[38]

Finally, the memo echoed Dean's suggestion that the counsellors be depicted as an experiment, a point that Ehrlichman explicitly verbalized at the press briefing. According to the memo, "Working with this untried and novel arrangement will undoubtedly result in adjustments in any plan now set forth."[39] It was a work in progress, but it was not intended to be temporary or short lived. It was expected to be a permanent feature of the second term, since no one in the administration had any serious expectations that the Democratic-majority Congress would pass the reorganization legislation creating the three super-departments. So, while some details in the super-secretary structure might need to be fine tuned, the basic role was firmly set. The memo had described a grand presidential reorganization, more sweeping than some of the previous ones, but well within the tradition of all twentieth-century presidents. However, unlike most of the predecessor plans, this one was being done without congressional approval and was actually being implemented, not just proposed. It was audacious and revolutionary.[40]

SENATE CONFIRMATION

Ehrlichman wanted a fast start, but Congress remained an obstacle, not in terms of approving reorganization legislation but instead due to the requirement for Senate confirmation of Nixon's nomination of Weinberger as HEW secretary and Lynn as HUD secretary (since Butz was one of the few incumbent Cabinet secretaries asked to stay on, and in the same position, for the second term). As would be expected, secretaries-designate had no formal power to run their intended departments. In fact, to do so would be illegal. Given that the counsellor roles were closely related to the departments they would be heading (as the core of the informal super-department), they could not realistically begin any overt activities as super-secretaries until sworn in to the Cabinet. (As counsellors per se, they were the president's personal appointees to his White House office and did not need Senate confirmation.)

While congressional reaction to the administrative reorganization was low key (except for Ribicoff's and Byrd's responses), general issues of congressional prerogatives were important nonetheless. By emphasizing that he would quickly submit reorganization legislation to Congress and that the counsellor structure would not affect how Congress dealt with agencies, Nixon had finessed major congressional concerns in that regard. However, another issue was looming large in January 1973. The view from Democratic-majority Capitol Hill was that Nixon was more aggressive about asserting executive privilege than his predecessors, which is why the subject came up during the January 5 congressional breakfast. The concept had largely come to the fore in the post–World War II era, with presidents asserting that they had the right to prohibit senior administration officials from testifying before Congress if the subject related to personal conversations with the president, advice given to the president, and other activities that would impinge on the ability of a president to receive frank advice and frame policies. The Constitution vested in the president "the executive Power," and, therefore, if Congress demanded testimony by certain senior administration officials, such testimony would harm presidents' ability to execute their executive powers. From that perspective, executive privilege was inherent to the president's exercise of constitutional duties. This privilege was usually invoked relating to members of the president's immediate official family, especially senior White House staff. Therefore, it was rare for the White House chief of staff, legal counsel, national security advisor, special assistants, and the like to testify before Congress.[41]

In late 1972 and early 1973, some Democrats were convinced that the FBI investigation of the break-in at the Democratic National Committee offices in the Watergate building had been manipulated to protect the president and that the indictment of only the direct participants in the break-in was another demonstration of some kind of cover-up. (Around the same time, Bob Woodward and Carl Bernstein of the *Washington Post* were trying to find links between Watergate—and other shady activities of the Committee to Reelect the President—and the White House.) Some on Capitol Hill were convinced that any invocation of executive privilege to block congressional investigations would be part of such a cover-up.

In that context, the January 5 announcement of the counsellor structure was seen as possibly motivated to make some key Cabinet secretaries simultaneously part of the White House staff and, therefore, subject to assertions of executive privilege. During the first term executive privilege was invoked in precisely this context, when some agency heads who were also White House staff members declined to testify.[42] Furthermore, the combined jurisdiction of the three counsellors encompassed almost all the domestic policy activities of the federal government. Therefore, the counsellor structure could put the officials in charge of a major swath of federal operations beyond the reach of Congress, exempt from testimony, oversight, and consultation. Now *that* was an issue of legislative prerogative that struck a deep chord.

Majority-party senators decided on a coordinated basis that they would use confirmation hearings to force all presidential nominees, not just the secretaries-designate who would also be counsellors, to promise not to broaden the use of executive privilege to exclude Congress from involvement in matters in which it previously had been involved. If a presidential nominee refused to make such a promise, then there was a quiet internal consensus not to confirm the appointee. The Senate might not stand up to the president about an administrative reorganization that appeared to be in lieu of legislation, but they would draw the line on accountability to Congress and its role as a coequal branch of the federal government.

Weinberger's Confirmation

The first super-secretary to face senators at a confirmation hearing was Weinberger. Jurisdiction over HEW's programs was shared by the Finance

Committee and the Committee on Labor and Public Welfare. Therefore, Weinberger had to testify before both.[43] On January 11 (the Thursday after the Friday congressional breakfast), the Finance Committee held a hearing on his nomination. The senators mostly wanted to talk about their pet projects at HEW, but some of the conversation was about his counsellor role. Weinberger blandly said that the plan had not yet been finalized, so he did not know for sure what non-HEW programs would be within his purview. Weinberger emphasized that he viewed his counsellor role as coordinative, whether from the president to all relevant federal programs dealing with human resources or vice versa. He would not be administering any programs outside of HEW but merely trying to bring greater consistency to federal operations and federal policy.

Regarding executive privilege, he emphasized that as OMB director (and before that as deputy director) he had testified many times on Capitol Hill and had not claimed that, as a presidential advisor, he was protected by executive privilege.[44] That statement gave him credibility when he said that he would not use his presidential counsellor status to avoid testifying at congressional hearings. He would do so only when it related to advice he was giving the president and for which the president had not yet decided on a policy. Weinberger also ingeniously argued that with counsellors in place the Congress would get more consultation and information than under the Domestic Council structure of Nixon's first term. DC staff members were viewed as White House staff, and they usually declined to testify. However, as a counsellor who was a Cabinet secretary confirmed by Congress, Weinberger and his two colleagues were more likely to come before Congress to discuss the policy matters with which they were dealing. The members of the Finance Committee were generally satisfied with his explanations and promises.[45]

A week later, Weinberger went before the Senate's Committee on Labor and Public Welfare and largely repeated his testimony. Again, the members did not challenge his statements relating to the counsellor role and accepted his pledge not to invoke executive privilege solely due to his White House super-secretary status.[46] However, Weinberger's appointment was controversial for other reasons. Liberal Democrats correctly assumed that Nixon's choice of "Cap the Knife" (a nickname he earned at OMB and which he disliked) for HEW was to rein in social service spending programs. Weinberger's appointment was controversial enough that to make a point, the floor vote on his confirmation was delayed beyond those of the other Cabinet members. He was called back to appear before the committee a second time, on February 2 and thus Weinberger was not able to participate in the swearing-in ceremony for all other Cabinet secretaries that took place that day. His wife claimed that the delay "was just a TV show for Teddy" Kennedy.[47] When the Senate debated his nomination on February 8, his co-terminus status as counsellor for human resources was mentioned but was not a subject of debate or controversy. He was approved by a vote of 61 to 10.[48]

Lynn's Confirmation

On the same day that Weinberger first appeared before the Committee on Labor and Public Welfare Undersecretary of Commerce James Lynn came before the Senate Committee on Banking, Housing, and Urban Affairs as the nominee for HUD secretary. As with Weinberger, the subject of his counsellor role was brought up, especially regarding executive privilege. Lynn, too, stated that he would not use his role as White House counsellor to claim executive privilege and refuse to testify before Congress regarding his HUD responsibilities. Like Weinberger, he said he would come before Congress as counsellor and invoke executive privilege only when the matter related to communications with the president in the pre-decision stages of policy making. Shrewdly, Lynn also reminded the committee members that the law creating HUD explicitly assigned the department's secretary a *coordinating* role relating to housing and urban programs located in other departments. Therefore, his role as CD counsellor would merely be reinforcing a duty that HUD secretaries were already expected to perform.[49]

The committee recommended approval of the nomination, 11 to 4. It filed a formal report about its recommendation, a relatively unusual practice and an indication of the significance of the divided views. The committee report noted that "the majority of the committee were satisfied with Mr. Lynn's explanation that his coordinating duties as Counselor to the President on Community Development would help in many ways to carry out his statutory obligations as Secretary of HUD. He stated firmly that the added duties would not prevent him from meeting his statutory obligation as Secretary of HUD." In the same report, in a dissenting opinion, William Proxmire (D-Wisc.) gave as one of the reasons for his opposition that Lynn supposedly equivocated on the subject of executive privilege.[50]

When Lynn's nomination came up on the floor of the Senate on January

31 (before Weinberger's), several senators stated their opposition. Using a different argument, Senator Proxmire complained, somewhat oddly, that if Lynn's major office was to be his counsellor office in OEOB and that if most of his time would be spent there, then he would be "removed from the pressures of the mayors and community groups which he would have if his office were at HUD." However, as with Weinberger, the opposition was not focused on Lynn's super-secretary role. Rather the senators' concerns related to other second-term initiatives, such as the administration's impoundment of appropriated HUD funds and a freeze on additional public housing construction. Lynn was confirmed by voice vote.[51]

During the four committee hearings on the Weinberger and Lynn nominations, senators referred to the nominees' counsellor roles using a wide range of terminology, including "super-cabinet officer," "human resources special assistant (to the president)," and "super-secretary." Other terms used on Capitol Hill included "supercrats" and "super heads."[52] Senator Javits referred to the position as "a new brand of official. We do not know what the protocol is" for it, compared to a run-of-the-mill Cabinet secretary.[53] This confusion indicated not only the lack of precedent involved in the Nixon's new structure but also a lack of clarity as to what exactly the office was called, let alone what it would do.

At those hearings, one of the few members to express substantive support for Nixon's counsellor structure was Senator John Tower (R-Tex.). During Lynn's hearing, Tower said the reorganization "is, I think, a constructive move from the standpoint of the Congress because it has resulted in a closer integration of the policy-making process and the implementation process. Coupled with the expressed willingness of Mr. Lynn to appear before the committee, this gives us a better conduit of congressional opinion into the White House."[54] Most other senators, however, while noting and discussing Weinberger's and Lynn's co-terminus appointments as counsellor and Cabinet secretary, cautiously avoided such an open endorsement. This was the president's initiative; let him carry it on his political back, not theirs.

Confirmation of the "Second Class" Secretaries

The issue of the super-secretaries also came up at some of the confirmation hearings of a few other Cabinet nominees. At the Commerce Committee hearing on January 9 for Claude Brinegar to be secretary of transportation, Senator Warren Magnuson (D-Wash.), the committee chair, asked if it was true that Brinegar would be reporting to Counsellor Lynn, who would be reporting to Ehrlichman, who would be reporting to the president. Brinegar, an oil company executive with no previous public service experience, was well prepared: "The President expects me to serve as the Nation's principal transportation adviser to him, and to enforce the 1966 statute that established the Department." Playing that role, however, did not require him to meet solely with the president. Based on his business experience, he viewed counsellors as "chairmen of the committees that have been appointed to resolve issues that reach across several lines," and he welcomed that role. Furthermore, he would prefer to resolve issues with Counsellor Lynn than "with some White House assistant whose role I am not sure of." Upon prompting from the committee chair, he said what the senators wanted to hear: "If I feel strongly about certain matters I feel that I have a right to go higher," that is, to the president. The committee was satisfied with his answer, and the subject did not come up again in the hearing. Still, the touchiness and significance of a downgrading of the non-counsellor secretaries was indicated by the *Washington Post*'s coverage of the hearing, which led with that angle.[55]

A week later, Labor Secretary-designate Peter Brennan faced the Committee on Labor and Public Welfare. Committee chair Harrison Williams (D-N.J.) told Brennan, "I want to make one final observation in an area which has caused great confusion here—the superimposing of a new layer of bureaucracy between the departments and the President, the so-called Presidential counselors, the super cabinet, or whatever the colloquial expression is. If nominated, you will be the Secretary of Labor. This is an area of human resources which Mr. Weinberger has been designated to oversee. Have you thought through your problems as to how you are going to communicate with the President through this new layer when matters of importance arise[?]"[56] Brennan, a labor union official, was ready with the same message that Brinegar had provided. He, too, said that he viewed a counsellor as an effort "to cut a lot of redtape [*sic*] and cost, and expedite the relationships with the department heads with the President." But, like Brinegar, he said he would not hesitate to go directly to the president as needed.[57] Again, the committee was apparently satisfied because the subject was not raised again during the confirmation hearing.

Congress's more-than-cursory review of Nixon's Cabinet appointments led to a delay in the swearing in of his second-term Cabinet. Instead of the tradition of holding the ceremony a day or two after the January 20 inauguration, it did not take place until February 2, two weeks into the term. Even by then, Weinberger had not been confirmed. Weinberger eventually had his delayed swearing-in ceremony as HEW secretary on February 12.[58]

Sworn In—Or Were They?

Of the three counsellors, only Lynn was sworn in, as secretary of HUD, on February 2 at the major ceremony for all new Cabinet and major White House appointments. (Butz did not need to be sworn in again.) However, a minor detail during that swearing-in ceremony signaled an odd, but important, aspect of the new counsellor project. Lynn was sworn in as a Cabinet member but *not* as counsellor. Yet, at the same ceremony that day, Anne Armstrong was sworn in as a "Counsellor to the President," that is, a high-ranking White House official (unconnected to the reorganization).[59]

Armstrong's swearing in paralleled the legal and official status of others holding the rank of counsellor to the president during the first term (again, not related to the reorganization), such as Arthur Burns and Robert Finch.[60] The seemingly minor detail of Lynn not taking the oath of office also as a counsellor that day was not noticed at the time. The same thing happened (or, more precisely, did not happen) when Weinberger was sworn in ten days later: no oath as a White House counsellor, only as Cabinet secretary. The missing event indicated that Weinberger, Lynn, and Butz had been given an *administrative* appointment and title as counsellor but not a formal position that entailed receiving a commission of office.

This situation may have been driven partly by Haldeman's and Ehrlichman's efforts to square a round peg. In the official protocol listing of the status of White House aides, counsellors such as Armstrong, Burns, and Finch outranked assistants to the president such as Haldeman and Ehrlichman. Yet Weinberger, Lynn, and Butz were to report *to* Ehrlichman; they would not outrank him. Lacking official commissions, the three held a title (that of counsellor) that carried no official weight for the protocol list. In fact, since they did not hold a White House commission, they did not even appear on any official protocol lists of White House staff.[61]

The counsellors' absence from the protocol lists was no accident. In early March 1973, Staff Secretary Bruce Kehrli had submitted to Haldeman (his boss) a draft listing of the White House "Precedence List" to be used in the upcoming edition of the *Congressional Directory* and by the White House Protocol Office. In his cover memo, he noted that his draft was the same as one approved earlier by Haldeman, except for one change. It was "with the addition of Counsellors Butz, Lynn and Weinberger and Assistants [to the President] Shultz and Ash." The list showed the three counsellors at the same rank as Anne Armstrong and, therefore, outranking all the assistants to the president, including Haldeman and Ehrlichman.[62] Haldeman vetoed listing any of the counsellors as well as listing Shultz and Ash as assistants to the president. Similarly, even though Kehrli had conscientiously arranged for legal commissions to be prepared and *signed* for the three counsellors and for Shultz and Ash as assistants to the president, they remained in his files, never released.[63] That was how Haldeman wanted it.

That the counsellors were not sworn into office and had no official protocol ranking is consistent with the earlier White House decisions not to issue an executive order establishing the counsellor structure and to keep secret the document outlining the powers of the counsellors. It was all being handled informally and secretly by Nixon, Haldeman, and Ehrlichman: no swearing in, no commission, no executive order, no formal appointment, no legal delegation of power, and no circulation of the document outlining their new positions.

4

IN OPERATION, JANUARY-APRIL 1973

It was one thing to announce the plan, as Nixon did on January 5, but it was another to have the new structure in place, operating, and making decisions. Despite the desire to implement the president's announced structure as quickly as possible, these things took time. Every detail and every decision was about a new approach to the managerial presidency. As there were no precedents or existing guidelines to follow, the routine administrative machinery of the White House could not always make those decisions. Everyone was to some extent making it up as they were going along. Some unresolved issues had to go to Ehrlichman and Haldeman, who were committed to the plan and absolutely sure that it was worthwhile. Some other presidential power centers, such as OMB and what remained of the Domestic Council, were not. Making a success of the super-secretary approach to presidential governance would take a lot of work and attention to detail.

HITTING THE GROUND RUNNING AND ORGANIZING AS QUICKLY AS POSSIBLE

When Weinberger and Lynn had appeared at their confirmation hearings (to be Cabinet secretaries, not counsellors), both said that they knew few details about their counsellor role beyond what had been discussed at the January 5 congressional breakfast. Weinberger testified there had not "been a very precise definition yet of all of the responsibilities" he would have as counsellor. Similarly, Lynn said he needed "to get a lot better briefed" before he knew the full details of his new role.[1] Their comments were white lies, given that by then they had received from Ehrlichman's assistant the January 6 packet of documents, including the confidential memo, "The Role of the Counsellors." But they were expected to keep its contents—even existence—secret, not just from Congress but even from their staff. Weinberger and Lynn worded their statements in ways that made them literally truthful but incomplete.

On January 4, the day before the public launch, Ehrlichman had hosted a breakfast with the three counsellors to brief them generally on the plans for the next day (see chapter 3). During that meeting he had given them a general outline of his conception of their role but not much detail. Then, on Saturday, January 6, they had received the packet of information from the Friday briefings along with the "eyes only" memo regarding their roles. The following Monday (the first workday after the launch), Ehrlichman met with the three again for about an hour to urge that they get started as quickly as possible in their counsellor roles, albeit in a behind-the-scenes fashion, not publicly, since two of the three had neither been confirmed nor sworn in (as Cabinet secretaries).[2]

One of the items Ehrlichman mentioned at the Monday meeting was what titles to give to the two or three professional staffers who would be in their EOB office. Kenneth Cole, the incoming head of the downsized Domestic Council, was concerned that the assistants would be called "deputy counsellors." Cole wanted a seamless relationship between the DC and the counsellors as well as protection for his shop's turf. He wanted to be sure that each counsellor's committee of principals would be constituted, formally, as a DC committee. Relatedly, he mentioned to Ehrlichman that he feared a deputy counsellor would outrank any DC associate director or assistant director (working in a counsellor's policy area), thereby subsuming his own staff to the counsellors instead of creating a more balanced role.[3] Ehrlichman agreed with Cole on both points. At that January 8 meeting, he mentioned the limitations on the titles the three could give their counsellor staff and their expected working relationship with the Domestic Council.

However, by late that first week, other problems were already cropping up. Ehrlichman informed Nixon that Weinberger was still holding tight to the reins of OMB (which he would officially head until he could be sworn in as HEW secretary) instead of playing the de jure role as head of the agency and letting Ash begin acting as the de facto OMB director. The FY1974 presidential budget proposal was about to be released, and Ash needed to be ready to serve as the administration's spokesman on it. Also, Weinberger did not want to give up his OMB director's office in the West Wing (a highly coveted location signifying power, although he was on the second floor) as long as he was officially OMB director.[4] As for Butz, Ehrlichman complained to Nixon that Butz was still "preoccupied" with agricultural issues instead of beginning to expand his scope of attention to natural resources issues and letting the USDA undersecretary assume day-to-day management of the department.[5] As far as Ehrlichman was concerned, only Lynn "appears to be taking hold."[6] It is significant that at this early stage Ehrlichman already felt that only a presidential intervention could get Weinberger and Butz to shift their foci.

Ehrlichman tentatively scheduled a fifteen-minute meeting for the super-secretaries with Nixon in the Oval Office on January 11. The brevity of the proposed meeting was an indication that it was not a working meeting, only a chance for Nixon to say what Ehrlichman wanted him to say. But Nixon intensely disliked confrontations or any in-person tensions, even though he often talked about being tough and that he was cool in heated situations.[7] Nixon preferred to let subordinates handle the confrontation. The meeting was canceled. Instead, Nixon signed a letter to Weinberger, drafted by Ehrlichman, which—buried in diplomatic and laudatory comments—specifically requested Weinberger to "turn over responsibility" for OMB and the FY1974 budget "at once."[8]

During the second half of January, the three counsellors began the steps to bring their offices into being. (Separate details about each are presented in the next three chapters.) Each counsellor met with the Domestic Council staff, especially the associate director whose portfolio was largely the same as the counsellor's, to review the scope of their policy areas. But Ehrlichman was impatient. By early February he thought that the three were only "*beginning* to understand the dimensions of their responsibility."[9]

The presidential meeting that Ehrlichman had tried to schedule in mid-January finally took place on February 5, 1973, in Nixon's OEOB office. (On the parallel Watergate track, Nixon was deeply involved that week in trying to blunt a Senate investigation and the efforts by Judge John Sirica to get the convicted Watergate burglars to talk.[10]) It was the first joint meeting the three counsellors had with the president. In a sense, the purpose of the meeting was for the president to give them their charge personally.

Based on Ehrlichman's choreography, the meeting would largely be the same as the one he had wanted in mid-January. He was still unhappy with Weinberger and Butz's pace of shifting their focus to their counsellor responsibilities, and he continued to be satisfied with Lynn's work. As far as Ehrlichman was concerned, the meeting needed to take only fifteen minutes. He wanted Nixon to tell them that they needed "to immerse themselves in their new subject matters."[11] In particular, they needed to take the lead in preparing administration bills for major legislation and other policy initiatives that needed to be submitted to Congress.

That was not what happened. The meeting lasted an hour, with Nixon expressing detailed opinions on some of the major issues, especially housing (Lynn), welfare and health (Weinberger), and energy (Butz).[12] By using his preferred indirect method of communication, Nixon hinted to Weinberger in passing the message that Ehrlichman had wanted him to send. According to Weinberger's recollection of the meeting, the president wanted them to "put our major efforts into the Counsellor role," and let "the Under Secretaries run the Departments." Following another of Ehrlichman's talking points, the president also strongly urged them to activate the DC committees of the principals under their rubrics, rather than just have those bodies exist on paper. If the three did not do that, then "the Counsellors would just sit on the top of the heap." Rather, he wanted the counsellors to get to "know the problems from the bottom" by meeting with agency representatives and finding out, for example, when they would convene the principals.[13]

At the end of the meeting, Nixon asked Butz (also as requested by Ehrlichman) if the upcoming reorganization legislation to create a Department of Natural Resources should include USDA or not. It had been included in the first version submitted during the first term, then deleted due to the strong lobbying of farmers who wanted their own agency.[14] Butz, predictably, said he doubted Congress would ever approve it. That gave Nixon a perfect opening to conclude the meeting with a firm message. Given that USDA would not be part of proposed legislation creating a Department of Natural Resources, the administration would nonetheless treat the department as part of the domain of the natural resources counsellor.[15] (However, this move also undermined the close correlation between a counsellor's home department and the counsellor's larger domain.) The president had wrapped up the meeting with a simultaneous shot at Congress, expression of personal support for the counsellor idea, and a spurring of his three counsellors to get to work.

Figure 2. President Nixon meeting with his counsellors in the president's working office in the Old Executive Office Building, February 5, 1973. From left: unidentified White House aide (probably from the Press Office), videographer (partly obscured, probably from a TV news outlet), Caspar Weinberger, Earl Butz, James Lynn, and President Nixon. John Ehrlichman also attended the meeting but stepped aside while the official photograph was taken, probably to strengthen a (false) visual impression that the counsellors worked directly for the president. Courtesy Nixon Presidential Library, National Archives

As late as mid-March Ehrlichman was still dissatisfied with Weinberger's development of his counsellor office. In preparation for a wideranging meeting with Weinberger, Ehrlichman's assistant, Tod Hullin, prepared some talking points for his boss. One of them related to the status of Weinberger's counsellor office, with Hullin noting that the "Counsellor's staff [was] very weak." However, the meeting was canceled, likely due to Ehrlichman spending more and more time on Watergate and becoming largely removed from domestic policy and overseeing the counsellors.[16]

Before the super-secretaries could begin delving into their substantive duties, there were dozens of minor administrative details that needed to be ironed out. The burden of identifying and implementing the management details needed to get the counsellors' offices up and running usually fell on Staff Secretary Kehrli. First, Kehrli had to figure out a way to give the counsellors office suites in the coveted OEOB, with adequate space not only for them personally but also for three professional staff members, as had been promised in the secret memo, "The Role of the Counsellors," and an adjacent office for the counsellors' counterpart associate CD directors.[17]

Kehrli also had to add the counsellors to the standard lists of required clearances for presidential documents relating to domestic issues. From now on, the super-secretaries were on the automatic clearance lists for all domestic presidential statements and all domestic legislation pending presidential action. However, they were not included in the required clearance lists for presidential proclamations, executive orders, or messages to Congress in the area of domestic affairs, although on a case-by-case basis there would be an option to include them.[18]

There seemed to be no end to the accoutrements of senior staff privileges for counsellors that needed to be arranged, including White House passes, use of the White House Mess as well as the Conference Dining Room for meetings, parking for their limos, access to meetings in the president's OEOB office, use of the Roosevelt Room for meetings, full membership in the White House Health Unit (i.e., the fitness room, located in OEOB) and use of the president's tennis courts.[19] Administrative rank also required use of burn bags for material to be destroyed, but did not qualify the counsellors to have their own copy machine.[20] Similarly, their professional and secretarial staff needed to be integrated into the standard operating procedures of the Nixon White House. The staff were issued building passes and parking spots on State Place or the Ellipse, and they were offered limited membership in the Health Unit and limited use of White House cars.[21] The senior professional staff member in each counsellor's office was given limited access to the Staff Mess, but the other two professional staffers were assigned to the OEOB Mess.[22] It was not until mid-April, more than three months after the president's January 5 announcement, that Kehrli could finally report to Haldeman that "the Counsellors are all in and settled."[23] The same month, an outside observer came to the same conclusion. The *National Journal* reported in April that the counsellors "are quietly fashioning staffs and internal committees to institutionalize their roles."[24]

GROWING PAINS

Nixon had some fence mending to do with his Cabinet right after announcing the counsellor structure at the January congressional breakfast. The grumbling by secretaries (whether holdovers or new) about who would be "under" the counsellors was getting noticeable. No one wanted to be depicted as a "junior" secretary, with the implied loss of personal political standing and perhaps downgrading of the department itself. For example, columnist Ernest Furgurson's criticism of the "demotion" of Interior Secretary Rogers Morton may well have been inspired by associates of Morton.[25] The first meeting of the second-term Cabinet occurred on February 8, 1973, about a week after the new Cabinet had been sworn in (except for Weinberger). It was partly a pep talk by the president to set the tone for the term. Nixon made a point to talk about his (now one month old) counsellor program. In his handwritten notes for the meeting, the first of the six points he wanted to cover was "No Super Cabinet."[26]

Presidential assistant William Safire attended the meeting and took notes, capturing Nixon's comments verbatim: "Another issue not to be defensive about is this: I notice the columnists say we have a 'super Cabinet' and a 'regular Cabinet.' That's a lot of baloney. Thick or thin, no matter how you slice it, it's baloney. We have a committee of Cabinet members to coordinate matters that cut across departments, but this new system does not downgrade anybody. There is no 'super Cabinet.'"[27] But it was all for show. While the term "super-Cabinet" had never been used in the planning documents for the counsellor structure or during the January 5 unveiling, that is exactly what it was. Nixon was saying one thing and meaning another.

White House staff were also unclear about the counsellors. David Parker, who handled presidential scheduling and some other matters under Haldeman, sent a plaintive note to Cole, the DC director: "Would you please outline for me exactly what the organization of your operation is going to be. As I understand it, the relationship between [Associate Director] Dana Mead and Jim Lynn will almost be one in [sic] the same, however, do you want me to work directly with Lynn on substantive matters and schedule proposals or Mead? The same would apply with [Associate Director] Fairbanks and Butz; . . . [and Associate Director] Cavanaugh and Weinberger."[28]

Given that Parker was asking *Cole* for guidance, rather than Ehrlichman or any of the three counsellors, Cole's answer was predictable from the perspective of turf protection and bureaucratic politics: "I would appreciate it if you would deal only through the Domestic Council staff. They will be keeping regular contacts with the Counselors [*sic*] and should be able to include their views in various proposals as well as the views of our staff. Perhaps as things develop we will want to change this, but right now I would like to insure that this operating procedure is followed."[29] Cole of course worked for Ehrlichman and the counsellors reported to Ehrlichman, but when given an opening by a Haldeman aide to protect the role of the Domestic Council and his own centrality in the policy process, Cole naturally took it. It was an indication of the orphan status of the counsellors. They were being grafted onto a preexisting system, and the White House bureaucrats were more comfortable preserving the old standard operating procedures. Cole's answer ever so slightly marginalized the centrality of the counsellors, their raison d'être.

Another chink in the counsellors' armor concerned congressional relations. The confidential memo, "The Role of the Counsellors," had stated that each counsellor's staff would include a full-time legislation liaison specialist. This arrangement was not intended to downgrade the White House's own congressional relations office but assumed that a full-time counsellor staffer would be needed, given the expected heavy involvement that counsellors would have with legislation. The counsellors were expected to be the central coordinators working with agencies to prepare legislative proposals and then to be the senior spokesmen for those proposals on the Hill. But, like Cole at the Domestic Council, William Timmons, director of the congressional relations office, did not want any impingement on his turf. The staffer planning the structure of Weinberger's counsellor office, Stephen McConahey, met with Timmons's top aide to develop a working relationship. But he was told that "Timmons' preference is that the Counsellors not create special congressional liaison positions for fear that this action would undercut the direct contact that Timmons' staff maintains with *agency* congressional staffs and that it would give the appearance of the Counsellor's office interfering in *agency responsibility*."[30] In other words, Timmons was not particularly concerned about direct contact between counsellors and senators or members of Congress. He did not want the counsellors to interpose themselves between him and the line departments and agencies. But that was exactly what the concept of the super-secretaries was premised on, and the secret memo specifically called for a legislative liaison specialist. Still, Timmons won.

THE ADMINISTRATION'S JOINT PUBLIC FACE
FOR DOMESTIC POLICY

In January, even though the counsellor offices were not really function-ing, the White House was quick to incorporate the new structure into the public face of the administration. Late that month, Nixon sent his first reorganization plan of the year to Congress. (This move was a use of the president's limited *statutory* powers to reorganize the executive branch, subject to legislative veto.) It involved reorganizing the Executive Office of the President by shedding units that had "the task of managing or admin-istering programs" such as the Office of Emergency Preparedness, which he transferred mostly to HUD. He wanted to end any line responsibili-ties within EOP, so that it would have a pure staff role. In his message to Congress accompanying the plan, Nixon noted that the EOP plan was only one part of his larger and coordinated effort to reorganize the presidency and the executive branch. Another related action was when he "appointed three Cabinet Secretaries as Counsellors to the President with coordinating responsibilities in the broad areas of human resources, natural resources, and community development." Three days later, when transmitting his budget proposal for FY1974 to Congress, Nixon's legislative message included reference to his goal of reorganizing the federal government and called on Congress to pass his proposals for super-departments. But, in the meantime (or, the message implied, absent congressional action), "I plan now to streamline the executive branch along these lines as much as possible within existing law."[31]

Weinberger, Lynn, and Butz were also active participants in major public events organized by the administration. When the National Governors Association had a conference in the capital in February, the administra-tion arranged for the governors to come to the White House for a briefing on its major domestic policies. Similarly, when 150 key state legislators were in town in March, they too were invited to the White House to be briefed by senior domestic officials. At both events, the audience heard from five administration officials: OMB director Ash, a representative of the Domestic Council, and the three counsellors. Each gave a ten-minute talk about his area of domestic policy and the major presidential initia-tives that would be of interest to the audience. At the end of each event, participants were given an opportunity to ask questions of the five.[32]

(Nixon also made a surprise appearance at the legislative briefing.[33]) In March, when a bipartisan delegation of governors came to the White House to talk about Nixon's planned budget cuts, the administration was represented at the meeting by six high-ranking officials, including Counsellors Lynn and Weinberger.[34]

In another instance, the three super-secretaries made a joint appearance on the television program *Meet the Press*. Ehrlichman favored the idea, thinking it would be a good platform for promoting the counsellor initiative; they could explain their roles and gain a greater public profile as spokesmen for the administration in domestic policy.[35] It took several months to schedule the appearance, which finally occurred on April 8, 1973. While normally a thirty-minute program, this one was lengthened to an hour to accommodate the panel of three. The advance publicity for the program identified them as "recently appointed counselors [*sic*] to the President."[36] At the beginning of the broadcast, host Lawrence Spivak pointedly described their counsellor roles. However, reporters on the panel were much more interested in headline topics, such as inflation, health care costs, and the rising price of meat. During the entire hour, only two questions mentioned the counsellor role, both addressed to Butz, and then only glancingly.[37] Compared to the issues du jour, government reorganization and public administration were boring subjects to reporters.

PART OF THE PRESIDENT'S SENIOR TEAM

On February 5, 1973, the president and Ehrlichman had met with the three counsellors. As discussed above, the purpose of the meeting was for the president to personally give the three a clear assignment to coordinate administration policy in their three respective rubrics. Nixon wanted them to take charge. His private comments at the meeting were fully in line with his public statements. The next time the three counsellors met with Nixon and Ehrlichman was a month later, on March 6. Ehrlichman said to a reporter that he was hoping to establish a routine pattern of such meetings, perhaps holding them as often as "once or twice a week."[38]

That estimate was almost certainly an exaggeration intended to create a false public image, but with a reason. From Ehrlichman's perspective, for the system to work, the counsellors needed to be *perceived* by others as

Figure 3. Joint appearance of the counsellors on Meet the Press, *April 8, 1973. From left: Lawrence Spivak (host), Earl Butz, Caspar Weinberger, and James Lynn. The inscription reads: "To Larry Spivak, With fond memories of my 'baptism' appearance on* Meet the Press *and thanks for the opportunity. James T. Lynn 4/24/73." Lawrence Spivak Papers, Library of Congress. Reprinted by permission of NBC News*

speaking for the president. They would truly be functioning as high-level and personal representatives of the president if they were seen by third parties as being close to the president. If that was accomplished, then there would be fewer reflexive appeals to the president from secretaries unhappy with a counsellor's decision. However, this perception of power was based more on image than reality. As far as Ehrlichman was concerned, *he* would be an intermediary between the counsellors and the president. Counsellors would report to him. Only important matters would involve Nixon personally, and sometimes that could be accomplished by Ehrlichman meeting with the president alone. Ehrlichman and Haldeman knew the president's time was precious and wanted to protect as much of it as possible.

Also, Nixon was most interested in spending his time on foreign policy, not domestic policy. This preference was so widely known that a "Doonesbury" cartoon strip lampooned it. Richard Fairbanks, DC associate director for natural resources, even framed that comic strip and hung it on the wall of his OEOB office. After he left office, even Nixon made fun of his own supposed lack of interest in domestic policy. John C. Whitaker had been Cabinet secretary during the first administration and undersecretary of interior in the second. After leaving office, Whitaker wrote about Nixon's (and Ford's) policies on the environment and natural resources, praising Nixon's initiatives and accomplishments. He suggested that Nixon's publicly unappreciated record was more substantial than his foreign policy successes. The story is told that Nixon reacted in mock horror, telling Whitaker he hoped that was not the case.[39]

The March 6 meeting of the president and the counsellors took place late in the afternoon in the Oval Office. It is a good example of how the counsellor system was supposed to work as a regular and permanent part of the organization of a presidency and the executive branch. Preparing the three counsellors for the presidential session later that day, Ehrlichman convened a one-hour breakfast meeting with them.[40] Based on Weinberger's summary of the breakfast, the points that Ehrlichman was planning to cover at the upcoming meeting with Nixon were almost all related to the administration's public relations, not to the policy and management coordination roles that were central to the conception of the super-secretary structure.

One of the major themes of the second term would be Nixon's war on excessive (Democratic) congressional spending. He could govern by veto, needing only one-third of the votes in one of the two houses of Congress to prevail. However, some vetoes would be in politically sensitive areas, such as veterans affairs (Weinberger's area, especially relating to health care) and farmers (Butz's area). Ehrlichman urged the counsellors to help stage "some visible activity for the President" and for vulnerable Republican senators to counteract such images. Similarly, they were asked to prepare lists of potential surrogate speakers to defend administration policies in public appearances around the country. Also, Ehrlichman specifically asked Weinberger to prepare an op ed column for the *New York Times* as a response to a series of articles by John Herbers about Nixon's governing style that the administration considered unfair. The only non-PR related item concerned improving coordination between the counsellors and the White House congressional liaison office so that counsellors would be kept up to date on legislative developments in their respective policy areas.[41]

After the breakfast meeting, Ehrlichman sent Nixon the usual premeeting memo. Consistent with his comments to the counsellors at breakfast, he concentrated on public relations–related topics. What Ehrlichman was hoping Nixon would accomplish through the meeting included a consistent message to the public (and Congress) about cutting spending, the need for more public communication regarding the administration's effort to control spending, and Nixon's desire that the three counsellors "get out and speak on the budget, i.e., carry our case to the people." However, a few topics related to policy coordination, such as welfare reform (Weinberger), special revenue sharing (Lynn, for community development revenue sharing), and funding levels for USDA's Rural Electrification Administration (Butz).[42]

The meeting of the three counsellors (and Ehrlichman) with the president took place in the Oval Office and lasted about an hour. (On the parallel Watergate track, earlier that day, Nixon met with John Dean in the Oval Office to talk about the difficulties of controlling L. Patrick Gray, the acting director of the FBI—and nominee for the permanent position—who was cooperating somewhat with the Senate Watergate Committee regarding access to FBI files about Watergate.[43]) According to Ehrlichman's contemporaneous notes, the five men had an extensive and detailed conversation. Nixon covered Ehrlichman's talking points regarding the need for a more effective public communications program in support of the administration's anti-spending policies and to avoid appearing tó be anti-veteran and anti-farmer. But the meeting was neither a presidential monologue nor limited to PR issues. The conversation also covered specifics of some of the policy conflicts in which the counsellors were involved. For example, Lynn discussed a jurisdictional dispute between two house committees that would affect the upcoming administration bill on rural economic development. He and Butz also went into detail about spending levels for some specific programs, and Nixon responded with his guidance.

Also, Nixon provided the counsellors with his political appraisal of the anti-spending effort, his opinion that many conservative politicians were big spenders regarding projects in their districts, his belief in the need to focus on the House rather than the Senate for a reliable one-third vote to sustain vetoes, and the need to try to elect a more sympathetic House in the 1974 election.[44] The veto strategy (which had so far been successful) was still sometimes awkward politically. There were two veterans bills in advanced stages on Capitol Hill that Nixon might have to veto. Even before this meeting, those two bills were on Nixon's mind.[45] At the meeting, he turned to Weinberger and asked him to submit his best thinking on how to deal with the political difficulties of vetoing a veterans bill.

Weinberger conscientiously followed up on the president's (and Ehrlichman's) request for public relations ideas to prevent the vetoes of appropriations bills from appearing to be anti-veteran. He conferred with the head of the Veterans Administration (VA), and one of his staffers asked for other ideas from a middle-ranking VA manager.[46] Weinberger's talking points for the first meeting of his Human Development Subcommittee included saying that the "President's strong interest requires we consider two items" relating to veterans.[47] A few weeks after the presidential meeting, Weinberger submitted his recommendations to the president. Two of his ideas were that Nixon should give a major speech on the administration's policies toward veterans and that the president should visit the successful veterans program in St. Louis.[48] Donald Johnson, VA administrator, had suggested St. Louis for policy and political reasons. He wrote that its hospitals and assistance programs were very well managed and because "St. Louis had one of the better organized Veterans for Nixon campaigns. At VA, we have on duty, three staffers who worked at CRP [Committee to Reelect the President] and in St. Louis."[49]

As a glimpse of what could have been, the March 6, 1973, meeting and Weinberger's follow-up memo provide a significant insight into the "normal" functioning of the counsellor structure. The three counsellors were jointly meeting with the president (and his senior domestic advisor), which gave them a broad perspective on the administration's policies rather than the parochial departmental perspective that an individual Cabinet officer would have. They would be able to understand how their individual responsibilities related to a larger theme and how their actions could have significant impact on the work of other counsellors. They were a *team,* one that jointly covered the entirety of the federal government's domestic activities (excluding economic policy).

Further, their policy responsibilities were broader than the management of their respective bureaucratic portfolios because they were the *president's* men. All aspects of a White House perspective were within their purview. They were the spokesmen for the administration on Capitol Hill, whether regarding appropriations bills under consideration, sustaining presidential vetoes, or introducing new program legislation. Similarly, they were the spokesmen for the administration to the public at large and were expected to travel around the country to explain the president's policies. Related to that responsibility, behind the scenes they were to help organize the administration's public relations efforts, through, for example, developing a better surrogates program. Finally, they were the president's *political* men as well. They were expected to understand the larger political goals of the administration and to work to achieve them, including helping friendly members of Congress and not rewarding unfriendly ones. Influencing future elections was expected to be part of their daily political math.

On the whole, this meeting was a fleeting depiction of President Nixon's super-secretary experiment at full flowering. The session demonstrated the possibility that it could perhaps be a viable management structure for a president to use in running the executive branch. He would delegate to senior officials major responsibility for pursuing the administration's domestic agenda on a comprehensive basis, covering the bureaucratic, legislative, public, media, and political fronts. Had Nixon's reorganization plan been approved by Congress, or had many of the other grand reorganization plans by other presidents been enacted, the March 6, 1973, meeting could have been a routine—if infrequent—component of the reorganization. A president could meet with a small number of super-secretaries who had responsibility for coherent and integrated policy areas rather than with the rickety contraption of the executive branch that had gradually and incrementally evolved into a confusing and hard-to-manage structure. The motivation and rationale for so many previous (failed) grand reorganization plans was the omnipresent subtext of the meeting.

COUNSELLOR-TO-PRESIDENT REPORTING RELATIONSHIPS

Of the three counsellors, Weinberger's office was the first to get organized, had the largest staff, was the most structured by policy areas, and was the most paperwork oriented. Lynn was a bit slower and Butz the most lethargic (for details, see chapters 5–7). As a result, the most extensive pattern of counsellor-to-president reporting occurred from Weinberger to Nixon.

Based on the model that Nixon and Ehrlichman developed, counsellors would report to the president (via Ehrlichman) on issues that the counsellor could not resolve on his own or jointly with one or both of the other counsellors. These items, theoretically, would be the only issues that the president would have to decide. However, given the brief duration of the counsellor experiment, only one archetypal example of such reporting occurred.

Legal Services Corporation

The issue at hand was the future of legal services for the poor in non-criminal matters. Would it be abolished as part of the administration's effort to dismantle the war on poverty? In 1971–1972, the administration had proposed legislation to take legal services from OEO and place it in a new Legal Services Corporation that would be responsible for providing such a service (and nothing else). The subject was highly controversial and politicized, largely framed as essential legal services for the poor in civil matters (the framework supported by most of the legal establishment, much of it Republican) versus government subsidizing left-wing political advocates who used the courts for anti-administration activities.

As HR counsellor, Weinberger had oversight of most of OEO but not all of it. (Lynn had the rest.) The question that arose was whether the administration would reintroduce its first-term proposal or take another tack. Briefly, the main in-house argument was whether the legislation should create a national and centrally directed corporation (the original administration position) or essentially shift money to the state level and let fights over it occur there. Weinberger's staff presented him with a six-page draft memo to the president about both positions. Weinberger—typically—went over it word for word, writing additions and deletions in his own hand.[50] On April 10, he submitted a five-page memo to the president presenting the two basic options.[51] He carefully described the pros and cons of both positions. On the last line of the memo, he identified which option he recommended (staying with the national approach). Nixon, in substance, essentially agreed with Weinberger's recommendation, although the bill the administration introduced included state-by-state *advisory* councils.[52]

Given Nixon and Ehrlichman's stated preference that any unresolved issues would be presented to the president by the counsellor, this memo was the quintessence of the counsellor system. Weinberger's report was a balanced presentation of the two options, fair to both sides. It was lucid, clear, concise, and to the point. Whatever the president eventually decided, everyone could feel like they had had their day in court. The only difference was that their "day" would now be in writing and would be through the counsellor rather than any direct personal appeals to the president.

Separately, Counsellor Weinberger weighed in with advice to the president on the side issue of whether the proposed Legal Services Corporation could fund legal "back-up centers" to engage in legal research, that is, whether there was potential for funding research at law schools around the country.[53] Weinberger recommended against permitting legal back-up centers.

As a postscript to this matter, it was two months later—four weeks after the counselor positions were abolished—that the House debated the bill creating a Legal Services Corporation during an eleven-hour floor session. However, atypically, the discord within the administration—justifying the need for Weinberger's April 10 options memo to the president in the first place—were publicly apparent. According to the *New York Times,* "In recent days, it had become clear that there was a deep division within the White House over what form of legislation should be pushed."[54] Pushing for a compromise version of the bill was Frank Carlucci, Weinberger's HEW undersecretary, and Leonard Garment, the White House counsel. The other faction, which opposed any significant ideological compromises with Democrats (the majority party in Congress), was led by Howard Phillips, the head of OEO, and William Timmons, the White House director of congressional relations.

The initial "final" version of the bill passed by both houses permitted funding legal back-up centers. The administration was united in its response to this outcome, with Nixon publicly saying he would veto the bill if that provision remained in the version sent to him. The provision was deleted before a final vote by each house.[55] Weinberger's advice on legal back-up centers had prevailed.

The final version of the bill (sans back-up centers) was sent to the president in July 1974. It created a relatively centralized national Legal Services Corporation, reflecting the basic recommendation in Weinberger's April 10 memo, but there was still much in it that could have justified a veto, which conservatives urged. Still, Nixon signed a bill on July 26, 1974 (two weeks before his resignation). Notwithstanding his politically weakened condition by that time as the result of Watergate, his veto might have been sustained due to conservative objections to the bill. But for him, the political math at that point was to avoid creating any more ill will from potential congressional supporters in case of impeachment.[56]

Food Stamps for Strikers

A different kind of counsellor-presidential interaction occurred when the president had a query. The issue of *Time* magazine dated March 5, 1973, had a short piece claiming that striking agricultural workers in Texas were obtaining food stamps and that this aid was helping them to continue striking.[57] Nixon asked Cole if that was true and, if so, what could be done to stop it. Cole, in turn, asked Weinberger (and Cavanaugh).[58] Weinberger asked his staff to look into to it, and one aide, responsible for human development issues, sent a quick query to USDA, writing that "the Counsellor wishes your comments on the Texas incident" and asking about current regulations on the subject.[59] Justine Farr Rodriguez, a Weinberger staffer who was in charge of his Income Security Subcommittee, made sure the topic would be discussed in more detail by putting it on the agenda of the next meeting, set for April 10.[60] Based on that discussion and other research, she submitted to Weinberger on April 18 a detailed report regarding strikers' eligibility for unemployment insurance and food stamps. At the end of her memo, she included some political gossip: "There is also discussion in OMB and elsewhere to the effect that Secretary [of Labor] Brennan should now 'win' something, and welfare for strikers has been specifically mentioned in this context."[61] A week later, she followed up with a few more policy options.[62]

The next meeting of the counsellor's Income Security Subcommittee took place on April 25. One of the agenda items was "development of a coordinated policy with regard to benefits for strikers" with "discussion of possible options and their pros and cons."[63] At the meeting, Rodriguez handed out her April 18 memo to Weinberger, which turned out to be a mistake. The gossip about Brennan was the kind of comment that can cause major Washington controversies. Weinberger's chief of staff, William Taft, left a panicky memo for Weinberger to see before the day was over. The memo indicated that Weinberger "may have a very serious problem with Secretary Brennan. . . . It seems to me quite likely that the substance of the memo will appear in the press. Even if it does not, it is a virtual certainty that Secretary Brennan will be aware of it. Evidently, this type of memo was intended for your personal use—and quite useful it would have been—should not ever be distributed at so large a meeting."[64] So, a relatively brief and casual inquiry by the president had now led to major conflicts within the administration about policy, power, and personality.[65]

Another example of counsellor-to-president reporting occurred when, on his own initiative, Weinberger sent (what was expected to be) a periodic status report to the president that was not decision oriented in the way his options memo on the Legal Services Corporation was.[66] In late March, he asked one of the staffers in his counsellor office to draft an update report to the president.[67] On April 3, he signed and submitted the two-page memo, which focused on his actions to organize the new counsellor office since his appointment three months earlier. He told the president about the subcommittee and staff structure of his office in three policy areas. "I have given the highest priority to welfare reform in accordance with your specific direction to me," he carefully noted, aware that many other White House eyes would be reading his memo. By making this point, he was flagging for those others that he worked *for* the president and that anyone tempted to say to him, "The President wants you to . . ." should think twice before doing so. A similar political message was contained in the penultimate sentence about some strains in his relationship with the Domestic Council and OMB: "Certainly the clear and visible support you have given the Counsellors has been critical in establishing our role."[68]

A key point that Weinberger wanted to convey was his self-definition of his counsellor role. According to his memo, he had the "major purpose of improving the coordination and execution of major human resource policy development. We also are trying to provide an effective and more manageable flow of communication between the White House and human resource agencies." Specifically, Weinberger identified his counsellor position as encompassing five responsibilities: policy analysis, policy formulation, objective setting, budgetary discussions, and resolution of major issues.[69] This view of his job was broad and expansive, not necessarily one with which his fellow counsellors agreed, and other power centers in the White House (such as OMB and DC) certainly would not agree with it. Nonetheless, Weinberger had asserted his role as that of an assistant president.

Nixon did not give personal attention to Weinberger's report, nor much of anything else around that time. Instead, he was preoccupied with trying to prevent the Senate Watergate Committee from successfully pursuing its mission.[70]

Still, the Haldeman White House had specific protocols about handling paperwork that flowed to the president and replying to it. Weinberger's status report was handled by Staff Secretary Bruce Kehrli, who first sent copies of Weinberger's report to Ehrlichman and Cole. Second, on April 9, Kehrli assigned low-ranking staffer Roland Elliot the task of drafting a presidential reply, with a deadline of April 11.[71] On April 12, Kehrli then sent Elliot's draft to another staffer, Craig Gosden, asking, "Is this reply acceptable to the Domestic Council?" The due date was the next day. Gosden replied that it was.[72] Nixon's acknowledgment to Weinberger of receiving the status report was then signed and sent. Its tone was positive but noncommittal:

> Dear Cap:
>
> It was good to have your April 3 memorandum . . . Your summary indicates you are off to a fine start—just as I anticipated—and I look forward to your next report on the substantive aspects which, clearly, will be of major importance to us in the months and years ahead.[73]

Clearly, Nixon had almost totally withdrawn from any role in domestic policy making due to Watergate.

COUNSELLOR-TO-COUNSELLOR WORKING RELATIONSHIPS

Sometimes, the counsellors had bilateral contacts. In late March, CD counsellor Lynn described at a congressional hearing this kind of interaction:

> Now, what I have found in my role as counselor [*sic*] is that when I have a problem that involves human resources, it has been made much easier to get to the right source material, information, or decisionmakers within HEW or another human resource agency by my being able to go to Counselor Weinberg [*sic*] and ask him the best way to proceed in that area. Likewise, in the area of natural resources, to be able to go to Secretary Butz with his hat on as counselor for natural resources supplements . . . helps the coordinating role that the Secretary of Agriculture has as to rural development.[74]

A month later, Lynn provided another example, this one relating to cooperation by Weinberger regarding the human resources aspects of a major housing study that HUD was in the midst of conducting.[75] Lynn was highlighting the benefits of the counsellor system on a horizontal basis, an aspect largely ignored in Washington, where vertical thinking dominated. His comments indicated one of the side benefits of the counsellor structure.

Yet another example of inter-counsellor cooperation related to regulating use of pesticides due to their impact on agricultural workers. Counsellor Butz hosted a meeting at his OEOB office with Counsellor Weinberger's staffer for health matters, an assistant secretary of the Labor Department who handled occupational safety and health (which was out of Butz's jurisdiction), a senior official from EPA, and an assistant USDA secretary.[76]

Another potential benefit of the counsellor project would derive from the full triumvirate working together on a broad domestic policy area. In theory, when the three of them were coordinating their activities they would rival and even overshadow the Domestic Council and could have dominated the field of all domestic public policy. This would truly have been a full implementation of Nixon's and Ehrlichman's objectives for the reorganization: moving decision making away from the president and the inner White House staff. Had it occurred, it would have been a major development in federal operations.

However, it does not appear that this potential all-counsellor joint action scenario occurred during the brief life of the project. The three counsellors met (without Ehrlichman or the president) at least twice, on February 19 and April 26. The February meeting was largely the impetus of Counsellor Weinberger.[77] Moving fast to set up his counsellor office, he had prepared an untitled paper on the role and office operation of a counsellor. The paper reflected his rather ambitious take on the potential of a counsellor, and Weinberger was hoping to develop a consensus among the three reflecting his view of their powers and roles. (For more discussion of the memo, see chapter 5.) However, Butz and Lynn ended up self-defining their roles less expansively (see chapter 6–7). One of Lynn's assistant directors characterized Weinberger's model as "a rather strictly structured system," one too structured for Lynn's style, perspective, and approach.[78] Nonetheless, the February 19 meeting demonstrated the benefits of the three staying in touch and the potential for them acting on a common front. (For a discussion of the April meeting, see chapter 8.)

Below the level of the principals, there were routine contacts between the staffs of the three offices. However, there never were pan-counsellor staff meetings, that is, meetings of all the staffers of all the counsellors to create a networking relationship, nor were there any regular meetings of the chiefs of staff of the three counsellors. Such meetings may well have evolved if the experiment had lasted longer. Nonetheless, it is noteworthy that the staffs were so atomized during the time that all three counsellor offices were fully functioning. This insular activity may have been a reflection of office geography because the suites of the three counsellors were far apart from each other in OEOB. Kehrli's success at giving the three counsellors perfectly equivalent personal offices and corner suites had the effect of dispersing the three to different sides of the building, even different floors.

Sometimes, the inter-counsellor staff contacts were comparative organizational and process issues, such as "How are you handling the issue of subcommittees?" For example, Butz's secretary asked Lynn's senior aide about the CD subcommittees and the reporting procedures that Lynn had imposed on agencies and departments in his domain.[79] One of Lynn's aides contacted Weinberger's office for a copy of its policy on agency reporting and compared it to the nascent one for the CD counsellor. Indicating a sense of sibling rivalry, or at least a political version of keeping up with the Joneses, Lynn's aide concluded that Weinberger's office operations were "getting organized and perhaps that is more than we can say for our system."[80]

On some occasions, the staff interacted about matters other than process and structure. For example, McConahey of Weinberger's office contacted Parker of Lynn's office to ask about the human resources angle of Lynn's work in the area of rural development.[81] The two met to work out a way to include the human resources perspective in Lynn's Rural Development Working Group. On another occasion, Weinberger's staff director Taft inquired of his counterpart in Lynn's office about the specifics of the administration's moratorium on new housing projects. However, the inquiry was precipitated by a political friend of Weinberger's in California, not by Weinberger's human resources portfolio. This was more akin to case work, but at a very high level.[82]

WITH OMB AND THE COUNSELLORS, TWO WAS A CROWD

In the middle of his first term, Nixon had reorganized the Bureau of the Budget (BOB). Ever since the passage of the Budget and Accounting Act of 1921, BOB had begun to emerge as a key staff agency in the world of the managerial presidency. Initially, BOB was organizationally part of the

Treasury Department, but in 1937 FDR's reorganization planning committee (the Brownlow Committee) recommended bringing it closer to the president. After much *Sturm und Drang* on Capitol Hill, Roosevelt's 1939 reorganization included establishing the Executive Office of the President (EOP) and transferring BOB to it as one of its original five agencies. However, from then until the 1970s, the bureau's work had focused largely on the powers it derived from its *budgetary* focus. BOB's nonbudgetary role was thus quite limited. Some of its initiatives survived (such as central legislative clearance), while others did not (such as a field service). Nixon introduced sweeping changes to its role. In implementing the first group of recommendations made by the Ash Council, in 1970 he renamed BOB the Office of Management and Budget and expanded its mission so that it would work much more on management, not just budgeting. Nixon said that "the budget function is only one of several important management tools that the President must now have. He must also have a substantially enhanced institutional staff capability in other areas of executive management—particularly in program evaluation and coordination, improvement of Executive Branch organization, information and management systems, and development of executive talent."[83]

But institutions change slowly. During the winter of 1972–1973, Roy Ash, as the incoming OMB director, and Fred Malek, as the incoming deputy director, intended to make the M in OMB much more important in the second term. They wanted the agency to *manage* the executive branch. Before the reorganization, BOB had about 30 professionals involved in management matters. By early 1974, Ash and Malek had expanded that number to 130.[84]

As they were preparing to take over and restructure OMB, Ash and Malek also wanted to be sure the planning for the new counsellor structure would be in harmony with their view of OMB's management role. Malek, at that time the White House staffer in charge of appointing loyalists to positions in the departments and agencies for the second term, sought to raise with Haldeman—ever so faintly—some concerns about the role of OMB versus the counsellors. Ash (with his concurrent appointment as one of the Big Five assistants to the president in the plans for the second term, his to be for management) and Malek viewed their roles as overseeing the management of the executive branch. They were planning to impose a management-by-objectives (MBO) approach on all departments and agencies. (MBO was a management decision-making tool very popular in the private sector at the time.[85]) OMB would be the locus for implementing and enforcing that new management approach. Nixon approved the initiative in principle during the interregnum, when he was at Camp David planning his second term.[86] To reflect this new orientation, Ash and Malek continued to seek to rename OMB as the Office of Executive Management.[87]

Regarding the counsellors, Malek wrote Haldeman, "We need agreement on the role of the Counsellors (*policy vs. line*), the Counsellors' staffing needs, the grouping of Agencies under [Super?] Departments, and the placement of Natural Resources. We also need to have some plan for orientation for Counsellors and other Cabinet Members to ensure everyone fully understands the method of operation and *what they are actually expected to do.*"[88] If OMB was to be in charge of managing the executive branch, Malek and Ash wanted to be sure that the three counsellors did not think *they* had such a responsibility. In Malek and Ash's view, what counsellors handled was policy, not management.

During the final drafting of the counsellor documents in late December 1972, Ash was successful in preventing the counsellors from having too extensive a role in managing the executive branch in general and the budget process in particular. Instead of a counsellor having "the right to make recommendation to the President on budget matters," the final version of the memo establishing the counsellor roles eventually stated they would "participate in major Presidential budget decisions." Regarding the right to review in advance major policy pronouncements of departments and agencies in a counsellor's domain, the long list of such pronouncements (e.g., speeches, press releases. and congressional testimony) no longer included "internal policy directions." Instead of the counsellor being "consulted" by OMB during the budget review process, counsellor staff "should attend [OMB] Director's review sessions as the Domestic Counsel staff does now." The section on policy evaluation was totally changed, shifting the counsellor from being an active overseer to being a passive consumer of OMB evaluations.[89]

Meanwhile, Weinberger was planning for his counsellor work. He had in mind ten professionals and seven secretaries, which alarmed Ehrlichman because it implied a much more extensive activity than he had in mind. It sounded like Weinberger was planning to *manage* his domain, not just coordinate policy (exactly what Ash and Malek were concerned about). Ehrlichman expected only two to three staff (plus clerical) in each counsellor office and wanted to convey that expectation, indirectly, to the counsellors as quickly as possible.[90]

The question revolved around separating policy from management and budget, which is akin to the hoary effort by early public administration reformers to delineate a bright line between politics and administration. The politics-administration dichotomy had been thoroughly discredited in academic public administration circles, but Ash and Malek came from a business management background. From their corporate perspective, policy was the "what" of government and OMB's mission was merely the "how," that is, managing and budgeting. However, in the reality of government, the "what" and "how" cannot be cleanly and clearly separated. One person's policy is another's management, or one person's budgeting is another's policy. For example, setting the budget to implement an agency's statutory (and presidential) mission can have major implications regarding the *implementation* of policy. Is such an issue purely one that OMB should handle? From the opposite perspective, the coordination of the implementation of public policy is at the heart of policy decision making.

Ash's and Malek's concerns during the interregnum about counsellors being a potential threat to OMB's role proved accurate. The issue burst forth on March 9, when Weinberger promulgated his requirements for reporting, monitoring, and clearance by all the entities in the HR counsellor's domain. He provided three forms, one for each category of activity:

Weekly Status Reports: For upcoming events, he wanted the report to cover "key human resource activities, events, and problems having important implications for human resource policy and program performance." For past events, the report should include a response to the counsellor's requests or specific assignments.[91]

Priority Item Monitoring: The purpose of this category of reporting would be "to monitor the status of critical issues, policies and objectives, and thereby assist the counsellor and his staff to focus their attention on top priority items."[92]

Review and Clearance Procedures: These reports would "ensure human resource policies and agencies' operations are consistent with the Administration approach and strategy, and to ensure coordination of policy formulation and execution." Six subjects were to be included in reports relating to review and clearance: budgetary proposals; major legislative and policy proposals; major program regulations; major policy statements, announcements, and congressional testimony; major agency operating changes; and key personnel appointments.[93]

This approach entailed an exceptionally broad scope for oversight.

Essentially, Weinberger was announcing that he would be functioning as a kind of assistant president, with *line* authority over just about everything an agency did. But, based on Ash and Malek's dichotomy of government's "what" versus "how," Weinberger's definition of policy coordination definitely included a lot of the "how." In fact, in a version of thumbing his nose at Ash and Malek, Weinberger elaborated on the budgetary proposals he expected: "FY budget proposals and major mid-year adjustments reflecting changes in policy, priorities, or operating nature of programs (*prior to submission to OMB*)."[94] Weinberger did not try to do this behind OMB's back. He made sure that a copy of his memo was sent to Paul O'Neill, OMB's assistant director for human resources, the chief OMB liaison to the HR counsellor.[95]

Ash and Malek hit the roof, the former sending a packet to Ehrlichman about the problem.[96] He included a draft memo that Ash hoped Ehrlichman would sign and send to Weinberger (and the other two counsellors). It would direct Weinberger to repeal the second and third reporting forms, relating to, respectively, priority item monitoring and procedures for review and clearance. Ash also helpfully shared with Ehrlichman a draft memo for Weinberger to sign that would inform the principals of the human resource agencies about the repeal of those two forms. A few days later, he handed Ehrlichman a slightly toned down version of the memo he hoped Ehrlichman would sent to Weinberger.[97]

Ehrlichman never signed the memo.[98] (On the parallel Watergate track, in the second half of March, Ehrlichman was deeply involved in efforts to contain the work of the Senate Watergate Committee.[99]) Perhaps part of the reason he did not act on Ash's request was the tension that existed between Ehrlichman and Ash at the beginning of the second term. For example, in a 1977 interview with a researcher, Malek said that he and Ash viewed the counsellor project as intended "to strengthen Ehrlichman's own role in the White House . . . and to provide a counterweight [to] the strength of OMB."[100] In an effort to work out the controversy, even though Ehrlichman would not intervene personally, several members of Weinberger's counsellor staff met with O'Neill and other OMB officials to talk about Weinberger's memo to the agencies.[101] They agreed to rescind the requirement on advance clearing of legislative proposals and congressional testimony. They also eliminated any independent counsellor role in the review of regulations, instead integrating the counsellor's reviewing role into OMB's existing sixty-day review period.[102]

OMB was not the only agency alarmed by Weinberger's reporting forms.

The Department of Labor was also taken aback, and Labor Secretary Brennan sent Weinberger a diplomatically worded memo on April 5, 1973. He suggested that "some additional consideration and discussion would be useful prior to implementing any specific procedure." He was unhappy with just about everything required by Weinberger's reporting template, including the overlap with Labor's reporting to George Shultz in Shultz's counsellor-like role in the second term regarding all economic policy, as well as the duplication of OMB activity, the excessive paperwork, and the lack of clarity in the scope of some of the terms in Weinberger's forms. Brennan pointedly noted that copies of the memo were going to Shultz and Ash, both of whom, as assistants to the president (i.e., Ehrlichman equals) outranked Counsellor Weinberger.[103]

Weinberger replied in a conciliatory tone on April 19. He told Brennan of the changes in reporting that he had already agreed to (clearance of legislative matters and review of regulations) when his staff met with OMB. He further informed Brennan that he was rescinding any review of key personnel appointments, saying, "I think there are enough people involved in this circuit already." He stood his ground on several areas. He declined to rescind the requirement of weekly reports on program activities. However, Weinberger clarified that he intended them to be very short reports and that most of the reporting could be accomplished by sending him copies of relevant documents that would have been prepared for internal departmental use anyway. But on two other major matters involving Assistants to the President Ash and Shultz, he declined to retreat: "my participation in the budgetary process and overlapping jurisdictions" with Shultz's economic portfolio. To help resolve those two items of contention, Weinberger wrote Brennan that he would arrange a four-way meeting with Ash and Shultz.[104]

That is where the matter stood when the counsellor roles were abolished on May 10. In sum, Weinberger can be perceived as winning. His initial hand was admittedly aggressive and ambitious, but, after some modest compromises with OMB and Labor, he still had in place an extensive—but seemingly more reasonable—oversight regime. (For a discussion of the weekly reports that were submitted to Weinberger, see the section on reporting in chapter 5.) The other two counsellors were glad to be on the sidelines while the elephants trampled the grass. Lynn and Butz more slowly enacted reporting requirements, generally reflecting the precedents that Weinberger had established. (For more details on the reporting policies they promulgated, see the sections on reporting in chapters 6 and 7.)

Management by Objectives

The counsellors and OMB also bumped up against each other when Ash and Malek were getting ready to unveil their management-by-objectives initiative. Here was another interesting effort to define the "what" versus the "how" of government. Certainly, one would expect objectives to be part of the "what." Were not objectives about *policy?* In this case, however, the very term "*management* by objectives" disguised the fact that OMB (the "how" agency) was leading an effort to define the "what."

In late March, Ash and Malek submitted to Haldeman a draft of a presidential memorandum to all department and agency heads announcing the new MBO effort, led by OMB and endorsed by the president. The memo explicitly stated that the counsellors and the Domestic Council would be involved in working on finalizing departmental objectives (thus papering over the potential conflict of OMB being involved in the "what" of government). Haldeman okayed it in principle but thought the specific language "is not Nixonian." He asked that it be redrafted "to Nixonize it a bit."[105]

Meanwhile, Tod Hullin (Ehrlichman's top aide) convened a meeting of OMB, DC, and the counsellors' staffs to iron out the process regarding upcoming departmental MBO submissions. The result was clearly a compromise. Even though submissions (due May 15, 1973) would be addressed to OMB, OMB would not do anything with them except "cut and paste." Instead, the first substantive review would be by the counsellors. Hullin ambiguously stated that "this would be the first point at which the Domestic Council would be *inserted* into the process."[106] The Domestic Council's role was clear as mud but notably subordinate to the more defined and explicit roles of OMB and the counsellors.

Ultimately, the last step in the process would be five memos to the president specifying the administration's objectives for those areas. Each of the three counsellors would submit a memo that integrated all objectives in their functional areas, along with one from George Shultz on economic goals and from the attorney general outlining law enforcement objectives. This plan demonstrated the central role that the White House wanted for the counsellors: integrating executive branch activities by goals, objectives, and functions in order to overcome the centrifugal effects of the legal structure of the executive branch. But the plan also demonstrated the centrality of OMB as the lead agency on the MBO project.

With Ash's memo now revised and the relationship between the counsellors and OMB firmly established for the MBO project, on April 12 Haldeman approved issuing the presidential memo on MBO.[107] Nixon's document imposing a management-by-objectives structure on the executive branch was quietly disseminated on April 18 and only slowly became known publicly.[108]

As the next step in the MBO project, Ash and Malek met with Counsellor Butz to discuss "OMB's ideas for setting objectives and monitoring projects for natural resources."[109] Here was an example of a joint partnership between OMB and a counsellor on the MBO effort *before* agency submissions. An example of counsellors giving input after initial agency submissions occurred when Weinberger's aide McConahey sent his reactions on USDA's initial draft of its human resources activities (such as child nutrition and food stamps) back to the department with suggestions for clarifications and modifications.[110]

Weinberger also saw the potential of the MBO project for developing goals that crossed departmental lines. At the April 25 meeting of his Income Security Subcommittee, the group discussed the status of the MBO project. By now, two agencies had already submitted their statements of general goals. Weinberger urged the subcommittee members to think broadly rather than in departmental terms. In a "Tasks" list circulated at the meeting, he asked, "Where do you perceive commonality of interests with the other income security members? Program interfaces?"[111] Similarly, at the May 3 meeting of Weinberger's Health Subcommittee, his talking points included noting that "we are also interested in identifying objectives that, because of their interdepartmental nature, may not have been proposed by an agency. Hopefully, the Counsellor's office can identify a set of these interdepartmental objectives and ensure they are achieved."[112]

In contemporary jargon, Weinberger was trying to get them to break out of their stovepipes and develop policy with a horizontal perspective. The counsellor structure was perfect for this approach to the MBO project. That was precisely what Ehrlichman and Nixon were hoping for, namely, a functional approach to government programs rather than a structural one. However, at this point, the counsellor project was terminated and OMB "happily" carried forward the MBO campaign on its own, without any meddling from counsellors.[113]

The events recounted here clearly demonstrate that at the beginning of the second term the Nixon White House engaged in major in-house and public efforts to give substance and power to the new super-secretary structure. The administration worked to operationalize the declared duties of the three counsellors, gave them face time with the president, integrated them into the decision-making machinery, assigned them public roles to contribute to their credibility, and protected their essential roles in conflicts with other central management agencies. The next three chapters report individually on the activities and record of the three counsellors during the existence of their positions.

5

COUNSELLOR FOR HUMAN RESOURCES CASPAR WEINBERGER

The Super-Secretary as Assistant President

The memorandum the three counsellors received in early January from Ehrlichman outlining their duties and responsibilities (discussed in chapter 3) was strictly confidential, which meant that no one else knew precisely what their roles were. The three were not supposed to share the memo even with their counsellor staff, let alone with the Cabinet and subcabinet members who were in their domain. That secrecy bred internal and external ambiguity about their roles. Whether intentional or not, this situation gave the each counsellor the opportunity to develop his office and exercise powers based on his particular self-conceptualization of this unprecedented position. Weinberger had the most expansive approach. He saw himself as an assistant president, with direct line powers to supervise the agencies that were his responsibility. His was an audacious and bold approach to being the president's counsellor for human resources.

SCOPE

Based on Ehrlichman's congressional briefing of January 5, 1973, the jurisdiction of the human resources counsellor was described as encompassing eight functional policy areas: health, education, manpower development, income security, social services, Indians and native peoples, drug abuse treatment, and consumer protection.[1] In John Dean's early January memo, the jurisdiction of the HR counsellor was described according to administrative entities:

- Department of Health, Education, and Welfare (HEW): all except National Institute for Occupational Safety and Health, and public library construction grants
- Department of Labor: Manpower Administration, Employment Service Women's Bureau, unemployment compensation for federal employees and ex-servicemen only, unemployment insurance benefits, and Bureau of Employee's Compensation
- Department of Interior: only Native American programs
- HUD: college housing program
- Department of Commerce: product safety programs of the National Bureau of Standards
- USDA: Economic Research Service (Human Resources Branch), Agriculture Research Service (human nutrition and consumer research programs), Food and Nutrition Service, and meat, poultry, and egg inspection
- OEO (a unit in EOP): all except Community Action Programs and special impact programs
- Special Action Office for Drug Abuse Prevention (the drug "czar") (a unit in EOP)
- Office of Consumer Affairs (a unit in EOP)
- Veterans Administration (VA)
- National Cancer Institute
- ACTION
- Equal Employment Opportunity Commission (EEOC)
- Railroad Retirement Board
- Fine Arts Commission
- National Foundation for the Arts and Humanities[2]

Notwithstanding this long list of relevant agencies, the *National Journal* later opined that of the three counsellors, Weinberger's coordinative duties were the least cumbersome "since most policy issues fell solely within the jurisdiction of HEW." However, contradictorily, the same article identified Weinberger as the counsellor who "tried hardest to make the system work," spending about a third of his time at his OEOB office.[3] Had it been true that most policy issues fell within his secretarial scope, he would not have needed to spend so much time at his OEOB office and could have functioned largely out of his HEW office. Indeed, based on the preceding list of the administrative units under his jurisdiction, he had at least as broad an interdepartmental scope as the other two counsellors. That, along with his self-definition of the super-secretary role, made him the most involved of the three counsellors. Weinberger viewed his role as an assistant president, responsible for overseeing all aspects of the agencies in his domain.

During his confirmation hearings, Weinberger was asked to explain what his role as counsellor would be. He blandly stuck to the themes used by the president and Ehrlichman at the congressional breakfast. However, he also hinted at the central role that he expected to play, interposing himself between the president and the departments, both on an incoming and an outgoing basis: "I would transmit *to* the President their [the departments' and agencies'] requirements, their recommendations, their thoughts, and their reactions to various events. I would transmit to them, *from* the President, Presidential policy and Presidential requirements, and would insure that there is a coordinated response, that there is *a coordinated series of activities.*" This did not sound like he was going to be a mail forwarding service. He was going to be the one to ensure coordination. Weinberger explicitly disclaimed any "administrative, day-to-day, operational kind of task," limiting himself to policy.[4] But the difference between policy and administration is easier to assert than define.

SETTING UP

Weinberger's service as OMB director late in Nixon's first term meant that he directed the agency as it was preparing the FY1974 budget, the primary product of the agency's traditional role. Given his deep involvement in preparing that budget, Weinberger preferred to be in place at OMB when the president's annual budget proposal would be released publicly. After all, he had worked hard on it, and he wanted some public identification with the end result. So, despite some nudging from Ehrlichman and even the president to transition (if only unofficially) to his new role, he was reluctant to do so. On January 29, three and a half weeks after the congressional breakfast, the president's annual budget was released, with OMB chief Weinberger leading the press briefing.[5] Formal events finally obligated action. Ash was sworn in as OMB director on February 2, 1973, with the rest of the Cabinet (except Weinberger). Weinberger took the oath of office as HEW secretary ten days later, on February 12.[6]

Despite appearances, even to Ehrlichman and the president, Weinberger was actually moving the fastest of the three counsellors in organizing his area of responsibility. On January 18, his top aide, William H. Taft IV, submitted initial thoughts. Given Taft's work with Weinberger at FTC and OMB, Taft had a good sense of how Weinberger liked to work. Weinberger was a precise, focused, and organized administrator. He liked structure and liked to be personally involved in activities. He was no figurehead. Also, Weinberger and Taft had been at OMB when it coordinated the president's first-term reorganization effort. They were familiar with the proposals for the super-departments, including a Department of Human Resources (DHR). Therefore, they were well prepared to master the scope of the counsellor's responsibilities and organize a staff to manage those responsibilities.

Taft suggested organizing the HR counsellor's office as though the proposed HR department were already in place. That would mean subdividing the counsellor's policy involvements into the four categories that DHR would comprise: income security, health, human development and "other," the latter encompassing veterans, Native Americans, EEOC, and "special concerns." Structurally, Taft suggested a fifth area of activity in the counsellor's office for coordination with the White House on congressional relations and "political matters." As for staffing, he suggested one person for each area to start with, perhaps eventually increasing to two each. Taft's memo was generally approved by Weinberger and served as the basic plan for his operations. It also presciently presented how Weinberger approached his counsellor role: first came structure. From that flowed functional areas of public policy, as well as roles, responsibilities, staffing, and relationships.[7]

With Weinberger's okay in principle, Taft asked Stephen McConahey to flesh out the proposal, with more specifics on staffing and responsibilities. McConahey at the time was a White House Fellow who had worked as a management consultant at the elite McKinsey & Company consulting firm. McConahey understood the importance of thinking through the details (such as roles and responsibilities) and then stating them in print unambiguously. But he was also a sophisticated and shrewd observer of organizational politics. He understood the importance of moving quickly and assuming command in a lightning-fast strike—before opposition could be mustered.[8]

On January 31, McConahey submitted a plan for the counsellor's office to have nine professional staffers and six secretaries, a staffing level significantly higher than the three professional staff and four secretaries the White House would fund. Still, even that many staff members could not do all the necessary detail work. McConahey suggested (and Taft agreed) that "for the most part, the Counselor's staff should outline and assign analyses [to agencies] and then review results rather than personally initiate and undertake analysis."[9] The basic premises embodied in Taft's and McConahey's memos reflected the ambitiousness of Weinberger's approach to the counsellorship.

McConahey's blueprint also sought to enumerate the specific responsibilities of the counsellor in implementing the relatively vague mandate given to the three counsellors. He suggested specific and discrete roles for Weinberger vis-à-vis the agencies in his domain, including:

"Provide overall guidance to agency personnel through issuance and follow-up of policy directives, priorities and objectives"

"Issue budgetary guidelines, review agency submissions, resolve conflicting claims[,] . . . and submit consolidated human resource budget to President and OMB"

"Monitor and evaluate program performance"

"Ensure coordinated and consistent communication and information eminating [sic] from . . . reporting agencies—to include personal review of key speeches, press releases, testimony and internal policy statements"

"Outline and monitor legislative strategy for introduction of new legislation or the presentation of testimony and information to Congressmen and related committees on human resource matters"

"Review performance of key personnel in program areas reporting to him and where deemed appropriate participate directly in selection of individuals to fill position vacancies."[10]

This was not merely coordinating. This was control. McConahey was making a breathtaking assertion of responsibility, far greater than coordination, only stopping short at day-to-day management of all HR entities.

McConahey envisioned the same thing as Taft, that the counsellor for human resources would function as though he were already the secretary of the proposed the super-Department of Human Resources. He would be *in charge*. (Weinberger's eventual implementation of some of these proposals is discussed in chapter 4's section on OMB.)

To Weinberger's way of thinking, performing as the de facto super-secretary was only logical. If he was to be held accountable by the president (and Congress) for the activities and policies of all the HR agencies and bureaus, then he had to have commensurate authority. How could he be responsible for policies if he was a mere bystander, heckler, kibitzer, or paper shuffler when they were adopted? The only reasonable interpretation of the inherent powers of a counsellor's platform, from Weinberger's perspective, was possessing true authority that would, in turn, justify subsequent accountability. McConahey's planning premises fundamentally appealed to Weinberger. Coordination without accountability was, as a theoretical construct, an impossibility. A person was either in charge or not.

A week later—still a week to go before Weinberger was sworn in as HEW secretary—McConahey followed up with a proposed start-up timeline. He predicted that the counsellor structure "does pose a real threat to many members of the executive and legislative branches and to many public interest groups." Therefore, he emphasized the need for "*dispatch* to ensure the Counselor role becomes a force to be reckoned with and to prevent 'business as usual' at the agency level; *thoroughness* to ensure a systematic assumption of responsibilities."[11]

Finally, before leaving on an international trip with other White House Fellows on February 10, McConahey submitted his suggestions for agency reporting to the counsellor. He proposed that there be three such reporting categories: (1) weekly status reports, (2) program/priority monitoring, and (3) review and clearance procedures.[12] In three memos over ten days, McConahey had created a blueprint for a counsellor who wanted to be in charge, which was Weinberger's preferred approach. With only minor modifications, all of McConahey's suggestions were approved by Weinberger and implemented.

The initial staffing of the office had four professionals (one more than the White House reimbursed), with the plan to increase that figure to seven. Taft, the chief of staff, used the title of executive assistant to the counsellor and initially the other three were assistant directors for the three major policy areas of the counsellorship: Julia Vadala for health, Justine Rodriguez for income security, and McConahey for human development.

A few months later, the titles of the three were listed on an office directory as "Deputy Director" for, respectively, "Health," "Income Maintenance," and "Human Development." All three were policy professionals by background and all had worked in federal offices previously. Like McConahey, Vadala had been a White House Fellow. Rodriguez had been an economist at OMB while Weinberger was there.[13]

Weinberger's office used notepads that, along with the usual letterhead of "The White House, Washington," also were inscribed "Counsellor to the President for Human Resources."[14] In big ways and small, Weinberger was indicating to the bureaucracy that he was important and could not be dismissed as presidential window dressing.

PREPARING FOR THE FIRST MEETING OF
THE COMMITTEE ON HUMAN RESOURCES

On February 15, three days after Weinberger was sworn in as HEW secretary (and therefore after he had formally assumed the counsellorship), he sent a memo to the thirteen principals in his HR domain, notifying them of the inaugural meeting of what he called the Council on Human Resources (CHR), scheduled for February 21 in the Roosevelt Room of the White House.[15] This announcement was another demonstration of Weinberger's fast start as counsellor, especially given that he had not been able to undertake any public actions until being sworn in as HEW secretary. While this first meeting of the committee was seven weeks after the president's congressional breakfast, it was about as soon as reasonably possible given his delayed confirmation.

Weinberger wanted to set the right tone and worked in detail with his staff to prepare for the meeting. For him, the key was to create a document that would specifically state the role and responsibilities of the counsellor and how he would operationalize them through his office's activities. This document would be the basis for his introductory comments at the first meeting and would guide all of his subsequent actions. It was important, from his perspective, to get it right and do so from the start.

The first draft of the document is unsigned, untitled, and undated.[16] It essentially codified McConahey's three memos and enumerated in detail the responsibilities of the counsellor, including "involvement in *major* phases of key policy formulation," review of budgetary proposals, coordination and monitoring of priority operating activities, and coordination of politically sensitive actions (including major matters relating to Congress, press relations, and appointments).[17] The operations of the counsellor's office would be conducted by a staff other than his HEW staff, divided into four groups according to major HR subcategories: income security, human development, health, and consumer protection/special concerns. The principals would meet only about once every two months. CHR would have four subcommittees, reflecting the four policy areas of the counsellor's staff. This is where the major interagency work would occur and would involve subordinates, not the principals. Other temporary subcommittees, called ad hoc teams, would be created as needed. Finally, the departments and agencies would be required to submit three kinds of reports: weekly, program monitoring, and a clearance system.

This memo operationalized Weinberger's perception of his counsellor role as de facto assistant president. As mentioned in chapter 4, Weinberger convened a meeting of the three counsellors on February 19, two days before the first CHR meeting, and shared with them the contents of the memo. He wanted them to be acquainted with his conception of the job, and he hoped to potentially influence their own thinking. A common front was desirable, but Weinberger was not interested in making any major changes in his draft. He apparently did not even leave copies of the draft with his fellow counsellors.

The importance and sensitivity of the document came through in the final preparations for the CHR meeting. Taft reminded Weinberger that Weinberger's talking points at the first CHR meeting could be based on the document, "though this *will not be handed out.*"[18] This phrase again suggests the potentially controversial nature of the document and Weinberger's desire that others not have written evidence of what Weinberger was intending to do as counsellor. Weinberger was keeping things close to the vest. By now, at least, the draft finally had a title: "General Comments by Counselor [*sic*] Weinberger."[19]

THE COMMITTEE ON HUMAN RESOURCES

The first meeting of the Committee on Human Resources (formally a committee of the Domestic Council) took place in the Roosevelt Room of the White House on February 21. By hosting the meeting there, Weinberger was sending a clear message to the principals of the departments and agencies that he was counsellor to the president, not some bureaucratic flunky from the EOP. The highlight of the meeting was Ehrlichman's presence, to personally charge the principals and make clear what his expectations were regarding their cooperation with the counsellor. His presentation led off the meeting, followed by comments from Cole and then from Weinberger.

The key points they left with the attendees were "that we have only one client—the President" and "that the President will work through the option paper system *which must start with an agreed-upon set of facts,* difficult as this is."[20] These comments were clear signals that Ehrlichman did not want to see any end runs to the president, there would only be one channel for decision making, and he would not permit anything to reach the president if the agencies were not in agreement about the basic facts of the matter. There would be discipline in the second term, more so than in the first, and the counsellor system was a very prominent element of the new system. After Ehrlichman spoke, Cole explained the relationship between the counsellor and the Domestic Council. No doubt, he worded it carefully so as not to antagonize Weinberger in front of their common boss, Ehrlichman.

The focus of the meeting then shifted to the composition of the subcommittees. Weinberger outlined the four rubrics of the subcommittees: health, income security, human development, and "consumer protection and important concerns." He said that the first subcommittee to come into existence would be on welfare reform/income security and would be headed by HEW's undersecretary. He asked the attendees to keep the subcommittee list "absolutely confidential" because he had not finalized it and did not want any drafts circulating prematurely. Representing Interior Secretary Morton (who was convalescing from cancer), Interior Undersecretary Whitaker suggested that the placement of Indian affairs in the "consumer protection and important concerns" subcommittee struck him as misdirected and that instead Indian affairs should be shifted to the human development rubric. His suggestion was accepted.[21]

After the February meeting, two more agencies and their principals were added to CHR's membership: the Council of Economic Advisors and ACTION, the new Nixon name for the Peace Corps and VISTA (the "domestic" Peace Corps).[22] Based on a bimonthly meeting schedule, the next meeting of the principals would have been in late April. Weinberger never scheduled it, though, perhaps because of the demise of the counsellor project, but a more plausible explanation was that Weinberger did not want CHR to be active, preferring the subcommittees to be his instruments, rather than CHR's. That approach would give him more control and influence over the work products while simultaneously decreasing the potential influence of the principals. Weinberger was cutting them out of the action. The committee, for him, was ceremonial. One meeting in a blue moon was more than enough.

THE PRESIDENT'S SPOKESMAN ON HUMAN RESOURCES

The White House took care that Weinberger's counsellorship would be highlighted in its public actions relating to human resources and that Weinberger would be its chief spokesperson for relevant White House press events. So, for example, when the White House released the names of the president's new appointees to the Advisory Commission on Intergovernmental Relations, it identified Weinberger as HEW secretary "and Counsellor to the President for Human Resources."[23]

On March 1, Nixon sent to Congress one of the series of messages that constituted his State of the Union report for that year. Nixon's disregard for Congress in his second term included a decision not to deliver a State of the Union address in person in early 1973.[24] Rather, he was going to send a series of messages, each on a specific subject. His message on human resources was sent to Congress on March 1. As part of the release of that message, Weinberger was sent to brief the White House press corps on its contents. He told them that his new role as counsellor for human resources "is designed to try to insure that all of these programs are administered and treated in a unified and coordinated way."[25] But the press was interested only in headline topics and controversies, not the dull details of improving public administration. None of their questions during the press conference related to Weinberger's counsellor role. The text of the president's message on human resources itself highlighted the new counsellor role, saying it "should materially increase the unity, coherence, and effectiveness of our policies."[26]

Generally, Weinberger was more accessible to the media than his counterparts were. His comfort with the media made it possible for him not only to defend the president's policies (always welcomed and closely monitored by Haldeman) in a public way but also to strengthen his leverage as counsellor. Based on the Washington dictum that perception equaled reality, the stronger the public perception of his role as HR counsellor, the more influence Weinberger would really have. On February 8, the Associated Press released to its members a long profile of Weinberger that centered on his new role as one of the three "supercounselors." The article stated that Weinberger's new position would "give him a strong policymaking hand across the entire range of social issues, both in and out of the department, and will keep him at the White House—and thus close to the President's ear—much of the time."[27] That same day, Weinberger attended a breakfast session with Washington-based reporters who worked for California news outlets.[28]

Weinberger talked with some of the administration's media favorites. In a long interview with *US News & World Report,* he mentioned his counsellor role once, in connection with the Task Force on Welfare Reform he was overseeing.[29] He was also the (sole) guest on NBC's Sunday interview program, *Meet the Press,* on February 25, 1973. Lawrence Spivak, the moderator and host, pointedly introduced him not only as the new HEW secretary but also stated that "he also holds the newly created post of Counselor to the President for Human Resources." However, only the last question of the program was about his second role, specifically about the reorganization of HEW into DHR. In his answer, Weinberger was careful to emphasize that his counsellor role was related, but legally different from, any formal reorganization. He said that "the Counselor's role to the President, for Human Resources, is designed to secure the advantages of an overall combined and consistent approach to these problems we have been talking about, and many others. . . . That is what we are trying to do with this, to get a unified, constructive approach to all of these problems so that we can utilize all of the resources of the federal government."[30] (As noted in chapter 4, in early April all three counsellors appeared on an expanded one-hour edition of the program.)

Weinberger's comfort with the press (and shrewd understanding of the role of media coverage in Washington power politics) meant that he was willing to talk to administration enemies as well as friends. On February 18, the *Washington Post* published an interview with him that had been conducted by political reporter David Broder. While the earlier interview with AP would reach a national readership, the interview with Broder was for the inside-the-Beltway cognoscenti. (The Nixon White House hated the *Post* for its aggressive Watergate coverage in 1972, but Weinberger was not deterred by that.) Broder was on the A-list of national political reporters. He practically *was* the A-list. For Weinberger to survive a combative interview with Broder and then be thought well of by Broder would immeasurably increase Weinberger's influence in Washington. The interview ran in transcript form in the Sunday issue of the newspaper. Weinberger could not have asked for a better platform.

In the interview, Broder asked Weinberger two questions about the reorganization but blurred any distinction between the existing counsellor role and a proposal to Congress to create the Department of Human Resources. Was the purpose of the reorganization "to break up what you call the natural alliances between people administering programs and the beneficiaries of the programs?" Yes, answered Weinberger. A president needed "to have more control over the administration and the direction of these programs. . . . I think it's important for the President to have people who have what you might call the overall chief executive viewpoint in positions of responsibility where their coordination can be effective." Question: Is that the purpose of DHR? Answer: "Yes, . . . the more unified and coordinated approach you can get to problems that are broadly within one field, the better it will be for all."[31] Weinberger was plainly stating to the Washington establishment how he planned to act as the president's counsellor for human resources.

Also in February, Weinberger was the guest at a luncheon hosted by the *New York Times*'s Washington bureau. The informal tenor of the lunch meant that it was off the record and more of a get-acquainted session, and no interview or article appeared about his visit. Despite the White House's animosity to media outlets like the *Times*, Weinberger was unafraid to develop relations with the newspaper's key people.[32] He understood the importance of not only media coverage in public administration but also a back-channel relationship for the future, to facilitate solving problems that otherwise could become bigger and get out of control.

IN OPERATION

A week before he was sworn in as HEW secretary, Weinberger had already performed his first act as counsellor. In response to an inquiry from Nancy Hanks, who chaired the National Endowment for the Arts (which was in his HR domain), he suggested that the subject was important enough that they talk about it rather than merely correspond.[33]

Of the three counsellors, Weinberger spent the most amount of time in his counsellor role, had plans for the largest staff, and most aggressively asserted his centrality as the president's delegate to oversee just about everything occurring in human resources–related agencies (all discussed in chapter 4). He liked structure, formal subcommittees, and comprehensive staff paperwork. He was a voracious reader of everything that crossed his desk, paying attention to detail and specifics.

According to the *National Journal,* Weinberger spent a third of his time in OEOB. Generally, he was at his counsellor office every day from 7:30 to 9:30 A.M. Then, he usually would spend the rest of the day at his HEW office, as did Taft.[34] Usually, there was a counsellor staff meeting every morning at 7:30, with the three policy area professional staffers (Vadala, Rodriguez, and McConahey) joining Weinberger and Taft. Weinberger would ask each, "What are you working on?" Then, after hearing their answers, he would often orally give instructions for the follow-through he wanted, such as talking to a particular person, getting input from a particular agency, and so on.[35] Most meetings of the subcommittees were scheduled to begin at 8:30 A.M. so that Weinberger could personally chair them.[36]

An example of the thoroughness of his office operations was reflected in an "action forcing event" memo in mid-April. The term "action forcing" was Washington nomenclature for giving a heads up to a senior official about an upcoming deadline (that was beyond his own control) on an important issue. (Counsellor Lynn based his reporting system on the action forcing concept. See the section on reporting in chapter 6.) Weinberger's health staffer sent the memo to be sure that Weinberger would not be blindsided at a social event that evening. She made sure he knew what the subject was, who would be raising it, who cared about it (in this case, Vice President Spiro Agnew), and what its status was in the policy process. She suggested that, if asked, he say that his staff was already looking into it and that Weinberger himself had already committed to a meeting of principals to discuss the subject.[37] This was the kind of well-oiled machine that Weinberger liked.

However, Taft, his chief of staff, thought that Weinberger was overextending himself. About two months after Weinberger's swearing in, Taft wrote in a memo to him that "your schedule is out of control." Besides his counsellor and HEW duties, Weinberger wanted to travel to stay in touch with his political home base in California, and he accepted speaking engagements and invitations to social activities. Taft suggested that one of the reasons for his overly full schedule was the frequency with which congressional committees and subcommittees required, or requested, his attendance. In March and April, Weinberger had testified nine times (mostly as HEW secretary, a few times as counsellor). These appearances were especially time consuming because they required adequate preparation of testimony. Weinberger's schedule was so packed that "it does not permit the addition of important meetings or appointments which develop quickly, and, most important of all, does not permit any time for you to work by yourself . . . to make decisions on important policy matters." These comments raise the question that serving as both counsellor and secretary involved taking on too much responsibility. However, the record suggests that these time problems were largely self-inflicted, due to Weinberger's micro-management working style, his preference for structure, meetings, and paperwork, and his expansive view of the counsellor position.[38]

Weinberger's activist style and expansive self-definition of his role as counsellor included avoiding the typical Washington syndrome of always "playing defense." The conventional wisdom about the Domestic Council during the first term was that, notwithstanding Ehrlichman's grand goals, most of the staff's time was spent on putting out fires—the ever-changing list of headline problems. Weinberger was hoping to overcome that, partly with active subcommittees and partly by initiating policy inquiries. Manpower revenue sharing is an example of his system at work, in this case to stake his claim to a substantive, behind-the-scenes policy role, a role that was neither offered to him nor welcomed by others.

Manpower Revenue Sharing

The previous chapter discussed three of Weinberger's policy area involvements in the context of the overall counsellor initiative. They related to veterans, the Legal Services Corporation, and food stamps for strikers. Another example of his policy-related activities as counsellor related to manpower revenue sharing. This matter is significant in that it represents efforts by OMB and a line department to *prevent* a counsellor from adopting a particular role, notwithstanding his public association with the issue.

When Weinberger briefed the White House press corps on March 1 regarding the president's State of the Union message relating to human resources, he was performing his public role as spokesman for the administration on human resource issues. One of the subjects of the president's message and the press conference that day related to Nixon's desire to merge many categorical grant programs relating to work force training into a form of special revenue sharing. During the first term, Nixon had urged the adoption of a "New Federalism," with increased decision making at the state and local levels. As part of this goal, Nixon had proposed what was called "special" revenue sharing, that is, the federal government giving funding to local governments to cover broad policy areas, such as community development and work force training in lieu of dozens of highly specific categorical grant programs. (Community development special revenue sharing is discussed in chapter 6.) However, by spring 1973, Congress had not acted on this proposal. Therefore, one of the items in Weinberger's White House press briefing on March 1 was the announcement that the administration was not going to keep waiting for Congress to act on the issue. Instead, the administration was going to try to implement special revenue sharing for work force issues through administrative means—precisely the same approach used to create the counsellorships.

The oddity of the situation related to Weinberger's public and behind-the-scenes roles. Even though he was the public spokesperson on manpower revenue sharing, the counsellor's office (and HEW) had been wholly excluded from the planning for its administrative version. It was being prepared by the Department of Labor and OMB. About a month after Weinberger briefed the White House press corps about the plan, counsellor staffer Steve McConahey plaintively suggested to Weinberger that "we should be directly involved and represented" on the planning group; the counsellor and HEW staff had not been involved up to that point. McConahey mentioned several ticklish policy decisions that had yet to be made and that, if rushed, would lead to bad decisions. McConahey's strong suggestion to slow down the timetable for implementing manpower revenue sharing was a way of giving the counsellor more time to assert his authority over the planning. A way to insert himself into the decision making, McConahey suggested to Weinberger in mid-April, was to "elevate this interagency discussion through a special task force of the Counsellor's office."[39]

One of the delicate political subjects on McConahey's list was the role of governors versus mayors. As would be expected, governors were strongly opposed to a diminution of their current power over these federal funds. And more governors than mayors were Republican. Comically, given his public role on the subject, Weinberger was the one receiving complaints from Republican governors about the tentative reduction of their roles in manpower funding while he had in fact had no role in the decision making.[40] Much more politically attuned than OMB and lower-ranking Labor Department officials, Weinberger thought it important to try to accommodate Republican governors' concerns.[41]

Despite their discouragement of such uninvited meddling, other internal power players such as OMB and Labor could not totally ignore a counsellor's presidential standing or prevent the counsellor from having a role in policy making. To do so would be an open rebellion against Nixon's counsellor system. Gradually, they gave way, though neither very much nor very fast. The Labor Department's representative on Weinberger's Human Development Subcommittee said during its meeting on May 1, 1973, that the department had already been given clearance by OMB "to proceed with testimony and regulation for administratively implementing manpower revenue sharing."[42] McConahey was alarmed; he identified five counsellor concerns that had not yet been resolved in the plan for manpower revenue sharing.

In reaction to Labor's preemptory announcement that it was going ahead, Weinberger finally succeeded only in scheduling a three-way meeting with the top DC and OMB officials for the subject, with James Cavanaugh, the DC associate director for human resources, and with Paul O'Neill, OMB assistant director.[43] In advance of the meeting, set for May 14, Taft shared with Cavanaugh McConahey's list of unresolved issues of concern to the counsellor.[44] Had the counsellor project lasted longer, it is inevitable that Weinberger's role in manpower revenue sharing would have continued to grow. The operating system he had put into place would not lose sight of a problem once identified.

Yet, all this time, the public fiction of his central role continued. In mid-May, *National Journal* reported that in his capacity as counsellor, "he [Weinberger] and [Labor Secretary] Brennan worked together on one important interagency issue—development of guidelines for manpower revenue sharing."[45]

As a postscript to this matter, after the demise of the counsellorships, on December 28, 1973, Nixon signed into law the Comprehensive Employment and Training Act (CETA) of 1973, which contained a compromise version of manpower revenue sharing and funding for public service jobs.[46] Nixon's threat to implement manpower revenue sharing administratively had helped persuade opponents of the concept in Congress that they would be better off with a statutory program they helped craft than what Nixon might do on his own. But to get statutory manpower revenue sharing, Nixon had to agree to a part of the bill he opposed: federal funding of jobs in local government. It was, under normal circumstances, a political compromise, with each side getting about half of what they wanted and half of what they opposed.[47] But in the context of his go-it-alone anti-congressional tone of early 1973 (including counsellors, impoundment, and governing by veto), Nixon's approval of the bill was interpreted as reflecting how much Watergate had weakened him over one calendar year.

Notwithstanding the manpower revenue sharing example, Weinberger did not *always* insert himself into any topic that could possibly be connected to his counsellorship. For example, his health staffer recommended that "you not get involved" in the issue of pesticide standards for agricultural workers. The heads of the Labor Department, USDA, and Environmental Protection Agency (EPA) already were "quite concerned about the turf question." She suggested he stay out of it, "unless you can side (for political reasons) with Brennan," the secretary of labor. Weinberger accepted her recommendation and did not insert himself actively or significantly in this policy issue.[48]

SUBCOMMITTEES

At the February 21 meeting of the Committee on Human Resources, Weinberger emphasized the differences between the committee and its subentities. While the membership of the full committee comprised the principals, its substructure would be of key agency and program personnel. In other words, the members would form what Washington considered the *working* level, such as assistant secretaries, bureau heads, and so on. Weinberger viewed these subcommittees as the venue for the "performance of major staff work and support" for the full committee. Besides the subcommittees, he also expected some ad hoc teams to work on specific and short-term projects.[49]

As previously noted, at the principals meeting Weinberger had mentioned organizing the work of the committee and the counsellor into four rubrics: health, income security, human development, and consumer protection and special concerns (such as Indian affairs). However, the fourth topic was eventually merged into the third, so that the HR counsellor had three active subcommittees: health, income security, and human development. Each of the subcommittees would be staffed full time by one of the professional staffers specializing in that area in the counsellor's office.[50]

Weinberger wanted to proceed quickly, but in an organized, methodical, and formal fashion. He convened a joint meeting of all three subcommittees on March 9, two and a half weeks after the first meeting of the HR committee, in one of the larger meeting rooms on the fourth floor of OEOB. He discussed his view of the counsellor role (similar to his comments at the HR committee meeting) and his expectations about reporting from agencies to him. Then he described what he expected from the subcommittees, distributed membership lists of the three subcommittees, and handed out a meeting schedule.

The timetable for their meetings was firmly set for twice a month, with no overlapping meetings of the three subcommittees. He could thus attend and chair all of them, which he planned to do. In fact, his handout explicitly stated that the subcommittees "will meet separately *with* the Counsellor."[51] That simple detail conveyed his deep involvement. All subcommittee meetings would take place in his office suite on the second floor of OEOB.[52] The message was clear. Weinberger was not some genial dilettante serving in a titular capacity. He intended to be in charge, personally. He was a hands-on, detail-oriented, and policy-involved assistant president.

But a major player was still missing. The Department of Defense (DOD) was, understandably, very active in the areas of health and human development, but it was not within the scope of the counsellor plan that the president had announced on January 5. Nonetheless, on April 11 Weinberger called Defense Secretary Elliot Richardson (who had been Weinberger's predecessor at HEW). Weinberger asked Richardson if he would be willing to appoint a departmental representative at the subcabinet level to sit on two of Weinberger's subcommittees. This was a significant request, logically extending the policy areas of the counsellor program to other relevant departments but creating a precedent of noncounsellor departments accepting (implicitly) the coordinating role of the counsellor. Richardson agreed and named the assistant DOD secretary for health and environment (who was a physician) to Weinberger's Health Subcommittee and the assistant DOD secretary for manpower to the Human Development Subcommittee.[53]

Weinberger also asked OMB to name a representative to the three subcommittees.[54] Having that representative on his counsellor subcommittees would help establish his policy primacy in the ongoing power struggles with OMB.

Health Subcommittee

The Health Subcommittee started with nine members, including representatives from HEW, VA, Commerce, USDA, and the President's Consumer Affairs Office, and the drug czar.[55] By early May, it had fourteen members, including individuals from OEO, the Council of Economic Advisors, DOD, OMB, and the Cost of Living Council.[56] The subcommittee was staffed by Julia Vadala, and it met three times: March 30, April 12, and May 4, with Weinberger attending all the meetings.[57] At the May 4 meeting, Weinberger announced (based on Vadala's recommendation) that he was changing the subcommittee meetings from biweekly to monthly. The next meeting would have been on June 1.[58]

At the subcommittee's first meeting, Weinberger set the tone by giving an "enthusiastic welcome" that helped convey his personal commitment to the topic and his hope for their perception of the potentially significant impact the subcommittee could have.[59] The topics that came up for discussion and that the subcommittee sought to coordinate included a national blood supply policy, national drug strategy, veterans' health care benefits, hospital reimbursement, and use of prosthetics for rehabilitation.[60] The importance and touchiness of the subjects they were discussing prompted Weinberger at the beginning of the second meeting to emphasize the confidentiality of the discussions at the subcommittee level.[61] He was hoping to develop a culture within the subcommittee (and, for that matter, all the subcommittees) in which members from different agencies could trust each other to the point of talking frankly about issues and concerns. Certainly, premature leaks could have the effect of preventing evolution of policy options or discussion of controversial options. He wanted authentic give and take to accomplish the presidential mandates of coordinating policy making and policy implementation.

The subcommittee created a temporary National Health Insurance Task Force to develop an administration policy in that area. The task force had twenty-one members, including those from the agencies already represented on the subcommittee as well as representatives from the Civil Service Commission, the Social Security Administration, HUD, and the vice president's office. It met on May 8, 1973.[62] That the task force for this major (if intractable) policy topic was based in the counsellor's office and included representation from agencies outside the HR counsellor's domain was another signal of the presumed centrality of the counsellor's role in developing administration-wide policy recommendations.

In order to increase the value of meetings, whenever possible Vadala circulated copies of position papers and drafts of policy proposals in advance. These items included HEW's draft proposed national blood policy and a health insurance options paper.[63] The counsellor's staff also worked to prevent the subcommittee from being exclusively reactive to developments or captive to the agendas put forth by the departments and agencies. Rather, Weinberger wanted his counsellorship to be proactive by identifying subjects and collecting information that could be discussed by the subcommittee. For example, in early March, McConahey sent letters to appropriate agencies asking for information for the subcommittee on such diverse subjects as the legality of VA hospitals admitting patients from Public Health Service hospitals, the status of prosthetic and orthotic education programs, long-term drug abuse prevention strategy, and the impact of new regulations on methadone treatment programs.[64]

Income Security Subcommittee

The Income Security Subcommittee started with five members, from HEW, Labor, USDA, VA, and the Railroad Retirement Board. It was staffed by Justine Rodriguez. The subcommittee met three times: March 27, April 10, and April 25, with Weinberger attending all the meetings. Topics for the meetings included developing administration positions on some long-running social service subjects, including the minimum wage (especially the youth differential), pension reform, workers' compensation, food stamps, welfare reform, and supplemental security income (SSI).[65]

The administration's welfare reform task force, chaired by HEW's undersecretary, was merged into the subcommittee as a "committee of the whole."[66] This move made the subcommittee the center for welfare reform in the second term (after the administration abandoned the negative income tax proposal of White House staffer Daniel Patrick Moynihan in the first term). It also had the effect of bringing part of the Treasury Department's work under the wing of the HR counsellor for that topic.

Human Development Subcommittee

The Human Development Subcommittee started with ten members, who came from HEW, Labor, USDA, Interior, VA, OEO, ACTION, EEOC, the National Endowment for the Humanities, and the National Endowment for the Arts. Staffed by Stephen McConahey, the subcommittee met April 3, April 18, and May 1, with Weinberger attending each meeting.[67]

In preparation for the third meeting, McConahey suggested to the counsellor that biweekly meetings might be too frequent. He feared that so many meetings might mean that "the Assistant Secretary level people may choose not to attend as frequently." Also, "a two week interval does not allow enough time for major changes in status to occur and, therefore, hinders the development of a productive and well-prepared agenda." Weinberger accepted the recommendation and announced it at the May 1 meeting. The next meeting was scheduled for June 5, 1973.[68]

Veterans and manpower revenue sharing were two of the policy areas within the subcommittee's purview (see discussion of veterans in chapter 4 and revenue sharing earlier in this chapter). Other topics for the meetings included the occupation of Wounded Knee, South Dakota, by Indians protesting government policy, transferring OEO to HEW, educational financing, consumer legislation, the economic role of women, programs for the aging, and services to migrant workers. The subcommittee created two temporary task forces to develop recommendations in the areas of school vouchers and migrant workers.[69]

AGENCY REPORTING TO THE COUNSELLOR

As recounted in the previous chapter, OMB created a brouhaha over the forms that Weinberger wanted agencies in his domain to use in reporting to him. As a result of the controversy, Weinberger pulled back from oversight of some issues, such as clearance of legislative testimony and personnel appointments, but he did not withdraw his requirement of weekly reports on important upcoming and past events.

Based on the slightly evolving membership on the Human Resources Committee (comprising the principals of his empire), fifteen government entities (including HEW) were accountable to Weinberger.[70] Of the fifteen, ten submitted at least one weekly report: HEW (only the assistant secretary for education), Interior, Commerce, USDA, OEO, the drug czar, the President's Office of Consumer Affairs, Railroad Retirement Board, National Endowment for the Arts, and National Endowment for the Humanities. No reports were submitted by five: the Department of Labor, VA, ACTION, EEOC, and the Fine Arts Commission.[71] The well-organized and detail-oriented Weinberger and his staff noticed that lack of reporting. For example, in early May, McConahey wrote to the director of ACTION, gently chiding him for not submitting any weekly reports so far.[72] Also in early May, he wrote to the deputy assistant secretary of interior for Indian affairs that the reports were not being submitted "on a regular basis." Only one report from that office had been submitted so far.[73]

OEO was the most conscientious about submitting the reports, sending seven consecutive weekly reports. The counsellor's staff were reading them, too. In some cases, they commented to each other that the reports lacked enough detail to make them helpful for coordination and oversight purposes. For example, Rodriguez attached a note to one that said, "This does not seem adequate. . . . Should someone (Steve?) give them a call & ask for more [details] next time?"[74] Another time, Taft thought that "perhaps informally [we should] encourage a more detailed report next time."[75] Their comments do not seem to convey a bureaucratic insistence on filling out a form correctly but instead seem to suggest the need to have enough information to understand major developments and coordinate across agencies as necessary. Other reactions to OEO reports were explicit about using the reports for helpful coordination. For example, on one OEO report, McConahey asked, "Should we track [this] court case & its possible impact"?[76] Another time, one of the staffers wrote next to an item, "Need to know where we stand" on this issue.[77]

Some of the other smaller agencies in the HR counsellor's domain were also scrupulous about submitting their weekly reports: six arrived from the National Endowment for the Arts and three each from the National Endowment for the Humanities and the Railroad Retirement Board. The record for the larger departments varied. As would be expected, the assistant HEW secretary for education was regular in his reporting, given that Weinberger was his direct boss. USDA submitted four, but Commerce produced only one.

In general, the reports were one to three pages long, identifying just past or upcoming major events such as congressional hearings and important public speaking engagements. Besides OEO's reports, many showed notations indicating that Weinberger and/or staff had read them; there were various underlinings, check marks, and circles around important points. A prime example of the full potential of the reporting system in fulfilling its underlying purpose occurred in a report from the National Endowment for the Humanities. The agency noted that the next week it would be testifying before a House Appropriations Subcommittee on the administration's FY1974 budget request for the Endowment. The agency was expecting questions about the relatively large (in percentages) increase in its budget, at a time that the president was publicly trying to cut spending across the board. One counsellor aide wrote on the margins, "Should follow this."[78] This notation signified a reaction about the authentic need for interdepartmental coordination, an inkling of what could have been.

RELATIONS WITH THE DOMESTIC COUNCIL

From the beginning, relations between Weinberger and the Domestic Council were awkward to the point of being strained. He seemed to have little use for it, acting as though it was a minor irritant more than anything else. After all, Nixon's and Ehrlichman's plans for domestic policy in the second term included the establishment of the counsellor system and a simultaneous downsizing of the DC staff and role. It was a zero sum game. Weinberger was counsellor to the president and wrote on White House stationery. The Domestic Council was an entity within the Executive Office of the President, and Kenneth Cole, its lead staffer, had the title of executive director.[79] Even in the context of both reporting to Ehrlichman, Weinberger saw himself as a higher level and more important policy player than Cole, let alone the DC's associate director Cavanaugh, who was assigned the human resources portfolio.

As mentioned previously, in February Weinberger had prepared an untitled draft describing his expansive view of the role of the counsellor but did not give copies of it to the other two counsellors during a meeting he convened on February 19 to discuss the general subject. He was still trying to keep things close to the vest. Nonetheless, word was leaking out about the document. The draft would be of particular interest to the Domestic Council because any hints of Weinberger engaging in a power grab would be particularly alarming to the DC. They really wanted know what the document said.

On February 20, Cole and Weinberger spoke with each other by telephone, and later that day, Weinberger sent Cole the still untitled draft document outlining his view of a counsellor's responsibilities and operations. Suggesting some tension, Weinberger's cover note was terse: "Attached is a draft copy of the document we discussed on the phone this date." He did not invite comments or suggestions. Cole read the draft and then returned it later that day along with a similarly terse reply: "Thanks," and his signature. That he returned the draft suggests that Weinberger insisted Cole could see the document but not keep it.[80] That Cole wrote no reactions or proposals for revisions also suggests that Weinberger did not invite reactions and perhaps had made clear that he was not accountable to Cole but only to Cole's boss, Ehrlichman.

Meanwhile, a few days earlier, Weinberger's chief of staff had had a similarly odd exchange with Cole's associate director for human resources, James Cavanaugh. Cavanaugh was supposed to have a one-on-one relationship with the HR counsellor, and he had apparently asked Taft to see how Weinberger was planning to proceed. Taft sent Cavanaugh a copy of his January 18 memo to Weinberger (which was the original conceptualization of the counsellor's operations). Then, Cavanaugh *returned* the memo on February 16, with a cover note as enigmatic and cryptic as Cole's had been to Weinberger: "Returned from Jim Cavanaugh with thanks."[81]

Other small details indicated Weinberger's attempt to downgrade DC's importance. For example, the meetings of principals were to be as a committee of the Domestic Council. Yet, when Weinberger convened it for its first meeting, he called it the *Council* on Human Resources, implying it was on the same level as other councils, such as—by no coincidence—the Domestic Council.[82] After attending the February 21 CHR meeting, Interior Undersecretary John Whitaker (who had been the White House's Cabinet secretary and then a DC staffer in the first term) picked up on that nuance. In an internal Interior memo summarizing the meeting, Whitaker wrote, "I attended an organizational meeting conducted by Cap Weinberger to set up the *Council* on Human Resources. There will be a standing Human Resources Committee; that is, a *Cabinet committee* to coordinate human resources. It will be a standing committee, unlike many other Cabinet committees that come into being to solve a problem and then go out of existence."[83]

Given Whitaker's White House service in the first term and that both Ehrlichman and Cole spoke at the February 21 meeting, Whitaker's summary of what CHR was must be interpreted as an accurate representation of what occurred at the meeting. In a memo to DOD Secretary Richardson, Weinberger referred to CHR as the "Cabinet Committee on Human Resources." In some of her correspondence, Vadala used the title "Deputy Director to the Cabinet Committee for Human Resources (Health)." Again, the wording is significant. A committee of the *Cabinet* would be different from a committee of the Domestic Council and would certainly not be subordinate to the DC.[84]

On March 9, Weinberger convened an initial joint meeting of the members of CHR's three subentities. The terminology he preferred for them was "working committees." That also subtly conveyed a message. If CHR was a committee, then its subentities would probably not also have the title of committee. But, if CHR was a *council*, then "working committee" would be more fitting and not cause confusion.[85] At that kick-off meeting, Weinberger told the assembled members what his vision for the counsellor's position was. In the typewritten notes prepared for him for the meeting, he was to include in his talk a discussion about the role of the "Domestic Council Committee on Human Resources." By hand, he crossed out the DC reference, so his talking notes instead were: "~~Domestic Council~~ Committee on Human Resources."[86]

It appears that Cavanaugh was also excluded from most of the work of the HR subcommittees. None of the prepared agendas for any of the three subcommittee meetings assigned him a speaking part. The attendance list for the Health Subcommittee meeting of May 4 does not list him as attending, nor was his name on the membership list of the subcommittee.[87] The Health Subcommittee's membership list, updated through April 11, 1973, included the name of an OMB representative but not Cavanaugh or anyone else from the Domestic Council.[88] A revised membership list, updated through April 24, named him on the list of "Resource Personnel/FYI Offices." Unlike almost all the other people on the two lists, Cavanaugh's organizational affiliation was *not* provided. Further, the notation next to the name of the OMB member was "copy of all issues and meeting agenda," but no such wording was next to Cavanaugh's name.[89] Similarly, Cavanaugh was not listed as attending an early May meeting of the subcommittee's Health Insurance Task Force, a gaggle of twenty-one people, including two from OMB.[90] One of Vadala's rare written communications with Cavanaugh related to the release of a report by a presidential committee.[91] With that communication, she was acknowledging that presidential matters needed to go though DC. So, in general, Cavanaugh's contacts were largely limited to (somewhat unwelcome) personal contacts with Weinberger and not with the counsellor's staff, two doors away.[92]

In all, a fair inference from this pattern of behavior is that Weinberger sought to marginalize the Domestic Council vis-à-vis his work as a counsellor. The reason Cavanaugh's office was next to Weinberger's was to encourage seamless cooperation between the Domestic Council and "his" counsellor. But Weinberger would have none of that; his contacts with Cavanaugh were formal and distant. Cavanaugh's office may as well have been on the moon, not next door. Weinberger wanted to make it indisputably clear who was in charge.

In all, Weinberger's counsellorship was the largest, most active, most organized, most structured, and fastest out of the gate of the three counsellors. Personally, he invested the most time and attention in the role. For example, he attended (and, of course, chaired) all the meetings of the three subcommittees he created. Weinberger also had the most expansive view of his responsibilities. He considered himself the overseer of almost all aspects of the departments and agencies in his domain. By demonstrating the opportunities for a counsellor to manage a particular empire as an assistant president, Weinberger came the closest to exemplifying the full functioning and potential of a counsellor.

6

COUNSELLOR FOR COMMUNITY DEVELOPMENT JAMES LYNN

The Super-Secretary as Presidential Coordinator

In terms of public service, James Lynn was the most junior of the three counsellors. Prior to joining the administration in 1969 as general counsel (later rising to the position of undersecretary) for the Commerce Department, he had been in private legal practice in Cleveland for eighteen years, whereas Weinberger had been a three-term state senator in California and then the state's finance director during part of Ronald Reagan's governorship. Weinberger had joined the Nixon administration during the first term as chair of the Federal Trade Commission (FTC) and then was quickly promoted, first to OMB deputy director, then director. Similarly, Earl Butz had been an assistant secretary in USDA during the Eisenhower administration and then a professor and senior administrator at Purdue University, which was Indiana's land-grant public university. (He had also run, unsuccessfully, for governor of Indiana.)

With no major public sector experience before Nixon's first term and no obvious external political constituency, Lynn viewed himself as part of the president's team and did not "go native" as had happened to so many Cabinet and subcabinet officials. This team-player attitude was a major attribute that put him in good stead with the Nixon White House during the first term. It led to his promotion in the second term to Cabinet secretary and counsellor. Lynn's tenure as counsellor was a case study of two important aspects of senior-level governmental management. First, he was a political appointee seeking to be a vigorous advocate for the chief executive's priorities vis-à-vis the permanent bureaucracy. Second, he was a generalist administrator who did not have any specialized expertise in the policy areas he was overseeing. All these factors contributed to Lynn's approach to his counsellorship, which was very different from Weinberger's self-definition as an assistant president.

SCOPE

In an effort to describe Lynn's unprecedented job, the White House press secretary's office explained that "as Counsellor, Mr. Lynn has coordinating responsibility in the area of community development and heads a Committee of the Domestic Council[,] which provides a mechanism for interdepartmental cooperation."[1] Lynn led a White House press briefing on March 8 but was accompanied by a delegation of lower-ranking officials from HUD, DOT, USDA, and the Office of Emergency Preparedness (then in EOP). This entourage was another way for the White House to convey publicly what Lynn's counsellorship encompassed and where he stood in the hierarchy.[2]

Based on policy areas, the scope of the counsellor for community development was well defined and rational, covering the rubrics of community planning, community institutions, housing, highways, public transportation, regional development, disaster relief, and national capital affairs.[3] In organizational terms, these functions were scattered throughout the executive branch. As discussed in chapter 2, the CD counsellor's domain touched eleven separate federal agencies:

1. HUD (all except the college housing program)
2. USDA:
   Rural Electrification Administration
   Farmers Home Administration (water and waste disposal grants and loans, rural housing, and field offices)
   Economic Research Service (only the Economic Development Division, not the Human Resources Branch)
   Rural Development Service
   Rural Telephone Bank
3. DOT:
   Federal Highway Administration (except motor carrier safety)
   Urban Mass Transit Administration (UMTA)

4. Commerce Department:
   Economic Development Administration (EDA)
   Regional action planning functions of the secretary
   (except business development and technical assistance)
5. HEW: only public library construction grants
6. OEO: Community Action Programs (including Senior
   Opportunities and Services) and special impact programs
7. Small Business Administration (SBA): residential disaster
   loans only
8. Appalachian Regional Commission
9. District of Columbia (municipal government)
10. National Capital Housing Authority
11. National Capital Planning Commission[4]

However, some of these were relatively minor entities, either small programs within large departments and agencies or small agencies. Therefore, in terms of actual and active operations, the scope of Lynn's oversight quickly shrank to HUD (the department of which he was secretary), DOT and USDA. These were the "big three" of his focus. Lynn avoided trying to oversee from the start the politically charged programs of OEO, knowing that congressional Democrats would pounce on the administration's supposed insensitivity to poor people.[5] In public, Lynn argued that his scope of responsibility as counsellor was even less than the "big three" departments. In an appearance before a congressional committee, he said there was little that the counsellorship really added to his scope as HUD secretary. A careful lawyer, he reminded the committee that the executive order President Johnson had issued to implement the just-passed law creating HUD had assigned to the secretary of the new department the "convenor [sic] authority with respect to problems of communities"—not the narrower scope of *urban* communities. So, from that perspective his involvement in, for example, transportation or economic development would be inherent in promoting solutions to problems that cities and rural areas were having.[6]

Lynn and his staff sought a way to convey in shorthand fashion the scope of the CR counsellor. One of his staff members (probably the office director, Calvin Collier) suggested that Lynn could think of it this way: Weinberger was the "people" counsellor, Lynn the "place" counsellor, and Butz the natural resources counsellor.[7] This categorization almost perfectly echoed the traditional mantra that was used to define geography in American grade schools: people, places, and things. Lynn would benefit in several ways if he presented himself as the "places" counsellor. First, many Americans often identify themselves based on where they live, whether region, state, or locality. Second, "places" conveyed spatial distribution, the entire territory of the United States. Third, *places* was a very inclusive term, covering urban, suburban, and rural areas. Finally, "places" gave some slightly more tangible meaning to the (already) empty cliché of "community."

Lynn tried out that terminology at his first congressional appearance after becoming counsellor. At a public hearing of the Subcommittee on Rural Development of the Senate's Agriculture and Forestry Committee on March 27, 1973, Lynn described "place" as the common theme of his counsellorship responsibilities: "Mr. Moynihan [said] some time ago that everything is related to everything else and certainly when you are dealing with *a place,* whether it is rural America or urban America, but *a place* like urban America or rural America, all of these things come together and relate to each other."[8] However, the term never caught on, perhaps because of the brevity of the counsellor project and/or because Lynn did not endlessly flog the term with the press and in public.[9]

Lynn quickly developed a philosophy of what his job was and how he would approach it. In three congressional appearances he focused on the need for high-level coordination of executive activities. He said he never encountered any serious problems of "disagreement with regard to what our policy ought to be." In other words, he never had to *arbitrate* policy disputes. Rather, the problem at that level of government, he said, was *coordination,* adding that "there is a great need for this kind of coordination" on an interdepartmental level.[10] On another occasion, he said that "coordination is an extremely difficult thing across departmental boundaries" and that as counsellor he was in a better position to pursue it than he would have been able on an informal basis.[11] At a third congressional hearing, he said that "we are trying very, very hard to coordinate efforts the best we can."[12] For Lynn, his primary job as counsellor was to be the president's interdepartmental coordinator.

Nearly thirty-five years later, Lynn was still emphatic and focused on the positive contribution (or potential) that a counsellor could have on interdepartmental coordination. He said that to get something done in the federal government, one had to be able to "break down walls." To be able to do that, it made "a great deal of difference based on *where* you are." A person in the White House could do that (regardless of any particular title) but not someone in the departments or agencies. Lynn also believed that the counsellors could have served two other presidential functions besides coordination. One possibility was that the existence of a counsellor offered "a chance for the president to have someone to think forward about policy issues from a broad perspective." Further, Lynn said the counsellorship project "expose[d] Cabinet officers to the presidential perspective when it came to decision making," which, he believed, was a good counterbalance to the natural tendency for presidential appointees in the departments and agencies to become parochial advocates for their bureaucracies.[13] These three functions—interdepartmental coordination, forward planning, and a central perspective—all have in common that they are about the *president's* role. Lynn thought that a counsellor could serve the president by handling the difficult tasks of meshing the activities of the federal behemoth, breaking out of daily crisis mode, and countering the centrifugal forces that tend to push bureaucracies away from the perspective of the elected chief executive. A counsellorship represented the opportunity to enhance the centripetal forces that the president needed in order to truly run the executive branch. Lynn wanted to help the president.

GEARING UP

Lynn had a slower start than Weinberger, even though he was sworn in earlier. He had made an important legal and political point on January 17 during testimony at his confirmation hearing when he indicated that he had "no official capacity either as counselor or Secretary of HUD to be doing" any work related to those positions until confirmed and sworn in.[14] He was being careful, which contributed to the slower pace of his start-up compared to Weinberger's.

Lynn decided that for the small three-person office in OEOB he would designate Calvin Collier as office director. Collier, son of then-Representative Harold Collier (R-Ill.), was a lawyer and had worked continuously with Lynn since Lynn joined the Nixon administration in 1969 as general counsel at the Commerce Department.[15] When Lynn was appointed undersecretary of commerce, he took Collier with him. Lynn viewed Collier as a "wunderkind" and "brilliant."[16] Also, with his political background,

Collier was unusually attuned (for a policy wonk and lawyer) to the political environment. Therefore, it was natural for Lynn to appoint Collier to run his counsellor office.

In turn, Collier hired two other lawyers for the remaining professional slots (with Lynn's concurrence, of course): Michael Raoul-Duval and Douglas M. Parker. Raoul-Duval was a former Marine Corps officer.[17] He began his federal service in 1967 (i.e., before Nixon became president) as a staff lawyer for the general counsel of the Federal Aviation Administration (FAA, a unit within DOT). In 1970, he became a low-level staff assistant to Haldeman in the White House, mostly dealing with travel scheduling. He had no special expertise in community development, which was also true of Parker, who had specialized in corporate law at a firm in New York City before coming to Washington. But in American culture, a lawyer was viewed as someone trained at thinking rigorously and who—if smart and hard working—could master just about any subject matter.

Collier functioned as the "primary aide for all Counsellor functions."[18] Parker's and Raoul-Duval's roles were divided by policy areas, with Parker handling rural development and economic development and Raoul-Duval overseeing transportation. The title Collier generally used outside the office was director of the Community Development Committee (CDC), while Parker and Raoul-Duval were called assistant directors of CDC.[19] While the White House budget limited counsellor staff funding (actually, reimbursement) to three professional staffers, Lynn's office sometimes listed a fourth staff member, most likely funded solely by the HUD budget. Peter A. Michel focused on program coordination.[20]

Lynn's counsellor office opened for business on February 22 with two memos from Collier to Lynn on White House stationery. Collier focused on basic organizational and start-up issues, especially the need to call a first meeting of the Community Development Committee and to define Lynn's approach to the counsellorship. Regarding the latter, Collier suggested a typology of reactive issues and positive thrusts. For reactive issues, Collier identified a process definition and a policy agenda. For a process approach, he suggested that the Lynn counsellorship play a central role in (1) clearing testimony and legislation from the administration, (2) responding to congressional initiatives, (3) responding to special interest groups lobbying to influence the administration's positions, and (4) reviewing budget requests from programs under the CD counsellor's jurisdiction. In general, this scope of operation seemed a bit too broad for Lynn's liking. He did not want to be an assistant president like Weinberger. Rather, he preferred to focus on being a presidential interdepartmental coordinator.

The other reactive dimension that Collier outlined dealt with the pending policy issues that were already in play and that the counsellor could and should step into and thereby play a central role. Collier's list of policy issues included (1) the administration's desire to close out the Commerce Department's Economic Development Administration (EDA) and its affiliated regional development commissions, such as the Appalachian Regional Commission; (2) highway legislation; (3) implementation of the Rural Development Act of 1972; (4) housing; (5) revenue sharing (i.e., converting scores of categorical grants into a revenue sharing program in the area of community development); and (6) implementing the president's professed support for decentralization.[21] In handwritten notes, Lynn suggested expanding the highway topic to include mass transit (which was explicitly in his domain) and adding several other potential topics. One topic was substantive, regarding the "effect of energy challenge & environmental controls on CD."[22] The others were process oriented, regarding coordinating with the White House congressional liaison office and coordinating public information activities.

Looking to the future and to the counsellor creating a policy agenda, Collier suggested four "positive thrusts" that HUD would centrally be involved in: (1) coordination of federally funded local planning activities; (2) coordinating program delivery and generally delegating more of such decision making to state and local governments; (3) a national growth policy; and (4) what the federal government's role should be if CD revenue sharing were enacted. A fifth area would come more from the Commerce Department's activities and related to evaluating the effectiveness of targeted tax incentives for businesses to locate jobs in areas of high unemployment.[23]

IN OPERATION

One of the difficulties that Lynn faced (somewhat more than the other two counsellors) was that he was trying to jump on board a moving (policy) train. Many major policy decisions were already near completion when he became counsellor. The most obvious topic was that of the four new super-departments that Nixon had proposed in his 1971 reorganization plan to Congress; the DCD plan had advanced the farthest and Nixon had already approved resubmitting it. Thus, there was little input that Lynn could have at this late stage. Other policy subjects were also already in motion. As noted in chapter 5, Nixon had decided not to deliver a State of the Union address in person in early 1973. Instead, he was going to send a series of messages, with each message on a specific subject. The message on community development was already largely blocked out. For example, the president's weekly Saturday radio address on March 4 was set to preview the CD message that would be released on March 8. While this was two months after the congressional breakfast and one month after Lynn's swearing in, the presidential documents on community development were going to be released only about two weeks after the counsellor office was up and functioning.

Similarly, the proposal to collapse several categorical grant programs into a community development revenue sharing program was also quite advanced, but not finalized. In general, Lynn was inheriting a largely already-determined policy agenda, but one that he was expected to be the major spokesperson for. But Lynn was a quick study and fleet footed. And he had no substantive disagreements with the initiatives he would be advocating.

Besides policy timing, Lynn faced another issue—policy and organizational "geography." As the public face of the administration, Lynn's context was somewhat different than that of the other two counsellors. The close correlation between HUD's urban focus and Lynn's counsellorship portfolio meant that distinguishing between his two hats seemed less significant to outsiders. So, for example, when he addressed a conference of mayors meeting in Washington in early March, newspaper coverage identified him only as HUD secretary. Similarly, Senator Strom Thurmond (R-S.C.) used only Lynn's HUD title in a short speech on the Senate floor.[24]

Still, the administration tried its best to give him the counsellor brand as well as the secretary brand. For example, Nixon's radio address and congressional message on community development made a point of identifying Lynn's central role as counsellor for implementation of the ideas contained in the address and message.[25]

The three major policy (and legislative) topics that Lynn was most closely involved in as counsellor, both behind the scenes and publicly, were rural development, special CD revenue sharing, and the proposed Department of Community Development (DCD).

Rural Development

Rural development was both a political issue and a policy issue. In 1971–1972, the Nixon administration did not want to take on the farm lobby, which is why it dropped—and received nothing in return—its original plan to include USDA in the proposed Department of Natural Resources.[26] Taking advantage of that weakness, the Democratic-majority Congress shrewdly passed a rural development bill in 1972. The bill gave some explicit duties to USDA regarding rural development, even though the topic could just as easily be related to Nixon's incipient Department of Community Development. Nixon blinked and signed the bill.[27] Now, in early 1973, Counsellor Lynn needed to deal with this policy wreck and figure out how to harmonize his counsellorship and the DCD bill with the administration's implementation of the new law, the Rural Development Act of 1972. The chair of the Senate Agriculture and Forestry Committee's Subcommittee on Rural Development, Dick Clark (D-Iowa), had already announced that he would be holding hearings in March on the administration's *implementation* of the 1972 act. The politics of the issue revolved around how to pull rural development into the orbit of community development rather than agriculture. It was easy enough for Nixon to coalesce the two with his assignment of responsibilities to Lynn as counsellor, but it was another thing to make it work in face of the farm lobby and a hostile Congress.

The policy issue, as generally framed at the time, was that America's rural areas were in decline, with its population migrating to urban areas and no prospects for an improved economic situation for those who stayed. The question was what, if anything, the federal government could do to stop, even reverse, that decline. What followed from that question was whether this topic could most effectively be worked on from the perspective of the larger agriculture policy or community development. The pro-agricultural approach argued that community development was really a synonym for urban development and that rural development would therefore get lost in the shuffle if it was removed from the agriculture orbit. An example of this debate occurred in this exchange during Senator Clark's hearings:

SENATOR HENRY BELLMON (R-Okla.): It seems to me that the very fact that your primary duties are as Secretary of Housing and Urban Development may cause the rural development part of your responsibilities [as counsellor] to take a second seat. Is this the case or not?

SECRETARY LYNN: Not at all. . . . I don't think anyone can dis-
charge their duties properly as to the urban communities without looking at what is happening in rural America.[28]

Parker was given the rural development portfolio and quickly worked
to master the policy and politics of the issue. He found, contrary to the
conventional wisdom of bureaucratic turf wars, that the assistant USDA
secretary for rural development, William W. Erwin, was more than glad
to work with him. Erwin did not exhibit any fears of the policy area being
"taken away" from USDA. Parker recalled that Erwin was instead simply
happy that someone in the White House was interested in his work. Parker
and Erwin quickly departed for South Carolina to meet with the governor
and get his perspective on the general subject. Just before the first meeting of the Community Development Committee, Parker gave his quick
assessment to Lynn, pointing out, for example, that the pending draft of
the president's message to Congress on community development did not
even mention rural issues until page 14.[29]

About a week later, Parker reported to Lynn on the status of the
preparations for Lynn's testimony before Senator Clark's subcommittee.
He had been working with HUD, OMB, and Commerce to pull together
a consensus view within the administration and lay out for Lynn some
policy choices that needed to be made sooner or later.[30] The key question
was whether the administration considered rural development still part
of a community development department or if it would abandon that
position and maintain the status quo of that area's placement in USDA.

Lynn testified on March 27.[31] He was well prepared and handled as many
of the questions as those he let Erwin and others answer. He focused on
the need for coordination among all community development–related
activities. Without disparaging current law, he argued strongly for the
benefits of his administrative counsellorship and for Congress to enact
the president's DCD proposal. However, he finessed whether the upcoming DCD bill would include rural development or leave it in USDA. That
policy and political decision had not been made yet. Lynn focused on the
issue of coordination regarding rural development (and so many policy
areas in general): "Very frankly, coordination is an extremely difficult thing
across departmental boundaries, no matter what the circumstances . . .
I do believe, though, that with the move toward the counselors that the
President has put into place, we should have some better results than in
the past."[32] Lynn's performance demonstrated his ability to absorb new

information quickly and to handle the cut and thrust of congressional hearings—where every question can be a political trap—with confidence and without any gaffes.

Better Communities Act

The second major political and policy issue during Lynn's counsellorship was the Better Communities Act of 1973 (BCA), which was Nixon's proposal to fold seven categorical aid programs (i.e., created to fund very specific purposes) into a revenue sharing program, in this case in the area of community development. Like manpower revenue sharing, in Washington jargon this bill was an example of several administration initiatives called "special revenue sharing," in contradistinction to "general revenue sharing," a program that gave money to local governments on an across-the-board basis, without any limitation on policy area. The initiative reflected several strands of Nixon's "New Federalism," a presidential perspective that gave state and local governments more freedom to decide how to spend federal monies, thus depriving the Washington bureaucracy of its power to nitpick policy, reducing the size of government, and decreasing Congress's leverage and control over such federal operations. BCA was already in advanced form by the time Lynn's counsellor office was up and running. He had little input in the substance of the initiative, but in an effort to bolster Lynn's credibility as counsellor, the White House chose him to be its senior spokesperson at a press briefing on the president's upcoming State of the Union message relating to community development. It included BCA as one of its foremost legislative initiatives.[33]

Deputy White House Press Secretary Gerald Warren tried to lighten the atmosphere in the White House Press Room (which was extremely strained at the time because the Watergate cover-up was beginning to unravel and some of the reporters' antagonism focused on Warren's boss, Ron Ziegler). Warren began by introducing Lynn and said dryly, "This is his baptism of fire as Counsellor and Secretary in the White House Briefing Room, and we welcome him."[34] Lynn again demonstrated his ability to absorb large amounts of new information through his Q&A with the press.

After the March 8 message to Congress and press briefing, the next deadline was March 28, two and a half weeks later, when the BCA bill itself (as opposed to a message about it) needed to be ready for release "at a time to be determined by the White House."[35] Lynn and his staff were deeply involved in all aspects of that internal process. It was eventually released on April 20, again with Lynn as the administration's spokesman.[36] Congressional Democrats and local mayors promptly complained to the press that the bill was a conservative and anti-city subterfuge for cutting urban financial aid. Trying to keep control of the media's spin, Lynn gave an interview to a reporter from a national wire service, thus having the potential of being carried in hundreds of newspapers. The lead of the article (before the Q&A transcript) was: "Presidential counselor James T. Lynn says politics lie behind many objections" to the bill. He was right, but it was not an explanation that played well. A news analysis in the Sunday *New York Times* described Lynn's no-win situation of being stuck between criticism from the right as well as the left: "Congress greeted with skepticism the newest version . . . Some conservatives complained that with Federal deficits already at record levels the plan amounted to 'debt sharing.' And Housing Secretary James T. Lynn confirmed the fears of urban liberals that some of their communities 'might receive less' in aid from Washington under the new program."[37]

After the bill's release, Lynn's office continued to be the central address for the bill, meaning that, when DOT raised some questions about the scope and interpretation of the just released version of the bill, those questions were directed to Lynn's office.[38]

The bill did not have a major public hearing before Lynn's counsellorship was abolished. A compromise version of community development revenue sharing was ultimately signed into law by President Ford on August 22, 1974, about two weeks after Nixon resigned.

Department of Community Development

Lynn and his staff dedicated large amounts of their time to show the good faith connection between the administrative counsellorship and congressionally approved reorganization. Of all the reorganization proposals Nixon sent to Congress in 1971–1972, the bill to create a community development super-department went the farthest, with a House committee recommending its passage. Therefore, the strong political logic in early 1973 was that the DCD bill should be the first reorganization bill that the administration would pursue in the Ninety-third Congress. Also, the external legal foundation of the entire counsellorship concept was somewhat tenuous. The administration argued (partly legally, partly politically) to Congress that the counsellorships were not a presidential power grab but merely a step toward formal statutory reorganization that needed congressional approval. If so, then that argument needed to be buttressed with some overt action. The DCD bill was the obvious choice to be introduced first, and quickly.

Lynn was already familiar with the 1971–1972 version of the bill. As undersecretary of commerce, in April 1972 he had testified on its behalf at a hearing of the Senate Government Operations Committee.[39] On February 23, 1973, the day after the counsellor's office was launched with Collier's initial two memos to Lynn, Collier immediately turned his attention to the DCD bill.[40] A few details of the bill needed to be ironed out internally. For example, would rural development be included in the DCD bill or left in USDA? From the standpoint of legislative strategy, several angles needed to be considered. An intra–White House political assessment bluntly demonstrated that, in Washington politics, everything is related to everything else. Could House Government Operations Committee Chair Chet Holifield's (D-Calif.) support be counted on again? That "may depend upon the positions that the Administration takes in other matters," including a consumer protection agency and atomic energy policy. Senate Government Operations Committee Chair Sam Ervin "has not been particularly interested in the DCD proposal in the past," and his degree of cooperation might be linked to his fight with the administration on impoundment. The chairman of the committee's reorganization subcommittee, Abraham Ribicoff (D-Conn.), "has been generally ineffective in the past" and his cooperation might be linked to some federal projects back in his home state.[41] Two weeks later, OMB reported that "apparently, Holifield intends to reintroduce the DCD bill as the Committee reported it" in 1972. The latest on Ribicoff was that he was "at best, indifferent to DCD."[42]

On April 9, Lynn provided his policy guidance on the DCD bill by writing comments on a memo Parker had submitted three days earlier.[43] Yes, rural development should be included in the DCD bill, and no, there should not automatically be a separate Rural Community Development Administration within the super-department. The counsellor's office should be the central coordinator of the effort to finalize and pass the bill but "only if Cal thinks we have manpower to handle it." Who would be the administration's point person and chief spokesperson for the bill? Lynn conceded that he should be, but as counsellor he was already very involved in BCA. As HUD secretary, he was also deeply involved in several other major initiatives. Therefore, he agreed to the central public role but "not a lot." He would agree to do the "initial testimony," but after that Floyd H. Hyde, the HUD undersecretary, "would have to carry ~~a lot~~ most of it." Regarding Parker's proposed timetable of introducing the bill by the end of April, Lynn was more cautious, preferring to choreograph it with Congress, especially Holifield: "should depend on sound-out of Committees in part—hearing schedules, etc."[44] Lynn did not want any inadvertent blunders of timing that would doom the bill nor did he want it introduced with great hoopla as the administration's first step in the statutory reorganization of the executive branch and then have it just sit there. In politics, sometimes timing was everything.

Further strategizing was needed. In an exchange between Parker and Raoul-Duval, they agreed that OMB's public and congressional role should be much reduced compared to the 1971–1972 legislative effort. OMB "must maintain a low profile . . . because of their obvious role on the impoundment question," a big issue to Senator Ervin. Also, DOT needed to be more involved in the pre-introduction planning because urban mass transit was likely to shift from DOT to DCD. But before the principals (Lynn and Transportation Secretary Brinegar) met to sanction the plans, staff would need to clear the path with lower-level meetings.[45] At first, they assumed they would start with Undersecretary Egil "Bud" Krogh Jr., but they ultimately decided to work with Theodore Lutz, the deputy undersecretary.[46]

Plans for introducing DCD at the end of April (or whenever Representative Holifield decided) melted away in the policy chaos of Watergate. By the time the counsellorships were abolished on May 10, the bill had not yet been introduced. It never was.[47] An August 1973 memo by Raoul-Duval demonstrated the political, organizational, and policy sea change that had taken place during the previous one hundred days. Having become a DC staffer, he presented a summary of the Nixon administration's ongoing plans "in the field of Community Development." He did not mention DCD.[48]

THE COMMUNITY DEVELOPMENT COMMITTEE

One of Collier's kick-off memos of the CD counsellorship on February 22 was about agenda items for the Community Development Committee (CDC).[49] This early appearance reflected the importance of the committee to the counsellorship concept and the desire to show tangible follow-up activity as soon as possible after the president's congressional breakfast. Lynn set CDC's first meeting for March 5, exactly two months after the breakfast—an indication of the difficulty of starting up the counsellor office quickly (which included the delay in Lynn's confirmation as HUD secretary). However, in the context of the office opening for business on February 22, this action was quite prompt.

Lynn and his staff invested a lot of thought in the first CDC meeting, asking themselves how they would define its mission, how it would operate, what powers it had, and so on. For a while, the nomenclature for CDC was unsettled; they initially referred to it as a "sub-committee" and did not identify it as a committee of the Domestic Council. Based on the scope of Lynn's counsellorship, if CDC had included all of the governmental bodies in his domain, the committee would have had about ten members (see the "Scope" section above). Instead, however, Lynn and his staff decided they wanted a small committee, consisting only of the principal principals:

DOT Secretary Claude Brinegar or his major alternate (Undersecretary Egil Krogh Jr. on a de jure basis but Deputy Undersecretary Theodore Lutz on a de facto basis)

USDA Secretary Earl Butz (also, of course, the natural resources counsellor) or his major alternate, Undersecretary Phil Campbell Jr.

Commerce Secretary Frederick B. Dent or his major alternate, William Letson, the department's general counsel

Darrell M. Trent, acting director, Office of Emergency Preparedness (temporary committee member)[50]

The tone and agenda of the first meeting were important. Lynn had to walk a tightrope in the same way that Nixon had at the congressional breakfast. This time, with an audience of Cabinet and subcabinet principals, Lynn had to vigorously assert the presidential coordinator role he conceived without triggering a defensive and turf protection reaction from the committee members. Parker emphasized that Lynn "shouldn't appear to be power grabbing."[51] Lynn also needed to be specific about how the committee itself would operate and what his expectations were vis-à-vis the members' roles and, in general, to create a collegial relationship that would set a positive tone. The hope was that when the principals returned to their bureaucracies and recounted the meeting to subordinates it would be with a positive message of cooperation rather than a grumbling one of having yet another intrusive boss. One internal memo discussed tactics for accomplishing these goals. For example, perhaps the principals could give their reactions to the pending draft of the president's State of the Union message on community development: "Such a tactic would serve several useful ends. First, it would encourage the joint resolution of those issues which need to be agreed upon before the President's Message is delivered. Second, it would allow the Counsellor to clear up any confusion concerning appropriate emphasis or directions in the Community Development area."[52]

Raoul-Duval suggested the benefit of holding the meeting in the Roosevelt Room in the West Wing of the White House proper (instead of OEOB), permitting only the principals to attend (excluding an entourage of departmental staff), and having a more senior official there, such as Ehrlichman, to help be sure the principals understood what the White House wanted of them to make the counsellorship work.[53] Parker thought the meeting should help to clarify for the principals the role of the counsellor staff. For example, should Lynn's staff be expected to "participate in the dialogue between Departments (Agriculture, Transportation, Commerce) and OMB? Should requests and responses be forwarded through the Counsellor or should the Counsellor receive copies?"[54]

The last few days before the meeting, set for Monday, March 5 (the first work day after the president's radio address on community development) generated a slew of more pre-meeting documents: a revised agenda for the meeting, an annotated agenda for the counsellor, and talking points for Lynn for the meeting.[55]

As it turned out, Ehrlichman did not attend the kick-off meeting. Instead, Cole did.[56] In terms of signals, Cole's presence sent a very different message than Ehrlichman's would have. For the second term, Ehrlichman was one of the "Big Five" top-tier assistants to the president. The counsellors and Cole, as head of the Domestic Council, all reported to Ehrlichman. The counsellorship project was, of course, directly tied to the halving of DC's size, and counsellors were, in effect, to take over part of DC's first-term role. Therefore, with Cole attending the first CDC meeting instead of Ehrlichman, Cole would have an implicit bureaucratic imperative to discount any supposed downgrading of the DC and instead to insinuate a greater role for DC vis-à-vis the counsellors and the principals. He could emphasize, correctly, that CDC was a committee of the Domestic Council. The rest of the agenda was, as expected, mostly process (e.g., role of the counsellor, CDC operating procedures) but partly about substance (e.g., input on the upcoming presidential message to Congress on CD). Under the agenda item "Other Current Issues," they were briefed about and then discussed upcoming legislative activity and the need to defend the president's budget in their public appearances.[57]

Lynn wanted the committee to be a working committee, not a symbolic gathering of Cabinet officers. So, he first encouraged the three secretaries to designate a representative to the committee who was at the working level, such as undersecretary or even assistant secretary (such at Erwin at USDA). Second, he wanted CDC to meet regularly, on a monthly cycle. Shrewdly, he decided that the next CDC meeting, on Monday, April 12, should also be in the West Wing. Especially with secretaries sending lower-ranking representatives, he wanted those representatives, too, to be affected by the venue of the meeting. Lynn was the *president's* counsellor.[58]

The agenda of the second meeting was more focused on policy issues than process, including the problem of the railroads in the Northeast (several were on the verge of financial collapse), HUD's housing study, and implementation of the Rural Development Act.[59] Here, as in some other examples of counsellors' operations, was a glimpse of what might have been. This was a substantive meeting of under- and assistant secretaries all engaged in matters relating to community development. The committee meeting demonstrated the value of interdepartmental meetings and imbued the multidepartmental representatives with a sense of teamwork and the idea that all were working on matters of mutual interest, regardless of where they were currently located in the bureaucracy. This was a working meeting, not a symbolic one. Another inkling of the role that the counsellors and their DC committees could have played came from a memo from UMTA's director of program development. He suggested that CDC could be a very useful venue for "a positive executive role . . . on the need for an overall Federal direction in Federal/city relationships and on the move toward flexibility."[60]

SUBCOMMITTEES

During his brief tenure as counsellor, Lynn decided he did not want to have any formal standing subcommittees with permanent meeting schedules, membership, and scope.[61] Rather, he preferred a more fluid substructure to reflect the ad hoc and changing public policy agenda.

CDC had a rural development working group chaired by Will Erwin, USDA assistant secretary for rural development.[62] However, as of mid-April, its membership had not yet been finalized.[63] Besides contacting the obvious representatives from HUD, USDA, and Commerce (home of the Economic Development Administration), HEW also notified the CD counsellor's office that it would welcome being a member of the working group, even though that part of HEW was in the domain of the human resources counsellor.[64]

A major administration reevaluation of housing policy was led by HUD but was actually an interagency project. For example, the USDA had the Farmers Home Administration under its purview, so that department provided from three to six staffers to assist in staffing the housing policy review task force. In total, eight to ten agencies were expected to participate.[65] However, this study was so closely aligned with HUD that it was only marginally viewed as a CDC subunit. Similarly, a DOT study of the impact that the bankruptcy of railroads in the Northeast would have on the country was also lightly associated with CDC because of the interdepartmental aspect of the subject. It was a recurring item on the agendas of CDC's meetings.

Lynn had an especial interest in using the counsellorship as a vehicle for legislative coordination. For example, he had personally decided that the subject should be on the agendas of the two CDC meetings. To further implement Lynn's desires, Collier arranged for the congressional liaison staffers from CDC's membership to meet weekly in his OEOB office.[66] The purposes of the meetings were to keep each other informed, improve coordination, and, whenever possible, help each other. At least one meeting took place, on April 11, 1973. The agenda focused mostly on the highway bill, then about to be debated on the floor of the House.[67]

Lynn also was interested in exploring the potential for a counsellor to coordinate public information and media relations activities within the rubric of community development. In a handwritten note to Collier on the margins of an early draft agenda for CDC's first meeting, he wrote, "How about PA [public affairs]?"[68] Pursuing that idea, Lynn's annotated agenda for the meeting included a reminder for him to discuss his desire to improve coordination of public affairs matters. For example, public information officers (PIOs) in the CD domain should get to know each other. He hoped to see improved coordination and cooperation with the

White House Press Office, too.[69] However, it appears that Collier did not create a weekly PIO meeting as he did for the congressional relations people.

AGENCY REPORTING TO THE COUNSELLOR

Based on his experience at senior levels of the Commerce Department in the first term, Lynn understood that if information is power, then heads-up reports from the bowels of the bureaucracy to the top echelons were essential. As the new HUD secretary, he had instituted a uniform system of reporting on upcoming "action-forcing" events. As counsellor, he wanted to implement the same system, as an essential way of exercising his role of representing the president. At CDC's first meeting on March 5, he told the principals that he wanted this type of report from them, and he handed out a format for them to follow.[70] However, as his staff prepared for the next monthly meeting, set for April 2, they noticed that no such reports had been submitted.[71] Clearly, Lynn needed to handle the subject in a more direct fashion at the April CDC meeting than he had at the March meeting.

By then, Weinberger had released his own highly structured and de-tailed reporting system for human resources. Lynn's handwritten talking points for the April CDC meeting indicated that he wanted the constituent departments to fill out and submit his action-forcing reports. He emphasized that he was requiring only one kind of report. He would "refer to what Cap is doing" but also note that such a formalized, detailed, and multiform approach was "*not yet* for us."[72] The implication was clear. At the April meeting, Lynn redistributed the "Standard Form for Action-Forcing Events Report." He wanted those reports submitted twice a month, and they were to cover events in the upcoming three weeks. But he also emphasized that the reports should cover more than those obvious short "time-fuse" items. Rather, he wanted the reports also to include a rolling (and continuously updated) six-month projection of such events.[73] The format for the report was:

Description of event: "(Terse)"
Anticipated Timing

Background
Source of Interest
   Congressional
   Press
   Interest Groups
   Other Federal Agencies
   Other
Proposed Action
Contact for Additional Information
Date Submitted[74]

Few such reports were submitted before the counsellorship project was canceled. Those reports, in the format Lynn had required, came from three USDA subunits: the Rural Development Service, the Farmers Home Administration, and the Rural Electrification Administration.[75] The reports provided precisely the kind of detail that Lynn wanted. For example, in its report the Rural Development Service mentioned joining Federal Regional Councils as a way of implementing its new rural development role, as determined in the Rural Development Act of 1972. Had Lynn's counsellorship lasted longer, reports such as these would indeed have helped him fulfill his self-defined role as presidential coordinator.

RELATIONS WITH THE DOMESTIC COUNCIL

The self-defined role that counsellors chose to play greatly influenced their relationship with the Domestic Council, especially with their corresponding associate DC directors. For Lynn, that associate DC director was Dana G. Mead.

Mead, who had a PhD in political science, served in Viet Nam, and was a former West Point instructor, had started as a White House Fellow in 1970. After the completion of that fellowship, he stayed on as a member of Ehrlichman's staff. (As noted previously, in the second half of Nixon's first term Ehrlichman was director of the Domestic Council.) Mead had several assignments, including preparing domestic policy initiatives to be unveiled in the 1972 State of the Union address. That work acquainted him with special revenue sharing, including the proposal for CD revenue sharing. Another of his assignments related to liaison with the District of Columbia government, again in the community development portfolio. As a result, during the post–November 1972 transition, he was tabbed to be the Domestic Council's associate director for community development. This gave him a one-on-one relationship with Counsellor Lynn.

Mead and Lynn had a good working relationship and were frequently in touch. In interviews, both acknowledged some tensions in the institutional relationship between a counsellor and the Domestic Council.[76] Occasionally they disagreed but only on a professional level, and such disagreements never interfered with ongoing work. Lynn recalled some tensions due to the downsizing of the DC and with the counsellors being allocated "all the fun parts," that is, policy initiatives. Mead recalled some disagreements about spending, Lynn (partly wearing his Cabinet hat) for more and Mead for less. Their different perspectives were also a reflection of the arm's-length relationship that traditional Republicans had with HUD and its policy issues. Many viewed housing and urban issues as a "Democratic" policy area. Lynn brought new enthusiasm to community development and related policy making, while Mead sometimes had to keep Republican priorities in mind. There was only so much that a Republican White House and Republican legislators would support regarding community development. Lynn had a good political antenna and recognized the policy realities of his position. Still, he was the more policy-oriented member of the duo. Mead sometimes provided a kind of downbeat reality check.

However, whatever disagreements Lynn and Mead had, they were never significant or impossible to resolve, largely because of Lynn's self-defined role. For Lynn, the counsellor was always the *president's* coordinator. That meant both Lynn and Mead were attuned to reflecting the administration's priorities and being loyal to Nixon's domestic policy program. They were both pulling in the same direction.[77]

Nonetheless, as the *president's* counsellor, Lynn had a sense of independence from the Domestic Council, as did his staff. Thus, although Mead's OEOB office was next door to Lynn's, Mead was not routinely included in the circulation list of internal staff memos that always went to Collier, Parker, Raoul-Duval, and/or Michel. Mead was viewed as *outside* the counsellor's office. His name was, however, on distribution lists for the kinds of paperwork that also went to OMB, a linkage that hinted at an "other side of the street" mentality. This was organizationally accurate, given that a counsellor was part of the White House, while DC and OMB were part of the Executive Office of the President, an important distinction in terms of status and power.

Lynn and his staff wanted to work well with DC but made clear in their paper flow that DC was a separate, outside entity. The counsellor would be functioning independently of the Domestic Council, not seamlessly integrated *into* it and certainly not subordinate to it. The counsellor was the *president's* personal appointee. Cutting off Mead from routine staff paperwork said volumes about power—who had it and who did not.

Still, CDC was formally a DC committee, permitting Mead to make the argument that *he* was the *committee's* staff, while Collier, Parker, and Raoul-Duval were the counsellor's staff.[78] Nevertheless, it was the counsellor's staff that prepared and distributed the agendas of upcoming CDC meetings, not Mead. Lynn was careful to show through his own behavior a desire for a good, cooperative working relationship, especially regarding meetings of CDC, given that it was an entity within DC, Mead's territory. For example, one of Collier's two February 22 memos that kicked off the operation of the counsellor office related to calling a first meeting of CDC. Lynn wrote in the margins, "Clear with Mead."[79] On a partially blank draft Lynn reviewed for calling the second CDC meeting, the handwritten notes included a list of the three principals to whom it should be addressed, followed by a list of those who should get a blind carbon copy or "bcc." Mead was the first name on the handwritten bcc list, indicating that he came to mind first.[80] Mead also had leverage because of DC's role in clearing domestic legislation, a role it had had during the first term that was not changed in the transition to the second. Thus, counsellor staff had no choice but to liaise with Mead as they prepared the BCA legislation and documented the administration's stance on EDA legislation then being considered in Congress.[81]

This pas de deux, with countervailing designated and formal roles, helped keep the relationship between Lynn and his counsellor staffers and Mead on a relatively balanced plane. In this case, the mix of personalities, desire to cooperate, self-definitions of roles, and formal powers contributed to a modus vivendi for this counsellor and his DC counterpart.

Few external observers appeared to understand the importance of the associate DC directors, notwithstanding the halving of the size of the DC staff and the importance of the close linking of each counsellor to an associate DC director. One of the few that did was the *Journal of Housing*, the publication of the National Association of Housing and Redevelopment Officials. In its issue of February 28, 1973, the journal not only summarized Lynn's new HUD and counsellor duties but also focused on those of Cole, the new DC head replacing Ehrlichman, and Mead. It reported of Mead that "his primary task will center on the federal commitment to community development," a statement that indicated Mead's position was an important role and not overshadowed by Lynn's counsellorship. The article included not only a photo of Lynn but also photos of Mead and Cole, another signal to readers that Mead was an important player on matters of interest to the organization's membership, notwithstanding the new higher-profile CD counsellor.[82] It was an astute insight.

Based on his self-defined role as the president's policy and program coordinator, Lynn demonstrated that this approach could be a constructive one. He used his platform to coordinate, both internally and externally, the administration's policy activities in community development. He was a public face on issues outside HUD (such as rural development) and sought to keep all executive branch entities working together. The criticism that the counsellor's role added yet another layer of bureaucratic hurdles did not appear to be borne out in Lynn's case. With the limits that Haldeman and Ehrlichman imposed on the size of counsellor staff, there did not seem to be significant overt duplication between Lynn's work and Mead's on behalf of the Domestic Council.

Lynn's staff, based on their activities, seemed to focus largely on coordinating rather than on actually doing the detailed and time-consuming background work that was usually done in the agencies. They let such work stay in those agencies. Also, Parker's recounting of how the USDA assistant secretary for rural development did not seem to resent Parker's role was telling. According to Parker, the assistant secretary was delighted that *someone* in the White House was interested in his work. This rings true, even if coming from a subjective source. Their joint trip to South Carolina indicated collegiality rather than a superior-subordinate relationship. If anything, the counsellor structure permitted the assistant secretary to be more of a central player rather than playing only a bit part in the lowly subcabinet. After all, he had been named to chair the CDC's Rural Development Working Group, which was to be a White House committee, right where the action was. So, had the counsellorship project continued beyond May, Lynn's performance as a presidential coordinator would likely have been a creditable and constructive, but modest, one. Nixon and Ehrlichman had created a structure that, with such realistic expectations, could have worked.

7

COUNSELLOR FOR NATURAL RESOURCES EARL BUTZ

The Dutiful and Passive Super-Secretary

When Nixon met with Agriculture Secretary Earl Butz on November 20, 1972, at Camp David to notify him of his appointment as counsellor, they discussed two issues that signaled how Butz would approach the position. (Chapter 2 described Nixon's bellicose comments at that meeting about wanting a tough and ruthless counsellor.) First, Butz mentioned that at sixty-three he was the oldest member of the (outgoing) Cabinet and that he felt he had been subject to "enormous wear & tear" during the first term and the reelection campaign. They talked about both Roosevelt presidents dying in their early sixties. Using a football analogy (a nod to Nixon's favorite sport), Butz said that "when [a person is] a step too slow, [you] take yourself out" of the game. Second, Nixon pitched the appointment as signaling the preeminence of USDA over the Interior Department. For Butz, who had dedicated his career to the American farmer, it was validating to have the USDA secretary reign over Interior. Given the usual conflicts and rivalries between Cabinet departments, accepting the appointment was a way for Butz to further his own parochial policy interests. He had little interest in promoting environmental protection, especially if it conflicted with the interests of farmers. Loyal to the president and wanting to serve him (as well as advancing farming interests), Butz accepted the appointment as counsellor. He also accepted all the conditions in the loyalty check-off list developed by Ehrlichman and Haldeman, but cagily, he did not sign it. Given Butz's concern about his age and health, they agreed that his acceptance was conditional on his passing a physical exam and the understanding that he was making a commitment to serve as counsellor (and, it was understood, as USDA secretary) for only two years.[1]

Clearly, Butz was not enthusiastic about the counsellor appointment and did not bring to it eagerness, freshness, or broader policy goals. For him, the appointment was a capstone to his pro-farmer career, and he would serve only two years—assuming his health held up. This stance did not mesh well (or, for that matter, at all) with Nixon's stated desire for a tough and ruthless activist counsellor who would fight the bureaucracy. Instead, Butz's record in office provided a case study of a dutiful but relatively passive and uncurious counsellor, significantly different from Weinberger's assistant president and Lynn's presidential coordinator.

SCOPE

In his most extensive public discussion of the counsellorship, Butz articulated his views of the new position. First, he would be involved in "policy formulation," especially in "the resolution of differences" among departments and agencies in the natural resources area. When agreement could be accomplished, then there would be no need to go to the president for a decision. This would push decision making farther away from the president. If the counsellor was unable to achieve unanimity, then he would serve as "arbiter," that is, decision maker.[2] However, the losing department or agency could still appeal Butz's decision to, as appropriate, the Domestic Council, OMB, or, if necessary, to the president personally. This function could be deemed as dealing with "incoming" matters, although Butz did not use that terminology.

Second, the counsellor would be "articulating the policies and programs of the President" internally, to his constituent departments and agencies—a form of "outgoing" communication (again, not his term). Thus, in Butz's view, a counsellor generally had a role in preparing for policy decisions, deciding (sometimes), and then in disseminating the decisions. According to Butz, these activities should help "in making the whole process of Government flow more smoothly." Super-secretaries would be "a mechanism to focus on problems of this kind to get action."[3]

Third, externally, counsellors would be available to testify before Congress on administration positions relating to their respective policy areas. This would, theoretically, be helpful to Congress when it was interested in a policy area that was broader than an individual department or agency. Butz told Congress that the doctrine of executive privilege (becoming very controversial due to Watergate) would generally not apply to counsellors. It would apply only to direct contacts with the president or confidential pre-decision situations.

However, Butz was careful to focus on the *internal administrative* nature of the counsellorship (the line determined by Dean and Ehrlichman back in November and December). The *statutory* duties of Cabinet secretaries and heads of administrative agencies were unaffected. If the *law* deemed them "the senior advisor to the President on ___," that did not change. Most importantly, the president had given no directives to ignore laws relating to the organizations of government, as was happening concurrently regarding Nixon's impounding of legally appropriated funds (or, at least, so said the Democratic-majority Congress). Furthermore, departmental reporting relationships to congressional committees had not changed. In general, counsellors were not arrogating to themselves the powers of de facto super-secretaries above and beyond what a president could legally accomplish without congressional action. Such line powers could be exercised only when (and if) Congress enacted any of the proposed departmental reorganization bills. Yes, a counsellor was a step in the direction of reorganized departments, but only Congress could decide on such large reorganization questions.[4]

When Ehrlichman briefed the congressional leaders on January 5, he outlined the duties of the NR counsellor according to policy areas: natural resource use, lands and minerals, environment, outdoor recreation, water navigation and control, and park and wildlife resources.[5] The scope of the NR counsellorship based on administrative entities was enumerated in John Dean's memo of January 2, 1973:

Department of Interior: all except Native American issues
USDA: only the Forest Service and Soil Conservation Service
Agricultural Research Service: only the Soil and Water Conservation Division
Economic Research Service: only the Natural Resources Economics Division
Farmers Home Administration: only the watershed loan program
Department of Transportation: only oil and gas pipeline safety
Department of Commerce: only the National Oceanic and Atmospheric Administration (NOAA)

Department of Defense (U.S. Army, Army Corps of Engineers):
  civilian programs only
Atomic Energy Commission (AEC): only uranium enrichment
  and raw materials program
  policy planning and funding of the Plowshare program
  civilian power and non-nuclear energy programs
Tennessee Valley Authority (TVA)
Environmental Protection Agency (EPA)
Council on Environmental Quality (CEQ) (a unit in the EOP)[6]

However, the policy scope of Butz's counsellorship was quickly and significantly narrowed soon after his appointment, when control of the energy portfolio was shifted out of his purview. At first, it was assumed that energy was part of his area of responsibility. For example, only a week after Nixon's congressional breakfast, Butz said in a press conference in his home state of Indiana that "his first priority as counselor would be to look at ways of meeting energy shortages." Similarly, in early March, Butz was quoted in the press as the administration's spokesperson on the price and supply of natural gas. Both times, Butz's public statements to reporters indicated that he was the senior administration person on energy matters.[7]

Notwithstanding that public visage, behind the scenes he was being stripped of that portfolio. As early as February, the White House explicitly severed energy from his jurisdiction and appointed Charles DiBona as a new presidential assistant to coordinate the administration's response to energy problems. Butz was not involved in the decision and did not fight back to protect his turf. In a congressional appearance on March 5, he had to admit that, despite being the counsellor for natural resources, he was not a member of the highest-level administration planning group on energy.[8]

Butz's lack of standing in the energy policy area was further highlighted as DiBona prepared the text of a presidential message to Congress that was to be released on April 18. Even though Butz was totally excluded from energy policy making, Glenn Schleede, a member of his counsellor staff, was deeply involved in drafting the message, as was the DC's associate director for natural resources, Richard Fairbanks.[9] This was another indication of Butz's voluntary abdication of power, even acceding to a White House rival temporarily commandeering his staff.

A week before the release of the president's message on energy, Ehrlichman aide Tod Hullin asked Ehrlichman to decide who should be the public spokespersons for the president on the issue. (DiBona, as White House staffer, was ineligible, partly because of Nixon's continued insistence that his personal staff not testify before Congress and partly because faceless White House staff did not have the official rank and high profile that would be needed for the role.) Ehrlichman pointedly skipped over Butz and selected Treasury Secretary George Shultz, William Simon (Shultz's deputy secretary), and John Whitaker (Interior undersecretary).[10] Hullin then notified Fairbanks by stating diplomatically that "if necessary and appropriate, he [Ehrlichman] would also recommend Earl Butz. He [Ehrlichman] recognizes, however, that Secretary Butz is not up to speed on the energy initiative."[11]

Fairbanks, reading the draft of the presidential message, saw the chance that Butz would be humiliated publicly if he was not even mentioned in the message, which implied that Fairbanks's own power within the White House would also diminish by association. Fairbanks thought there should be a "Mention of Counsellor's Role in Energy Message." He told DiBona that "not mentioning the [counsellor's] assignment would seem to add even more chance of confusion and questioning."[12] But DiBona (and, by implication, Ehrlichman and Shultz) would have none of it. There was only one reference to Butz in the energy message, which never explicitly stated that the NR counsellor had had jurisdiction over energy policy. The wording only implied it and then indicated that such an implied assignment was an "interim" one, anyway, now superseded by the policy statement encompassed in the message.[13]

REAL AND PERCEIVED DEMOTIONS

A major potential problem inherent to the counsellor project reared its predictable head even before Butz moved into his OEOB office. Less than a full week after Nixon's announcement of the counsellor project on January 5, a problem about the reorganization arose with Russell Train, chair of the Council on Environmental Quality (CEQ), which was part of the Executive Office of the President. Based on the plans Nixon and Ehrlichman released on January 5, CEQ would be within the rubric of the natural resources counsellor.

Train had a short list of issues on his mind and was willing to resign his position if he did not get satisfactory resolutions to those issues. His pointed demand led to a relatively rare one-on-one meeting in the Oval Office with the president on January 11. From his November reelection to his January 20 inauguration, Nixon had kept himself even more separate from his appointees than during his first term, since he especially disliked personal confrontations or awkward conversations. Also, he spent little time in the White House, preferring Camp David or his homes in warmer climes. During those three months, the White House regularly issued lists of appointees whose resignations "were accepted," that is, whose service was no longer desired.

Emboldened by his election victory and plans for his second term, Nixon did not feel any need to be a supplicant urging appointees to stay. Yet Nixon wanted Train to stay or at least not resign with a politically potent blast. Nixon was willing to meet with Train and hear his conditions for remaining. Train was unhappy that CEQ was apparently being downgraded, not only by redirecting him to report to the NR counsellor instead of the president but also by proposed cutting of his budget and staff as part of Nixon's parallel initiative to reduce EOP's size and hold down spending in his FY1974 budget plan (not yet released publicly at that point). Nixon could smoothly assure Train, as he had told all his Cabinet secretaries, that they would continue to have direct access to the president as appropriate. Train told reporters after the meeting that he had agreed to stay notwithstanding the cuts and also, according to another reporter, that "CEQ had not been downgraded in the least." However, a third reporter at the briefing pointedly noted that "the White House indicated that Train now will report" to the NR counsellor. Train had been placated, but Nixon was not willing to change his grand reorganization plan just because a member of his administration was unhappy.[14]

A second case of ruffled feathers occurred with Interior Secretary Rogers Morton. Like Butz, Morton was one of the few Cabinet officers asked to stay, but having the USDA secretary as his boss was a public humiliation, especially considering the institutional rivalry between the two departments. In fact, at the time of these events, all of Interior's publications contained a standard branding paragraph that described the department as "America's 'Department of Natural Resources.'"[15] Based on Butz's appointment as NR counsellor, USDA was at the core of Nixon's de facto Department of Natural Resources (in contradistinction to formal legislative proposals to Congress, in which USDA was retained intact outside a new Department of Natural Resources). The humiliation became semi-public at a kick-off event for all senior officials from the departments, agencies, and bureaus within the NR counsellor's domain on February 7. It took place in a large theater-style room on the top floor of OEOB. Sitting on the stage were the president, Butz, Cole (DC director), and Fairbanks (associate DC director for NR). Sitting in the audience with the hoi polloi of assistant secretaries and bureau chiefs was Interior Secretary Morton. It was a stark visualization of Nixon's reorganization. Some secretaries were less important than others. If in Washington the *perception* of power *is* power, then that event conveyed to all the officials from Interior that they and their boss had indeed been demoted. They were now part of a second-class Cabinet department.[16]

Yet this perception of demotion was inevitable in the way that Ehrlichman and Nixon tried to short-circuit any official and legal reorganization through the administratively implemented counsellor structure. Placing Cabinet officers with broad powers of coordination inside the White House apparatus created a more powerful and, by implication, a more important office than had first-term efforts at coordination by Whitaker as Cabinet secretary or his (and his counterparts') later efforts as associate DC directors. A Cabinet officer had more standing in protocol-conscious Washington than White House staff. Not all Cabinet officers could be counsellors—that would defeat the inherent purpose of the reorganization. Therefore, despite public denials to Congress and the press, some Cabinet officers were indeed "more equal" than others.

The problem with Morton burst out publicly in February. *Baltimore Sun* writer Theo Lippman Jr. wrote a nationally syndicated column entitled "The Ordeal of Interior's Rogers Morton." (Morton had previously been a member of Congress from Maryland, so Lippman already knew him.) The *Los Angeles Times,* among others, published it. Lippman opined that because of Butz's appointment as counsellor, Morton's "influence as a policy maker has been cut off above, too." Furthermore, Lippman claimed that Morton "wanted the job, and may have expected to get it. After Nixon indicated he hoped to create such an office, Morton's speeches in support of it sounded to many people like campaign speeches." Lippman was referring to the formal plan in the first term for a statutory Department of Natural Resources, but there is no doubt that Morton would have wanted the counsellorship appointment (if only as a prelude to a formal reorganization). In general, the column was sympathetic to Morton and critical of the way the Nixon White House was treating him, including the demotion as part of the counsellorship initiative.[17]

It is possible that the sense of demotion was felt particularly strongly in Interior because so much of that department was assigned to one counsellor, with only its Indian programs under the HR counsellor. Therefore, the senior officials at Interior may have felt more of a sense of being swallowed by a competing Cabinet secretary than the DOT or Commerce department might have. The latter had units scattered to several counsellors and some units wholly outside the counsellor structure. While those departments had been scattered, Interior was swallowed almost whole.

However, in the spring of 1973, Morton had some serious health issues caused by cancer. He was absent for several months for medical treatment and (understandably) physically weaker before and after. He was not in a position to fight it out publicly. And the abrupt firing in 1970 of his predecessor, Walter Hickel, was a reminder that Nixon expected Cabinet officers to keep their disagreements private. Also, Morton did not have as combative a personality as some politicians did. When Fairbanks personally apologized to him for the incident at the OEOB briefing, Morton graciously accepted it and did not carry a public grudge.[18]

While the Train and Morton incidents highlighted the difficulties of making the counsellorship plan work, the immediate and public results demonstrated that the Nixon White House was going to hold the line and try to give the counsellorship initiative a chance to work.

STAFFING THE OFFICE

One element of the plan for the second term was to sprinkle White House staff throughout the bureaucracy to make agencies and departments more responsive to the president. It was not enough that all Cabinet officers and the subcabinet (such as undersecretaries and assistant secretaries) were nominated by the president and subject to Senate confirmation. If the goal was to prevent presidential appointees from "going native," then White House staff from the first term were viewed as more likely to retain their loyalty to Nixon. The transition plans paid special attention to the appointment of undersecretaries, who held the number-two position in each department. Given the amount of outside and public duties that a secretary would have (congressional testimony, Cabinet meetings, speeches to groups, media interviews, international conferences, etc.), the Nixon team viewed undersecretaries as the "inside" and day-to-day managers of the departments. If the goal was to get control of the bureaucracy, then each departmental undersecretary would be the person to spearhead that effort. The White House Personnel Office made clear that, unlike the Washington culture in earlier times, the secretary did not have the prerogative of naming the undersecretary. Rather, it would now be solely a White House decision.

At the Interior Department, Nixon had decided to retain Rogers Morton as secretary. For undersecretary, he picked John C. Whitaker. Before 1968, Whitaker had been a long-time supporter of Nixon's, with strong credentials in natural resources, including a doctorate in geology. In the first term, he began as the secretary of the Cabinet and then served as assistant director of the Domestic Council for natural resources. He was a natural for undersecretary of Interior.

Beginning in mid-1971, Whitaker's assistant at the Domestic Council had been Richard W. Fairbanks III, who had started in the Nixon administration as special assistant to EPA's first administrator, William Ruckelshaus. With Whitaker leaving, Fairbanks was perfect to fill Whitaker's job—although it was not *exactly* the same job. Ehrlichman's plan for the second term had been to reduce the staffing of the Domestic Council as a corollary to creating the counsellorship positions, and he expected close cooperation between the staff of the Domestic Council and the counsellors. As discussed in chapter 2, the OEOB office assignments paired each counsellor's office side by side with the associate DC director for that same policy area.

Fairbanks already had a good working relationship with Butz. The two got along well during the first term and had thus already established a basis for a cooperative relationship in the new, uncharted territory of counsellor and counterpart DC associate director. The template for their particular pairing was established right after the announcement of the counsellor plan on January 5. Butz asked Fairbanks to recommend to him candidates for his counsellor staff.

By January 11, Fairbanks had some suggestions. Knowing that the plan anticipated only a small staff for each counsellor, Fairbanks suggested "a small group of highly talented people" to staff Butz's office. Given Butz's relative depth of knowledge in agriculture policy, Fairbanks perceptively focused on identifying staffers who had expertise in some of the other policy areas of the NR counsellor. He recommended well-educated policy wonk types, such as OMB analysts and budget examiners. These were not "political" or partisan types per se, but all had already proved they could operate in a politicized policy environment. Fairbanks listed three recommended individuals and attached the résumés of two lesser candidates. Of the three he listed, the first was Norm Ross, "a neg[r]o (a group which we are actively trying to make more visible at the top level)." The other two were Glenn Schleede and Roger Strelow.[19]

Butz had given such an open mandate to Fairbanks that the latter felt it necessary to urge Butz to be a bit more involved in the hiring: "In view of the close personal relationship that you will obviously have to develop with whatever staff you select, I would assume you would not want to make any decision without interviewing a few of these people." From Fairbanks's list, Butz ended up hiring two, neither of whom he had worked with before: Ross and Schleede. This move was an indication of how much he trusted Fairbanks as well as Butz's big-picture approach to public policy. He was not a detail man.[20]

Both Ross and Schleede were hired with the title of assistant director of the Natural Resources Committee. Ross was thirty-one and had worked as an OMB budget examiner in the area of the environment. As such, he knew the subject matter and agencies in Butz's domain well. He was also a former army officer and had served in Viet Nam. Schleede, thirty-eight, was also a veteran (air force) who at that point was chief of OMB's environmental branch and had worked for James Schlesinger briefly at the Atomic Energy Commission. He did not join the staff until March 20, another indication of the gradual pace of establishing Butz's counsellor operation.[21]

To run the office and oversee Ross and Schleede, Butz chose John W. Larson. Larson's formal title was executive director of the Natural Resources Committee and his informal title was chief of staff to the counsellor. Larson, thirty-seven, was a lawyer and had been assistant secretary of interior for public policy from 1971 to 1973. In that capacity, he oversaw program coordination, regional planning, environmental reviews, international activities, and the Bureau of Outdoor Recreation.[22] Larson was a substantial appointment. After all, an assistant secretary is a member of the subcabinet and is nominated by the president and confirmed by the Senate. Larson was no run-of-the-mill policy wonk. In that respect, appointing him as head of the counsellor staff was an indication of the importance of the counsellorship and the high-level policy role he and his staff would engage in.

In general, the three professional staff members all brought expertise in the areas of natural resources, environment, and energy, thus balancing out Butz's own expertise in agriculture and related USDA activities. These three male professional staffers, plus a full-time clerical assistant for each, rounded out the NR counsellor's operation. It was fully staffed as of March 21, 1973, two and a half months after Nixon's congressional breakfast.[23]

IN OPERATION

Even though he was still in the midst of establishing his office, Butz was responsive to Fairbanks's suggestion (which reflected the president's and Ehrlichman's desires) to have some tangible indications of the counsellorship as soon as possible, even before the staff was fully in place. Fairbanks arranged for a kick-off event (briefly mentioned earlier in relation to the slighting of Secretary Morton) at 11:00 A.M. on February 7, 1973, a month after the president's congressional breakfast. Butz convened a meeting of all Cabinet, subcabinet, and independent agency officials as well as bureau chiefs for a briefing on his plans for the counsellorship. It was a major event, with fifty-two people slated to attend. However, at least based on the agenda Fairbanks prepared, DC Director Cole's subject matter and role were more extensive than Butz's.[24] It was almost as though Butz was merely the host of the meeting, with the detailed policy substance being handled by others. (Cole was, of course, Fairbanks's supervisor.) In his comments at the meeting, Butz tried to alleviate the fears of a power takeover. "Don't let's use that word 'super cabinet,'" he recalled saying. He emphasized that "those of us who are counselors continue as cabinet secretaries just like any other cabinet secretary."[25]

But not much happened after that kick-off event. In late February, Butz appeared along with a retinue of Interior officials at the initial public hearing of a subcommittee of the House Appropriations Committee on the president's budget request for Interior for FY1974. Again, Butz did not do any heavy lifting at the congressional hearing, leaving to Whitaker and others the job of providing substantive and detailed answers.[26] Nonetheless, it was a glimpse of what might have been if the counsellor project had survived. Butz was viewed by Congress as the line person in the White House (i.e., he was not staff, like OMB officials) overseeing the Interior budget and that his views should therefore be solicited. The slow start in staffing was only one of the signals of Butz's style of counsellorship. According to the *National Journal,* throughout the spring "Butz showed no great interest" in non-USDA policy areas he was ostensibly responsible for as NR counsellor.[27] This statement was valid in part but also partly unfair.

After the slow ramp-up in staffing and the reduction in the scope of his empire, Butz's work as counsellor finally seemed to hit its stride in mid-March, about the same time his staffing was complete. Unique among the counsellors, Butz embarked on a grand tour of his domain. Beginning on March 12, he scheduled visits to the agencies he was overseeing, allotting an hour for the appropriate officials to brief him on their agency's activities. His itinerary included stops at AEC (with a one-hour lunch at the commission's headquarters building before the briefing), the TVA's Washington office, the NOAA, the Army Corps of Engineers, and EPA.[28] In one sense, it was to his credit to admit via his behavior how little he knew about federal operations beyond USDA. On the other hand, the visits represented a deft bureaucratic maneuver. They demonstrated that he was on the job fulfilling his counsellor appointment, but the number of agencies he needed to visit also justified delaying any policy involvement until he finished becoming familiar with all the departments and agencies he was to oversee. It was also significant that he left it to each agency to decide what to brief him on, instead of sending in advance of his visit a common (or specific) list of questions he wanted addressed. He was not taking control of the agenda but letting the agencies do that. It was another indication of his passivity and collegiality.

Still, the *National Journal's* knock on his seeming lack of engagement as a counsellor is also somewhat unfair. An examination of his daily schedules in April 1973 shows Butz spending a creditable amount of time on his counsellor duties, whether working in his OEOB office (though certainly less than half the time) or conscientiously (though usually passively) handling the paperwork that flowed to him.[29]

There were several examples of Butz the counsellor (rather than Butz the USDA secretary) serving as the public face of the administration for natural resources. On April 9, 1973, he was the spokesperson for the administration when briefing the White House press corps on the rationale for Nixon's veto of the rural water and sewer bill and the upcoming override vote in Congress.[30] He focused on the president's contention that the Democratic-majority Congress was too free with spending and that fiscal conservatism was needed. Also, behind the scenes regarding the same issue,

Butz was asked by the White House congressional liaison office to make some telephone calls to Republican members of Congress to urge them to vote to sustain the president's veto.[31] Nixon's veto was sustained. (It is important to see the link between "governing by veto" and the counsellor project as two components of Nixon's larger second-term strategy for marginalizing Congress and going ahead with his own policy priorities.) Even when the news media seemed interested in his comments about agricultural issues, such as rising food prices, reporters sometimes identified Butz as a presidential counsellor or, in the preferred media usage, counselor.[32] However, while referring to this new, more senior position, some journalists preferred using more evocative and self-explanatory terms such as "super-secretary" and "Super-Cabinet."[33]

On another occasion, Butz was asked to address the National Coal Association. Schleede explained that "the group has previously heard from Secretary Morton" and that it "is particularly interested in having someone from *a very high level in the Administration* and have specifically asked for you since John Ehrlichman will no longer be able to appear."[34] Again, this sort of public representation was exactly what Nixon intended as one of the roles of a counsellor. However, of course, this was really a sort of mis-invitation, given that the coal producers were interested in energy policy and Butz had by then been stripped of that portfolio. Another speaking engagement Butz accepted as counsellor was for the Environmental Writers Association.[35] The group was eager to hear his views about the environment now that he had a portfolio for all natural resources, including EPA.

Conversely, sometimes Butz acted as the in-house representative of the president. In early April, the secretary of commerce sent to the president a compilation from the National Industrial Pollution Control Council, which was organizationally attached to the Commerce Department. A question arose about who should sign the acknowledgment letter. To signal the president's position that the counsellor was his supra-departmental representative, Butz was assigned the duty of thanking the secretary of commerce. It was the kind of small, but bureaucratically important, detail that underlined Nixon's commitment to the role of the counsellors.[36]

An example of Butz fulfilling the policy coordination role that Nixon and Ehrlichman envisioned for counsellors occurred in April. At the time, the administration was pushing for coordinated decision making about possible development of the coal reserves in the Great Plains, especially in Montana and Wyoming. Understandably, several agencies had legal roles to play, including the Department of Interior, EPA, and USDA's Forest

Service. Butz issued a policy directive on April 23 that declared Interior the lead agency for supervising and coordinating the effort, while all other agencies were to remain involved "both at the policy and working levels." It was a detailed memo, further declaring his desire that the program not "be treated as a 'step child' by the various agencies" due to the absence of a line appropriation from Congress and his desire that the coordinated effort yield "useful information and a plan for action within the next year."[37] This memo was another glimpse of what the NR counsellorship concept could have accomplished.

Another example of Butz acting in the counsellor's supra-agency role occurred in early May regarding the AEC and its feisty chairperson, Dixy Lee Ray. On one occasion, Ray wanted "an unequivocal restatement" from an authoritative person in the administration regarding AEC's continuing role in uranium enrichment under the new energy policy (as embodied in the president's recent message to Congress). Her letter bounced around the White House bureaucracy between high-ranking Assistant to the President Peter Flanigan, OMB, and the Domestic Council. Finally, it was agreed internally that Butz should sign the letter (which merely restated current policy). He did.[38] Ray was satisfied. Again, however, this was all a bit odd, given that Butz had already been stripped of the energy portfolio.

A few days later, Ray was on the warpath again, unhappy with EPA's critical views of AEC's environmental stewardship. Schleede gave Butz a heads up that Ray would probably try to talk to him after the May 2 meeting of the Natural Resources Committee. Schleede suggested Butz should "indicate our preference is that AEC and EPA work out problems with each other—without our involvement." This was precisely the approach that Ehrlichman had planned for counsellors: pushing coordination out from the center to the agencies and departments themselves to the greatest extent possible.[39]

Generally, Butz deferred to his staff on such matters and signed the paperwork they presented him. However, at least once he overturned a staff recommendation and substituted his own perception of the adminis-tration's policy priorities over staff's. The issue related to how EPA would implement a legal requirement in the Clean Air Act that violators of the act be denied eligibility for federal contracts. EPA suggested that "a facility could be lis[t]ed upon a criminal conviction and a determination by the [EPA] Administrator of continuing or recurring violations." However, the secretary of commerce (following the department's pro-business agenda) argued that the draft EPA regulations were onerous and largely unnecessary. Fairbanks and Ross sided with EPA and, following their routine practice, asked Butz to sign off on their stance. Butz disagreed with them, however. To Ross's observation that there probably would be very few companies affected, Butz dictated a reaction: "Norm, this really is a very thin defense of the effect of the proposed regulations. The mere existence of a regulation like this causes companies to incur the cost of compliance, whatever that may be, even in the absence of citation of violation. . . . I had considerable doubt about them in my own mind."[40]

This, too, was another example of the potential of the counsellorship project and of Butz living up to the general expectations for the new office. The counsellor could make a difference in the policy process by taking care that broad principles of the administration would be applied in specific circumstances while eliminating the need for the president to be the conciliator between warring agencies. The counsellor's existence was indeed pushing decision making down the hierarchy and away from the White House.

THE NATURAL RESOURCES COMMITTEE

Given his relative passivity as counsellor, Butz was content to follow the operational precedents being set by Weinberger, the exemplar of a hands-on counsellor. In mid-February Weinberger had issued his first memorandum to the agencies within his domain about his plans to create a Council on Human Resources (see chap. 5). A month later, Butz followed suit. Having used the same structure as Weinberger's memo and at times the same wording, on March 12 Butz sent a memo to the seven principals within his area of responsibility: the undersecretary of interior, the undersecretary of USDA, the AEC chairperson, the general who was chief of the Army Corps of Engineers, the administrator of NOAA (in Commerce), the EPA administrator, and the CEQ chairperson.[41] Lesser members of the committee were the head of TVA's Washington, D.C., office and DOT's assistant secretary for safety and consumer affairs. The latter was included because the Office of Pipeline Safety was one of seven units under his jurisdiction and the only DOT unit assigned to the NR counsellor. In his memo, Butz informed the principals of his decision to establish a Natural Resources Committee: "This will be a standing committee with regularly scheduled meetings to provide an opportunity for communication and coordinated action on the critical natural resource issues. I am asking you to participate actively on this committee since this is the only way we will be able to more toward the goals the President wishes to achieve."[42] He stated that the committee would meet monthly. The NR Committee was deemed a committee of the Domestic Council, although this structural issue was not raised in the memo.

The first monthly meeting was set for March 21 in Butz's OEOB office. By now it was nearly eleven weeks after the president's congressional breakfast, another indication of Butz's leisurely pace. Shrewdly, Butz issued invitations to join him for a pre-meeting breakfast at the White House Mess, one of the prestige political venues in Washington.[43] Further adding distinction to the breakfast, he invited only the major principals, not the lesser-ranked officials. It would truly be a power breakfast and a good reminder to the invitees of the source of Butz's authority.

The Natural Resources Committee met three times: March 21, April 3, and May 2. Almost all the meetings involved a gradual creation of the modus operandi for the NR counsellor and the programs within his domain. These were process issues. The infrastructure and this venue never progressed to the point of extensively dealing with many substantive policy issues. So, while Weinberger's work was the most fully operationalized case study of a counsellor interested in heavily involving himself in details, Butz's was the least operationalized. Instead of the (relatively) preemptory approach by Weinberger of simply promulgating the requirements he was imposing on his empire, Butz was encouraging a more collegial and consensus process for establishing standard operating procedures. Inevitably, this took more time than Weinberger's approach.

At the first meeting, after the breakfast in the White House Mess, Butz (and his staff and DC Associate Director Fairbanks) and the seven attending principals discussed the role of the counsellor, role of the committee, proposed subcommittees for the committee, and procedures for the operation of the counsellor office in relation to the departments and agencies. (For discussion of subcommittees and reporting, see sections below.)

The last agenda item of the March 21 meeting tried to begin identifying upcoming issues. Circulated in advance to the invitees, this item was titled "Major Problems in which the Counsellor's Office will be involved during the month of April (Agency representatives should be prepared to outline the nature of any such problems.)" Interior Undersecretary

Whitaker, who had represented the department at the committee meeting, followed up promptly. The next day, he sent Butz a list of five upcoming interagency issues that could be taken up by the counsellor and the NR Committee. As would be expected, he raised several issues of concern to Interior regarding other agencies. For example, he suggested that CEQ's proposed revisions of guidelines for each environmental impact statement (EIS) would convert the EIS into "a decision document" rather than an overview of the environmental aspects of a decision. Here was conflict between Interior and CEQ, both of which were under Butz's jurisdiction. Another suggestion related to the sale of water from dammed reservoirs controlled by Interior's Bureau of Reclamation and those of the Army Corps of Engineers. The duplication could lead to undesirable price competition, he said. Again, both agencies were in the NR counsellor's domain.[44]

However, some issues Whitaker raised affected even more agencies, reflecting the difficulty of policy coordination in the federal behemoth. What about exports of lumber from federal lands? At that time, lumber prices were increasing, partly due to scarce supply. This inflation had the potential of becoming a major media issue, with news outlets asking why timber from federal lands was being diverted from domestic consumption. The issue, of course, affected Interior and USDA's Forest Service, but Whitaker correctly noted that it also affected State, Treasury, Commerce, the Council of Economic Advisors, and the Office of the Special Trade Representative (an entity in EOP). Who was to be the lead administration person on this issue: Shultz as the majordomo for all economic issues or Butz as NR counsellor?

All in all, Whitaker's memo was a substantive and serious effort to contribute to the counsellor's work. That it reflected concerns by his department about other agencies—making the list somewhat parochial and self-serving—does not diminish its utility. In fact, Whitaker's list was a good embodiment of Nixon and Ehrlichman's desire that counsellors involve themselves in interagency problems to keep those issues away from the president. Here was an effort to get a bit ahead of the curve and deal with potential policy problems *before* they became public controversies. Whitaker's memo gives a glimpse of the kind of interagency and policy issues that the NR counsellor would have been involved in if the counsellorship concept had been longer lived. At the same time that Whitaker submitted his list, the three counsellor staffers and Fairbanks were also considering possible policy areas for Butz. Some of the policy areas they thought might be worthwhile included land use policy, weather modification, power plant location, and improved coordination of units involved in geophysical sciences.[45]

At the April 4 meeting of the Natural Resources Committee the principals continued to discuss architecture and kept on reviewing the proposed subcommittee structure, expected reports, and review procedures. Similarly, they discussed "proposed areas for major policy guidance from the Committee."[46] A large part of the meeting was a briefing by DiBona on the presidential energy message due to be released mid-month. The last meeting of the committee was on May 2. Despite the upheaval in the White House (which included Ehrlichman's resignation on April 30), the principals continued taking their assignment to the committee seriously. Attendance at the meeting included John Whitaker, Robert Long (USDA assistant secretary, representing Undersecretary Campbell), Dixy Lee Ray (AEC chairperson), Russell Train (CEQ chairperson), Robert M. White (NOAA administrator), and Robert Fri (EPA deputy administrator, representing Ruckelshaus, the agency's head).[47] The agenda included one substantive item, a detailed briefing on "current policy regarding implementation of Clean Air Act."[48] Here, at last, was a policy matter on the agenda for the committee's consideration. Several officials from OMB attended, given OMB's role in overseeing federal regulations. An agenda item on the proposed Department of Energy and Natural Resources (DENR) was deleted at the last minute. The third and last agenda item was the recurring topic of "discussion of significant items for decision during the month of May."[49]

SUBCOMMITTEES

In advance of the first meeting of the Natural Resources Committee, Butz circulated to the principals his tentative thinking about the committee's substructure. The purpose of these subunits "would be to coordinate implementation of policy emanating from the Counsellor and the Natural Resources Committee."[50] He proposed four subcommittees:

Subcommittee for Energy & Mineral Resources
Subcommittee for Land and Recreation Resources
Subcommittee for Oceanic, Atmospheric & Earth Sciences
Subcommittee for Water Resources

Another idea, floated informally, was to create a fifth group, the Subcommittee on Pollution Control and Abatement. It was not adopted.

Butz suggested to the principals that their representatives on subcommittees would "be a 'Bureau Chief' or the person holding a similar position in the organization represented." In the traditional structure of Cabinet departments at that time, bureau chiefs were at the level below assistant secretaries and reported to assistant secretaries. AEC and NOAA, lacking bureaus, would have to designate officials who would be at roughly the same bureaucratic level, so that the subcommittee members would be equals.

The simplest subcommittee was the one for oceanic, atmospheric, and earth sciences. Its membership would be limited to officials from NOAA and Interior's U.S. Geological Survey (and staff from the counsellor's office). The tentative subcommittee chair would (logically) be NOAA's administrator. But in discussions about its membership, the principals suggested adding to the subcommittee representatives from other agencies engaged in relevant activities: the Forest Service (USDA), Bureau of Reclamation (Interior), EPA (especially regarding its research and development activities), and CEQ.

The membership of other subcommittees was much more complicated and reflected the rationale for reorganizing the executive branch, whether through legislation or through a presidential counsellor system. The initial list for the Land and Recreation Resources Subcommittee (to be chaired by USDA Assistant Secretary Long—a significant decision by Butz, favoring his home department) consisted of five entities: Forest Service (USDA), Bureau of Land Management (Interior), National Park Service (Interior), Bureau of Sport Fisheries & Wildlife (Interior), and the Bureau of Outdoor Recreation (Interior). Other suggestions included the Army Corps of Engineers, NOAA, EPA, and CEQ. All but the Corps were added.[51] Similarly, the Water Resources Subcommittee started with five members: Bureau of Reclamation (Interior), Army Corps of Engineers, Soil Conservation Service (USDA), Office of Saline Water (Interior), and the Water Resources Council. EPA and CEQ were added.

The most extensive subcommittee was for energy and mineral resources. Given how federal energy policy and structure were in flux, this subcommittee's membership plan was the most tentative; eventual presidential and congressional decisions were likely to affect it. But, in the meantime, it was also the largest subcommittee, including AEC, several units from Interior, the Office of Pipeline Safety (DOT), and all of the power marketing agencies (such as TVA and the Bonneville Power Administration). Again, EPA and CEQ were added.

In sum, the most consistent change in subcommittee membership from Butz's March 20 proposal to his April 4 revision was that EPA and CEQ had been added to all four subcommittees. It was another indication of the problem of coordination in the capital, especially with some silo-style vertical agencies (such as the bureaus in USDA and Interior) versus the horizontal ones (EPA, CEQ). None of the subcommittees ever met. Within a month of finalizing the subcommittee structure and membership, the counsellor system was abolished. Similarly, Butz had originally envisioned that each subcommittee would establish temporary working groups to address "problems and opportunities identified by the subcommittees."[52] Like their parent subcommittees, no such working groups ever came into existence.

However, one example of an ad hoc and temporary subcommittee was the administration's Timber Supply Task Force. As mentioned in the preceding section, Interior Undersecretary Whitaker had suggested that the NR counsellor could get involved in the problem of rising lumber prices, but he noted that the subject affected more policy concerns and departments than just those within Butz's domain. A broad-based Timber Supply Task Force of the administration was indeed convened. Its membership included not only units in USDA and Interior (from Butz's area of responsibility) but also representatives of the Cost of Living Council and OMB.[53] Significantly, counsellor chief of staff Larson was tapped to chair the Task Force.[54] He hosted at least one of the meetings in Butz's OEOB office, amplifying the message of the centrality and power of the counsellor, even though the task force's membership and policy implications extended beyond Butz's domain. In terms of signaling power relationships to the bureaucracy, there was no mistaking who the big dog was in this case.

AGENCY REPORTING TO THE COUNSELLOR

Butz was also content to follow the precedents that Weinberger was setting regarding periodic reports from the agencies to the counsellor offices. As noted in chapter 4, Weinberger had issued his proposal to members of the Human Resources Committee on March 9. Butz issued his version on March 20, in anticipation of the first meeting of the Natural Resources Committee the next day.[55] However, reflecting the two counsellors'

different approaches, Butz's guidelines for reporting were much less stringent and controlling than Weinberger's. For example, Weinberger required weekly reports from the agencies in his domain, while Butz wanted only monthly reports. Weinberger's review and clearance procedures covered six categories of activities, while Butz listed only four, omitting "Major Program Regulations" and "Key Personnel Requirements." Finally, Weinberger's memo was essentially a promulgation of procedures and concluded with an almost perfunctory invitation: "Your comments would be welcome." Butz, on the other hand, described the procedures in his memo as "proposed" and ended with a full paragraph calling for feedback, including the statement, "I would appreciate it if you would review the attachments and let us have your comments, *negative, positive, or otherwise.*"[56] It was a much lighter touch than Weinberger's.

Indeed, on April 4, Butz issued a revision of the procedures based on feedback. The major substantive change was that he reduced the scope of the clearance procedures by deleting major regulatory proposals and instead limited the reporting to major legislative proposals.[57]

Based on the deadlines for the monthly reports, there was only one cycle of reports (in advance of the May monthly meeting of the full committee) before the termination of the counsellorships. Interior Undersecretary Whitaker submitted a three-page summary. In the category of "Priority Item Monitoring," he provided a listing of the department's implementation of the president's energy message (eight items), the trans-Alaska pipeline (one item), the Alaska Native Claims Settlement Act (three items), water resources management (three items), and land use reform legislation (two items). In the category of "Concern or Opportunity Alert" he listed three upcoming hearings, one hosted by the department's Bureau of Mines and two legislative hearings by Congress.[58]

NOAA administrator White's monthly report listed no items for priority monitoring and four categories of concern or opportunity. For "Continuing Major Concern," he listed the legislative status of a bill that would "have implications for funding the Coastal Zone Management Act" and the delays in appointments to the Marine Mammal Commission. Items "Of Clear Future Concern" included the legislative status of the High Seas Conservation Act and whether a move of NOAA offices should be delayed until it was certain if Congress would approve legislation creating DENR. For "Areas Offering Opportunities for Favorable Action by the Administration" he listed progress in consolidating the federal government's earthquake programs and asked if the committee wanted to recommend a consolidation of weather modification programs that were, at the time, ongoing in three departments. Finally, for "New Policies or Programs under Consideration," he suggested focusing on enhancing the federal government's monitoring of the environmental quality of the Great Lakes. He concluded the memo by noting that the agency "has no impending major policy statements or announcements and plans no major agency operating changes at this time."[59]

In all, these two reports were good indications of the wide scope of federal operations in the area of natural resources, of the preoccupations of departments and subdepartments with scores of issues, and the reactive nature of public administration.[60] Implicitly, the reports hint at the difficulties that a counsellor (or super-department secretary) would have with coordinating, let alone leading proactively. Big picture principles of public policy wear thin quickly when dealing with the substantive detail inherent in governmental operations.

RELATIONS WITH THE DOMESTIC COUNCIL

As discussed in chapters 2 and 3, Ehrlichman envisioned the counsellors taking over some of the work of the Domestic Council. DC staffing was being sharply reduced in the transition to the second term and replaced in part by the new staff for the counsellors. For Kenneth Cole, the new DC director, this was a sensitive situation. He did not want to see the council's centrality reduced, but he was loyal to Ehrlichman (to whom he reported) and understood that the counsellor structure represented Ehrlichman's preferences. As noted previously, Cole sought to achieve a good relationship between his staff and the counsellor offices by assigning to the three associate DC directors policy responsibilities identical to those of their respective counsellors. Also, the committees of principals that the counsellors established were viewed as committees within the Domestic Council. Finally, the offices of the three associate directors were adjacent to the office of "their" counsellor.

As with all other aspects of their performance in office, the relationship between the counsellor and the DC associate director reflected the personality and management style of the counsellor. As noted earlier, in the case of Counsellor Butz and Associate Director Fairbanks, there was a very harmonious relationship, which stemmed largely from Butz's passive and reactive approach to his responsibilities as counsellor. He had not coveted the job, had committed to the president to serve only two years, and was largely interested only in agricultural policy. Also, Butz and Fairbanks were not strangers; before the counsellor project, they had worked together on many issues. These factors contributed to a distinct working relationship, described by Fairbanks as "seamless." Butz treated Fairbanks practically as an equal rather than a subordinate. Their standard operating procedures were of Fairbanks proposing and Butz disposing. Fairbanks had hired at least two of Butz's three professional staffers (Schleede and Ross), had initiated the kick-off meeting in February, and saw just about every piece of paper that crossed Butz's (counsellor) desk. His input for all decisions was essential.[61]

Schleede considered Fairbanks his immediate boss, with Butz as the more remote and often absent public figure. "For all practical purposes," Schleede said, "Norm [Ross] and I were working for Dick Fairbanks as well as Secretary Butz and we saw a lot more of Dick, who was there all the time." Similarly, Whitaker (as probably the most important principal in the NR counsellor's cluster) had been Fairbanks's boss in the second half of the first term, so they had a close and trusting relationship.[62] If there was any rivalry for power, it would have been between Larson, a former assistant secretary, now Butz's chief of staff, and Fairbanks. However, the archival record and interviews (admittedly incomplete historical sources) did not document such tensions.

Perhaps the most accurate analogy to the working relationship between Counsellor Butz and Associate DC Director Fairbanks would be what Nixon sought for the leadership of Cabinet departments in the second term. The secretary would be the department's show horse, its public face to Congress, the media, and interest groups. Meanwhile, the undersecretary would be the department's workhorse, as the internal day-to-day manager of all manner of government business. Butz applied this model to the counsellorship, too—even though this was most definitely *not* what Nixon and Ehrlichman had in mind for a counsellor. Butz was the person of rank who gently presided over a complex working apparatus of experts, while Fairbanks was the in-house person who really made the wheels turn. Fairbanks was the master of substance, of the stupefying details of public policy. In their case it was a successful partnership, providing a model of one pattern of relationships between a counsellor and his counterpart associate DC director.

In all, did Butz's brief tenure contribute to improved public admin-istration? Or, from the opposite perspective, was it just another layer of bureaucracy? The difficulty of evaluating any of the counsellors is closely tied, of course, to the brevity of the experiment and the political chaos that was gradually engulfing the White House due to Watergate. In Butz's particular case, his light touch and lack of authentic interest makes it even harder to discern influence and impact. Further lowering expectations would be how quickly he lost the energy portfolio. From a minimalist viewpoint, it is difficult to make the case that Butz hampered the policy process or added another extraneous bureaucratic layer. As with all other counsellors, his staff was so small that they could produce almost no substantive policy work in that office. Butz and his staff tried to ride herd over developments and keep the administration on top of any impending issues. He and they really could not do much more than that. Perhaps the most accurate analysis would be to ask what would have happened if Butz's counsellor office had not existed. The porous relationship with Fairbanks was an indication that Butz and his staff did the work that the Domestic Council had done in the second half of the first term and then resumed doing after the counsellorship project was aborted. It was a lower-end staff coordination role. Butz did not want to be a majordomo or pooh-bah throwing his weight around. He was not a leader. Instead, he opted for a genial and almost symbolic role. His was a dutiful and passive counsellorship.

8

DEMISE, APRIL–MAY 1973

By April, the White House internal domestic policy structure seemed to have finally completed its shakedown cruise and settled into some degree of routine. The three counsellor offices were nearly fully staffed, and some minor office refurbishing of two of the counsellors' personal offices had been completed.[1] The triangular relationship between the counsellors, OMB, and the Domestic Council was somewhat untangled, at least enough to have ongoing working relationships. But trying to express the different roles of the three was still a bit tricky.

That spring, OMB Director Roy Ash was preparing to testify before a House Appropriations subcommittee on the FY1974 budget requests for various EOP components, including the Domestic Council. For his briefing book on DC's budget request, OMB staffers asked DC to submit proposed answers to questions that Ash might be asked. One dealt with the trilateral power structure of OMB, DC, and the counsellors. One could almost hear a member of Congress insinuate that this arrangement was duplicative. The answer suggested by the Domestic Council described the three-way relationship this way: "The role of the Domestic Counsel staff is to ensure the *coordination* amongst the various departments and agencies, the Congress, and the private sector *of information going to the President for his decision.* The Office of Management and Budget brings to these issues a critical *budget and technical expertise* and the Counsellors are, of course, responsible for the *development of the actual alternative proposals.*"[2]

In tandem to that seemingly definitive, yet vague, allocation of responsibilities, the administration continued to be careful to present the role of the counsellors as a prelude to a statutory reorganization that would have to be approved by Congress. So, for example, when a Senate subcommittee was considering the president's Reorganization Plan No. 1 of

1973 (which involved moving some agencies out of EOP), OMB Deputy Director Fred Malek emphasized that the counsellors were an internal administrative coordinating device. He said, "As far as the role of the counselors [is concerned], this is really only a very, very small step in the direction of the reorganization." Formal reorganization into the proposed super-departments continued to be "a very high priority. And we would be more appreciative of this subcommittee reserving an appropriate amount of time to deal with this very critical issue."[3]

In all, it looked like everything was going more as less as Nixon, Ehrlichman, and Haldeman had planned when they made their decisions about the super-secretaries right after the November election. The three counsellors were operating pretty much as they envisioned. The president could spend less time on domestic policy and his senior aides could spend less time on coordination and squabbles between agencies. But the pesky questions of possible White House ties to the June 1972 Watergate break-in, so successfully suppressed up to election day, just would not go away.

WATERGATE AND EHRLICHMAN

As winter turned to spring, Ehrlichman struggled mightily to maintain both the appearance and the substance of his role as one of the "Big Five" of the second term, as the assistant to the president for domestic affairs. As noted previously, Ehrlichman had arranged for the three counsellors to meet with the president on February 5 and March 6, he had spoken at the kick-off meeting of Weinberger's Committee on Human Resources on February 21, and on March 16 he expressed his dissatisfaction with Weinberger's pace as counsellor and as HEW secretary. In late March, Ash asked Ehrlichman to intervene with Weinberger because the OMB director perceived the HR counsellor's reporting requirements as impinging on his agency's role.

Another in-house activity in March involved Ehrlichman's desire to convene a large meeting of mid-ranking administration officials to discuss the administration's domestic policy goals for the second term. He wanted to hold this meeting so that the people who did not have routine direct contact with the top levels of the White House (or the president) would be able to have that opportunity. Ehrlichman intended this meeting to include the subcabinet (such as assistant secretaries and general counsels), heads of non-Cabinet agencies, the senior public information officer of each department and agency, and the senior congressional liaison officers. The tentative agenda included Ehrlichman giving an "overview on White House structure and the Counsellor system." Speaking later in the briefing would be "each Counsellor on the legislative outlook in their specific areas of responsibility." Ehrlichman wanted to achieve a greater coherence of the departments and for agencies to understand the underlying principles of what Nixon wanted to accomplish domestically in the second term and what their role would be in achieving those goals.[4]

Ehrlichman also continued in his public role as the chief domestic policy spokesperson for the administration. He briefed the White House press corps on February 8 and indicated that he would do so relatively regularly, perhaps every two weeks.[5] In early March, he granted interviews to CBS and *Newsweek*. At mid-month he talked to ABC and *US News & World Report*, and he lunched with PBS's Jim Lehrer. On February 19, he gave Jules Witcover of the *Washington Post* a one-hour interview.[6] That month he made several public appearances (such as the National League of Cities/Conference of Mayors) and held meetings in the White House with outside groups (such as the United States Chamber of Commerce) and with legislators. His in-house involvement with domestic policy and his attendance at decision-making meetings were routinely part of his daily schedule.[7] The developments about to consume him were apparently unexpected, because in mid-March he accepted a speaking engagement for May 7. It was for a national conference of finance analysts, and two of the counsellors had also accepted invitations to address that conference. Ehrlichman suggested they coordinate their messages and then seek to maximize media coverage of their remarks.[8]

As late as April 16, just two weeks before resigning, he was still providing advice and input about future counsellor activities. In mid-April Ehrlichman endorsed the idea of the three counsellors holding "public hearings" on spending proposals introduced by senators and members of Congress. It would be a turning of the tables on the legislative branch, with the legislators testifying and the counsellors and other Cabinet members grilling them. Ehrlichman thought it was a "first rate" idea.[9]

However, Ehrlichman's involvement with these in-house issues, including the counsellor structure and domestic policy, paled in comparison to the time he was having to spend on Watergate. By March, Ehrlichman was meeting almost daily with Nixon about Watergate and related matters (such as the "plumbers," the break-in at the office of Ellsberg's psychiatrist, etc.) as well as collateral meetings and telephone calls with John Dean, John Mitchell, and many others. On April 4, he met in Los Angeles with William Matthew Byrne Jr., the federal judge who was in the midst of the trial of Daniel Ellsberg over the release of the Pentagon Papers.

As Watergate took up more and more of his time Ehrlichman gradually abandoned any significant involvement in domestic policy in general and in the counsellor project in particular. At the last minute he backed out of the March 5 kick-off meeting of Counsellor Lynn's Community Development Committee. There is no paper record indicating any deep personal involvement on his part in late March when Ash had complained to him about Weinberger's proposed reporting procedures.

Ehrlichman's increasing preoccupation with Watergate was more discernibly apparent to the three DC associate directors. In the spring of 1973, they noticed that DC Director Cole was increasingly dealing directly with the president on domestic matters and that Ehrlichman was almost totally uninvolved in what was supposed to be his primary second-term role.[10] In fact, his presence was so rare that it was memorable when he did make an appearance. Associate Director for Natural Resources Richard Fairbanks recalled vividly a senior DC staff meeting (chaired by Cole) in February or March. Ehrlichman suddenly burst into the room and dramatically said that the president had just given him an assignment to investigate any possible links between the White House and Watergate. "If anyone in the room knows anything, please come and tell me," Fairbanks recalled Ehrlichman saying. Then, just as abruptly, he turned around and left.[11]

Watergate affected the counsellors not only by causing their supervisor, Ehrlichman, to be preoccupied with other matters but also by altering their relations with Congress. As described previously, when Weinberger and Lynn attended Senate confirmation hearings for their secretaryships, they were specifically asked if their presidential service as counsellor might reduce their availability to testify at future hearings due to presidential assertions of "executive privilege." No, Weinberger and Lynn assured the senators, they would not routinely invoke executive privilege regarding their presidential roles as counsellors. The only time they could imagine that their counsellorships would compel declining to testify related to drafts of policy proposals not yet decided by the president or personal conversations with the president. That was acceptable to the senators.

While Butz was not up for confirmation (because he was continuing as USDA secretary), he made a similar commitment at a more routine congressional hearing on March 5.[12]

But, as the congressional investigation of Watergate deepened, on March 12, the president drew the line on executive privilege more broadly than the degree to which Weinberger, Lynn, and Butz had already testified it would be drawn. As part of an overall statement on when he would invoke executive privilege, Nixon's new policy stated, "A Cabinet officer . . . who also holds a position as a member of the President's personal staff shall comply with any reasonable request to testify in his *non-White House capacity,* provided that the performance of his duties will not be seriously impaired thereby."[13]

While counsellors did not hold legally executed presidential commissions, they were funded by the White House office appropriation and used "The White House" stationery letterhead. This new policy seemed to ban them from testifying about much of their presidential service as counsellors. The impact of the statement would have harmed the credibility of Weinberger, Lynn, and Butz on Capitol Hill due to their earlier promises at congressional hearings, and it probably caused them to be unhappy about the situation Nixon had now put them in.

EXIT EHRLICHMAN, ENTER HAIG

From the perspective of anyone dealing with routine domestic policy making, by mid-April the White House had ceased functioning. Daily developments increasingly documented a stronger connection than Nixon had admitted up till then between the Watergate break-in and the White House staff and his reelection campaign. In early April, Haldeman discontinued his daily senior White House staff meetings (which had always included Ehrlichman). On April 19, the president met with the criminal lawyer whom Haldeman and Ehrlichman had hired to represent them regarding any potential criminal charges arising out of Watergate. On April 25, the White House press secretary said that Nixon was spending most of his time on Watergate.

On short notice, the three counsellors decided to meet to assess the situation. They got together on the morning of April 26 in Butz's counsellor office, from 8:55 to 9:40 A.M. No one else was in the room. They could talk frankly. At the same time that their counsellorships were finally hitting their stride, they could only feel abandoned by their senior patron, Ehrlichman. He had had no significant contact with them in more than a month. Not quite sure what, if anything, to do, the only decision they could make was to await further developments that were out of their control. In the meantime, they would do what was in their control—what they were charged by the president to do.[14]

The day after the counsellors met, the *New York Times* reported that the paralysis in the White House did not affect everything. It quoted one source as saying that "when it comes to issues, the agencies deal through *supercrats*... and there may not be any delays." The next paragraph quoted one of those "supercrats." Weinberger, identified both as "counselor" to the president and HEW secretary, was quoted as saying that "the fallout is not affecting the operations" of his department or other responsibilities. According to the article, that was because Weinberger (and others in his category) had "considerable authority to proceed on his own."[15] That is precisely how the counsellors behaved. Weinberger's Human Development Subcommittee met on May 1. The next day, Butz's Natural Resources Committee (of principals) had its regularly scheduled meeting. Also, on May 2, Lynn testified before Congress and was asked about an article in the *Journal of Housing* that discussed his counsellor role.[16] Weinberger's Health Subcommittee met on May 4. Until further notice, it was business as usual.

But not quite. For example, on May 4, Weinberger staffer Julia Vadala sent him an "Action Memorandum" on naming a chairperson for the Health Industry Advisory Committee. Things were being delayed at the top levels of the White House with no clear explanation of what was causing the delay. What the White House had already agreed to do was not being done. Vadala speculated that "perhaps the unsettling events surrounding the Watergate have caused the Domestic Council to delay the announcement which was to have been made in January." Still, the business of government needed to continue. The purpose of her memo was to suggest that Weinberger *call* Cole and maybe OMB Deputy Director Malek to get the necessary actions back on track. Given the fluidity of the situation, Weinberger more cautiously decided to *send* Cole a memo instead.[17] In general, according to the *Los Angeles Times,* little business was getting done in OEOB. "There has been a temporary hiatus in a lot of business," one OEOB source was quoted as saying.[18]

On April 30, four days after the three counsellors met with each other, Ehrlichman (and Haldeman) resigned.[19] The architect of the counsellor project was out. Ehrlichman remained physically in the White House for a few weeks (until May 16), but he no longer held any official position. Two days after his resignation, he sent to Weinberger (care of his counsellor office, not his HEW office) a short note, beginning "Dear Cap." Ehrlichman wrote that he wanted to ensure as smooth a transition as possible and urged Weinberger to continue serving on the White House staff. He wrote that if it would help in the transition, he would be glad to be in contact with Weinberger. However, "In view of the other demands on my time the best way to do this would be by appointment, I think."[20] Weinberger took his time replying, waiting more than a week. On May 10, he thanked Ehrlichman for the letter but explained that he had not followed up on Ehrlichman's offer because "I have not wished to bother you during this difficult time, so I have not called."[21]

After Ehrlichman's and Haldeman's departures, *US News & World Report* quickly speculated that "the 'super-cabinet' that Mr. Nixon set up a few months ago becomes more important now. President Nixon will rely heavily on these men who serve both as department heads and as counselors to the President."[22] Ostensibly filling the void of Ehrlichman's resignation, Nixon announced on May 2 that he was appointing Vice President Agnew to be vice chair of the Domestic Council. However, noted the *New York Times*, it was "a job that [Agnew] had been given and withdrawn twice before since 1969."[23] Still, dutifully, Weinberger quickly wrote to the vice president of the counsellor task force on national health insurance and very lightly invited Agnew's input, but not his participation or direction: "Due to your long-standing interest in the formulation of a health insurance policy, I welcome any ideas and suggestions which you would like us to explore." Weinberger pointedly explained that the task force was affiliated with "the Cabinet Committee on Human Resources," not mentioning any relationship with the Domestic Council.[24] Hence, he was not admitting to any formal connection Agnew might have, given his new appointment as DC vice chair, with Weinberger's work as counsellor.

On May 4, Nixon announced that he had appointed the U.S. Army's vice chief of staff, General Alexander Haig, to be Haldeman's replacement, at least on an interim basis. Haig was looking for fast, visible, tangible, and newsworthy ways for Nixon to break with the past, shake off Watergate, and restart the second term. Two days after arriving in the

White House, he proposed that Nixon cancel the counsellorships and the related push for congressionally approved reorganization: "Watergate had demolished Nixon's grand plan to reorganize the domestic Cabinet departments and some agencies into four superagencies (Human Resources, Natural Resources, Community Development, and Economic Affairs) under tighter control by the White House staff. It was clearly impossible under present circumstances for Nixon to push a grandiose reorganization of the federal government through a Congress that was on the verge of impeaching him."[25]

Haig's memoir is silent on the original source of the idea to disband the counsellorships. In an interview in 2007, Lynn said circumspectly that "the story is" that the idea came from OMB Director Ash, who saw Ehrlichman's departure and Nixon's political problems as an opportunity to accomplish something he had had in mind from the beginning regarding OMB's role.[26] A staffer in Lynn's office independently volunteered the same opinion.[27] Certainly, all that spring Weinberger's initiatives on agency reporting and his active role in OMB's management-by-objectives project had discomfited OMB. If it is accurate that Ash suggested to Haig that the super-secretary project should be canceled, it was a masterful maneuver in the cutthroat world of White House staff politics. Ash, in his later oral histories, did not indicate such a role (although he was never questioned directly about the matter). He merely said, "I'd let it atrophy on its own, as I knew it would."[28]

Theoretically, as an internal administrative mechanism, the counsellors could have continued even if Nixon dropped the pretext that counsellors were the first step to statutory reorganization. But Haig felt it was necessary to disband the counsellors and cancel the reorganization for a slightly different reason: "What was needed, instead, was decentralization of the decision-making process, a lower profile for the White House staff, and greater independence and visibility for the Cabinet."[29] In other words, the counsellors had come to represent the centralization of decision making in the second-term Nixon White House and the counterpart downgrading of the Cabinet. Here is how a White House aide described Haig's thinking at the time: "The feeling here was that it was in the President's interest to abolish the counselor operation for several reasons—to broaden his base of support, to wipe out any residual power left over from the Haldeman-Ehrlichman regime[,] and to illustrate his pledge to clean house."[30] Nixon, desperate to shake off Watergate, accepted Haig's suggestion with alacrity.[31]

CABINET MEETING, MAY 10, 1973

On May 9, the White House informed all Cabinet secretaries of a Cabinet meeting set for the next morning at nine o'clock. Also on May 9, in preparation for the Cabinet meeting, speechwriter Pat Buchanan had the relatively routine assignment to write talking points for the president to use in the meeting.[32] As usual, Weinberger was at his counsellor office first thing in the morning of May 10 and worked to catch up on correspondence and paperwork before walking across the alley to the Cabinet Room in the West Wing of the White House. He dictated a few letters, signing them "Counsellor to the President for Human Resources." He also sent a request to the print shop for five hundred routing slips with the letterhead "Office of the Counsellor to the President for Human Resources."[33] He had no idea what was about to happen.

The Cabinet meeting lasted nearly two hours, indicating it was a serious meeting, not a mere formality or photo opportunity. Nixon announced many sweeping personnel changes, including the naming of CIA chief James Schlesinger to be DOD secretary (Richardson had been named attorney general the previous week), the appointment of William Colby to replace Schlesinger at the CIA, the request for former treasury secretary John Connolly to be an unpaid presidential advisor with an office in OEOB, and the appointment of Fred Buzhardt Jr. as Watergate legal counsel.

Buchanan's talking points for the meeting suggested that the president make a more general point about the changes he was announcing. Nixon should discuss the "principle of de-centralization—putting decision-making power where problems are—[that] will be applied to the Executive Branch" and that "the door to the Oval Office will be open to every member of this Cabinet."[34] At the meeting, the president indeed made those points, emphasizing changing his relationships with the secretaries now that Haldeman and Ehrlichman were gone. Trying to put the best face on it, he said that "out of this may come a more effective operation" for the administration. He said, "We want the members of the Cabinet to take more of the responsibility for their particular department." He wanted a "lower White House profile" and to eliminate any "barrier" between him and the secretaries. He no longer wanted "Cabinet members as administrators" merely but also wanted them to engage in policy development, congressional relations, and selling the administration's programs to the public.[35]

Then, Nixon deviated from Buchanan's talking points and added a related topic Buchanan had not included. (This move suggests that Buchanan did not know about the additional topic and that Nixon and Haig did not share their decision with him or anyone else.) Nixon said that the counsellorships had been an "experiment" in anticipation of congressional approval of the reorganization bills creating the super-departments. But, "we have found that without the Congress approving those plans the ability to operate in a so-called counsellor level is very, very seriously impaired. Under the circumstances, therefore, I want you to know that I have decided that we will continue to expect that there be some coordination on a Cabinet committee basis. We cannot, it seems to me, go forward in a formal way on the counsellor basis as we had originally talked about." (The flimsiness of his excuse for canceling the counsellorships is demonstrated by the fact that none of the bills to create the Departments of Human Resources, Community Development, and Natural Resources had even been introduced in the new Congress.) He now wanted interdepartmental coordination to proceed on an "informal basis rather than a formalized basis." From now on, "the line of authority will run directly from each Cabinet officer to the President, rather than from the Counsellor to President." Nixon turned to Ash for verbal support, in part because the counsellorships had ostensibly been an implementation of the first-term Ash Council's recommendations (they were not, however, and as OMB director, Ash disagreed with the existence of the counsellors). Ash was delighted to help kill the concept. Of what Nixon had just announced, he said, "I think that most everybody involved would believe that would make a substantial improvement in the operating prospects." Nixon then moved on to the next topic in the Cabinet meeting. That was that. The counsellorship project was over.

White House Press Secretary Ron Ziegler then briefed the press on what the president had said at the Cabinet meeting. When he finished relaying the personnel appointments, he said,

In the Cabinet meeting this morning, the President also made reference to the fact that the White House or the Administration continues to move ahead . . . under a revised White House operational procedure, that he also intended to have, under this new procedure, more direct lines of communication with members of the Cabinet. And in this regard, he made reference to the fact that the Administration has sent to the Congress legislation suggesting certain reorganization of the various departments of government. As you know, earlier on, at the start of the second term, a procedure was set up where there would be three Counsellors to the President for the purpose of coordinating the overlapping activities of the various departments.

In the session this morning, the President pointed out that he wanted to have direct lines of communication with all members of the Cabinet and that the Counsellor role, as previously announced to you, would continue on an informal basis and not a formalized basis, as had originally been contemplated, pending the decision on the passing of the legislation which has been submitted to the Hill calling for such reorganization.

The President made the point that we have been experimenting with this particular Counsellor position as an operational procedure. . . . [T]he Counsellor role, as originally announced and conceived, would be moved aside at this time until legislation is passed.[36]

Reporters then wanted to clarify a few details about the disbanding of the super-secretaries:

Q. A point of clarification: Will Secretaries Butz, Lynn, and Weinberger give up their EOB offices and their extra titles as Counsellors to the President . . . ?

A. . . . In terms of the Counsellors giving up their offices in the EOB, that is something that I can't answer today. The President, in the Cabinet meeting this morning, simply made reference to the fact that he wants the interdepartmental coordination to move in a more informal way and not on such a formalized basis.

Q. . . . since that [reorganization] legislation has not gone anywhere in Congress, to speak of, and is not generally expected to go anywhere, is it a fair inference the President is dropping the Counsellor arrangement now for the foreseeable future?

A. . . . The Counsellor role, as earlier described to you, will not be in effect any longer.

Q. Butz, Lynn and Weinberger will not have the title of Counsellor any longer?

A. That is correct.[37]

Later, reporters continued to press Ziegler about the rationale for canceling the counsellors, beyond his talking point about increasing direct communication with Cabinet secretaries:

Q. What happened between the time that the Counsellor system
    was established and this new change in policy?
A. . . . the thing that has happened is that existing members of the
    White House staff who were here previously have left.[38]

A White House source restated Ziegler's answer more bluntly in the next day's *Washington Post*: "Ehrlichman was 'the key to the system—it couldn't work without him.'"[39] In other words, the counsellor setup was Ehrlichman's baby, and since he was gone, the project would be abandoned.

SHUT-DOWN

Weinberger, Lynn, and Butz were totally surprised. That Ziegler did not know if they would keep their OEOB offices was an indication of how hasty Nixon and Haig's decision had been. There had not been enough time to work out some of the important implementation details before the decision was announced. But the ever-efficient White House staff secretary, Bruce Kehrli, brutally cut off the funding for their counsellor offices effective the day of the Cabinet meeting. No transition, no shutdown time.[40]

The day after they lost their counsellorships, the three counsellors met for the last time since their appointment. On May 11, they met with DC Director Cole to coordinate the hand-off of the issues they were working on.[41] That they met with Cole was an indication that the Domestic Council was the "winner," presumptively taking over the domestic policy coordination that the counsellors had been doing.

Weinberger

As would be expected, Weinberger's shutdown of his office was the most thorough and paper oriented. As the entire counsellor staff had come from

HEW (and was reimbursed by the White House), it was easy for him to move them back to HEW full time.[42] Given Weinberger's broad ambitions for the counsellorship, even by May 10 a staffer did not feel that "the office began full operations."[43] The staffer wrote to him that many of the subcommittee and task force members "share our disappointment that the Cabinet Committee on Human Resources was terminated before it could fully meet the goals it was designed to serve."[44] On May 23, still using the White House stationery, Weinberger sent a memo to the members of the three subcommittees on his transition plans. He was seeking to maintain some continuity, even without his counsellorship. As part of Nixon's May 10 announcement,

> however, the President recognized the importance and emphasized the necessity of continuing the interagency work that had begun in the Counsellors' offices.
>
> My staff and I are presently working with the Domestic Council and OMB to determine precisely how the work we have initiated can be continued most effectively.
>
> Until a final decision is made on these matters, we will continue working with you in special task groups that have been organized around such topics as welfare reform, health insurance, and manpower revenue sharing. However, we will discontinue formal meetings of the Health, Income Security and Human Development working committees.[45]

On July 5, Weinberger wrapped up his work as counsellor with a final twelve-page report to Cole, Ash, and the new counsellor to the president for domestic affairs, Melvin Laird.[46] He reviewed all the projects his office had been actively working on and coordinating as of the termination of his counsellorship. Weinberger listed five projects in the area of health (national health insurance, health care cost control, emergency medical services, drug abuse prevention, and strategy for technological development for the handicapped); four in income security (welfare reform, workers' compensation, retirement income, and poverty statistics); and six in human development (manpower revenue sharing, education financing, Indian affairs, aging, veterans, and migrants).[47] For each of the fifteen subjects, he summarized the purpose of his involvement in that policy area, its current status, the participants in the effort, and his suggestions for future actions. It was typical Weinberger, to the very end.

Lynn

For Lynn, the president's announcement at the Cabinet meeting was a bolt out of the blue. His senior staffer, Cal Collier, was out of town that day, and in an interview thirty-five years later, Lynn laughingly recalled telling Collier over the telephone that he had no job to come back to.[48] Four days after the end of the counsellorships, Lynn had a previously scheduled appearance before a Senate appropriations subcommittee on HUD's FY1974 budget request. As an indication of the fast pace of events, Lynn still had not been told about the fate of his OEOB office:

SENATOR [WILLIAM] PROXMIRE [subcommittee chair (D-Wisc.)]:
 Will you still have that office in the Executive Office Building?
LYNN: I don't know whether that final decision has been made, but
 my guess would be that we will not.[49]

Lynn believed he had a responsibility to his staff members and made sure all were taken care of. Most of the staff reverted back to HUD. Before the counsellorship was abolished, Parker had transferred to the office of Len Garment, an attorney on the White House staff (who had worked with Nixon at a law firm in New York City). Garment was expanding his legal staff because he was—as it turned out, only briefly—Nixon's Watergate legal counsel. Then Parker rejoined Lynn at HUD. According to news reports at the time, of the three counsellors, Lynn was the most "upset at [the counsellor project's] early demise, and felt that the structure should have been given more time."[50]

Butz

Butz took the decision in stride. He had invested the least in the counsellor job. An hour after the May 10 Cabinet meeting, he had lunch with chief counsellor aide John Larson in the White House Mess and discussed the termination of the counsellor project. As soon as he got back to his OEOB office after lunch, he talked with another counsellor staffer, Glenn Schleede. Butz called Weinberger and Ash and then went out for a haircut.[51]

Butz signed two last letters that day. Both acknowledged receipt of a publication on minerals issued by the U.S. Geological Survey, a unit within the Interior Department. Early in the day he wrote a thank-you note to the Survey's director, stating that "this is a very welcome addition to my office here at the White House and contains a great deal of information to which

I shall refer frequently in my role as Counsellor for Natural Resources."
He signed the letter "Counsellor to the President for Natural Resources."[52]
Later that day, he signed another thank-you letter to the official who had
transmitted the publication to him, Interior's assistant secretary for congressional and public affairs. He signed it as USDA secretary.[53]

Two post–May 10 magazine articles summarized his thinking and his
counsellor record. One quoted "persons close to the Secretary" conveying that "he was not happy with the counselor concept" and that he now
"feels more comfortable in a Cabinet that is back fulfilling its traditional
role."[54] Another stated that he "showed no great interest in the affairs of
a department other than Agriculture" and that aide Larson's efforts to
energize the counsellor's work "were 'shot down by Butz's disinterest.'"[55]

All three of the professional NR counsellor staffers shifted quickly to
the Domestic Council and kept working on the same natural resources
issues. Fairbanks moved up DC's hierarchy, and Raoul-Duval replaced him
as the associate director for natural resources. Ross and Schleede became
assistant DC directors for natural resources.[56] They did little more than
change payrolls.

The month after he abolished the counsellor for natural resources position, Nixon formally submitted a reorganization bill to Congress to create
a Department of Energy and Natural Resources (DENR).[57] However, with
the disbanding of the super-secretary project in May and the broader effort
at grand statutory reorganization, his DENR plan was now in a wholly different political context. As a result of the energy crisis of 1973, Nixon was
seeking multiple initiatives to demonstrate that he was "doing something"
about the problem. Reorganization was one such "something."[58] The bill
was also part of a parallel effort by the White House to try to shake off
Watergate by demonstrating that it was engaging in business as usual. It
never passed.[59]

Less than a week after the May 10 Cabinet meeting ending the counsellorships, Cole met with Haig and laid out a plan for the DC to pick up the
counsellors' workload. Based on Cole's count, the three counsellors had
twenty staffers (professional and secretarial). Cole said he did not need all
twenty, that only eleven (five professional and six clerical) "were necessary
to replace Counsellor staffs."[60] Haig approved it. Ziegler announced the
new arrangement on May 24 but obscured the expanded staffing, focusing
on the promotion of five *current* staff members to higher positions in the
DC hierarchy and the addition of more principals to the council itself.[61]
Writing a year later, a British political scientist concluded that the abolition

of the counsellorships was not a "devastating blow to the new structure" of organizing White House staffing by functional policy areas. Rather, he agreed with an emerging consensus that the termination of the counsellor project was "just window dressing" because their coordinating roles in functional policy areas were merely shifted to the Domestic Council, not discontinued.[62] So ended Nixon's grand domestic reorganization. In terms of the White House power structure, it evaporated practically in an instant, leaving almost no trace behind and little discontinuity in the policy process.

9

LEGACY AND SIGNIFICANCE

History is dynamic. For example, the presidential hit parade changes over time. Truman's and Eisenhower's standings were low in the first decades after leaving office, but now (2009) each is much better regarded. In that vein, the story of Nixon's super-secretaries had a relatively permanent historical reputation. Something lasting less than half a year was assumed, ipso facto, to be of little consequence or importance. Then, Richard Nathan's negative, even sinister, judgment about it was widely accepted as the definitive post-hoc interpretation. In this revision of the given history, the counsellors have been presented as an interesting effort by a president seeking actually to *be* the chief of the executive branch. In particular, he used the novel variation of administrative reorganization for the grand reorganization template that had mostly been a dead-end and nonstarter for his twentieth-century predecessors. Besides the potential historical value of this recounting, it may also be relevant to studies of the presidency, Congress, and public administration.

The comparison in chapter 1 of the presidential and congressional *record* regarding grand reorganization pre- and post-counsellors documented that the super-secretary event may well have underestimated the counsellors as a significant hinge of history. Grand reorganization plans were routinely proposed by Nixon's twentieth-century predecessors but not by his successors. Instead, they opted at most for incremental and single-department reorganizations. At the other end of Pennsylvania Avenue, Congress had routinely passed reorganization acts, delegating to presidents the power to submit reorganization plans that were subject only to legislative veto. All presidents from Hoover to Nixon were given that power. After Nixon, Congress was increasingly hesitant, not giving it to Ford but giving it to Carter, only with more strings attached, and then giving Reagan even less reorganizing power. After Reagan, Congress stopped passing these across-the-board reorganization acts that gave broad restructuring powers to presidents. In that context, the super-secretaries were the last grand presidential reorganization effort.

Evaluating the super-secretaries or drawing lessons applicable to the future must be pursued with caution. There is a large political science and public administration literature on structural and statutory reorganization and, using the more recent term, organizational design. While much of the early literature was normative or descriptive, more recent work seeks methods of assessment and evaluation.[1] However, those approaches are not applicable to administrative reorganization at the top, absent structural and statutory reorganization. Therefore, this historical assessment uses two different approaches as a way of drawing conclusions about it. The super-secretaries are first evaluated as a stand-alone event with criteria that emerge directly from the stated and behind-the-scenes purposes of the project itself. This evaluation is an internal one based on the historical record. Second, the super-secretary reorganization is compared to other relatively similar presidential reorganizations. This is an effort at an external evaluation.

ASSESSING THE COUNSELLORS IN MEETING PRESIDENTIAL GOALS

Based on the information developed from this case study, there were three discernible types of goals that gave birth to the project: political, managerial, and structural. Some were stated openly and publicly, others indirectly or confidentially. Each of these three rationales needs to be examined in terms of the desired goals versus accomplishments.

Nixon's Political Goals for the Counsellors

President Nixon had had several overriding political goals for the second term. First, the counsellor project was part of his larger strategy of assuming more control over the executive branch during the second term. Other components of the strategy included administering loyalty questionnaires before appointing anyone to a Cabinet post, appointing first-term White House staffers to positions of responsibility in the departments and agencies, and strengthening the OMB's new management role (the "M" in OMB). The last included naming OMB Director Ash to serve concurrently as assistant to the president for management and approving OMB's management-by-objectives project.

Therefore, the first political evaluation question is, Did the counsellors contribute to giving the president more control over the executive branch? It appears that, had the experiment lasted longer, the counsellors would have helped assert presidential control over federal departments and agencies. The strongest indication comes from Weinberger's counsellor activities. He created three active subcommittees that met regularly (at first every two weeks, then monthly) and consisted of the working-level bureaucrats for that policy area. Rather than the sometimes figurehead secretaries, his subcommittee membership included the worker bees of federal administration. Some were assistant secretaries (presidential nominees in the subcabinet who were subject to Senate confirmation), administrators, assistant administrators, and sometimes bureau heads. These bureaucrats were where the action really was. So, it appears reasonable to conclude that had the super-secretary structure lasted longer, Weinberger would probably have contributed to greater presidential control over—or at least coordination between—executive branch agencies.

Nixon's second major political theme for the second term was to marginalize Congress and strengthen the executive's power vis-à-vis the legislative branch. Besides implementing an administrative (rather than legislative) reorganization through the counsellors, this political effort included impounding appropriated funds that fit the president's agenda, moving to implement manpower revenue sharing administratively, and vetoing spending bills that went beyond what Nixon wanted.

So, the second political evaluative question is, Did the counsellors help Nixon marginalize Congress? Based on the short time frame that the counsellors were in office, the answer would probably have to be no. During their confirmation process, Weinberger and Lynn both testified that they would not use their White House status to avoid dealing with Congress. Subsequent to becoming counsellors, there were several examples of all three counsellors testifying at congressional hearings in their capacity as counsellors rather than in their secretarial roles. They were functioning truly as super-secretaries, accepting the routine obligation of senior federal managers to appear before Congress to justify their proposals, policies, and budgets. They never invoked executive privilege.

Nixon's Management Goals for the Counsellors

One argument for the super-secretaries was that the new structure would rationalize the management of the federal executive branch. This is the rationale that had been strongly supported by the field of public administration ever since the Brownlow Committee. The discipline and literature accepted as a normative goal that the management of the federal government would be improved by reorganizations that placed all similar programs within the same department. Indeed, even in March 1974, after some of the Watergate revelations (but before the House Judiciary Committee's vote recommending impeachment and Nixon's subsequent resignation), a report by the National Academy of Public Administration to the Senate Watergate Committee (chaired by Ervin) continued to state the orthodoxy of the discipline's support for reorganization so that activities "which are closely related and interdependent" will be in the same department.[2]

Did Nixon's super-secretaries improve the rational management of the government? Yes. By giving the counsellors duties based on functions, Nixon had created a structure that brought together all like activities under one roof—albeit an administrative roof rather than one approved by Congress. The counsellors were dealing with people working in overlapping policy areas, which was relatively symbolic at the principals' level. However, especially regarding counsellor subcommittees, task forces, and ad hoc working groups, the super-secretaries were convening at the working level people and programs coming from different departments and agencies with overlapping policy roles. Weinberger demonstrated especially well the rationality of function-based federal organization and management.

Another argument behind the counsellor structure was the desire to minimize the issues that had to go to the president and to reduce the number of people who reported (at least theoretically and legally) to the president. Generally, public administration has supported reducing the number of direct reports and making the span of control more manageable. In part, this is about *incoming* policy matters that needed to be decided. Ehrlichman had described the goal of pushing decision making out of the White House. Did the super-secretaries accomplish this goal? It is certainly true that the coordinative work of the counsellors and their staffs appeared to suggest the potential of placing more decision making at their level and less at the presidential level. However, the scant historical record is insufficient to construct a definitive answer to the question.

A third managerial argument for the counsellors related to outgoing co-ordination. Nixon and Ehrlichman were hoping that the super-secretaries would help ensure the implementation of administrative policies as they filtered out from the center to the periphery. Was this goal accomplished? Again, the skimpy record is ambiguous. However, the potential for effective coordination of policy implementation was glimpsed from time to time. In particular, the self-appointed roles that Weinberger and Lynn adopted, as assistant president and as presidential coordinator, respectively, held out the distinct potential that this goal might have been accomplished over the longer term.

However, these management arguments for counsellors, based on co-ordinating incoming and outgoing policy matters, raise a final issue. Was it possible for the super-secretaries to be policy coordinators (whether incoming or outgoing) and not be the de facto line managers of all the departments, bureaus, and agencies in their domains? Weinberger tried to resolve this dilemma by simply asserting that he did not want day-to-day management responsibilities, but he created a reporting structure that in essence reflected precisely such control. Lynn tried for an "action forcing" reporting approach, believing it would be less likely to entangle him in management issues rather than policy matters. However, his approach did not last long enough to prove or refute his intent. Certainly, public administration concluded in the aftermath of World War II that, just as it is impossible to separate politics from administration, it is equally im-possible to separate policy from administration.[3] The literature suggests that it would stretch credulity to assume that the counsellors could have succeeded in threading the administrative needle so finely as to include policy without affecting management. Had the project lasted longer, this issue probably would have become more apparent.

Organizational Structure of Nixon's Counsellors

One of the critics of the super-secretary experiment was by Roy Ash, who said it was doomed to failure because the counsellors were concurrently serving as secretaries of departments. From this perspective, they were not neutral policy makers because there would always be the *appearance* (whether true or not was virtually irrelevant) that they would be parochial in protecting the interests of their respective departments. The National Academy of Public Administration also expressed disapproval of the "two-hatted" approach.[4] Alternately, this potential conflict of interest could lead to the opposite outcomes, of secretary-counsellors always deciding against their home departments to keep proving that they were impartial. There is little in the brief historical record that would confirm that either of such hypotheticals actually occurred, which may be taken as a refutation of the critique, but it would not be persuasive given the lack of opportunities for the circumstances to arise repeatedly.

Another critique of Nixon's counsellors was that he created two classes of Cabinet secretaries. The ones who were not counsellors were demoted to a kind of second-class secretaryship. The *Wall Street Journal*'s instant verdict the day after Nixon canceled the counsellors project was a validation of this perspective: "The counselor setup didn't seem to be working particularly well anyway, although top Nixon officials were saying as recently as last week that there hadn't been time for a fair test. Transportation Secretary Claude S. Brinegar made it known some time ago, for instance, that he didn't intend to go through Mr. Lynn on major transportation issues. Mr. Brinegar explained that he wasn't going 'to take orders from somebody who isn't involved in my affairs.'"[5]

In an interview, Lynn confirmed this situation as an ongoing problem inherent in the way Nixon and Ehrlichman constructed the super-secretary project (but not referring to his personal relationship with Brinegar). The problem could not be avoided given the structure. The only way to overcome that aspect of the project, he said, would be to rotate the counsellorship on a regular basis among the secretaries within that functional policy area.[6] This solution, of course, carries with it different potential negatives, such as inconsistency, varying personalities, and different Cabinet members possibly having different levels of presidential trust.

A third critique of the way Ehrlichman and Nixon structured the counsellor initiative related to overburdening the three men. Would it be possible to serve simultaneously as department secretary and counsellor? Of the three, Weinberger spent the most time in his counsellor office, estimated at about one-third of his time, yet his chief of staff quickly noted how overscheduled he was, believing he was stretched to the breaking point. Butz was the least dedicated to his counsellor responsibilities and made the least effort to exercise his powers. Lynn appeared to be the middle ground, trying to fulfill his secretarial duties and his self-definition of the counsellor as presidential coordinator. Still, it is asking a lot of one person to take on both roles. This problem may have become more apparent had the counsellor experiment lasted longer.

The last structural critique of Nixon's super-secretaries was that they merely created another bureaucratic layer of approvals and paperwork and, thereby, slowed down the already slow policy decision-making process. Was this indeed the case? From the modest historical record, it does not appear to be the case that the counsellors added a whole new (and implicitly unnecessary) step in the policy process. Ehrlichman made sure that the Domestic Council staff was cut back roughly in proportion to the size of the new counsellor staffs. A related effort by Ehrlichman to prevent duplication was by constituting the counsellors' committees of principals as DC committees.

Somebody at the senior levels of the federal government needs to coordinate different agencies involved in overlapping functional and policy areas. It would be unfair to judge the counsellors on the criterion of whether they *solved* any domestic problems. The big issues they dealt with were not subject to definitive and one-time solutions. A good example of this situation was Weinberger's subcommittee on national health insurance, an issue that was still on the front burner of U.S. domestic policy at the time of writing (2009). Rather, a more reasonable evaluation criterion might be to inquire if the counsellors moved the policy process along. Did they keep the policy ball rolling forward? Based on some of the few extant examples, whether through subcommittees or their own work, the counsellors indeed kept the policy process moving toward consensus and resolution. The unanswered historical question is how the mechanism would have fared in a highly contentious, zero-sum, and controversial policy area.

COMPARING THE COUNSELLOR PROJECT TO OTHER PRESIDENTIAL *ADMINISTRATIVE* REORGANIZATIONS

Historical comparisons and judgments are notoriously difficult to operationalize, especially accounting or discounting for time, place, and national culture.[7] Nonetheless, there are three examples from the period between World War II and the present (2009) that can be viewed as somewhat comparable to the counsellor project. These are instances of White House-based supra- or super-departmental reorganizations, partly or wholly implemented by a president through his administrative powers: FDR's appointment of a director of war mobilization (James Byrnes),

Nixon's elevation of George Shultz to be economic affairs super-secretary, and George W. Bush's appointment of Tom Ridge to serve as head of the White House's Office of Homeland Security (before the creation of the Department of Homeland Security).

As with many historical efforts at comparison, the *n* is too small for quantitative evaluation. However, qualitative assessments of the performance of Byrnes, Shultz, and Ridge can provide a modest basis for comparative juxtaposition with Nixon's three counsellors. The most significant evaluation approach comes from Herman Miles Somers's study of Byrnes. Somers adduced seven guiding principles undergirding Byrnes's success and then generalized that these were lasting principles for subsequent presidential policy coordinators:

> institutional status in the president's office
> jurisdiction over all relevant agencies
> focus limited to major policy issues
> noninvolvement in routine agency management
> exercising power to ensure implementation of decisions
> qualified for the role in terms of personal characteristics and
>   public standing
> overseeing only a small staff[8]

Somers's work had a lasting impact. It was republished by a commercial press in 1969 and continues to be cited broadly, for example, in Harold Relyea's evaluation of Ridge. Therefore, Somers's seven principles for the success of a presidential supra-agency policy coordinator are used here to provide a degree of evaluative analysis of Nixon's super-secretaries, especially in comparison with these three similar historical examples. However, there is a major limitation, too. Byrnes and Ridge wore only one hat, as presidential coordinators, while the counsellors and Shultz had two. This is a significant difference that cautions against excessive or simplistic historical comparisons.

President Roosevelt's general managerial style was to give senior civilian officials vague and overlapping roles. From his perspective, this built-in confusion and competition helped ensure that all important decisions would have to cross his desk. This practice, he believed, preserved his indispensability and centrality. As a result, he strongly preferred governance structures that were based solely on his administrative powers to create, modify, and cancel (usually by executive order) rather than structures requiring a congressional role. During the defense buildup (1939–1941) and the beginning of the war (1941–1942), he created an alphabet soup of temporary civilian agencies, almost all within EOP's Office for Emergency Management (OEM).

However, after the first year of the war, the vortex of inflationary pressures on wages and prices, shortages, economic mobilization, manpower supply, and conflicting priority-setting was beginning to spin out of control. In October 1942, Congress passed the Stabilization Act. After signing it, FDR asked Supreme Court Associate Justice James Byrnes, a former senator and member of the House, to resign and become director of the new Office of Economic Stabilization (OES).[9] When Byrnes assented, Roosevelt issued an executive order implementing the new legislation. In it he delegated extensive powers, tantamount to making Byrnes an economic czar. The president "turned over to Byrnes the management of the civilian economy in order to allow FDR to preside over the military and diplomatic management of the war."[10] Byrnes received an office in the newly built East Wing and hired a small staff. He "scrupulously avoided involvement in administrative details and operating responsibilities."[11] Rather, he would be involved in high-level decisions and policy and program coordination, and he would arbitrate disputes between agencies. In May 1943, another presidential executive order changed his title but not his role. The new title was director of the Office of War Mobilization (OWM). Eventually, Congress intervened to make that new agency statutory based and changed its name to the Office of War Mobilization and Reconversion (OWMR). However, in all these changes, Byrnes's role remained the same. He engaged in interagency adjudication and supervision of agencies and planning. A running theme of his work was ongoing conflict with the Bureau of the Budget. Reflecting his centrality, Byrnes was often referred to colloquially (and at least once by FDR) as the "Assistant President."[12]

A macro-evaluation of FDR's management of the civilian effort in support of the war (not Byrnes's work specifically) concluded that the president's "insufficient coordination of American war production impeded the efforts of the armies" and was one of his biggest mistakes in World War II.[13] Appraising Byrnes's own record shortly after the war, James Fesler et al. concluded that he had indeed been "*coordinating* in character, [and] contributed to the process of *smoothing out relationships* between WPB [War Production Board] and other agencies charged with responsibility for specific phases of the war program."[14] This was mild praise but reflected the difficulty of assessing the precise impact of any single office in a large and complex administrative effort. Applying Fesler's evaluation criterion to the super-secretaries, it is accurate to describe them, too, as presidential coordinators who tried to smooth out relationships between agencies and had ongoing run-ins with the president's budget agency.

Somers was much more definitive than Fesler that Byrnes had been successful, and he viewed OWMR as a template for future presidential coordinators. His seven principles for future successful White House initiatives were all extrapolated from Byrnes's work. Somers's somewhat reverse logic was that Byrnes had implemented the seven post-hoc principles that Somers drew from the Byrnes case and that they were the reason for Byrnes's success. Applying these principles to Nixon's counsellors shows several similarities. Both Byrnes's and Nixon's organizational strategies were super-departmental, based in the White House, staffed with a small number of aides, and were coordinative in nature. Most pointedly, the appointed officials were the *president's* men, holding positions that were administratively created (at least in part) by the president, that exercised powers delegated by the president, that served as the president's personal representative, and that reflected a president-centric approach to managing the executive branch. The counsellors largely met six of Somers's criteria. Weinberger, Lynn, and Butz had institutional status in the president's office and accordingly occupied suites in OEOB, had White House status (albeit via an administratively confidential presidential memorandum), had jurisdiction over all agencies operating in the scope of their portfolios, tried to limit themselves to top policy issues, tried to avoid involvement in routine operations of agencies and departments, had discernible amounts of power and control over agencies (delineated in Nixon's public statement of January 5, 1973), and had small staffs.

The most significant deviation from Somers's principles (besides the one-hatted versus two-hatted context) was whether they were qualified for their positions compared to Byrnes. All three counsellors had held subcabinet- or Cabinet-level positions in the Nixon's first term, but these were not comparable to the breadth and length of Byrnes's Washington experience. Weinberger came the closest to meeting Somers's qualification criterion. He, too, had been an elected legislator (California State Assembly) before his administrative career. He started as Governor Reagan's budget director, and Nixon appointed him to chair the Federal Trade Commission, then tapped him to be OMB's deputy director and, eventually, director. Weinberger had no specific experience in the HR area but had a record as an able political administrator. Lynn had been a corporate lawyer in private practice in Cleveland for almost twenty years before joining the Nixon administration. He evolved into a generalist administrator, shifting smoothly from general counsel to undersecretary at Commerce. He was chosen to be CD counsellor in part due to his apparent managerial competence and in part because of his loyalty and responsiveness to the White House. He was the kind of "organization man" that Nixon liked. Butz, the reluctant counsellor, was interested only in agricultural issues based on his academic and administrative careers. He viewed natural resources and environmental issues through that prism. In summary, based on their short record in office, the three counsellors most likely would be judged as meeting at least six of Somers's seven principles for success as a presidential super-departmental coordinator, with Weinberger coming the closest to meeting the seventh criterion, on qualifications.

The second historical comparison is to Treasury Secretary Shultz's role as assistant to the president for economic affairs at the same time the three counsellors were in place (and then for about another year until he resigned to work in the business sector). As noted in chapter 1, there were some similarities, as well as differences, between them. Notwithstanding the differences, it is compelling to compare Shultz's performance and impact in a super-secretary role with that of the counsellors because they served at the same time, were all two-hatted administrators, and occupied their positions via the same presidential administrative reform rather than being congressionally sanctioned. Little has been written by scholars assessing and evaluating Shultz's super-secretary role. Roger Porter came close, concluding that "Shultz personally *succeeded* in presiding over a process" of economic policy making for two reasons. First, he "involved most senior administration officials in issues that affected their interests," and, second, he "was by temperament more collegial in his approach." Porter did not express any parallel conclusions about the three counsellors. He noted the advantages and disadvantages of the "Super Secretary or Czar" approach but believed their work was too "short-lived" to evaluate.[15] Still, using Porter's two criteria for judging Shultz, roughly the same could be said about the counsellors. They developed organizational and communication infrastructures to involve relevant senior officials in policy discussions that pertained to their responsibilities. However, regarding collegiality, Butz had the lightest touch, Lynn was the most focused on active coordination, and Weinberger the most authoritarian. So, based on Porter's two measures, the three counsellors would generally be viewed as moderately or relatively successful in comparison to Shultz.

Given the similarities in the structure and context of Nixon's counsellors and Shultz, one can summarily judge that Shultz's work reflected the same six of Somers's seven principles that Weinberger, Lynn, and Butz did. However, somewhat unlike Lynn and Butz, Shultz also reflected Somers's principle regarding qualifications. His nongovernmental qualifications included earning a PhD from MIT and serving as a faculty member and dean of the University of Chicago Graduate School of Business. Shultz's governmental experience before serving as Nixon's super-secretary included a staff position on Eisenhower's Council of Economic Advisors and then, for Nixon, as labor secretary and then OMB director. Therefore, Shultz reflected all seven of Somers's principles. His reflecting all seven principles would then call for the conclusion that he was as successful as Byrnes, while the three counsellors were largely similar to Byrnes but not as completely similar as Shultz was.

This conclusion would then call attention to history's seeming blind spot about Shultz versus the counsellors. One of the major critiques of the counsellors was that they were doomed to fail because of potential conflicts of interest between their Cabinet roles and their White House positions. Shultz had the same two roles, but history judged him successful. As mentioned in chapter 1, Shultz himself believed the difference was that the economic affairs role involved more policy-making coordination than did the counsellors' responsibilities over entrenched bureaucracies. Still, the similarities in their two-hatted roles suggest that if history deems Shultz successful, then it must give the counsellors something of a passing grade, short of using a major criterion not yet raised.

The third example of a president's administratively executed reorganization relates to the immediate post-9/11 period. In October 2001, President George W. Bush appointed Pennsylvania governor Tom Ridge as assistant to the president for homeland security and head of the White House's new Office of Homeland Security (OHS). Ridge served in that position for about a year, until Bush signed a bill creating the Department of Homeland Security in November 2002 and named Ridge its secretary. Relyea specifically used Somers's seven standards to compare Ridge's OHS service to Byrnes's White House role but only glancingly mentioned the three counsellors as another somewhat similar historical example.[16] He identified several of Ridge's variances from Somers's seven principles as contributing to his limited degree of success. Like Byrnes, Ridge's power was based on presidential (rather than statutory) action, he had the president's personal confidence, and he had an office in the White House. However,

Ridge did not appear to have as much authority as Byrnes, he occasionally intervened in day-to-day operational decisions, he publicly lost some turf battles, and he had a large staff (numbering more than a hundred). Relyea concluded that Ridge and his OHS were "not altogether successful" and speculated that this limited success contributed to the president changing direction and asking Congress to create a new Cabinet department.[17] Like the three counsellors, Ridge served only briefly as a presidential coordinator. Therefore, conclusions and comparisons are equally tentative. The three counsellors more closely reflected Somers's criteria for success than Ridge did, suggesting that they were *positioned* to be somewhat more successful than Ridge, had all of their offices continued.

In this comparative context, Nixon's three counsellors can tentatively be judged moderately successful. More precisely, they possessed the presidential, organizational, and operational factors and some of the personal characteristics that probably would have led to generally positive results had their counsellor positions not been eliminated after less than half a year.

AN OVERLOOKED MODEL FOR THE MANAGERIAL PRESIDENCY

Nixon's super-secretaries may have closed the door on efforts at grand presidential reorganization, but his successors have energetically pursued other venues for increasing their ability to manage and govern the executive branch. The number of official and unofficial "czars" in the modern White House is an indication of the persistence of conditions similar to what motivated Nixon (in part). The central conclusion, of course, about Nixon's super-secretary experiment is the obvious and inescapable one, namely, that it did not last long enough to yield firm historical lessons. Still, from the tentative conclusions presented here, Nixon's super-secretary experiment deserves a modest presence in a discussion of presidential organizational design and management effectiveness. At the very least, it adds to a textured historical and institutional understanding of presidential efforts to manage the federal behemoth.

Lynn reflected on his counsellor experience thirty-five years later, after having served as OMB director for President Ford and then as a private sector CEO (for a large insurance company) for eight years. He suggested that the counsellors had the potential of balancing out the younger, "eager-beaver" types that so typically populate the White House and OMB staff. Counsellors, in theory, would usually be more senior people who had already proven themselves. Based on their station in life, they would not hesitate to say, if necessary, "I don't need this" and then walk out the door. The constructive conflict of the two types of people would, he believed, serve the president well.[18] The post-Watergate report of the National Academy of Public Administration (NAPA) also saw some positives in Nixon's idea. While criticizing some aspects of the counsellors, this blue ribbon panel of public administration's venerable scholars nonetheless proposed that future presidents be able to appoint "secretaries without portfolio," subject to Senate confirmation. They would be empowered to take on temporary assignments on behalf of the president, with a rank and place in the hierarchy that would permit them to break bureaucratic logjams.

These recommendations from Lynn and NAPA get to the essence of the super-secretary model. It was not merely another cluster of advisors to the president, another expansion of the White House and EOP staff. Counsellors were not *staff*. They were *line*. They spoke for the president as part of the management chain of decision making and policy making. Whether adopting the role that Weinberger accorded himself as assistant president or that Lynn assumed as presidential coordinator, they were speaking *for* the president. They could make decisions that did not need approval from any higher in the hierarchy, not the Domestic Council, not Ehrlichman, not the president. The super-secretaries had been given the power to make decisions in the president's name. It was precisely this characteristic that generated so much criticism, whether from rank-and-file Cabinet members or legislators protecting their pet policy areas. If only for that reason, it is no wonder the structure lasted less than half a year. The point was highlighted by the White House announcement in May 1973 explaining why Nixon had killed his counsellor project. The president now claimed he wanted more direct contact with his Cabinet secretaries, more open communication. No wonder there was such a collective sigh of relief and why no voices called for keeping the super-secretaries. Opposition to diminution of one's power is always fierce. Washington's status quo could not be overturned easily. Perhaps a powerful president just reelected and willing to fight could do so, but certainly not a weakened president struggling for survival. It is regrettable that this novel approach did not have a chance to play itself out, to demonstrate if such a relatively unorthodox template had something to offer future presidents who, whether they like it or not, are enveloped by the modern managerial presidency.

NOTES

PREFACE

1. Mazmanian and Lee, "Tradition Be Damned"; Mordecai Lee and Daniel Mazmanian, "Nixon's DENR Plan—Reorganization to What End?" unpublished article manuscript (typescript), September 1973, author's files.

2. Lee, "President Nixon Sees a 'Cover Up.'"

3. E-mail to the author from Mark Fischer, reference archivist/team leader, Nixon Presidential Library at National Archives II, College Park, Md., October 29, 2007.

CHAPTER 1. INTRODUCTION

1. Robert C. Toth, "Reorganization: Old Headache, New Twists," *Los Angeles Times,* November 29, 1972; Jack Rosenthal, "Nixon's Reorganization," *New York Times,* December 23, 1972.

2. Arnold, *Making the Managerial Presidency,* chaps. 8–9. The Ash Council also recommended strengthening the institutional presidency's managerial and policy-making roles. In 1970 Nixon submitted to Congress a reorganization plan for the Executive Office of the President (EOP). It refashioned the Bureau of the Budget (BOB) as the Office of Management and Budget (OMB) and established the Domestic Council (DC) to oversee policy making. The House Government Operations Committee recommended exercising the legislative veto to disallow the plan, but a House floor vote permitted Nixon's plan to go into effect. R. Moe, "Domestic Council," 255–56. John Ehrlichman, head of DC staff, had high hopes for it but gradually recognized its limitations. This realization directly influenced his planning to (largely) replace DC with super-secretaries in the second term.

3. Nixon, *Public Papers of the Presidents: 1971,* 56, 472–89; U.S. OMB, *Papers Relating to the President's Departmental Reorganization: March 1971;* AP, "Rep. Holifield Derides Agency Overhaul Move," *Washington Post,* February 21, 1971; Helen Thomas, "Nixon in San Clemente," *Redlands (Calif.) Daily Facts,* March 27, 1971. Beginning with the Kennedy administration, Holifield was involved in many reorganizations. Dyke and Gannon, *Chet Holifield,* 8–9, 117–20, 273, 299–300.

4. Nixon, *Public Papers of the Presidents: 1972,* 505–12; U.S. OMB, *Papers Relating to the President's Departmental Reorganization: Revised, February 1972;* House Committee on Government Operations, *Department of Community Development Act,* 92nd Cong., 2nd sess., H. Report 92–1096, 1972; Courtney R. Sheldon, "Congress Ignores Nixon Calls," *Christian Science Monitor,* August 8, 1972.

5. Carroll Kilpatrick, "Little Hope Seen on Hill for Nixon's Programs," *Washington*

Post, July 22, 1972; Nixon, *Public Papers of the Presidents: 1972,* 834, 919; Mansfield quote from *Congressional Record* 118:23 (September 8, 1972): 29814.

6. Pfiffner, *The President, the Budget, and Congress;* John F. Lawrence, "Tighter Rein on Bureaucracy to Be a Major Goal If Nixon Is Reelected," *Los Angeles Times,* August 23, 1972. At that time, the federal fiscal year ran from July 1 to June 30 and was named by the year in which it ended. Hence, Nixon's FY1974 budget proposal was submitted to Congress in January 1973 with the goal of passing all appropriations bills by July 1.

7. Counsellor and super-secretary are used synonymously in this text.

8. Arnold, *Making the Managerial Presidency;* R. Moe, *Administrative Renewal.*

9. Arnold, *Making the Managerial Presidency,* 336–37; Balogh, Grisinger, and Zelikow, *Making Democracy Work,* 46; J. Carter, *Why Not the Best?* 113; Seyb, "Reform as Affirmation."

10. The text of Reorganization Acts from 1932 through 1969 can be found in Emmerich, *Federal Organization and Administrative Management,* app. III-B. The 1971 act is in 85 Stat. 574.

11. Berg, "Lapse of Reorganization Authority," 197; R. Moe, *Administrative Renewal,* 103–17.

12. More recently, Congress has sometimes delegated to presidents the authority to submit a reorganization plan but usually limited the reorganization to one department or topic. During the George W. Bush administration, the statute creating the Department of Homeland Security required a final presidential reorganization plan. Earlier, President Clinton was given authority to reorganize the State Department and related activities (Sec. 1601, PL 105–277). In 2003, the House Committee on Government Reform held a hearing titled *Toward a Logical Government Structure: Restoring Executive Reorganization Authority* (108th Cong., 1st sess.), but no general reorganization legislation resulted.

13. Nathan, *Plot That Failed,* 68–69, 78–79; Nathan, *Administrative Presidency,* 51–53.

14. In reverse chronological order: Lewis, "Revisiting the Administrative Presidency," 61; Mason, *Richard Nixon and the Quest for a New Majority,* 204; Rudalevige, *Managing the President's Program,* 58; Light, *President's Agenda,* 116; Small, *Presidency of Richard Nixon,* 270–71; Arnold, *Making the Managerial Presidency,* 299; Hoff, *Nixon Reconsidered,* 74; T. Moe, "Politicized Presidency," 255–57; Lowi, *Personal President,* 144–45; Reichley, *Conservatives in an Age of Change,* 246; Schick, "Coordination Option," 108. David Crockett also cited Nathan but only in the context of all of Nixon's reorganization efforts, not just the 1973 super-secretaries. Crockett, *Running against the Grain,* 182n24.

15. In reverse chronological order: Rudalevige, *New Imperial Presidency,* 62; A. Dean, "Organization and Management of Federal Departments," 149; Heale, *Twentieth-Century America,* 265; Hess, *Organizing the Presidency,* 110; Patterson, *White House Staff,* 16; Aberbach and Rockman, *In the Web of Politics,* 31–32; Warshaw, *Powersharing,* 63.

16. Shultz and Dam, *Economic Policy,* 169; Malek, *Washington's Hidden Tragedy,* 233–34; A. Dean, "General Propositions of Organizational Design," 150.

17. Meier and Bohte, "Span of Control"; Wildavsky, *Politics of the Budgetary Process* (1974), xvii–xviii; (1979), xxvii–xxviii.

18. In reverse chronological order: Seidman, *Politics, Position, and Power,* 86–89; Fox et al., "Mini-Symposium"; Fox, "President's Proposals for Executive Reorganization"; Stenberg, "Some Comments on Reorganizing."

19. Fox et al., "Mini-Symposium," 493.

20. Newbold and Terry, "President's Committee on Administrative Management"; Milkis, "Remaking Government Institutions," 55; Gilmour in Fox et al., "Mini-Symposium," 495.

21. Emmerich, *Essays in Federal Reorganization;* Emmerich, *Federal Organization,* 203.

22. West, *Controlling the Bureaucracy;* T. Moe, "Politicized Presidency."

23. Klein, *Making It Perfectly Clear,* 364–68; Ehrlichman, *Witness to Power,* 211 (emphasis added).

24. Cronin, "Swelling of the Presidency," 36; R. Moe, "Domestic Council," 260, 263 (emphasis added).

25. Hoff, *Nixon Reconsidered,* 74.

26. Haldeman, *Ends of Power,* 168–69 (emphasis added).

27. Schell, *Time of Illusion,* 313 (emphasis added).

28. [Memo] For Ken Cole [staff director of the Domestic Council]; From Tod R. Hullin [Ehrlichman's executive assistant]; Subject: Counsellor Hearings; April 16, 1973, Folder: 2 April 1973–16 May 1973 [2 of 4], Box 65, Chronological File 1969–1973, John D. Ehrlichman Papers, SMOF, WHSF, NPL.

29. Ehrlichman, *Witness to Power,* 211; Reichley, *Conservatives in an Age of Change,* 246; Pious, "Sources of Domestic Policy Initiatives," 104; A. Dean, "Organization and Management of Federal Departments," 149.

30. *Weekly Compilation of Presidential Documents* 8:49 (December 4, 1972): 1711–12; 8:50 (December 11, 1972): 1728.

31. Kutler, *Abuse of Power,* 266.

32. Shultz and Dam, *Economic Policy,* 170, 176. Shultz continued as economic policy overseer after the three counsellors were relieved of their duties. He resigned a year later. However, after Haldeman and Ehrlichman resigned, Shultz's role had much less formality.

33. Seidman, *Politics, Position, and Power,* 86–87; Patterson, *White House Staff,* 26; T. Moe, "Politicized Presidency," 257; Tubbesing, "Predicting the Present," 494; Shani, "U.S. Federal Government Reorganization," 206.

34. Rudalevige, *New Imperial Presidency,* 62; Mason, *Richard Nixon and the Quest for a New Majority* 204; Hess, *Organizing the Presidency,* 110; Small, *Presidency of Richard Nixon,* 270; Milkis, "Remaking Government Institutions," 55.

35. Counselor of the Department, http://www.state.gov/s/c/ (accessed June 21, 2009).

36. Memorandum for: Bob Haldeman, John Ehrlichman; From: Ray Price; Re: "Counsellors" in the new reorganization; January 3, 1973, Folder: [Reorganization-EOP Part II], Box 174, Alphabetical Subject Files, H. R. Haldeman Papers, SMOF, WHSF, NPL.

37. Robert B. Semple Jr., "Nixon Executive Style Combines Desires for Order and Solitude," *New York Times,* January 12, 1970; Lawrence Laurent, "'President's Men,'"

Washington Post, October 30, 1969; Godfrey Sperling Jr., "Directives Stake Out Nixon's Domestic Program," *Christian Science Monitor,* April 1, 1969.

38. Paul Light defined staff as "those units that facilitate the activities of 'line,' or service delivery units." Light, *Thickening Government,* 29, table 1–8, note b.

39. Nixon, *Public Papers of the Presidents: 1969,* 12; *Official Congressional Directory* (1969), 421; *U.S. Government Organization Manual, 1971/72,* 58; *Official Congressional Directory* (1974), 467.

40. Nixon, *Public Papers of the Presidents: 1970,* 493, 517–18, 599.

41. Ibid., 1102. Rumsfeld was defense secretary during most of the George W. Bush administration (2001–2006).

42. Haldeman, *Haldeman Diaries,* 556–57.

43. *Weekly Compilation of Presidential Documents* 9:23 (June 11, 1973): 740–44.

CHAPTER 2. PLANNING, NOVEMBER 1972–JANUARY 1973

1. Kutler, *Wars of Watergate,* 245; Perlstein, *Nixonland,* 746 (original emphasis).

2. Memorandum Re: Post-Election Activities; November 6, 1972; n.a., p. 1 (emphasis added), Folder 4: August–December 1972, Office of Management and Budget, Box 72, Government File, William H. Taft IV Papers, MD/LoC.

3. Kutler, *Abuse of Power,* 146; Nixon, *RN,* 682; Haldeman, *Ends of Power,* 172. There are two authoritative transcripts of the Watergate part of the September 15, 1972, conversation: Kutler, *Abuse of Power,* 146–52, and the House Judiciary Committee's 1974 impeachment inquiry, http://nixon.archives.gov/forresearchers/find/tapes/watergate/trial/exhibit_04.pdf (accessed May 27, 2009). A summary of the conversation is in Kutler, *Wars of Watergate,* 222–26.

4. Memorandum for H. R. Haldeman; From Peter Flanigan; November 6, 1972; "Eyes Only," Folder: [CF] FG-10 The Cabinet [1971–1974], Box 18, Subject Files: Confidential Files 1969–1974, WHSF, NPL.

5. Memorandum for: The President; From: Peter Flanigan; Re: The Cabinet; November 6, 1972, p. 2, Folder: [CF] FG-10 The Cabinet [1971–1974], Box 18, Subject Files: Confidential Files 1969–1974.

6. This gender-specific nomenclature reflects the corporate world at that time.

7. The OEOB was originally the State, War, and Navy Building when constructed in the 1880s. It is now (2009) the Eisenhower Executive Office Building.

8. Memorandum for: The President; From: Peter Flanigan; November 6, 1972, pp. 2–3.

9. Ibid., p. 4.

10. Garnett D. Horner, "Transcript of Interview with President Nixon," *Washington Evening Star and Daily News,* November 9, 1972; Robert B. Semple Jr., "Aides Say Nixon's Plans Could Expand His Power," *New York Times,* November 10, 1972.

11. AP, "Nixon Holds Talks on Reorganization," *New York Times,* November 15, 1972; Spencer Rich, "Nixon Confers with Cabinet Aides on Reorganization," *Washington Post,* November 18, 1972; UPI, "Nixon Goes to Camp David to Work on Reorganization," *New York Times,* November 20, 1972.

12. Memorandum for: The President; From: Caspar W. Weinberger; Subject: Reor-

ganization along lines of "Corporate Executive Vice-Presidencies"; November 14, 1972, p. 1 (original emphasis), Folder: Caspar Weinberger 1972, Box 107, Alphabetical Name Files, Haldeman Papers. There is no record that Haldeman acted on the memo, and the fact that it was never returned to Weinberger with any of the adopt/do-not-adopt options check-marked suggests that he did not, thus diminishing the possibility that Reagan's super-secretaries at the state level were a precedent influencing Nixon's plan.

13. Dean, *Blind Ambition,* 155.

14. Haldeman, *Haldeman Diaries,* 534.

15. Diagram marked "II 11–16–72," Folder: Staff Reorganization: Concept & Reporting Relationships, Box 280, Alphabetical and Chronological Files—L. Higby [aide to Haldeman], Haldeman Papers.

16. Dean, *Blind Ambition,* 156–58. Ehrlichman's comment about making the birds sing presumably reflected his happiness at the president's approval of the reorganization concept. There also is a subtle, ominous undertone to the phrase—the implication of *making* the birds sing, that is, forcing them to.

17. Role of the Executive Secretaries, n.a., n.d., Folder: Staff Reorganization: Concept and Reporting Relationships, Box 280, Alphabetical and Chronological Files—L. Higby, Haldeman Papers.

18. Open Questions, n.a., n.d., Folder: Staff Reorganization: Concept and Reporting Relationships, Box 280, Alphabetical and Chronological Files—L. Higby, Haldeman Papers.

19. Joy Aschenbach, "Nixon Will Bypass Legislative Route in Reorganization," *Washington Sunday Star,* November 19, 1972.

20. Conversations 33–104 and 33–106, Tape 33, November 19, 1972, Nixon White House Tapes—Online, Nixon Presidential Library, http://nixon.archives.gov/for researchers/find/tapes/tape033/tape033.php (accessed May 15, 2009).

21. Conversation 33–108, in ibid.

22. Weinberger, *In the Arena,* 216.

23. Questionnaire administered to George H. W. Bush (relating to his service as ambassador to the United Nations) by John D. Ehrlichman, November 20, 1972, Folder: Notes 8/7/72–12/13/72 [5 of 9], Box 13, John D. Ehrlichman Notes of Meetings, SMOF, WHSF, NPL.

24. Loyalty questionnaire administered to Agriculture Secretary Earl Butz by John D. Ehrlichman, November 20, 1972, in ibid.

25. Ehrlichman, notes of Nixon meeting with Butz on November 20, 1972, at Camp David, in ibid. Butz, who could be politically savvy about the politics of agriculture, was tone deaf on this issue. After the inauguration, he sent the president a letter renewing his suggestions for more substantive and frequent Cabinet meetings. Nixon replied, "I appreciate having your views on this matter," a relatively overt rejection of the idea. Folder: (Material staffed in January 1973, #2), Box 57, Memoranda Files, Staff Secretary Files, SMOF, WHSF, NPL.

26. Meeting of President Nixon and John Ehrlichman with James Lynn, November 28, 1972, Folder: Notes 8/7/72–12/13/72 [7 of 9], Box 13, John D. Ehrlichman Notes of Meetings.

27. Weinberger's non-DOD memoirs do not mention his counsellor service. He recounts his Camp David meeting with Nixon solely regarding HEW, not the second

appointment as counsellor. Weinberger, *In the Arena,* 216–17. Weinberger eventually was defense secretary in the Reagan administration.

28. Rowland Evans and Robert Novak, "Nixon's Masterbureaucrats," *Washington Post,* November 22, 1972; "Nixon Courts Trouble on Hill," *Washington Post,* November 24, 1972.

29. Nixon, *Public Papers of the Presidents: 1972,* 1149–50.

30. Warber, *Executive Orders and the Modern Presidency;* Meyer, *With the Stroke of a Pen.*

31. Executive Order: Presidential Staff Assignments; Draft No. 2; November 19, 1972, Folder: Reorganization 1972/73 [4 of 5], Box 64, Subject Files, John W. Dean III Papers, SMOF, WHSF, NPL.

32. Addendum: Legal Status of Counsellors for Policy; n.d. (probably November 21, 1972), Folder: Reorganization 1972/73 [4 of 5], Box 64, Subject Files, Dean Papers.

33. Roy Ash, President's First Statement Re Organization; November 27, 1972, p. 3, Folder: Presidential Statements Re: Organization, Box 190, White House Budget Files, Staff Secretary Files.

34. Roy L. Ash, oral history, January 13, 1988, p. 42, NPL. He made a similar point when Reichley interviewed him. April 30, 1978, p. 8, Box 1, A. James Reichley Interview Transcripts, 1977–1981, Ford Presidential Library.

35. [Human Resources], Draft No. 1; November 22, 1972, Folder: General 1973, Box 471, Caspar Weinberger Papers, MD/LoC.

36. Reordering the President's Staff to Improve the Management of the Executive Branch, November 24, 1972, n.a., p. 3; Assignment of Assistants and Principal Advisers, Executive Office of the President (organization charts), n.a., n.d., p. 2, Folder: General 1973, Box 471, Weinberger Papers.

37. *Weekly Compilation of Presidential Documents* 8:49 (December 4, 1972): 1711–12.

38. Ibid., 8:50 (December 11, 1972): 1728.

39. Ibid., 8:51 (December 18, 1972): 1752–53.

40. Ibid., 1757.

41. Nixon, *Public Papers of the Presidents: 1972,* 1154–55.

42. Memorandum for: H. R. Haldeman and John Ehrlichman; From: Roy L. Ash; December 14, 1972, Folder: [Reorganization-EOP Part II], Box 174, Alphabetical Subject Files, Haldeman Papers.

43. Memorandum for: H. R. Haldeman; From: Bruce Kehrli; Subject: EOB Space Plan; December 15, 1972, Folder: Space [#2], Box 145, Memoranda Files, Staff Secretary Files.

44. Dana Mead, interview by author, June 1, 2007, p. 7.

45. Memorandum for: H. R. Haldeman; From: Bruce Kehrli; Subject: Payment of Counsellors' and Assistants' Staffs; December 18, 1973, Folder: Chronological December 1972, Box 74, Memoranda Files, Staff Secretary Files.

46. Memorandum for: John Ehrlichman—Via Walter Minnick; From: Mark W. Alger; Subject: Presidential Counsellors; December 18, 1972, p. 7, Folder: General 1973, Box 471, Weinberger Papers.

47. Ibid., p. 2.

48. Memorandum for: Mr. Weinberger; From: Mark W. Alger; Subject: Memo to Mr. Ehrlichman, December 19, 1972, Folder: General 1973, Box 471, Weinberger Papers.

49. The Role of the Counsellors (memo); December 29, 1972; n.a., Folder: General 1973, Box 471, Weinberger Papers.

50. OMB Route Slip; To: Mr. Weinberger; From: MWA [Mark W. Alger]; January 3, 1973, Folder: General 1973, Box 471, Weinberger Papers.

51. Nixon, *Public Papers of the Presidents: 1972*, B-20.

52. Rowland Evans and Robert Novak, "Some Get Power, Others Long Black Limousines," *Washington Post*, December 21, 1972; "Behind Nixon's Reorganization," *US News & World Report* 74:1 (January 1, 1973). Newsmagazines post-dated their issues. While the date of this issue was 1973, it would have been released in late December.

53. Jack Rosenthal, "Nixon's Reorganization: President Seems Determined to Take Firm Control of U.S. Bureaucracy," *New York Times*, December 23, 1972; David S. Broder, "Nixon Acts to Take Control of Agencies," *Washington Post*, December 24, 1972.

54. Letter from Senator Sam J. Ervin Jr. to President Nixon; December 20, 1972; Letter from Tom C. Korologos, Special Assistant for Legislative Affairs, to Senator Ervin, December 21, 1972, both in Folder: [Reorganization-EOP Part II], Box 174, Alphabetical Subject Files, Haldeman Papers. Separately, and more publicly, Ervin also opposed Nixon's impoundments of appropriated funds in late 1972 and early 1973.

55. John Dean, interview by author, February 13, 2007. As the third-ranking member of the Senate Government Operations Committee in the 1971–1972 Congress, Ervin evinced no interest in reorganization, attending none of the nine hearings on Nixon's reorganization bills.

56. Ervin, *Whole Truth*, 5.

57. Bob Woodward and Carl Bernstein, "Oct. 15 Halt to Hearings Seen Likely," *Washington Post*, August 8, 1973.

58. Memorandum for: Roy Ash, John Ehrlichman, H. R. Haldeman; From: John Dean; Subject: Reorganization of Executive Branch; January 2, 1973, Folder: [Reorganization-EOP Part II], Box 174, Alphabetical Subject Files, Haldeman Papers.

59. Memorandum; From: John Dean; Subject: Methods for Reorganizing the Executive Branch; January 2, 1973, p. 2, Folder: [Reorganization-EOP Part II], Box 174, Alphabetical Subject Files, Haldeman Papers.

60. [Draft] Presidential memorandum, Subject: Restructuring of Staff Assignments in the Executive Office of the President, Tab H, p. 3, Folder: [Reorganization-EOP Part II], Box 174, Alphabetical Subject Files, Haldeman Papers. This undated memo was ultimately distributed to the three counsellors without change. Folder: Counsellor Butz–Correspondence [2 of 2], Box 1, Earl Butz Papers, SMOF, WHCF, NPL.

61. Ibid.

62. Ehrlichman, *Witness to Power*, 364–65.

63. Memorandum for: Bob Haldeman and John Ehrlichman; From: Ray Price; Subject: "Counsellors" in the new reorganization; January 3, 1973, Folder: [Reorganization-EOP Part II], Box 174, Alphabetical Subject Files, Haldeman Papers. Oddly, in Price's memoirs, he spells Weinberger, Lynn, and Butz's title "counselor." Price, *With Nixon*, 197. Perhaps that reflected his unhappiness with the decision that they would have the identical titles as the other (and, for him) real counsellors.

64. Schedule for Thursday, January 4, 1973, Folder: [Appointment Schedule for John D. Ehrlichman, 1969–1973], Box 2, Appointment Calendars and Diaries 1969–1973, Ehrlichman Papers.

65. Memorandum for: H. R. Haldeman; From: Bruce Kehrli; Subject: Reorganization Documents; January 4, 1973, Folder: Chronological January 1973 [#2], Box 74, Memoranda Files, Staff Secretary Files.

66. [Memo] For Bruce Kehrli; From Tod R. Hullin; January 5, 1973, Folder: 2 January–31 January 1973 [1 of 5], Box 63, Chronological File 1969–1973, Ehrlichman Papers. OMB had been the lead agency in pushing the president's 1971–1972 requests to Congress to approve legislation for the super-departments, based on the recommendations of the Ash Council.

67. Memorandum for: The President; From: Ken Cole; Subject: Domestic Policy, n.d. [stamped "Received Jan 4 1973 Central Files"], Folder: Domestic Council Issues (2), Box 12, Norman Ross Papers, Ford Presidential Library.

68. A recording of the January 4, 1973, meeting was released by the Nixon Presidential Library in mid-2009. While the sound quality is low, Nixon's comments clearly demonstrate his commitment to the project and his understanding of its details. Conversation 393–11b, http://nixon.archives.gov/forresearchers/find/tapes/tape393/393–011b.mp3 (accessed June 23, 2009).

69. Memorandum for: Mr. Roy Ash; From: Bruce Kehrli; Subject: Reorganization Legislation Options; January 5, 1973, Folder: Chronological January 1973 [#2], Box 74, Memoranda Files, Staff Secretary Files.

70. Memorandum for: Caspar Weinberger; From Tod R. Hullin, January 4, 1973, Folder: 2 January 1973–31 January 1973 [1 of 5], Box 63, Chronological File 1969–1973, Ehrlichman Papers.

71. "Presidential Policy Guidance: Economic Affairs," Redirecting Executive Branch Management (slides), Folder: Bi-Partisan Leaders Organization Briefing, Box 68, Speeches and Briefing 1970–1973, Ehrlichman Papers. See also appendix A in Memorandum; From: John Dean; Subject: Methods for Reorganizing the Executive Branch; January 2, 1973, p. 2, Folder: [Reorganization-EOP Part II], Box 174, Alphabetical Subject Files, Haldeman Papers.

CHAPTER 3. LAUNCH, JANUARY–FEBRUARY 1973

1. Carroll Kilpatrick, "Nixon Vows Future Hill Consultation," *Washington Post*, January 6, 1973. Senator Sam Ervin, as incoming chair of the Government Operations Committee, was invited. When Ehrlichman met with the president the day before the breakfast, he said that Ervin was expected to attend. Recording of Nixon-Ehrlichman meeting, http://nixon.archives.gov/forresearchers/find/tapes/tape393/393–011b.mp3 (accessed June 23, 2009). However, an ice storm in North Carolina prevented him from returning to the capital for a few days. Ervin, *Whole Truth*, 18.

2. Folder: Friday, January 5, 1973, Leadership Meeting, Box 82, President's Speech File 1969–1974, President's Personal File, NPL.

3. Transcript, Remarks of the President at a Bipartisan Leadership Breakfast, January 5, 1973, Office of the White House Press Secretary, p. 2, Folder: Friday, January 5, 1973, Leadership Meeting, Box 82, President's Speech File 1969–1974.

4. Redirecting Executive Branch Management (slides), Folder: Bi-Partisan Leaders Organization Briefing, Box 68, Speeches and Briefing 1970–1973, Ehrlichman Papers.

5. Transcript, Remarks of the President at a Bipartisan Leadership Breakfast, January 5, 1973, pp. 3, 5–6. Anderson ran as a third-party candidate in the 1980 presidential election, getting slightly less than 7 percent of the popular vote.

6. Transcript, Remarks of the President at a Bipartisan Leadership Breakfast, January 5, 1973, p. 12.

7. Ambrose, *Nixon,* vol. 3, *Ruin and Recovery,* 47, 600n31.

8. Press Conference of John D. Ehrlichman, Assistant to the President for Domestic Affairs, January 5, 1973 (transcript), Office of the White House Press Secretary, p. 6, Folder: Bi-Partisan Leaders Organization Briefing, Box 68, Speeches and Briefing 1970–1973, Ehrlichman Papers.

9. Emmerich, *Federal Organization,* app. I.

10. Letter from Tod R. Hullin, Executive Assistant to John D. Ehrlichman, to Congressman Chet Holifield, January 5, 1973, Folder: 2 January–31 January 1973 [1 of 5], Box 63, Chronological File 1969–1973, Ehrlichman Papers.

11. Nixon, *Public Papers of the Presidents of the United States: 1973,* 3.

12. Ibid.

13. UPI, "Cabinet Powers Extended," *Greenville (Miss.) Delta Democrat-Times,* January 5, 1973.

14. Press Conference of John D. Ehrlichman, Assistant to the President for Domestic Affairs, January 5, 1973, p. 13.

15. Ibid., p. 10.

16. Ibid., pp. 3, 14, 18.

17. Schedule for Friday, January 5, 1973, Folder: [Appointment Schedule for John D. Ehrlichman, 1969–1973], Box 2, Appointment Calendars and Diaries 1969–1973, Ehrlichman Papers; Eugene V. Risher, "Nixon Ready for Second Term," *Coshocton (Ohio) Tribune,* January 17, 1973; UPI, "Muscle Power Given to Four in Cabinet," *Hartford Courant,* January 6, 1973.

18. John Herbers, "Nixon Increases Scope of Duties for 3 in Cabinet; Executive Order; Reorganization Plans Advanced without Congress Action," *New York Times,* January 6, 1973.

19. Lou Cannon, "President Realigns His Staff: Butz, Lynn, Weinberger in Super-Cabinet," *Washington Post,* January 6, 1973.

20. Norman Kempster, "Nixon Reorganizes Executive," *Lowell (Mass.) Sun,* January 6, 1973.

21. John Herbers, "Nixon Increases Scope of Duties for 3 in Cabinet; Executive Order; Reorganization Plans Advanced without Congress Action," *New York Times,* January 6, 1973.

22. "Executive Reorganization," *Congressional Record* 119:1 (January 6, 1973): 432–33. Ribicoff mistakenly referred to the president's plan as an executive order. Adding to the peculiarity of Ribicoff not convening his subcommittee to consider his opposition to the counsellor reorganization is the fact that, later, in 1973–1974 he held seven hearings on Nixon's post-counsellor proposal for a Department of Energy and Natural Resources. Senate Subcommittee on Reorganization, Research, and International Organizations, Committee on Government Operations, *Establish a Department of Energy and Natural Resources* (hearings), 93rd Cong. 1st sess., 1973; *To Establish a Department of Energy and Natural Resources* (hearings), 93rd Cong., 2nd sess., 1974.

23. Quotes from "*Today Show* Transcript," *Congressional Record* 119:1 (January 16, 1973): 1297–98.

24. "Nixon Evades Congress to Reorganize Cabinet," *Bennington (Vt.) Banner,* January 6, 1973.

25. "'Supercabinet'" (editorial), *New York Times,* January 14, 1973.

26. "Creating a 'Supercabinet'" (editorial), *Washington Post,* January 15, 1973.

27. Ernest B. Furgurson, "Felony Committed against U.S. Natural Resources," *Los Angeles Times,* January 14, 1973.

28. *The Proceedings of* Meet the Press, January 7, 1973 (transcript), 17:1 (Washington, D.C.: Merkle Press, 1973), Box 259, Lawrence Spivak Papers, MD/LoC.

29. Role of the Counsellors, n.a., n.d., attached to Memorandum for: Honorable Earl Butz; From: Tod R. Hullin; n.t.; January 6, 1973 (original emphasis), Folder: Counsellor Butz—Correspondence [folder 2 of 2], Box 1, Butz Papers. Identical memos went to the other two counsellors. For Weinberger's, see Folder: General 1973, Box 471, Weinberger Papers. For Lynn's, see Folder: 2 January–31 January 1973 [1 of 5], Box 63, Chronological File 1969–1973, Ehrlichman Papers. Undoubtedly, this memo was from and by Ehrlichman and probably included his revisions to Dean's draft of January 2.

30. Dean interview.

31. Ibid.

32. Role of the Counsellors memo, pp. 1, 2.

33. "Presidential Policy Guidance (Domestic Affairs)," Redirecting Executive Branch Management (slides), Folder: Bi-Partisan Leaders Organization Briefing, Box 68, Speeches and Briefing 1970–1973, Ehrlichman Papers.

34. Role of the Counsellors memo, p. 4.

35. Ibid., p. 2.

36. Ibid., p. 3.

37. Ibid., p. 6 (emphasis added).

38. Ibid., pp. 5–6.

39. Ibid., p. 2.

40. The memo explicitly stated on page 1 that the counsellors were part of the Executive Office of the President. On the other hand, it described the counsellor's staff as needing to be seen as "'the President's men.'" Role of the Counsellors memo, p. 5. The ostensible organizational location of the counsellors in EOP was contradicted by three details. First, the letterhead used was "The White House," not "Executive Office of the President." Second, the counsellors' staff salaries were paid (reimbursed, actually) from the budget of the White House Office. Third, their formal title was "Counsellor *to the President* for ____." The one-time wording in the secret memo would yield to actual practice. Therefore, the counsellors are described here as part of the White House, not EOP.

41. U.S. Constitution, Article II, sec. 1; Fisher, *Politics of Executive Privilege,* 72–73, chap. 10; Rozell, *Executive Privilege,* chap. 3.

42. Rozell, *Executive Privilege,* 58.

43. This already fragmented committee jurisdiction over one department gives lie to the criticism that approval of Nixon's super-department reorganization would be difficult politically because it would force Congress to reorganize its committees.

44. OMB directors were not subject to Senate confirmation until shortly thereafter.

45. Senate Committee on Finance, *Nominations of Caspar W. Weinberger, of California, to Be Secretary of Health, Education, and Welfare, and Frank C. Carlucci, of Pennsylvania, to Be Under Secretary of Health, Education, and Welfare* (hearing), 93rd Cong., 1st sess., 1973, 3–18.

46. Senate Committee on Labor and Public Welfare, *Caspar W. Weinberger to Be Secretary of Health, Education, and Welfare* (hearings), 93rd Cong., 1st sess., 1973, 2–6, 28, 39.

47. J. Weinberger, *As Ever,* 53. Weinberger, circumspect and diplomatic in public, was more candid in private. He told the president, "I regarded Teddy Kennedy as the worst demagogue in the Senate and 'the least of the Kennedys.'" Memorandum for the File; Subject: Meeting with the President on September 17, 1973; p. 3, Folder 3: DHEW [2 of 3], Box 67, Government File, W. Taft Papers.

48. "Executive Session," *Congressional Record* 119:4 (February 8, 1973): 4087–98.

49. Senate Committee on Banking, Housing, and Urban Affairs, *Nomination of James T. Lynn* (hearing), 93rd Cong., 1st sess., 1973, 8–10, 21–22, 50, 58.

50. Ibid., Executive Report 93–4, pp. 1–2, 6–7.

51. "Nomination of James T. Lynn to Be Secretary of Housing and Urban Development," *Congressional Record* 119:3 (January 31, 1973): 2783–95.

52. House Committee on Appropriations, *Treasury, Postal Service, and General Government Appropriations for Fiscal Year 1974* (hearings), 93rd Cong., 1st sess., 1973, 376.

53. Senate Committee on Labor and Public Welfare, *Caspar W. Weinberger to Be Secretary,* 39. In another variation, Weinberger was called "one of three new 'super-counselors.'" Lee Byrd, "Cap the Knife: Blade Honed for HEW Post," *Los Angeles Times,* February 8, 1973.

54. Senate Committee on Banking, Housing, and Urban Affairs, *Nomination of James T. Lynn,* 10.

55. Senate Committee on Commerce, *Nominations—January 1973* (hearings), 93rd Cong., 1st sess., 1973, 14–15; Peter Braestrup, "DOT Nominee Plans to Run Show," *Washington Post,* January 10, 1973.

56. Senate Committee on Labor and Public Welfare, *Nomination [of Peter Brennan to Be Secretary of Labor]* (hearings), 93rd Cong., 1st sess., 1973, 11.

57. Ibid., 11–12.

58. Nixon, *Public Papers of the Presidents: 1973,* 87–88.

59. Ibid., 72.

60. Nixon, *Public Papers of the Presidents: 1969,* 56–57; *1970,* 517–18.

61. *Congressional Directory* (1973), 467–68. Similarly, Shultz and Ash were not in the official protocol list in the *Congressional Directory* for 1973 even though they, too, had been named assistants to the president.

62. Memorandum for: H. R. Haldeman; From: Bruce Kehrli; Subject: White House Precedence List; March 8, 1973, Folder: Chronological March 1973 [#2], Box 75, Memoranda Files, Staff Secretary Files.

63. Memorandum for: David Parker; From: Bruce Kehrli; Subject: Oath Ceremony for Roy Ash, George Shultz, Earl Butz, James Lynn, and Caspar Weinberger as Assistants

and Counsellors to the President; February 12, 1973 (emphasis added), Folder: Chronological File February 1973 [#2], Box 74, Memoranda Files, Staff Secretary Files. A signed commission would provide no legal standing until the official had taken the oath of office.

CHAPTER 4. IN OPERATION, JANUARY–APRIL 1973

1. Senate Committee on Finance, *Nominations of Caspar W. Weinberger*, 10; Senate Committee on Banking, Housing, and Urban Affairs, *Nomination of James T. Lynn*, 10. Lynn's use of the passive tense had the effect of emphasizing the subordinate role of the counsellor vis-à-vis senior White House staff.

2. Schedule for Monday, January 8, 1973, Folder: [Appointment Schedule for John D. Ehrlichman, 1969–1973], Box 2, Appointment Calendars and Diaries 1969–1973, Ehrlichman Papers.

3. Memorandum for: John Ehrlichman; From: Ken Cole; January 6, 1973, Folder: [9 of 27] January–February 1973, Box 4, Domestic Council (FG 6–15), Subject Files, WHCF, NPL.

4. "*Note to Haldeman ONLY*" from John Ehrlichman, appended to the draft of a proposed letter that Nixon would send to Weinberger, January 9, 1973, p. 2 (original emphasis), Folder: 2 January–31 January 1973 [2 of 5], Box 63, Chronological File 1969–1973, Ehrlichman Papers. To be close to their staff, OMB directors also had an office in OEOB. Apparently, Ehrlichman had developed an impatience with Weinberger during Weinberger's OMB years. Weinberger wrote that Ehrlichman "rarely returned phone calls. When I walked over to his office to get answers I needed for my budget work, he was annoyed, distant, and buttoned up." Weinberger, *In the Arena*, 196.

5. Another factor contributing to Ehrlichman's concern about Butz not shifting to a natural resources perspective was the rumor that Butz would name outgoing Assistant Secretary Richard Lyng as his top counsellor staffer. Lyng would not have added any natural resources expertise and would duplicate Butz's policy expertise. Also, Cole and Ehrlichman did not think highly of Lyng. Memorandum for: John Ehrlichman; From: Ken Cole; January 6, 1973, Folder: [9 of 27] January–February 1973, Box 4, Domestic Council (FG 6–15), Subject Files. Lyng did not receive an appointment to Butz's counsellor staff, nor any other administration position in the second term. In 1986, President Reagan named him agriculture secretary.

6. Memorandum for: The President; From: John Ehrlichman; Subject: Meeting with newly appointed Counsellors; January 10, 1973, Folder: January–February 1973 [9 of 27], Box 4, Domestic Council (FG 6–15), Subject Files.

7. Nixon's reluctance included saying no to a request made in person. According to Dana Mead, associate DC director, one secretary developed a technique of lingering after a presidential meeting. As everyone was leaving, the secretary would suddenly develop a coughing fit. Nixon would come over and say, "Are you OK? Can I get you a glass of water?" This meant the secretary was briefly alone with the president because staff had already left the room thinking the meeting was over. The secretary would take

advantage of the opportunity to quickly ask the president for a few more million dollars for a project and Nixon would assent. Mead emphasized this was not an apocryphal story, that he had personal knowledge of it happening, but he declined to identify the secretary. Mead interview, p. 3.

8. Letter from President Nixon to Caspar Weinberger, January 11, 1973, Folder: 2 January–31 January 1973 [2 of 5], Box 63, Chronological File 1969–1973, Ehrlichman Papers.

9. Memorandum for: The President; From: John Ehrlichman; Subject: Meeting with newly appointed Counsellors; February 5, 1973 (emphasis added), Folder: 1 February–28 February, 1973 [1 of 3], Box 63, Chronological File 1969–1973, Ehrlichman Papers.

10. Kutler, *Abuse of Power*, 204–209.

11. Ehrlichman memo to the president, February 5, 1973, p. 1.

12. The President's Schedule, Monday—February 5, 1973; Revised: 2/5/73, 10:30 A.M., Folder: The President's Schedule—February 1973, Box 98, Administrative File, President's Meetings Files, President's Office Files, NPL.

13. Memorandum on the Meeting of the President and the Three Presidential Counsellors; February 5, 1973, Folder: General 1973, Box 471, Weinberger Papers.

14. Seidman, *Politics, Position, and Power*, 85.

15. Memorandum on the Meeting of the President and the Three Presidential Counsellors, February 5, 1973.

16. Memorandum for: John Ehrlichman; From: Tod Hullin; Subject: Meeting with Cap Weinberger, Friday, March 16, 1973, 2:30 P.M.; March 16, 1973, Folder: [CF] FG 999–26, Human Resources, Department of [1971–1974], Box 27, Subject Files: Confidential Files 1969–1974, White House Central Files, WHSF, NPL. The cancellation of the meeting is noted in an undated cover note attached to the memo.

17. Memorandum for: Bruce Kehrli; From: John Campbell; January 18, 1973, Folder: Domestic Council Staff, Box 189, White House Budget Files, Staff Secretary Files.

18. Memorandum for: Ken Cole; From: Bruce Kehrli; Subject: Clearances on Material Presented to the President Concerning Domestic Issues; March 14, 1973, Folder: Chronological March 1973 [#2], Box 75, Memoranda Files, Staff Secretary Files.

19. On White House passes: Memorandum for: Jane Dannenhauer; From Bruce Kehrli; February 23, 1973; on use of dining areas: Memorandum for: Bill Gulley; From: Bruce Kehrli; February 1, 1973; on limo parking: Memorandum for: Mike Farrell; From: Bruce Kehrli; Subject: Parking for Counsellors' Limousines; February 13, 1973; on access to president's OEOB office meetings: Memorandum for: Chief Laurence B. Quimby, Executive Protective Service; From: Bruce Kehrli; Subject: Access List for President's OEOB Office; February 26, 1973, all in Folder: Chronological February 1973, Box 74, Memoranda Files, Staff Secretary Files. On use of the Roosevelt Room: Memo for: The White House Staff; From: Bruce Kehrli; Subject: Reservations for Use of Roosevelt Room; February 27, 1973, Folder: Procedures 1973, Box 472, Weinberger Papers. On use of recreation facilities: Memorandum for: Caspar Weinberger; From: Bruce Kehrli, Staff Secretary; Subject: Your White House Office Arrangements; March 6, 1973, p. 3, Folder: Chronological March 1973 [#2], Box 75, Memoranda Files, Staff Secretary Files. Lynn and Butz received identical memos.

20. On burn bags: Memorandum to: Inspector M. J. Riordan; From: Isabelle I. Bethel, Secretary to Counsellor Weinberger; Subject: Continuation of Burn bag pickup; March 16, 1973, Folder: Procedures 1973, Box 472, Weinberger Papers. On photocopier: Memorandum for: Honorable Earl Butz; From: Bruce Kehrli; Subject: Your Request for Xerox Equipment; March 1, 1973, Folder: Chronological March 1973 [#2], Box 75, Memoranda Files, Staff Secretary Files.

21. On building passes: Memorandum for: Jane Dannenhauer; From: Bruce Kehrli; February 2, 1973, Folder: Chronological February 1973 [#2], Box 74, Memoranda Files, Staff Secretary Files. Kehrli also conferred with Legal Counsel John Dean for help in drafting a policy on White House and OEOB passes in advance of the expected slew of applications for passes from counsellors' staff. Memorandum for: John Dean; From Bruce Kehrli; Subject: White House/EOB Pass Policy; February 23, 1973, Folder: Chronological February 1973, Box 74, Memoranda Files, Staff Secretary Files. Kehrli knew that counsellors' staff were actually departmental employees whose salaries were reimbursed from a White House account. Therefore, in legal terms, they were not White House or EOP *employees*. That Kehrli felt he needed legal help drafting a pass policy indicated the ripple effects of the corner-cutting decisions Haldeman and Ehrlichman made about the official status of the counsellors. On staff parking: Memorandum for: Caspar Weinberger, The Secretary of HEW; From: Michael J. Farrell; Subject: Revision of Parking Arrangements; March 12, 1973, Folder: Staff 1973, Box 472, Weinberger Papers. It is interesting that Farrell addressed his memo to Weinberger as HEW secretary, not as HR counsellor. This was another indication of the somewhat ambiguous status of the counsellors and their staff. On Health Unit membership: Memorandum for: Bill Gulley; From: Bruce Kehrli; Subject: White House Health Unit; March 1, 1973; on White House cars: Memorandum for: Bill Gulley; From: Bruce Kehrli; Subject: "B" Car List; March 3, 1973, both in Folder: Chronological March 1973 [#2], Box 75, Memoranda Files, Staff Secretary Files.

22. On Staff Mess: Memorandum for: Bill Gulley; From: Bruce Kehrli; Subject: White House Staff Mess; February 28, 1973, Folder: Chronological February 1973 [#1], Box 74; on OEOB Mess: Memorandum for: Honorable Caspar Weinberger; From: Bruce Kehrli, Staff Secretary; Subject: Your White House Office Arrangements; March 6, 1973, p. 2, Folder: Chronological March 1973 [#2], Box 75; Memorandum for: Charlie Rotchford; From: Bruce Kehrli; April 6, 1973, Folder: Chronological April 1973, Box 75, all in Memoranda Files, Staff Secretary Files.

23. Memorandum for: H. R. Haldeman; From: Bruce Kehrli; Subject: White House Budget and Personnel, January 1–March 31, 1973—Report for Third Quarter; April 18, 1973, p. 4, Folder: Chronological File April 1973, Box 75, Memoranda Files, Staff Secretary Files.

24. "Three Presidential Counselors Establish Staffs to Institutionalize Functions," *National Journal* 5:14 (April 7, 1973): 508.

25. Ernest B. Furgurson, "Felony Committed against U.S. Natural Resources," *Los Angeles Times,* January 14, 1973.

26. Folder: Wednesday, February 7, 1973, Cabinet Meeting, Box 84, President's Speech File 1969–1974, President's Personal File.

27. Safire, *Before the Fall,* 684.

28. Memorandum for: Ken Cole; From: David Parker; February 21, 1973, Folder: [20 of 27, March–April 1973], Box 4, Domestic Council (FG 6–15), Subject Files.

29. Memorandum for: David Parker; From: Ken Cole; March 5, 1973, Folder: [20 of 27, March–April 1973], Box 4, Domestic Council (FG 6–15), Subject Files.

30. Memorandum for Counsellor Weinberger; Through: Will Taft; From: Steve McConahey; Subject: Congressional Relations within the Counsellor's Office; March 14, 1973 (emphasis added), Folder: Reading File 1973, Box 472, Weinberger Papers.

31. Nixon, *Public Papers of the Presidents: 1973*, 21, 39.

32. Memorandum for: Honorable Earl Butz, Secretary of Agriculture; Honorable Caspar Weinberger, Secretary of Health, Education, and Welfare; Honorable James T. Lynn, Secretary of Housing and Urban Development; Honorable Roy Ash, Director, Office of Management and Budget; From: James H. Falk, Associate Director, Domestic Council; Subject: White House Briefing for National Legislative Council; March 28, 1973, Folder: March 30, 1973—10:30 A.M. Mtg. with the Counsellors and Natl. Legislative Conf., Box 4, Butz Papers.

33. Nixon, *Public Papers of the Presidents: 1973*, 239–45.

34. AP, "Governors, White House Discuss Cuts," *Des Moines Register,* March 1, 1973.

35. [Memo] For: Ken Cole; From: Tod R. Hullin; Subject: "Meet the Press"/The Three Counsellors; February 14, 1973; and [Memo] For: Al Snyder; From: Tod R. Hullin; Subject: "Meet the Press"/The Three Counsellors; February 16, 1973, Folder: 1 February–28 February 1973 [2 of 3], Box 64, Chronological File 1969–1973, Ehrlichman Papers.

36. "TV Revisions," *Chicago Tribune,* April 8, 1973.

37. *The Proceedings of* Meet the Press, April 8, 1973 (transcript), 17:13 (Washington, D.C.: Merkle Press, 1973), pp. 6, 9, Box 260, Spivak Papers.

38. Jules Witcover, "Ehrlichman Sees Nixon as a Time-Conscious President," *Washington Post,* March 27, 1973.

39. Whitaker, *Striking a Balance;* Richard W. Fairbanks III, interview by author, February 6, 2007, p. 10.

40. Schedule for Tuesday, March 6, 1973, Folder: [Appointment Schedule for John D. Ehrlichman, 1969–1973], Box 2, Appointment Calendars and Diaries 1969–1973, Ehrlichman Papers.

41. Memorandum for the File; From: Caspar W. Weinberger; Subject: Minutes of Breakfast Meeting with John Ehrlichman, Secretaries Butz, Lynn, and Weinberger; March 6, 1973, Folder: Presidential Meetings 1973, Box 472, Weinberger Papers. As the dictated recollections of a participant, Weinberger's summary may be incomplete. Still, he was a very methodical person, so the summary is likely to be comprehensive, at least as a "to do" list. Weinberger's column was published later that month ("Congress as the Crisis" [op ed column], *New York Times,* March 27, 1973). Lynn, too, wrote one ("Pork-Barrel Waste" [op ed column], *New York Times,* April 10, 1973).

42. [Memo to the President]; From: John Ehrlichman; Subject: Meeting with the Counsellors, Tuesday, March 6, 1973, 4:00 P.M., The Oval Office; Folder: 1 March–31 March 1973 [1 of 5], Box 64, Chronological File 1969–1973, Ehrlichman Papers.

43. Kutler, *Abuse of Power,* 220–22.

44. Handwritten notes by Ehrlichman on President Nixon's meeting with Butz,

Weinberger, and Lynn, March 6, 1973, Folder: Notes 1/4/73–5/2/73 [3 of 6], Box 14, John D. Ehrlichman Notes of Meetings.

45. Memorandum for: Jim Cavanaugh; From: Ken Cole; February 26, 1973; cc Cap Weinberger, Paul O'Neill [OMB associate director], Bill Timmons [White House congressional liaison director], Folder: General 1973, Box 471, Weinberger Papers.

46. [Memo to] Rufus Wilson, Associate Deputy Administrator, Veterans Administration; From: Stephen G. McConahey; Subject: Income Security Working Committee Assignment; March 9, 1973, Folder: Health Resource Programs—General—1973, Box 471, Weinberger Papers. To be sure that Wilson understood the priority of the request, he pointedly included at the bottom of the memo "cc: Counsellor Weinberger."

47. Memorandum to Counsellor Weinberger; From: Steve McConahey; Subject: Suggested Agenda for Human Development Meeting, Tuesday, April 3, 1973; April 3, 1973, p. 3, Folder: Health Resource Programs—General—1973, Box 471, Weinberger Papers.

48. Memorandum for: The President; From: Caspar W. Weinberger; March 27, 1973, Reading File 1973, Box 472, Weinberger Papers. Based on White House policies, written submissions to the president usually required a response, but not necessarily in the name of the president. In this case, the staff secretary passed Weinberger's letter to DC head Kenneth Cole, with the notation "for your handling," meaning that a presidential reply was not called for. White House Staff Secretary Action Memorandum; Subject: Weinberger memo, 3–27, re Vietnam veterans; March 28, 1973, Folder: Material Staffed in March 1973 [#2], Box 58, Memoranda Files, Staff Secretary Files. Cole, in turn, gave it to Associate Director James Cavanaugh because Cavanaugh handled health issues and was paired with Weinberger to handle human resources issues. Cavanaugh replied to Weinberger in his own name with a bland and noncommittal two-paragraph memo. He noted that Nixon had met with Donald Johnson, the VA administrator, subsequent to Weinberger's memo to the president and that Nixon had told Johnson "to get our Veteran's [*sic*] story out to the public," an implied implementation of Weinberger's recommendations. Memorandum for: Counsellor Caspar Weinberger; From: James H. Cavanaugh; March 30, 1973, Folder: Material Staffed in March 1973 [#2], Box 58, Memoranda Files, Staff Secretary Files. That it was *Cavanaugh* who replied to Weinberger's memo to the president was a not-so-subtle signal to Weinberger not to ignore Cavanaugh.

49. Memorandum for: The Honorable James H. Cavanaugh, Staff Assistant to the President for Health Affairs; From: Donald E. Johnson, Administrator, Veterans Administration; Subject: Possible Presidential Visit to Underscore Jobs for Veterans Interest; February 5, 1973. This letter was Tab A in Memorandum for: The President; From: Caspar W. Weinberger; March 27, 1973, Reading File 1973, Box 472, Weinberger Papers. The proposed presidential visit to St. Louis never happened.

50. Draft memo on Legal Services Corporation Legislation, Reading File 1973, Box 472, Weinberger Papers.

51. Memorandum for: The President; [From: Caspar W. Weinberger]; Subject: Legal Services Corporation Legislation; April 10, 1973, Reading File 1973, Box 472, Weinberger Papers.

52. Linda Charlton, "Nixon Again Asks Legal Aid to Poor: Independent Agency Would Replace O.E.O. Unit," *New York Times,* May 12, 1973.

53. Memorandum to: The Counsellor; From: Steve McConahey; Subject: Legal Services Backup Centers; March 30, 1973; Memorandum for: Jim Cavanaugh; From: Caspar W. Weinberger; April 2, 1973, both in Folder: Staff 1973, Box 472, Weinberger Papers.

54. Marjorie Hunter, "House Passes Legal Aid Bill with Amendments That Backers Say Cripple It," *New York Times,* June 22, 1973.

55. Warren Weaver Jr., "Congress Passes Legal Aid to Poor," *New York Times,* July 19, 1974.

56. John Herbers, "President Is More Yielding in Clashes with Congress," *New York Times,* July 29, 1974.

57. "Cash Crop," *Time,* March 5, 1973, http://www.time.com/time/magazine/article/0,9171,903870,00.html (accessed May 18, 2009).

58. Memorandum for: Caspar Weinberger and Jim Cavanaugh; From: Ken Cole; March 5, 1973, Folder: Health Resources Programs—General—1973, Box 471, Weinberger Papers.

59. Memorandum to: Mr. Ed Heckman, Administrator, Food & Nutrition Services, Department of Agriculture; From: Stephen G. McConahey; Subject: Human Development Working Committee Assignment; March 9, 1973, Folder: Health Resource Programs—General—1973, Box 471, Weinberger Papers.

60. Income Security, Agenda—April 10, 1973, Folder: Health Resource Programs—General—1973, Box 471, Weinberger Papers.

61. Memo to: Counsellor Weinberger; From: Justine Farr Rodriguez; Re: Strikers; April 18, 1973, p. 3, Folder: Health Resource Programs—General—1973, Box 471, Weinberger Papers.

62. Memo to: Counsellor Weinberger; From: Justine Farr Rodriguez; Re: Additional Options on Welfare for Strikers; April 23, 1973, Folder: Health Resource Programs—General—1973, Box 471, Weinberger Papers.

63. Income Security [Subcommittee]; Agenda—April 25, 1973; p. 2, Folder: Health Resource Programs—General—1973, Box 471, Weinberger Papers.

64. To: Mr. Weinberger; From: Will Taft IV; April 25, 1973, Folder: Health Resource Programs—General—1973, Box 471, Weinberger Papers. In an interview, Taft said that Weinberger generally had a good relationship with Brennan. William Taft IV, interview by author, August 14, 2006. That good relationship may have helped prevent this minor matter from exploding into a very major one.

65. Like so many Washington issues, food-stamps-for-strikers went on for a long time, with the center of action shifting to Capitol Hill. AP, "Food Stamp Ban in Strikes Voted," *New York Times,* July 20, 1973, p. 16; AP, "Senate Votes Rises in School Lunch Aid," *New York Times,* May 22, 1974, p. 46.

66. In an interview, Weinberger's chief of staff did not recall that specific memo but vividly remembered the context of the times. He dryly suggested that the motivation for the memo was most likely "to remind the President that we were there." W. Taft interview. By April 1973, Watergate had sucked up so much of the president and Ehrlichman's time and attention that Weinberger (and many others) were feeling somewhat abandoned. Weinberger was not getting the kind of routine policy guidance, oversight, and feedback he was used to from his service at OMB in the first term.

67. Memorandum to: The Counsellor; From: Steve McConahey; Subject: Status Report to the President; March 29, 1973, Folder: Reading File 1973, Box 472, Weinberger Papers.

68. Memorandum for: The President; From: Caspar W. Weinberger; April 3, 1973, Folder: [Material Staffed in April 1973], Box 58, Memoranda Files, Staff Secretary Files.

69. Ibid.

70. Kutler, *Abuse of Power*, 290–98.

71. Action Memorandum; For: Roland Elliot; From: The Staff Secretary; April 9, 1973, Folder: [Material Staffed in April 1973], Box 58, Memoranda Files, Staff Secretary Files. Elliot was deputy special assistant to the president and in charge of the White House Correspondence Office, a low-prestige position. That Elliot was assigned the task of drafting the president's response to Weinberger's status report most likely reflected the inner circle's relative unhappiness with Weinberger's job performance so far and annoyance at having to deal with unnecessary correspondence when more important issues (e.g., Watergate) were pressing.

72. Action Memorandum; For: Craig Gosden; From: The Staff Secretary; April 12, 1973 [and handwritten response from Gosden to Kehrli on cover sheet], Folder: [Material Staffed in April 1973], Box 58, Memoranda Files, Staff Secretary Files.

73. Letter from President Nixon to Caspar Weinberger; April 11, 1973, Folder: [Material Staffed in 1973], Box 58, Memoranda Files, Staff Secretary Files.

74. Senate Committee on Agriculture and Forestry, *Implementation of the Rural Development Act (Part 1)* (hearings), 93rd Cong., 1st sess., 1973, 137.

75. Senate Committee on Banking, Housing, and Urban Affairs, *Oversight on Housing and Urban Development Programs: Washington, D.C. (Part 1)* (hearings), 93rd Cong., 1st sess., 1973, 286.

76. The Secretary's Schedule, Monday—April 23 [1973], Folder: White House—Counsellor Butz's Schedules, Box 1, Butz Papers.

77. The meeting is referred to in a memo to Weinberger from his top aide, William Taft. Memorandum to: The Secretary [of HEW]; From: William H. Taft IV; Subject: Talking points for the Human Resources Committee opening meeting; February 20, 1973, p. 1, Folder: General 1973, Box 471, Weinberger Papers.

78. Memorandum for Cal Collier; From: Michael Raoul-Duval; Re: Human Resources Committee Procedures; March 15, 1973, Folder: Community Development [1 of 2], Box 9, Alpha-Subject Files, Michael Raoul-Duval Papers, SMOF, WHCF, NPL.

79. Memorandum for: Bobbie J. Crider [Counsellor Butz's secretary]; From: Calvin J. Collier; April 10, 1973, Folder: White House—Memoranda to U.S.D.A., Box 2, Butz Papers.

80. Memorandum for: Cal Collier; From: Michael Raoul-Duval; Re: Human Resources Committee Procedures; March 15, 1973, Folder: Community Development [1 of 2], Box 9, Alpha-Subject Files, Raoul-Duval Papers.

81. Memorandum to: Doug Parker, Office of the Counsellor for Community Development; From: Steve McConahey [Office of the Counsellor for Human Resources]; Subject: Social Service Component of Rural Development Strategy; March 15, 1973, Folder: Reading File 1973, Box 472, Weinberger Papers. See also Memorandum to: The Counsellor, From: Steve McConahey; Subject: Human Resource Component of Rural Development Strategy; March 30, 1973, Folder: Staff 1973, Box 472, Weinberger Papers.

Inter-counsellor contact is also briefly mentioned in the section of chapter 6 regarding the subcommittees of the CD counsellor.

82. To: Mr. Calvin J. Collier; From: Mr. William H. Taft, IV; March 9, 1973, Folder: Reading File 1973, Box 472, Weinberger Papers.

83. Nixon, *Public Papers of the Presidents: 1970,* 260.

84. John Herbers, "The Other Presidency," *New York Times Sunday Magazine,* March 3, 1974.

85. MBO can be viewed as proto–performance measurement, a management fad dominating public administration in the early twenty-first century.

86. Malek, *Washington's Hidden Tragedy,* 24.

87. The term was not new and had its origins in the work of the Ash Council. In June 1970, when Nixon announced the reorganization of the Bureau of the Budget into the Office of Management and Budget, per the Ash Council recommendations, he referred to the new agency as the "Office of Executive Management and Budget." Nixon, *Public Papers of the Presidents: 1970,* 493.

88. Memorandum for: H. R. Haldeman; From: Fred Malek; Subject: Issues to Resolve; December 6, 1972, p. 1 (emphasis added), Folder: Reorganization Department and Agencies I [Part II], Box 172, Alphabetical Subject Files, Haldeman Papers.

89. Based on a comparison of mid-December and late December drafts on the role of the counsellor. Memorandum for: John Ehrlichman—Via Walter Minnick; From: Mark W. Alger; Subject: Presidential Counsellors; December 18, 1972; and Role of the Counsellors; December 29, 1972; n.a. (but identified as Ehrlichman in a related document), Folder: General 1973, Box 471, Weinberger Papers.

90. [Memo] For: Bruce Kehrli; From: Tod R. Hullin [Ehrlichman's personal assistant]; Re: Office Space for Counsellors; December 15, 1972, Folder: 21 November–31 December 1972, Box 63, Chronological File 1969–1973, Ehrlichman Papers.

91. Folder: White House—Memoranda to U.S.D.A., Box 2, Butz Papers. This form was later slightly revised, but more in format than content.

92. Memorandum to: Human Resource Committee Members; From: Caspar W. Weinberger; Subject: Reporting, Monitoring, and Clearance Procedures for the Counsellor's Office; March 9, 1973, Folder: Health Resources Council Committee: Contacts 1973, Box 471, Weinberger Papers.

93. Ibid.

94. Ibid. (emphasis added).

95. Note with the distribution list for the March 9 memo, in ibid.

96. [Memo] For: John Ehrlichman; From: Tod R. Hullin; March 26, 1973, Folder: [CF] FG 999–26 Human Resources, Dept. of [1971–1974], Box 27, Subject Files: Confidential Files 1969–1974.

97. Note for: Tod Hullin; From: Jim Edwards [executive assistant to the OMB director]; March 19, 1973, Folder: [CF] FG 999–26 Human Resources, Dept. of [1971–1974], Box 27, Subject Files: Confidential Files 1969–1974.

98. No such memo from Ehrlichman to Weinberger was located in any of Weinberger's counsellor files, Taft's office files, or Julia Vadala's personal files. Given how meticulous Weinberger and his counsellor aides were about recordkeeping, the absence of such a memo in any archives permits a reasonable inference that it was never sent.

99. Kutler, *Abuse of Power,* 234–40, 286–90.

100. Notes of interview with Fred Malek, September 13, 1977, by A. James Reichley, p. 6, Folder: Nixon White House—Malek, Fred, Box 1, A. James Reichley Interview Transcripts, 1977–1981, Ford Presidential Library.

101. Daily calendar for April 4, 1973, Folder 4: 1973 [1 of 3], Box 74, Appointment Books and Calendars, Miscellany, W. Taft Papers.

102. My conclusions are derived from the contents of: Memorandum for: The Honorable Peter J. Brennan, Secretary of Labor; From: Caspar W. Weinberger, Counsellor to the President for Human Resources; Subject: Procedures of the Counsellor's Office and the Department of Labor (Your memorandum of April 5); April 19, 1973, Folder: Cavanaugh, James H.: Memoranda 1973, Box 471, Weinberger Papers.

103. Memorandum for: The Honorable Caspar W. Weinberger, Counsellor to the President for Human Resources; From: Peter Brennan, Secretary of Labor; Subject: Reporting, Monitoring, and Clearance Procedures for the Counsellor's Office; April 5, 1973, Folder: Cavanaugh, James H.: Memoranda 1973, Box 471, Weinberger Papers.

104. Memorandum for: The Honorable Peter J. Brennan, Secretary of Labor; From: Caspar W. Weinberger, Counsellor to the President for Human Resources; Subject: Procedures of the Counsellor's Office and the Department of Labor (Your memorandum of April 5); April 19, 1973, Folder: Cavanaugh, James H.: Memoranda 1973; Box 471, Weinberger Papers.

105. Haldeman's handwritten comments on OMB's draft of a presidential memorandum on MBO, March 29, 1973, Folder: [Material Staffed in April 1973], Box 58, Memoranda Files, Staff Secretary Files.

106. [Memo] For: Ken Cole; From: Tod R. Hullin; Subject: Review of our meeting with Fred Malek, April 10, 1973; April 10, 1973, p. 1 (emphasis added), Folder: 2 April 1973–16 May 1973 [1 of 4], Box 65, Chronological File 1969–1973, Ehrlichman Papers.

107. [Memo] To: H. R. Haldeman; From: Bruce Kehrli; April 12, 1973, Folder: [Material Staffed in April 1973], Box 58, Memoranda Files, Staff Secretary Files. Haldeman wrote a check mark next to "Approve" and signed it "H."

108. Malek, *Washington's Hidden Tragedy,* 154. A month after the president's MBO document was released, Malek mentioned it in a speech in California. Brent Howell, "Nixon Aide Addresses S&L Forum," *Pasadena (Calif.) Star-News,* May 11, 1973. However, none of the wire services picked up the article mentioning it for their national distribution. References to the MBO project in the national news media did not appear until the next year. Fred L. Zimmerman, "Roy Ash and His OMB 'Hustlers' Expand Influence through Much of Government's Day-to-Day Work," *Wall Street Journal,* February 1, 1974; John Herbers, "The Other Presidency," *New York Times Sunday Magazine,* March 3, 1974.

109. [Memo] To: John Larson/Heidi Reaves; From: Bobbie [Crider, Counsellor Butz's personal secretary]; March 30, 1973, Folder: White House Interoffice Memoranda, Box 1, Butz Papers.

110. Memorandum to: Mr. Robert Hemphill; From: Stephen G. McConahey; Subject: Department of Agriculture objectives; May 18, 1973, Folder: Human Resources Programs: Weekly Status Reports 1973, Box 471, Weinberger Papers. This memo was sent one week after Nixon had canceled the counsellor project, but Weinberger's staff was still tying up loose ends. Before getting to the substantive purpose of the commu-

nication, McConahey noted, "As you are well aware, the role of the Counsellor's Office in developing and monitoring these objectives has changed considerably in the last few days. Nonetheless, I will comment in response to your memorandum."

111. Tasks; attachment to Income Security, Agenda—April 25, 1973, Folder: Health Resource Programs—General—1973, Box 471, Weinberger Papers.

112. Memorandum for: Counsellor Weinberger; From: Julia Vadala; Subject: Agenda for Health Working Group, 8:30 A.M., Friday, May 4; May 3, 1973, p. 4, Folder 3: DHEW 1973 [2 of 3], Box 67, Government File, W. Taft Papers.

113. John Herbers, "The Other Presidency," *New York Times Sunday Magazine,* March 3, 1974. That same year, Newland predicted that MBO had less of a chance of success because of the failure of the counsellor effort the previous year. He suggested there needed to be greater harmony between objectives and the structure of the executive branch for MBO to become institutionalized. Newland, "MBO Prospects and Challenges," 421–22. Ash and Malek never saw it that way. Nonetheless, their MBO initiative quickly "evaporated." Rose, "Implementation and Evaporation."

CHAPTER 5. COUNSELLOR FOR HUMAN RESOURCES CASPAR WEINBERGER

1. "Presidential Policy Guidance (Domestic Affairs)," Redirecting Executive Branch Management (slides), Folder: Bi-Partisan Leaders Organization Briefing, Box 68, Speeches and Briefing 1970–1973, Ehrlichman Papers.

2. Appendix C: Counsellor to the President for Human Resources; in Memorandum; From: John Dean; Subject: Methods for Reorganizing the Executive Branch; January 2, 1973, Folder: [Reorganization-EOP Part II], Box 174, Alphabetical Subject Files, Haldeman Papers.

3. Dom Bonafede and John K. Iglehart, "End of Counselor System Enlarges Policy-Forming Role of Cabinet," *National Journal* 5:20 (May 19, 1973): 727.

4. Senate Committee on Finance, *Nominations of Caspar W. Weinberger,* 4 (emphasis added).

5. Untitled photo, *New York Times,* January 30, 1973, p. 21. The caption read: "Caspar W. Weinberger, the director of the Office of Management and Budget, at a news conference in Washington on the new budget."

6. Nixon, *Public Papers of the Presidents: 1973,* 72, 87–88.

7. Memorandum for: Mr. Weinberger; [From: William H. Taft]; Subject: The Counsellor's Office; Date: January 18, 1973, Folder: General 1973, Box 471, Weinberger Papers. For the administration, "income security" was the synonym for welfare and descended from the president's first-term proposal for what was tantamount to a guaranteed annual income.

8. "Three Presidential Counselors Establish Staffs to Institutionalize Functions," *National Journal* 5:14 (April 7, 1973): 508.

9. Memorandum to: Will Taft, Executive Assistant to the Director [of OMB]; From: Stephen G. McConahey, White House Fellow; Subject: Organization of the Counselor's Office; January 31, 1973, p. 4, Folder: General 1973, Box 471, Weinberger Papers.

10. Position Description: Counselor to the President for Human Resources, Attachment B to memorandum to: Will Taft, Executive Assistant to the Director [of OMB]; from; Stephen G. McConahey, White House Fellow; Subject: Organization of the Counselor's Office; January 31, 1973, p. 4, Folder: General 1973, Box 471, Weinberger Papers.

11. Memorandum to: Honorable Caspar W. Weinberger; Through: Will Taft, Executive Assistant to the Director; From: Stephen G. McConahey; Subject: Start-up Strategy for the Counselor's Office; February 5, 1973, p. 1 (original emphasis), Folder: General 1973, Box 471, Weinberger Papers.

12. Memorandum to the Counselor; Through: Will Taft; From: Stephen G. McConahey; Subject: Draft Operating Procedures for Counselor's Office; n.d. [probably between February 6 and 9, 1973], Folder: Procedures 1973; Box 472, Weinberger Papers.

13. Letter from Taft to Aurora K. Reich, April 9, 1973, Folder: Reading File 1973, Box 472, Weinberger Papers; "Three Presidential Counselors Establish Staffs," *National Journal* 5:14 (April 7, 1973): 508. McConahey was listed as "acting" deputy director. Staff to Counsellor Weinberger, [handwritten: 5/10/73], Folder: Staff 1973, Box 472, Weinberger Papers.

14. Blank notepad example, Folder: Staff 1973; Box 472, Weinberger Papers.

15. Memorandum for: Members of the Council on Human Resources; From: Caspar W. Weinberger, Counsellor to the President; Subject: The Council on Human Resources; February 15, 1973, Folder: Health Resource Programs—General—1973, Box 471, Weinberger Papers.

16. Lacking a title, the first heading in the document is "I. Background and Purpose of Counsellor Role." The first time the document appears in the files is next to McConahey's Memorandum to the Counselor; Through: Will Taft; Subject: Draft Operating Procedures for Counselor's Office; n.d. [probably between February 6 and 9, 1973], Folder: Procedures 1973; Box 472, Weinberger Papers. However, the draft document was typed on a different typewriter and was not referred to in the McConahey memo.

17. Ibid., p. 1 (original emphasis).

18. Memorandum to: The Secretary; From: William H. Taft IV; Subject: Talking points for the Human Resources Committee opening meeting; February 20, 1973, p. 1 (emphasis added), Folder: General 1973, Box 471, Weinberger Papers.

19. General Comments by Counsellor Weinberger, n.d., n.a., Folder 2: DHEW [1 of 3], Box 67, Government Files, W. Taft Papers.

20. Memorandum to: Marvin Franklin, Special Assistant to the Secretary [of Interior] for Indian Affairs, and William L. Rogers, Deputy Assistant Secretary—Public Land Management; From: The Under Secretary [John Whitaker]; Subject: Interior's participation in the Council on Human Resources; February 27, 1973, p. 1 (original emphasis), Folder: Health Resource Programs—General—1973, Box 471, Weinberger Papers.

21. Ibid, p. 2.

22. Committee for Human Resources [membership list, as of April 20, 1973], Folder: White House—Memoranda to U.S.D.A., Box 2, Butz Papers.

23. *Weekly Compilation of Presidential Documents* 9:10 (March 12, 1973): 234.

24. Choosing not to give the traditional address was related to Nixon's second-term goals of marginalizing Congress and maximizing presidential action, including the establishment of counsellorships instead of seeking statutory reorganization.

25. Office of the White House Press Secretary, "Press Conference of Caspar Weinberger" (transcript), March 1, 1973, p. 1, Folder: General 1973, Box 471, Weinberger Papers.

26. Nixon, *Public Papers of the Presidents: 1973,* 137.

27. Lee Byrd, "Cap the Knife: Blade Honed for HEW Post," *Los Angeles Times,* February 8, 1973.

28. Letter to Benjamin Shore, Copley News Service; from Caspar W. Weinberger, Counsellor to the President for Human Resources; March 15, 1973, Folder: Reading File 1973, Box 472, Weinberger Papers.

29. "Why Welfare Costs Keep Rising: Interview with Caspar W. Weinberger," *US News & World Report* 74:12 (March 19, 1973): 47.

30. *The Proceedings of* Meet the Press, February 25, 1973 (transcript), 17:7 (Washington, D.C.: Merkle Press, 1973), pp. 1, 9, Spivak Papers.

31. David S. Broder, "Presidential Power: An Interview with Caspar W. Weinberger," *Washington Post,* February 18, 1973, B5.

32. Letter to Clifton Daniel, Washington Bureau, *New York Times;* from Caspar W. Weinberger, Counsellor to the President for Human Resources; February 22, 1973, Folder: Reading File 1973, Box 472, Weinberger Papers.

33. Letter to Nancy Hanks, Chairman, National Endowment for the Arts; from Caspar W. Weinberger; February 5, 1973, Folder: Human Resources Council Committee—General, Box 471, Weinberger Papers. The subject Hanks raised with Weinberger was not identified.

34. Bonafede and Iglehart, "End of Counselor System," *National Journal* 5:20 (May 19, 1973): 727; W. Taft interview. Differing with Taft's recollection, the *National Journal* reported that Weinberger came to his counsellor office only on Tuesday and Friday mornings.

35. Julia Vadala Taft, interview by author, August 9, 2006.

36. Attachment A: Meeting Schedule, Human Resources Committee and Functional Working Committees; Memorandum to: Human Resources Committee and Functional Working Committees; From: Caspar W. Weinberger, Counsellor to the President for Human Resources; Subject: Meeting Schedule; March 12, 1973, Folder: Health Resources Council Committee: Contacts 1973, Box 471, Weinberger Papers.

37. Note to Secretary Weinberger; from Julia Vadala; Action Forcing Event; April 10, 1973, Julia Vadala Taft Personal Files, NPL.

38. [Memo] To: The Secretary; From: William H. Taft IV; Subject: Your schedule; April 18, 1973, Folder 3: DHEW 1973 [2 of 3], Box 67, Government File, W. Taft Papers.

39. Memorandum to the Counsellor; From SGM [Stephen G. McConahey]; Subject: Status of Manpower Revenue Sharing; Cause for Counsellor Involvement; n.d. [probably April 2, 1973], p. 4, Folder: Manpower/Revenue Sharing, Box 472; Memorandum for the Counsellor; From: Steve Mc Conahey [*sic*]; Subject: Agenda for Human Development Committee Meeting: April 18; April 17, 1973, p. 2, Health Resource Programs—General—1973, Box 471, both in Weinberger Papers.

40. For example, see letter to Otis R. Bowen, M.D., Governor of Indiana; from Caspar W. Weinberger, Counsellor to the President for Human Resources; April 26, 1973, Folder: Reading File 1973, Box 472, Weinberger Papers. This letter was a response to an earlier letter from Bowen to Weinberger about the role of governors in an administrative implementation of manpower special revenue sharing.

41. Weinberger's handwritten reply on a memo from McConahey: "Steve: Discuss with ____'s [illegible] staff & tell them I urge that Gov Milliken [R-Mich.] be accommodated. CW." Memorandum for: Counsellor Weinberger; From: Steve McConahey; Subject: Discussion with Michigan Delegation; April 24, 1973, Folder: Health Resources Programs—General—1973, Box 471, Weinberger Papers.

42. Memorandum to: The Counsellor; From: Stephen McConahey; Subject: Manpower Revenue Sharing; May 2, 1973; p. 1, Folder: Manpower/Revenue Sharing, Box 472, Weinberger Papers.

43. Memorandum to: Counsellor Weinberger; From: Stephen G. McConahey; Subject: Manpower Revenue Sharing (MRS); May 11, 1973, Folder: Manpower/Revenue Sharing, Box 472, Weinberger Papers. O'Neill later served as treasury secretary during George W. Bush's presidency.

44. Cover note to Mr. Weinberger; from Will Taft IV; May 8, 1973; attached to a copy of Memorandum to: the Counsellor; From: Stephen McConahey; Subject: Manpower Revenue Sharing; May 2, 1973, Folder: Manpower/Revenue Sharing, Box 472, Weinberger Papers.

45. Bonafede and Iglehart, "End of Counselor System," *National Journal* 5:20 (May 19, 1973): 727.

46. Nixon, *Public Papers of the Presidents: 1973,* 1026–27.

47. Notes of interview with Kenneth Cole, December 21, 1977, by A. James Reichley, p. 4, Folder: Nixon White House—Cole, Kenneth, Box 1, Reichley Interview Transcripts, 1977–1981.

48. Memorandum to: Counsellor Weinberger; From: Julia Vadala; Subject: Pesticide Standards for Agricultural Workers; April 20, 1973, J. Taft Personal Files.

49. General Comments by Counsellor Weinberger, n.d., n.a., p. 3; attached to Memorandum to: The Secretary; From: William H. Taft IV; Subject: Talking points for the Human Resources Committee opening meeting; February 20, 1973, Folder 2: DHEW [1 of 3], Box 67, Government Files, W. Taft Papers. Some of the HR counsellor's records referred to these subentities as committees, working committees, or working groups. For clarity (in relation to the committee of principals) and consistency (in relation to the other two counsellors), "subcommittee" is used here.

50. Organization of the Counsellor's Office: Counsellor for Human Resource Programs [as of April 20, 1973], Folder: White House—Memoranda to U.S.D.A., Box 2, Butz Papers.

51. Meeting Schedule of Human Resource Committee and Functional Working Committees; Attachment C to Agenda for Initial Meeting of Functional Working Committees, March 9, 1973 (emphasis added), Folder: Staff 1973, Box 472, Weinberger Papers. The non-overlap of the subcommittee schedules was also intended to permit a department to appoint the same person to be its representative on more than one subcommittee.

52. Meeting Schedule of Human Resources Committee and Functional Working Committees; Attachment A to Memorandum to: Human Resources Committee and Functional Working Committees; From: Caspar W. Weinberger, Counsellor to the President for Human Resources; Subject: Meeting Schedule, March 12, 1973, Folder: Health Resources Council Committee: Contacts 1973, Box 471, Weinberger Papers.

53. Call Request for Wednesday, April 11, 1973; Secretary's call to Elliot Richardson, Folder: Health Resources Council Committee: Contacts 1973, Box 471; Memorandum for: Honorable Elliot L. Richardson; From: Caspar W. Weinberger; Subject: Cabinet Committee for Human Resources; April 20, 1973, Folder: Staff 1973, Box 472, both in Weinberger Papers.

54. Memorandum to: Mr. Paul O'Neill; From: Steve McConahey; Subject: OMB Representation for Human Resources Working Committees; March 14, 1973, Folder: Health Resources Council Committee: Contacts 1973, Box 471, Weinberger Papers.

55. Several agencies had more than one representative. Attendees of Initial Working Committee Meeting; Attachment A to Agenda for Initial Meeting of Functional Working Committees, March 9, 1973, Folder: Staff 1973, Box 472, Weinberger Papers.

56. Tab B: List of Attendees; Memorandum for Counsellor Weinberger; From: Julia Vadala; Subject: Agenda for Health Working Group, May 4; May 3, 1973, Folder 3: DHEW 1973 [2 of 3], Box 67, Government File, W. Taft Papers. The Cost of Living Council was the temporary agency implementing Nixon's anti-inflation wage and price stabilization policies. HEW had two members and VA had three.

57. Agendas for March 30 and April 12 meetings: Memorandum to Counsellor Weinberger; From: Julia Vadala; Subject: Meeting of Health Working Group, March 30 Suggested Agenda; March 29, 1973, J. Taft Personal Files. Agenda of May 4 meeting: Memorandum for: Counsellor Weinberger; From: Julia Vadala; Subject: Agenda for Health Working Group, May 4; May 3, 1973, Folder 3: DHEW 1973 [2 of 3], Box 67, Government File, W. Taft Papers.

58. Memorandum for: Counsellor Weinberger; From: Julia Vadala; Subject: Agenda for Health Working Group, May 4; May 3, 1973, p. 3, Folder 3: DHEW 1973 [2 of 3], Box 67, Government File, W. Taft Papers.

59. Memorandum to: Counsellor Weinberger; From: Steve McConahey; Subject: Suggested Agenda for Human Development Meeting, Tuesday, April 3, 1973; April 3, 1973, p. 1, Folder: Health Resource Programs—General—1973, Box 471, Weinberger Papers.

60. Memorandum for: Counsellor Weinberger; From: Julia Vadala; Subject: Health Issues in the Counsellor's Office; May 11, 1973, Folder: General 1973, Box 471, Weinberger Papers.

61. Weinberger's handwritten reminder notation to include in his comments at the beginning on the meeting, on Memorandum to: Counsellor Weinberger; From: Julia Vadala; Subject: Meeting with Health Working Group, April 12, 1973, Briefing Memorandum; April 11, 1973, p. 1, Folder: Health Resource Programs—General—1973, Box 471, Weinberger Papers.

62. List of members of the National Health Insurance Task Force, May 8, 1973, J. Taft Personal Files. The Civil Service Commission is now (2009) the Office of Personnel Management.

63. Memorandum for: Members of Health Task Force—Cabinet Committee for Human Resources; From: Julia Vadala; Subject: Health Insurance Options Paper; April 18, 1973; and Memorandum on National Blood Policy from Counsellor Weinberger, sent to DOD and Commerce secretaries and head of VA, May 1, 1973, both in J. Taft Personal Files.

64. Three memoranda from McConahey to Food and Drug Administration (HEW) and one to the drug czar, all "Subject: Health Working Committee Assignment," all March 9, 1973, Folder: Health Resource Programs—General—1973, Box 471, Weinberger Papers.

65. Attendees of Initial Working Committee Meeting; Attachment A to Agenda for Initial Meeting of Functional Working Committees, March 9, 1973, Folder: Staff 1973, Box 472, Weinberger Papers.

66. Letters from Weinberger to Dr. Michael H. Moskow, HUD Assistant Secretary, and Martin J. Bailey, Treasury Department Deputy Assistant Secretary; April 19, 2008, Folder: Staff 1973, Box 472, Weinberger Papers.

67. Attendees of Initial Working Committee Meeting; Attachment A to Agenda for Initial Meeting of Functional Working Committees, March 9, 1973, Folder: Staff 1973, Box 472, Weinberger Papers.

68. Memorandum for: Counsellor Weinberger; From: Steve McConahey; Subject: Agenda for Human Development Meeting, May 1, 1973; April 30, 1973, p. 2; Memorandum for: Members of the Human Development Working Committee; From: Stephen McConahey, Acting Director, Human Development Working Committee; Subject: Schedule of Human Development Committee Meetings; May 8, 1973, both in Folder: Health Resource Programs—General—1973, Box 471, Weinberger Papers.

69. Agendas of April 3, April 18, and May 1 subcommittee meetings, Folder: Health Resource Programs—General—1973, Box 471, Weinberger Papers

70. Membership/mailing list that Weinberger's office shared with Butz's office on April 20, 1973, Folder: White House—Memoranda to U.S.D.A., Box 2, Butz Papers. Several entities did not "count." The Council of Economic Advisors was on CHR more as an observer. The National Cancer Institute and HUD's college housing program were within the counsellor's formal domain but were not represented on the committee.

71. Based on various reports located in the archival files of Weinberger and Taft at the Library of Congress and in Vadala's personal files. Given Weinberger's detailed and structured approach to work, it is unlikely that a significant number of other agency reports were submitted but not retained in the files.

72. Letter to Michael P. Balzano, Director, ACTION; from Stephen McConahey, Office of the Counsellor for Human Resources; May 9, 1973, Folder: Health Resource Programs—General—1973, Box 471, Weinberger Papers.

73. Letter to William Rogers, Deputy Assistant Secretary [of Interior] for Indian Affairs; from Stephen G. McConahey, Acting Deputy Director, Human Development Working Committee; May 8, 1973, Folder: Health Resource Programs—General—1973; Memorandum to the Counsellor; From: The Under Secretary [of Interior, John G. Whitaker]; Subject: Weekly Status Report—Week Ending April 21, 1973; April 30, 1973, both in Folder: Human Resources Programs: Weekly Status Reports 1973, Box 471, Weinberger Papers.

74. Handwritten note attached to Memorandum to: The Counsellor; From: Howard Phillips [OEO director]; Subject: Weekly Status Report—Week Ending April 17; April 10, 1973, Folder: Human Resources Programs: Weekly Status Reports 1973, Box 471, Weinberger Papers.

75. Note from Taft to McConahey; March 28, 1973, attached to Memorandum to: The Counsellor; From: Howard Phillips; Subject: Weekly Status Report—Week Ending March 17; March 21, 1973, Folder: Human Resources Programs: Weekly Status Reports 1973, Box 471, Weinberger Papers.

76. McConahey's handwritten query on Memorandum to: The Counsellor; From: Howard Phillips; Subject: Weekly Status Report—Week Ending March 17; March 21, 1973; p. 2, Folder: Human Resources Programs: Weekly Status Reports 1973, Box 471, Weinberger Papers.

77. Handwritten note on Memorandum for: The Counsellor; From: Howard Phillips; Subject: Weekly Status Report—Week Ending May 2; April 25, 1973, Folder: Human Resources Programs: Weekly Status Reports 1973, Box 471, Weinberger Papers.

78. Memorandum to: Mr. Caspar W. Weinberger, Counsellor to the President for Human Resources, The White House; From: Robert J. Kingston, Deputy Chairman, National Endowment for the Humanities; Subject: Weekly Status Report—Week Ending Wednesday, April 4; April 2, 1973, p. 1, Folder: Human Resources Programs: Weekly Status Reports 1973, Box 471, Weinberger Papers.

79. The term *council* in Domestic Council connotes a high-level committee of principals. It rarely met. References to the Domestic Council usually meant its staff. Thus, when the relationships between counsellors and the Domestic Council are discussed, the latter are references to one cluster of EOP staff. There was also some confusion in the records because "Council staff" and "Counsellor staff" sounded similar in dictation.

80. Memo for: Ken Cole; From: Cap Weinberger; February 20, 1973, Folder: Human Resources Council Committee: Contacts 1973, Box 471, Weinberger Papers. Naturally, Cole could have used a photocopier to make a copy and then return the original, with or without Weinberger's permission.

81. Memo to: William H. Taft IV; From: James Cavanaugh; February 16, 1973, Folder 2: DHEW [1 of 3], Box 67, Government Files, W. Taft Papers. This sequence of events suggests that perhaps the exchange between Taft and Cavanaugh then escalated, going up one notch of the hierarchy, to the exchange four days later between Weinberger and Cole.

82. Memorandum for: Members of the Council on Human Resources; From: Caspar W. Weinberger, Counsellor to the President; Subject: The Council on Human Resources; February 15, 1973, Folder: Health Resource Programs—General—1973, Box 471, Weinberger Papers. However, later documents usually called it a committee.

83. Memorandum to: Marvin Franklin, Special Assistant to the Secretary [of Interior] for Indian Affairs, and William L. Rogers, Deputy Assistant Secretary—Public Land Management; From: The Under Secretary [John Whitaker]; Subject: Interior's participation in the Council on Human Resources; February 27, 1973, p. 1 (emphasis added), Folder: Health Resource Programs—General—1973, Box 471, Weinberger Papers.

84. Memorandum for: Honorable Elliot L. Richardson; From: Caspar W. Weinberger; Subject: Cabinet Committee for Human Resources; April 20, 1973, Folder: Staff 1973, Box 472, Weinberger Papers; Letter to Mr. Robert H. Kroepsch, Executive Director, WICHE; from Julia Vadala, April 18, 1973, J. Taft Personal Files.

85. Agenda for Initial Meeting of Functional Working Committees, March 9, 1973 (emphasis added), Folder: Staff 1973, Box 472, Weinberger Papers.

86. Ibid., Attachment B: General Comments by Counsellor Weinberger, p. 3.

87. Tab B: List of Attendees; Memorandum for: Counsellor Weinberger; From: Julia Vadala; Subject: Agenda for Health Working Group, May 4; May 3, 1973, Folder 3: DHEW 1973 [2 of 3], Box 67, Government File, W. Taft Papers.

88. Membership list of Health Subcommittee, April 11, 1973, J. Taft Personal Files.

89. Resource Personnel/FYI Offices, Health Working Committee, April 24, 1973, p. 4, J. Taft Personal Files.

90. Attendees, National Health Insurance Task Force, May 8, 1973, J. Taft Personal Files.

91. Memorandum for Dr. James Cavanaugh; From: Julia Vadala; Subject: Acknowledgment and Release of the Report of the President's Committee on Health Education; May 14, 1973, J. Taft Personal Files. Note that this memo was sent four days after the abolition of the counsellors, so Vadala no longer was a counsellor staffer.

92. James Cavanaugh, interview by author, March 2, 2007, p. 3.

CHAPTER 6. COUNSELLOR FOR COMMUNITY DEVELOPMENT JAMES LYNN

1. Office of the White House Press Secretary, Community Development Fact Sheet, March 8, 1973, p. 3, Folder: Community Development [1 of 2], Box 9, Alpha-Subject Files, Raoul-Duval Papers.

2. Office of the White House Press Secretary, Press Conference of James T. Lynn, Secretary of Housing and Urban Development and Counsellor to the President for Community Development (transcript); March 8, 1973, p. 1, Folder: Community Development [1 of 2], Box 9, Alpha-Subject Files, Raoul-Duval Papers.

3. "Presidential Policy Guidance (Domestic Affairs)," Redirecting Executive Branch Management (slides), Folder: Bi-Partisan Leaders Organization Briefing, Box 68, Speeches and Briefing 1970–1973, Ehrlichman Papers.

4. Appendix D: Counsellor to the President for Community Development; Memorandum; From: John Dean; Subject: Methods for Reorganizing the Executive Branch; January 2, 1973, Folder: [Reorganization-EOP Part II], Box 174, Alphabetical Subject Files, Haldeman Papers.

5. Presumably, had the counsellor positions lasted longer, Lynn might have sought more of a role in overseeing anti-poverty programs. Things definitely would have changed if the DCD bill had passed. Lou Cannon, "Plans Seen to Scrap OEO: Programs to Be Shifted" (column), *Victoria (Tex.) Advocate,* January 24, 1973.

6. Senate Committee on Appropriations, *Department of Housing and Urban Development, Space, Science, Veterans, and Certain Other Independent Agencies' Appropriations for Fiscal Year 1974* (hearings), 93rd Cong., 1st sess., 1973, p. 1654.

7. Annotated Agenda for Mr. Lynn [for first meeting of Community Development Committee, March 5, 1973], n.d., n.a., p. 1, Folder: Community Development [1 of 2], Box 9, Alpha-Subject Files, Raoul-Duval Papers.

8. Senate Committee on Agriculture and Forestry, *Implementation of the Rural Development Act,* 137 (emphasis added).

9. For example, Lynn did not use the "place" terminology in a speech in Anderson, South Carolina, on March 6 or at a White House press conference on March 8. "New Federalism," *Congressional Record* 119:8 (March 27, 1973): 9681–82; Office of the White House Press Secretary, Press Conference of James T. Lynn, Secretary of Housing and Urban Development and Counsellor to the President for Community Development (transcript), March 8, 1973, Folder: Community Development [1 of 2], Box 9, Alpha-Subject Files, Raoul-Duval Papers.

10. Senate Committee on Appropriations, *Department of Housing and Urban Development and Related Agencies Appropriations for Fiscal Year 1974* (hearings), 93rd Cong., 1st sess., 1973, 1655.

11. Senate Committee on Agriculture and Forestry, *Implementation of the Rural Development Act,* 136.

12. Senate Committee on Banking, Housing, and Urban Affairs, *Oversight on Housing and Urban Development,* 286.

13. James T. Lynn, interview by author, March 23, 2007.

14. Senate Committee on Banking, Housing, and Urban Affairs, *Nomination of James T. Lynn,* 22.

15. House Committee on Appropriations, *HUD-Space-Science-Veterans Appropriations for 1974 (Part 3)* (hearings), 93rd Cong., 1st sess., 1973, 7.

16. Lynn interview.

17. The Nixon White House had a general preference for hiring former military officers. Symbolism and partisan ideologies aside, officers were viewed as having demonstrated leadership and organizational skills.

18. Annotated Agenda for Mr. Lynn [for first meeting of Community Development Committee on March 5, 1973], n.d., n.a., p. 2, Folder: Community Development [1 of 2], Box 9, Alpha-Subject Files, Raoul-Duval Papers.

19. Community Development Committee [staff list], n.d., Folder: Community Development Committee, Box 2, Butz Papers; letter from William W. Blunt Jr., Acting Assistant Secretary for Economic Development, Commerce Department, to Michael Raoul-Duval, May 11, 1973, Folder: EDA I [1 of 3], Box 12, Alpha-Subject Files, Raoul-Duval Papers.

20. Michel was listed as a staff member handling program coordination on informal notes to be used by Lynn at the first CDC meeting. Annotated Agenda for Mr. Lynn [for first meeting of Community Development Committee, March 5, 1973], n.d., n.a., p. 2, Folder: Community Development [1 of 2], Box 9, Alpha-Subject Files, Raoul-Duval Papers. However, he was not listed on a formal staff list distributed externally. Community Development Committee [staff list], n.d., Folder: Community Development Committee, Box 2, Butz Papers. Also, when Staff Secretary Kehrli provided a final accounting for the costs of running Lynn's counsellor office after it had been canceled, only Collier, Parker, and Raoul-Duval were listed. Memorandum for: Honorable James T. Lynn;

From: Bruce A. Kehrli; June 13, 1973, Folder: Counsellor Lynn, Box 94, Memoranda Files, Staff Secretary Files.

21. EDA and the Appalachian Regional Commission continue to exist at the time of writing (2009).

22. Lynn's handwritten notes on Memorandum for: James T. Lynn; From: Calvin J. Collier; Subject: Possible Activities for Community Development Committee; February 22, 1973, Folder: Community Development/Committee Meetings, Box 10, Alpha-Subject Files, Raoul-Duval Papers.

23. Enumerated items from Collier memo, ibid.

24. Paul Delaney, "Cities' Aides See Easing of U.S. Stand on Funds," *New York Times,* March 6, 1973; Jim Squires, "Administration Is Seeking Funds to Aid City Programs: Opposition Is Softened," *Chicago Tribune,* March 6, 1973; "The Nation" (national news shorts), *Los Angeles Times,* March 6, 1973; *Congressional Record* 119:8 (March 27, 1973): 9681–82.

25. Nixon, *Public Papers of the Presidents: 1973,* 166, 174, 176, 179.

26. Memorandum for: James T. Lynn; From: Douglas Parker and Lawrence Goldberg; March 2, 1973, p. 2, Folder: Community Development [1 of 2], Box 9, Alpha-Subject Files, Raoul-Duval Papers.

27. Seidman, *Politics, Position, and Power,* 85.

28. Senate Committee on Agriculture and Forestry, *Implementation of the Rural Development Act,* 142.

29. Douglas Parker, interview by author, August 17, 2006; Memorandum for: James T. Lynn; From: Doug Parker; Subject: Community Development Message—Rural Development and the Department of Community Development; March 5, 1973, Folder: Community Development [2 of 2], Box 10, Alpha-Subject Files, Raoul-Duval Papers.

30. Memorandum for: James T. Lynn; From: Douglas M. Parker; Subject: Oversight Hearings on Rural Development Act—Department of Community Development; March 13, 1973, Folder: Community Development [2 of 2], Box 10, Alpha-Subject Files, Raoul-Duval Papers.

31. Testimony of James Lynn, Secretary of Housing and Urban Development, before the Senate Committee on Agriculture and Forestry, March 27, 1973 [pre-hearing prepared testimony], Folder: James T. Lynn—Counsellor for CD [*sic*], Box 20, Alpha-Subject Files, Raoul-Duval Papers.

32. Senate Committee on Agriculture and Forestry, *Implementation of the Rural Development Act,* 136–37.

33. Nixon, *Public Papers of the Presidents: 1973,* 171–80.

34. Office of the White House Press Secretary, Press Conference of James T. Lynn, Secretary of Housing and Urban Development and Counsellor to the President for Community Development (transcript); March 8, 1973, p. 1, Folder: Community Development [1 of 2], Box 9, Alpha-Subject Files, Raoul-Duval Papers.

35. Memorandum for: James T. Lynn; From: Peter A. Michel; Subject: Proposed Schedule for Preparing the Better Communities Act Legislation; March 13, 1973, p. 2, Folder: Better Communities, Box 9, Alpha-Subject Files, Raoul-Duval Papers.

36. Bill Kovach, "Nixon Seeks $2.3-Billion in a New Urban Plan," *New York Times,* April 20, 1973; UPI, "Nixon Proposes End of Urban Renewal Aid," *Los Angeles Times,* April 20, 1973.

37. Tom Seppy, "Politics in Fund Share," *Uniontown (Pa.) Morning Herald—Evening Standard,* April 23, 1973; James M. Naughton, "Striking a Bargain on the Elderly," *New York Times,* April 22, 1973.

38. Memorandum for: Jim Mitchell; From: Michael Raoul-Duval; Re: Better Communities Act; April 30, 1973, Folder: Better Communities, Box 9, Alpha-Subject Files, Raoul-Duval Papers.

39. Senate Committee on Government Operations, *Establish a Department of Community Development* (hearings), 92nd Cong., 2nd sess., 1972, 1318–22.

40. Memorandum for: Larry Goldberg; From: Cal Collier; Subject: Department of Community Development; February 23, 1973, Folder: Community Development [2 of 2], Box 10, Alpha-Subject Files, Raoul-Duval Papers.

41. Memorandum for James T. Lynn; From: Douglas Parker and Lawrence Goldberg; March 2, 1973, p. 1. Folder: Community Development [1 of 2], Box 9, Alpha-Subject Files, Raoul-Duval Papers.

42. Memorandum from OMB's Dwight Ink to Parker regarding status of DCD, p. 2, Tab A in Memorandum for: James T. Lynn; From: Douglas M. Parker; Subject: Oversight Hearings on Rural Development Act—Department of Community Development; March 13, 1973, Folder: Community Development [2 of 2], Box 10, Alpha-Subject Files, Raoul-Duval Papers.

43. Memorandum for: James T. Lynn; From: Doug Parker; Subject: Department of Community Development; April 6, 1973, Folder: Community Development [1 of 2], Box 9, Alpha-Subject Files, Raoul-Duval Papers.

44. To: Doug Parker; From: James T. Lynn; Subject: Department of Community Development; April 9, 1973 (handwritten notes over April 6 memo to Lynn from Parker, in ibid.).

45. Note for: Doug Parker; From: Michael Raoul-Duval; Re: April 6 Memo on the Department of Community Development; April 10, 1973, Folder: Community Development [2 of 2], Box 10, Alpha-Subject Files, Raoul-Duval Papers. It is unclear if the handwritten notes on the document are Parker's or Raoul-Duval's.

46. Seventeen days later, Ehrlichman revealed that Krogh had been involved in the "plumbers' break-in" at Daniel Ellsberg's psychiatrist's office.

47. The indices of the *Congressional Record* for the first and second sessions of the Ninety-third Congress list neither a DCD bill introduced at the administration's request nor a bill that Holifield introduced on his own.

48. Draft(2):Duval:8/28/73, n.t., Folder: Community Development [1 of 2], Box 9, Alpha-Subject Files, Raoul-Duval Papers. The first sentence of the untitled three-page draft was: "This Fall will see considerable activity by the Nixon Administration in the field of Community Development."

49. Memorandum for: James T. Lynn; From: Calvin J. Collier; Subject: Agenda Items for Community Development Sub-Committee Meeting; February 22, 1973, Folder: Community Development [1 of 2], Box 9, Alpha-Subject Files, Raoul-Duval Papers.

50. Senate Committee on Banking, Housing, and Urban Affairs, *Oversight on Housing and Urban Development,* 286. The membership of the Office of Emergency Preparedness on the committee was temporary. As part of his effort to reduce EOP's size, Nixon submitted Reorganization Plan No. 1 (for 1973) to Congress to disestablish the office and shift its major activities to HUD. The plan went into effect on July 1, 1973.

Nixon, *Public Papers of the Presidents: 1973,* 23–25; "Nixon Proposes Disaster Aid Unit: Office Would Meld Tasks Now Shared by Agencies," *New York Times,* May 9, 1973.

51. Handwritten comments by Parker on his "FYI copy" of Talking Points for First Community Development Committee Meeting, Draft: MRD [Michael Raoul-Duval]:jc 3/2/73, p. 1, Folder: Community Development [1 of 2], Box 9, Alpha-Subject Files, Raoul-Duval Papers.

52. Memorandum for: Cal Collier; From: Peter A. Michel; Subject: Community Development Committee Meeting; February 27, 1973, pp. 1–2, Folder: Community Development/Committee Meetings, Box 10, Alpha-Subject Files, Raoul-Duval Papers.

53. Memorandum for: James T. Lynn; From: Michael Raoul-Duval; Re: Community Development Committee Meeting; February 27, 1973, Folder: Community Development-/-Committee Meetings, Box 10, Alpha-Subject Files, Raoul-Duval Papers.

54. Memorandum for: Calvin J. Collier; From: Douglas M. Parker; Subject: Current Operations of the Counsellor's Office; February 27, 1973, p. 3, Folder: Community Development [1 of 2], Box 9, Alpha-Subject Files, Raoul-Duval Papers.

55. Memorandum for: James T. Lynn; From: Calvin J. Collier; Subject: Agenda Items for Community Development Sub-Committee Meeting; March 1, 1973; Annotated Agenda for Mr. Lynn, n.d., n.a.; Talking Points for First Community Development Committee Meeting, Draft: MRD [Michael Raoul-Duval]:jc 3/2/73, all in Folder: Community Development [1 of 2], Box 9, Alpha-Subject Files, Raoul-Duval Papers.

56. Annotated Agenda for Mr. Lynn [for first meeting of Community Development Committee, March 5, 1973], n.d., n.a., p. 1, Folder: Community Development [1 of 2], Box 9, Alpha-Subject Files, Raoul-Duval Papers. It is likely, but not documented, that Ehrlichman's absence was due to the Watergate crisis.

57. Community Development Committee, Agenda, March 5, 1973, Folder: White House—Memoranda to U.S.D.A., Box 2, Butz Papers. While the records are sketchy, apparently all three principals attended: Butz, Brinegar, and Dent.

58. Memorandum for: Community Development Committee Members [draft]; From: James T. Lynn; Subject: Community Development Committee Meeting; March 27, 1973, p. 1, Folder: Community Development/Committee Meetings, Box 10, Alpha-Subject Files, Raoul-Duval Papers. Lynn personally made many of these decisions. The first sentence of the typed draft read: "There will be a meeting of the Community Development Committee at ____ on ____ in the ____ Conference Room (____)." Here is how the last part of the sentence read with the handwritten additions provided by Lynn: "in the Roosevelt R[oo]m ~~Conference Room~~ (West Wing)."

59. Memorandum for: Community Development Committee Members; From: James T. Lynn; Subject: Community Development Committee Meeting; March 30, 1973, Folder: Community Development/Committee Meetings, Box 10, Alpha-Subject Files, Raoul-Duval Papers.

60. Memorandum to: Acting Associate Administrator for Program Planning [UMTA, DOT]; From: Bruce Barkley, Director of Program Development; Subject: Community Development Council [*sic*] Role; March 30, 1973, Folder: Community Development/Committee Meetings, Box 10, Alpha-Subject Files, Raoul-Duval Papers.

61. Memorandum for: Bobbie J. Crider [Counsellor Butz's secretary]; From: Calvin J. Collier; April 10, 1973, Folder: White House—Memoranda to U.S.D.A., Box 2, Butz Papers.

62. Senate Committee on Agriculture and Forestry, *Implementation of the Rural Development Act*, 136.

63. Memorandum for: Bobbie J. Crider; From: Calvin J. Collier; April 10, 1973, p. 1.

64. Memorandum for: James T. Lynn; From: Douglas M. Parker; Subject: Community Development Committee Meeting—Talking Points on Rural Development Act; March 30, 1973, Folder: Community Development/Committee Meetings, Box 10, Alpha-Subject Files, Raoul-Duval Papers.

65. Memorandum for: Bobbie J. Crider; From: Calvin J. Collier; April 10, 1973, p. 1.

66. Ibid., p. 2.

67. Memorandum for: Dana Mead & Cal Collier; From: Michael Raoul-Duval; Re: CDC Legislative Subcommittee Meeting; April 10, 1973, Folder: Community Development/Committee Meetings, Box 10, Alpha-Subject Files, Raoul-Duval Papers. Raoul-Duval's memo was issued the same day that Collier wrote Crider that CDC did not have subcommittees "as such." Memorandum for: Bobbie J. Crider; From: Calvin J. Collier; April 10, 1973, p. 1. Presumably the reference to the CDC Legislative Subcommittee was simply an incorrect use of the group's title.

68. Memorandum for: James T. Lynn; From: Calvin J. Collier; Subject: Possible Activities for Community Development Committee; February 22, 1973, p. 2, Folder: Community Development/Committee Meetings, Box 10, Alpha-Subject Files, Raoul-Duval Papers.

69. Annotated Agenda for Mr. Lynn [for first meeting of Community Development Committee on March 5, 1973], n.d., n.a., p. 3, Folder: Community Development [1 of 2], Box 9, Alpha-Subject Files, Raoul-Duval Papers.

70. Memorandum for: James T. Lynn; From: Calvin J. Collier; Subject: Agenda Items for Community Development Sub-Committee Meeting; March 1, 1973, p. 1, Folder: Community Development [1 of 2], Box 9, Alpha-Subject Files, Raoul-Duval Papers.

71. Memorandum for: Cal Collier; From: Michael Raoul-Duval; Re: Human Resources Committee Procedures; March 15, 1973, Folder: Community Development [1 of 2], Box 9, Alpha-Subject Files, Raoul-Duval Papers.

72. Handwritten notes on draft, p. 3 (emphasis added), of Memorandum for: Community Development Committee Members; From: James T. Lynn; Subject: Community Development Committee Meeting; March 27, 1973 [draft], Folder: Community Development-/Committee Meetings, Box 10, Alpha-Subject Files, Raoul-Duval Papers.

73. Memorandum for: All Members of the Community Development Committee; From: James T. Lynn; March 27, 1973, Folder: White House—Memoranda to U.S.D.A., Box 2, Butz Papers. Notwithstanding the date and purpose of the memo (and attached blank form), according to a typewritten notation both were redistributed at the April 2 CDC meeting.

74. Attachment, in ibid.

75. [Memo] To: Counsellor James T. Lynn, The White House; From Joseph R. Wright Jr., Assistant USDA Secretary for Administration; Subject: Action-Forcing Events for Rural Development, April 15, 1973; April 16, 1973, Folder: Community Development [1 of 2], Box 9, Alpha-Subject Files, Raoul-Duval Papers.

76. Lynn interview; Mead interview.

77. Mead said that whatever professional disagreements they had, it did not affect their later relationship. After both left government, their friendship increased; they even went on a fishing trip.

78. Mead interview.

79. Memorandum for: James T. Lynn; From: Calvin J. Collier; Subject: Possible Activities for Community Development Committee; February 22, 1973, p. 1, Folder: Community Development/Committee Meetings, Box 10, Alpha-Subject Files, Raoul-Duval Papers.

80. Memorandum for: Community Development Committee Members; From: James T. Lynn; Subject: Community Development Committee Meeting; March 27, 1973, p. 3 [draft], Folder: Community Development/Committee Meetings, Box 10, Alpha-Subject Files, Raoul-Duval Papers. However, the final document listed the bcc recipients in alphabetical order. Memorandum for: Community Development Committee Members; From: James T. Lynn; Subject: Community Development Committee Meeting; March 30, 1973, Folder: Community Development/Committee Meetings, Box 10, Alpha-Subject Files, Raoul-Duval Papers.

81. Memorandum for: James T. Lynn; From: Peter A. Michel; Subject: Proposed Schedule for Preparing the Better Communities Act Legislation; March 13, 1973, Folder: Better Communities, Box 9; Memorandum for Wally Scott [OMB]; From: Michael Raoul-Duval; Re: EDA; May 9, 1973, Folder: EDA I [1 of 3], Box 12, both in Alpha-Subject Files, Raoul-Duval Papers.

82. "HUD's New Secretary Has Special White House Role," *Journal of Housing* 30:2 (February 28, 1973): 62.

CHAPTER 7. COUNSELLOR FOR NATURAL RESOURCES EARL BUTZ

1. Ehrlichman notes of Nixon meeting with Butz on November 20, 1973, at Camp David; loyalty questionnaire administered to Butz by Ehrlichman, Folder: Notes 8/7/72–12/13/72 [5 of 9], Box 13, John D. Ehrlichman Notes of Meetings.

2. Senate Committee on Appropriations, *Department of the Interior and Related Agencies Appropriations for Fiscal Year 1974,* Part 1 (hearings), 93rd Cong., 1st sess., 1973, 8 (first and second quotes), 9 (third quote).

3. Ibid., 8 (first and second quotes), 16 (third quote).

4. Ibid., 39.

5. "Presidential Policy Guidance (Domestic Affairs)," Redirecting Executive Branch Management (slides), Folder: Bi-Partisan Leaders Organization Briefing, Box 68, Speeches and Briefing 1970–1973, Ehrlichman Papers.

6. Appendix B: Counsellor to the President for Natural Resources; Memorandum; From: John Dean; Subject: Methods for Reorganizing the Executive Branch; January 2, 1973, Folder: [Reorganization-EOP Part II], Box 174, Alphabetical Subject Files, Haldeman Papers.

7. L. Carter, "Earl L. Butz, Counselor for Natural Resources," 359; Reuters, "Nixon to Ask Increase in Natural Gas Price," *Los Angeles Times,* March 6, 1973.

8. Memorandum for: H. R. Haldeman; From John D. Ehrlichman; February 1, 1973, Folder: 1 February 1973–28 February 1973 [1 of 3], Box 63, Chronological File 1969–1973, Ehrlichman Papers; Senate Committee on Appropriations, *Department of the Interior . . . for Fiscal Year 1974,* 14.

9. [Memo] To: Glenn Schleede; From: Earl Butz; Re: Your Assistance with the Energy Message; April 19, 1973, Folder: Counsellor Butz—Correspondence, Box 1, Butz Papers.

10. Memorandum for: John Ehrlichman; From: Tod R. Hullin; Subject: Who Should Testify before the Congress on the President's Energy Initiatives? April 11, 1973, Folder: 2 April 1973–16 May 1973 [1 of 4], Box 65, Chronological File 1969–1973, Ehrlichman Papers.

11. Memorandum for: Dick Fairbanks; From: Tod R. Hullin; Subject: Who Should Testify before the Congress on the President's Energy Initiatives? April 12, 1973, Folder: 2 April 1973–16 May 1973 [1 of 4], Box 65, Chronological File 1969–1973, Ehrlichman Papers.

12. [Note] To: Dr. DiBona; From: Dick Fairbanks; Subject: Mention of Counsellor's Role in Energy Message; April 16, 1973, Folder: March–April 1973, Box 1, Chronological Files, Glenn Schleede Papers, SMOF, WHCF, NPL.

13. Nixon, *Public Papers of the Presidents: 1973,* 317.

14. AP, "Train to Remain as Head of Environmental Panel," *New York Times,* January 12, 1973; L. Carter, "Earl L. Butz, Counselor for Natural Resources," 359; UPI, "Train Agrees to Stay, Will Report to Butz," *Washington Post,* January 12, 1973.

15. Mordecai Lee and Daniel A. Mazmanian, "Nixon's DENR Plan—Reorganization to What End?" unpublished article manuscript (typescript), September 1973, p. 21n30.

16. Tab A: Counsellor Butz Briefing: "Policy Directions and Program Relations in Natural Resources," Memorandum for: Secretary Butz; From: Dick Fairbanks; Subject: Natural Resources Briefing—Wednesday, February 7, 1973; February 6, 1973, Folder: Natural Resources, Box 3, Butz Papers; Fairbanks interview; John Whitaker, interview by author, February 16, 2007.

17. Theo Lippman Jr., "The Ordeal of Interior's Rogers Morton," *Los Angeles Times,* February 25, 1973.

18. Whitaker interview; Fairbanks interview.

19. Memorandum for: Counselor Earl Butz; From: Dick Fairbanks; Subject: Your Staff; January 11, 1973, Folder: Natural Resources, Box 3, Butz Papers. Butz made a point of introducing Ross at a congressional hearing. Senate Committee on Appropriations, *Department of the Interior . . . for Fiscal Year 1974,* 8.

20. Fairbanks interview.

21. Glenn Schleede, interview by author, December 12, 2006.

22. Proposed Press Release on Natural Resources Committee [draft], n.d., Folder: April 4, 1973—8:30 a.m., Meeting of the Natural Resources Committee, Box 4, Butz Papers; *U.S. Government Organization Manual 1972/73,* 249.

23. Memorandum to: Mr. Paul Henry; From: Bobbie Crider [Counsellor Butz's assistant]; Re: The Staff of Counsellor Earl L. Butz; March 21, 1973, Folder: White House General Administration, Box 1, Butz Papers.

24. Memorandum for: Secretary Butz; From: Dick Fairbanks; Subject: Natural Resources Briefing—Wednesday, February 7, 1973; February 6, 1973, Folder: Natural Resources, Box 3, Butz Papers.

25. Senate Committee on Government Operations, Ad Hoc Subcommittee on Impoundment of Funds and Committee on the Judiciary Subcommittee on Separation of Powers, *Impoundment of Appropriated Funds by the President* (joint hearings), 93rd Cong., 1st sess., 1973, 556.

26. House Committee on Appropriations, *Department of the Interior and Related Agencies Appropriations for 1974,* part 1 (hearings), 93rd Cong., 1st sess., 1973, 1–95.

27. Bonafede and Iglehart, "End of Counselor System," *National Journal* 5:20 (May 19, 1973): 728.

28. [Memo] To: Messrs. Fairbanks, Larson, Ross; n.a.; March 6, 1973, Folder: White House Interoffice Memoranda, Box 1, Butz Papers; Letter to Lt. Gen. Frederick J. Clarke, Chief of Engineers, U.S. Army; from Earl L. Butz, Counsellor to the President for Natural Resources; March 20, 1973, Folder: Organization and Function of Counsellor for Natural Resources, Box 33, Schleede Papers; Memorandum to: Counsellor Butz; From: Bobbie [Crider]; April 5, 1973, p. 2, Folder: Bobbie J. Crider Memos to Counsellor Butz, Box 1, Butz Papers.

29. For example: The Secretary's Weekly Schedule, Monday, April 16–Saturday, April 21, 1973; The Secretary's Schedule, Monday—April 23 [1973]; Memorandum to: Martha Lord; From: Bobbie Crider; Re: Counsellor Butz' Schedule for the Period April 29, 1973, thru [*sic*] May 5, 1973; April 27, 1973, Folder: White House—Counselor Butz's Schedules, Box 1, Butz Papers.

30. Office of the White House Press Secretary; Press Conference of Hon. Earl Butz, Secretary of Agriculture and Counsellor to the Press (transcript); April 9, 1973, Folder: Press Conference on Water & Sewer Veto—April 9, 1973, Box 3, Butz Papers.

31. Memorandum to: Counsellor Butz; From: Bobbie [Crider]; April 5, 1973, Folder: Bobbie J. Crider Memos to Counsellor Butz, Box 1, Butz Papers.

32. "Food Prices Going Higher?" *US News & World Report* 74:6 (February 5, 1973): 32.

33. UPI, "Butz Still Foresees Chicken-Price Dip," *Hartford (Conn.) Courant,* January 22, 1973; "Butz Links U.S. Grain Sales to Detente with Russ [*sic*]," *Chicago Tribune,* April 23, 1973.

34. [Memo] For: Counsellor Butz; From: Glenn Schleede; Subject: Proposed Speech to the National Coal Association Meeting on May 18; May 2, 1973 (emphasis added), Folder: May–June 1973, Box 1, Chronological Files, Schleede Papers. Ehrlichman had resigned two days earlier.

35. Senate Committee on Government Operations, Ad Hoc Subcommittee on Impoundment of Funds, *Impoundment of Appropriated Funds,* 557.

36. Letter to Honorable Frederick B. Dent, Secretary of Commerce; from Earl L. Butz, Counsellor to the President for Natural Resources; April 16, 1973, Folder: March–April 1973, Box 1, Chronological Files, Schleede Papers.

37. Memorandum for: Honorable John Whitaker, Under Secretary of the Interior; From: Earl L. Butz, Counsellor to the President; Subject: Northern Great Plains Resources Program; April 24, 1973, Folder: Counsellor Butz—Correspondence, Box 1, Butz Papers.

38. Memorandum for: Counsellor Butz; Through: Dick Fairbanks; From: Glenn Schleede; Subject: Letter to Dr. Ray on Uranium Enrichment for your Signature; May 1, 1973; Letter from Earl L. Butz, Counsellor to the President for Natural Resources; to

Honorable Dixy Lee Ray, Chairman, Atomic Energy Commission; May 2, 1973; both in Folder: May–June 1973; Box 1, Chronological Files, Schleede Papers.

39. Memorandum for: Counsellor Butz; From: Glenn Schleede; Subject: Dr. Dixy Lee Ray's desire to talk briefly with you *today* about our involvement in AEC-EPA relationships; May 2, 1973 (original emphasis), Folder: May–June 1973; Box 1, Chronological Files, Schleede Papers. In early March, testifying before Congress, Butz said that there had already been several instances when he mediated a compromise for interdepartmental problems in his role as counsellor. Senate Committee on Appropriations, *Department of the Interior . . . for Fiscal Year 1974,* 10.

40. Memorandum for: Counsellor Butz; From: Norm Ross; Subject: Proposed EPA Regulations Limiting Federal Procurement from Violators of the Clean Air Act; May 3, 1973; Memorandum for Honorable Earl L. Butz, Counsellor to the President for Natural Resources, Honorable Roy L. Ash, Director, Office of Management and Budget; From the Secretary of Commerce; Subject: Clean Air Act; April 20, 1973; [Memo] To: Norm Ross; From: Earl L. Butz; Re: EPA Regulations on Clean Air Act; May 7, 1973, all in Folder: White House—Environmental Protection Agency, Box 2, Butz Papers.

41. Later, after some bureaucratic jockeying, the general heading the Corps of Engineers was replaced by a civilian, the undersecretary of the army. Memorandum to: Natural Resources Committee; From: Earl L. Butz, Counsellor to the President for Natural Resources; Subject: Modification of Memorandum of March 12, 1973, Establishing Natural Resources Committee; April 4, 1973, Folder: Organization and Function of Counsellor for Natural Resources, Box 33, Schleede Papers.

42. Memorandum from: Earl L. Butz, Counselor to the President for Natural Resources; Subject: Establishment of the Natural Resources Committee; March 12, 1973, p. 2, Folder: Organization and Function of Counsellor for Natural Resources, Box 33, Schleede Papers.

43. Memorandum from: Earl L. Butz, Counselor to the President for Natural Resources; March 13, 1973, Folder: White House—Natural Resources Committee Correspondence, Box 2; Memorandum Re: Initial Meeting of the Natural Resources Committee Staff—March 21, 1973, 7:30 A.M., Breakfast in the White House Mess followed by Meeting in 100 EOB; March 20, 1973, Folder: March 21, 1973—7:30 A.M. Breakfast and Initial Meeting of Natural Resources Committee Staff, Box 4, both in Butz Papers.

44. Agenda: Meeting of the Natural Resources Committee, March 21, 1973, Folder: April 4, 1973—8:30 A.M. Meeting of the Natural Resources Committee, Box 4; Memorandum to: Counsellor Earl W. [*sic*] Butz; From: John C. Whitaker; March 22, 1973, Folder: Counsellor Butz—Correspondence [2 of 2], Box 1, both in Butz Papers.

45. N.a., n.t., n.d., internal counsellor staff document [probably mid-March 1973], Folder: Role of Counsellors, Box 33, Schleede Papers. The opening phrase was "Possible areas for attention by the Committee on Natural Resources."

46. Memorandum to: Natural Resources Committee; From: Earl L. Butz, Counsellor to the President for Natural Resources; Subject: Agenda for Meeting, April 4; April 2, 1973, Folder: April 4, 1973—8:30 A.M. Meeting of the Natural Resources Committee, Box 4, Butz Papers.

47. [Attendance list] Re: May 2, 1973—8:30 A.M. Meeting of the Natural Resources Committee Staff; May 1, 1973, Folder: May 2, 1973—8:30 A.M. Meeting of the Natural

Resources Committee Staff, Box 4, Butz Papers. The reference in the title to a meeting of the committee's *staff* is misleading. This was a meeting of the principals with Butz. Butz's three counsellor staffers attended, but they were not *members*.

48. Clean Air Act Standards and Regulations, 5/1/73 [handout for the meeting], Folder: May 2, 1973—8:30 A.M. Meeting of the Natural Resources Committee Staff, Box 4, Butz Papers.

49. Memorandum for: Members of the Natural Resources Committee; From: Earl L. Butz; Subject: Meeting with the Committee, 8:30 A.M., Wednesday, May 2, 1973; April 30, 1973, Folder: May 2, 1973—8:30 A.M. Meeting of the Natural Resources Committee Staff, Box 4, Butz Papers.

50. Memorandum to: Natural Resources Committee; From: Earl L. Butz, Counsellor to the President for Natural Resources; Subject: Proposed Subcommittees of the Natural Resources Committee; March 20, 1973, Folder: Organization and Function of Counsellor for Natural Resources, Box 33, Schleede Papers.

51. Memorandum to: Natural Resources Committee; From: Earl L. Butz, Counsellor to the President for Natural Resources; Subject: Subcommittees of the Natural Resources Committee; April 4, 1973, Folder: Organization and Function of Counsellor for Natural Resources, Box 33, Schleede Papers.

52. Memorandum to: Natural Resources Committee; From: Earl L. Butz, Counsellor to the President for Natural Resources; Subject: Proposed Subcommittees of the Natural Resources Committee; March 20, 1973, p. 1, Folder: Organization and Function of Counsellor for Natural Resources, Box 33, Schleede Papers.

53. Re: March 31, 1973, 10:00 A.M. Meeting of the Timber Task Force in Room 100 EOB; March 30, 1973 [attendance list and agenda], Folder: March 31, 1973, 10:00 A.M. Meeting of Timber Task Force, 100 EOB, Box 4, Butz Papers.

54. [Job description of John W. Larson, executive director of the Natural Resources Committee and chief of staff to Counsellor Butz], n.a. [probably Larson]; n.d. [probably mid- to late March, 1973], Folder: White House General Administration, Box 1, Butz Papers.

55. Memorandum to: Natural Resources Committee Members; From: Earl L. Butz; Counsellor to the President for Natural Resources; Subject: Reporting and Clearance Procedures for the Counsellor's Office; March 20, 1973, Folder: Organization and Function of Counsellor for Natural Resources, Box 33, Schleede Papers.

56. Ibid., p. 2 (emphasis added).

57. Memorandum to: Natural Resources Committee; From: Earl L. Butz, Counsellor to the President for Natural Resources; Subject: Reporting and Clearance Procedures for the Counsellor's Office; April 4, 1973; Memorandum to: Natural Resources Committee Members; From: Earl L. Butz; Counsellor to the President for Natural Resources; Subject: Reporting and Clearance Procedures for the Counsellor's Office; REVISED April 4, 1973, both in Folder: Organization and Function of Counsellor for Natural Resources, Box 33, Schleede Papers.

58. Memorandum to: Earl L. Butz; From: John C. Whitaker; Subject: Monthly Written Report for Natural Resources Committee; April 27, 1973, Folder: May 2, 1973—8:30 A.M. Meeting of the Natural Resources Committee Staff, Box 4, Butz Papers. The memo was a cover letter transmitting the enclosed report.

59. Memorandum for: Honorable Earl L. Butz, Counsellor to the President for Natural Resources; From: Robert M. White, Administrator, NOAA; Subject: Monthly Written Report; April 27, 1973, Folder: May 2, 1973—8:30 A.M. Meeting of the Natural Resources Committee Staff, Box 4, Butz Papers.

60. Archival files did not contain reports from other major components of Butz's domain, such as EPA, CEQ, or TVA.

61. Fairbanks interview.

62. Schleede interview; Whitaker interview.

CHAPTER 8. DEMISE, APRIL–MAY 1973

1. House Committee on Appropriations, *Treasury . . . for Fiscal Year 1974*, 614; Jack Anderson, "Did Soviets Manipulate U.S. Market?" (Washington Merry-Go-Round column), *Washington Post*, July 27, 1973. According to Anderson, the sum of sixty-three hundred dollars was spent on "alterations and built-in cabinetry" for Weinberger's office and one thousand dollars went toward improvements in Lynn's office.

2. April 30, 1973, n.t., pp. 1–2 (emphasis added), Folder: January 1973–February 1973 [9 of 27], Box 4, Domestic Council (FG 6–15), Subject Files. The authorship of the untitled document is unclear, but it is a fair inference that DC Director Cole would at least have reviewed it.

3. Senate Committee on Government Operations, *Reorganization Plan No. 1 of 1973* (hearings), 93rd Cong., 1st sess., 1973, 28. This was the Subcommittee on Reorganization, Research, and International Organizations, chaired by Ribicoff.

4. Memorandum for: Kenneth R. Cole Jr.; From Tod Hullin; Subject: Briefing for Cabinet and sub-Cabinet; February 5, 1973, Folder: 1 February 1973–28 February 1973 [1 of 3], Box 63; Memorandum for: Ken Cole; From: Tod R. Hullin; Subject: Briefing for Cabinet and Sub-Cabinet; February 14, 1973, Folder: 1 February 1973–28 February 1973 [2 of 3], Box 64, both in Chronological File 1969–1973, Ehrlichman Papers.

5. Carroll Kilpatrick, "Ehrlichman Scores Critics of Budget Cuts," *Washington Post*, February 9, 1973; Aldo Beckman, "Nixon Attitude Alters Markedly: Seems to Be More Relaxed," *Chicago Tribune*, February 12, 1973.

6. Jules Witcover, "Ehrlichman Sees Nixon as a Time-Conscious President," *Washington Post*, March 27, 1973.

7. [Appointment Schedule for John D. Ehrlichman, 1969–1973], Box 2, Appointment Calendars and Diaries 1969–1973, Ehrlichman Papers.

8. [Memo] For: Ken Clawson; From: Tod R. Hullin; March 16, 1973, Folder: 1 March 1973–31 March 1973 [4 of 5], Box 65, Chronological File 1969–1973, Ehrlichman Papers.

9. [Memo] For: Ken Cole; From: Tod R. Hullin; Subject: Counsellor Hearings; April 16, 1973, Folder: 2 April 1973–May 16 1973 [2 of 4], Box 65, Chronological File 1969–1973, Ehrlichman Papers. The "public hearings" never happened, in part due to Watergate and the abrupt termination of the counsellor project.

10. Mead interview, p. 8; Fairbanks interview, p. 9; Cavanaugh interview, p. 8.

11. Fairbanks interview, p. 9. The incident left a strong impression on Fairbanks, seemingly proving that Ehrlichman had not been at all involved in the Watergate cover-up. Fairbanks felt personally let down when later events proved otherwise.

12. Senate Committee on Labor and Public Welfare, *Caspar W. Weinberger,* 3–4; Senate Committee on Banking, Housing, and Urban Affairs, *Nomination of James T. Lynn,* 8–9; Senate Committee on Appropriations, *Department of the Interior . . . for Fiscal Year 1974,* 8–9.

13. Nixon, *Public Papers of the Presidents: 1973,* 186 (emphasis added).

14. The Secretary's Schedule, Thursday—April 26, [1973], Folder: White House—Counsellor Butz's Schedules, Box 1, Butz Papers. Lacking any archival record or memoir of their discussion, these conclusions are the author's interpretation based on context, circumstances, and the subsequent behavior of the counsellors.

15. John Herbers, "Watergate Impact Found Slowing Work in Capital," *New York Times,* April 27, 1973 (emphasis added).

16. House Committee on Appropriations, *HUD-Space-Science-Veterans Appropriations for 1974,* 63, 65.

17. Memorandum for: Counsellor Weinberger; From: Julia Vadala; Subject: Health Industry Advisory Committee—Action Memorandum; May 4, 1973; Memorandum for Honorable Kenneth R. Cole; From Caspar W. Weinberger; Subject: Health Industry Advisory Committee; May 5, 1973, both in Folder: Health Industry Advisory Committee—1973, Box 471, Weinberger Papers.

18. Don Irwin, "Effect on Agencies Ranges from 'Paralysis' to 'Business as Usual,'" *Los Angeles Times,* May 1, 1973.

19. Nixon presented the resignations as part of a larger effort he was making to clean house and remove any possible links between his presidency and Watergate. He also fired Legal Counsel John Dean and accepted the resignation of Attorney General Richard Kleindienst.

20. Letter to The Honorable Caspar Weinberger, The White House; from John D. Ehrlichman; May 2, 1973, Folder: 2 April 1973–16 May 1973 [3 of 4], Box 65, Chronological File 1969–1973, Ehrlichman Papers. It was something of a form letter, but Ehrlichman sent it only to a select few. The archival records did not contain similar letters to Lynn or Butz.

21. Letter to the Honorable John D. Ehrlichman, The White House; from Caspar W. Weinberger, Counsellor to the President for Human Resources; May 10, 1973, Folder: Reading File 1973, Box 472, Weinberger Papers.

22. "As Nixon Picks Up the Pieces," *US News & World Report* 74:20 (May 14, 1973): 18. This issue, while dated May 14, came out before Nixon's May 10 Cabinet meeting.

23. Christopher Lydon, "Maneuvers among the Hopefuls," *New York Times,* May 6, 1973.

24. Memorandum for: the Vice President; From Caspar W. Weinberger; May 7, 1973, J. Taft Personal Files.

25. Haig, *Inner Circles,* 343.

26. Lynn interview, p. 1.

27. Parker interview, p. 1.

28. Roy L. Ash, oral history interview conducted by Frederick J. Graboske, August 4, 1988, Nixon Presidential Materials Staff, National Archives and Records Administration, p. 46.

29. Haig, *Inner Circles,* 343.

30. Bonafede and Iglehart, "End of Counselor System," *National Journal* 5:20 (May 19, 1973): 726.

31. Haig claimed "a doubling of my own work" by taking on Ehrlichman's domestic policy job as well as becoming chief of staff. Haig, *Inner Circles,* 345. This seems an exaggeration vis-à-vis Cole's work.

32. Cabinet Meeting, Thursday, May 10, 1973 [pre-meeting notes]; [to the President]; from Patrick J. Buchanan; May 9, 1973; Folder: Cabinet Meetings, Box 3, FG 10–1, Cabinet Files, WHCF, NPL.

33. Letters to Donald Rees, Executive Director, Yosemite Institute, Yosemite National Park; and Mrs. Henry Gibbons III, San Francisco; May 10, 1973; Memorandum for: Mr. Lindner; From: Caspar W. Weinberger; May 10, 1973, both in Folder: Reading File 1973, Box 472, Weinberger Papers.

34. Cabinet Meeting, Thursday, May 10, 1973 [pre-meeting notes]; [to the President]; from Patrick J. Buchanan; pp. 1–2.

35. All quotes from the May 10 Cabinet meeting are from an unofficial transcript prepared by the author from the then-secret tape of the meeting. Tape CAB 120–3, NPL. The sound quality is very poor. Therefore, the quotes reflect the author's best effort at transcription, but they are neither official nor authoritative. After most Cabinet meetings, a staff note-taker would routinely submit a relatively authoritative "Memorandum of Conversation," summarizing the meeting for the files. However, the National Archives does not have in its files such a document for the May 10, 1973, Cabinet meeting. E-mail to the author from Mark Fischer, Reference Archivist/Team Leader, Nixon Presidential Library, National Archives and Records Administration, College Park, Md., August 4, 2008, author's files. This absence of a summary of the meeting is likely an indication of the chaos in White House staff operations caused by the departures of Haldeman and Ehrlichman and the arrival of Haig.

36. *Weekly Compilation of Presidential Documents* 9:19 (May 14, 1973): 662–63. This is the published version of Ziegler's statement at the beginning of the press conference but not the subsequent Q&A. The differences between the transcript (see next note) and the published version of his statement are minor, such as cleaning up some punctuation and other negligible details. I have opted to cite these passages from the official version because it is from a published source and therefore is a more accessible source.

37. News Conference #1735, at the White House with Ron Ziegler at 11:40 A.M. EDT, May 10, 1973, Thursday (transcript), p. 6, Folder: James T. Lynn—Counselor for CD, Box 20, Alpha-Subject Files, Raoul-Duval Papers.

38. Ibid., p. 13.

39. Lou Cannon, "Nixon Junks 'Super-Cabinet' After 4 Months," *Washington Post,* May 11, 1973.

40. Memorandum for: Honorable James T. Lynn; From: Bruce A. Kehrli; June 13, 1973, Folder: Counsellor Lynn, Box 94, Memoranda Files, Staff Secretary Files. In contrast, after Vice President Agnew resigned, his staff remained funded for more than three months. Marjorie Hunter, "G.A.O. Challenges Guard for Agnew," *New York Times,* January 30, 1974.

41. Memorandum to: The Counsellor; From: Stephen G. McConahey; Subject: Human Development Activities to Date; May 11, 1973, p. 1, Folder: General 1973, Box 471,

Weinberger Papers. Apparently, it was Cole who suggested the meeting, but that cannot be confirmed.

42. Among those staff returning to HEW were Taft and Vadala, who were soon married. She had a long and constructive career in human services in the federal government and the nonprofit sector. He followed Weinberger to the Defense Department when Reagan was elected in 1980, becoming the department's general counsel. He concluded his public career as U.S. ambassador to NATO.

43. Letter to Dr. Nancy Milio, Adjunct Professor, Boston University; from Julia Vadala, Deputy Director to the Cabinet Committee for Human Resources (Health); May 15, 1973, J. Taft Personal Files. She joked in a 2006 interview that the office furniture she had ordered arrived the day the counsellorships were abolished. J. Taft interview.

44. Memorandum for: The Secretary; From: Julia Vadala; Subject: Health Issues Which Merit Interdepartmental Coordination; May 30, 1973, p. 8, J. Taft Personal Files.

45. Memorandum to: Human Resource Working Committee Members; From: Caspar W. Weinberger; May 23, 1973, Folder: Health Resource Programs—General—1973, Box 471, Weinberger Papers.

46. Memorandum for: Honorable Kenneth R. Cole, Honorable Roy L. Ash, Honorable Melvin R. Laird; From: Caspar W. Weinberger; Subject: Assignment of Responsibilities of the Counsellor for Human Resources; July 5, 1973, Folder: Responsibilities of the Job 1973, Box 472, Weinberger Papers. The memo was on Weinberger's HEW letterhead.

47. Weinberger omitted three subjects in the health policy area that Vadala had listed in her internal report to him: national blood policy, the President's Committee on Health Education, and rehabilitation/spinal cord injury. He may have felt that these three issues were primarily HEW issues and/or that they were far enough along to not need separate attention. In the area of human development, Weinberger omitted one topic that McConahey had included in his own wrap-up status report, that of social service revenue sharing. Again, Weinberger may have believed this topic was so closely linked to HEW's responsibilities that it did not need to be picked up by any White House coordinating agencies. Memorandum to: Jim Cavanaugh; From: Stephen G. McConahey; Subject: Status of Human Development Projects; May 29, 1973, Folder: Reading File 1973, Box 472, Weinberger Papers.

48. Lynn interview, p. 2. Collier transferred briefly to Lynn's HUD office. President Ford named him to the Federal Trade Commission.

49. Senate Committee on Appropriations, *Department of Housing and Urban Development . . . for Fiscal Year 1974*, 1657.

50. Bonafede and Iglehart, "End of Counselor System," *National Journal* 5:20 (May 19, 1973): 728.

51. The Secretary's Schedule, Thursday, May 10, '73 [*sic*], Folder: White House—Counsellor Butz's Schedules, Box 1, Butz Papers.

52. Letter to Mr. V. E. McKelvey, Director, U.S. Department of the Interior, Geological Survey; from Earl L. Butz, Counsellor to the President for Natural Resources; May 10, 1973, Folder: Counsellor Butz—Correspondence, Box 1, Butz Papers.

53. Letter to The Honorable John Kyl, Assistant Secretary for Congressional and Public Affairs, U.S. Department of the Interior; from Earl L. Butz, Secretary; May 10, 1973, Folder: Counsellor Butz—Correspondence, Box 1, Butz Papers.

54. "Earl Butz: Plowing New Furrows for U.S. Agriculture," *Nation's Business* 61:6 (June 1973): 29.

55. Bonafede and Iglehart, "End of Counselor System," *National Journal* 5:20 (May 19, 1973): 728.

56. Domestic Council Staff, n.d. [probably summer 1973], p. 1, Folder: Domestic Council Issues (1), Box 12, Ross Papers.

57. Nixon, *Public Papers of the Presidents: 1973,* 625–26.

58. Mordecai Lee and Daniel A. Mazmanian, "Nixon's DENR Plan—Reorganization to What End?" unpublished article manuscript (typescript), September 1973, author's files.

59. The reorganization subcommittees of the House and Senate Government Operations Committees held eight hearings in the summer of 1973 on Nixon's DENR proposal. Subcommittee on Legislation and Military Operations, House Committee on Government Operations, *Department of Energy and Natural Resources [Part 1],* 93rd Cong., 1st sess., 1973; Senate Subcommittee on Reorganization, Research, and International Organizations, Committee on Government Operations, *Establish a Department of Energy and Natural Resources* (hearings), 93rd Cong. 1st sess., 1973. Neither subcommittee acted on the proposal. The extant (2009) Department of Energy was created in 1977 and has no natural resources portfolio.

60. Tab attached to Memorandum for: Al Haig; From: Ken Cole; Subject: Domestic Council Operation; May 24, 1973, p. 2, Folder: Domestic Council Staff, Box 189, White House Budget Files, Staff Secretary Files. While the memo is untitled, the opening sentence states that it is "a follow up to our conversation of last week."

61. *Weekly Compilation of Presidential Documents* 9:21 (May 28, 1973): 701–702.

62. Hart, "Executive Reorganization," 183.

CHAPTER 9. LEGACY AND SIGNIFICANCE

1. For an overview of the literature, see Pfiffner and Boardman, *Managing the Executive Branch.*

2. Mosher et al., *Watergate,* 47.

3. Appleby, *Policy and Administration.*

4. Mosher et al., *Watergate,* 37–38.

5. Fred L. Zimmerman, "Nixon Names Schlesinger as Defense Chief, Moves Other Veterans, Junks Supercabinet," *Wall Street Journal,* May 11, 1973.

6. Lynn interview.

7. Pierson, *Politics in Time.*

8. Somers, *Presidential Agency,* 224–32. Somers's views were based in part on participant observation; he had worked briefly under Byrnes during the war before going on to write his Harvard dissertation.

9. Byrnes had been a Democratic ally of FDR on Capitol Hill. After Roosevelt named him to the Supreme Court, Byrnes maintained his direct involvement in high-level politics. Lee, *The First Presidential Communications Agency,* 132–33. An activist by nature, Byrnes welcomed FDR's invitation to leave the Court and return to the center of action.

10. Robertson, *Sly and Able,* 319–20.

11. Somers, *Presidential Agency,* 58. During the third quarter of the twentieth century the East Wing gradually became the exclusive domain for the offices of the president's spouse.

12. Byrnes, *All in One Lifetime,* chap. 12.

13. Brands, *Traitor to His Class,* 819.

14. Fesler et al., *Industrial Mobilization for War,* 556–57 (emphasis added). In June 1945, shortly after assuming the presidency, Truman named Byrnes secretary of state.

15. Porter, "Economic Advice to the President," 411 (emphasis added), 419–20. Porter was as much a participant as a detached academic observer; he joined the Ford administration in 1974.

16. Relyea, "Homeland Security," 405.

17. Relyea, "Organizing for Homeland Security," 614–16.

18. Lynn interview.

BIBLIOGRAPHY

Bibliographic information for congressional publications and journalistic sources is included in the endnotes.

MAJOR ARCHIVAL SOURCES

All sources are at the Nixon Presidential Library in Yorba Linda, California, unless otherwise noted.

Ash, Roy L. Oral history interviews by National Archives staff.
Butz, Earl L. Papers. Staff Member and Office Files, White House Central Files.
Cabinet Meetings, FG 10–1. Cabinet Files, White House Central Files.
Dean, John W., III. Papers. Staff Member Office Files, White House Special Files.
Domestic Council, FG 6–15. Subject Files, White House Central Files.
Ehrlichman, John D. Papers. Staff Member Office Files, White House Special Files.
Haldeman, H. R. Papers. Staff Member Office Files, White House Special Files.
President's Meetings Files, President's Office Files.
President's Speech File 1969–1974, President's Personal File.
Raoul-Duval, Michael. Papers. Staff Member and Office Files, White House Central Files.
Reichley, A. James. Interview Transcripts, 1977–1981, Ford Presidential Library, Ann Arbor, Mich.
Ross, Norman E., Jr. Papers. Ford Presidential Library, Ann Arbor, Mich.
Schleede, Glenn R. Papers. Staff Member and Office Files, White House Central Files.
Spivak, Lawrence. Papers. Manuscript Division, Library of Congress.
Staff Secretary Files. Staff Member Office Files, White House Special Files.
Taft, Julia Vadala. Personal Files.
Taft, William H., IV. Papers. Manuscript Division, Library of Congress.
Weinberger, Caspar W. Papers. Manuscript Division, Library of Congress.

Abbreviations
GPO: Government Printing Office
PAR: Public Administration Review
PSQ: Presidential Studies Quarterly

BOOKS AND SCHOLARLY ARTICLES

Aberbach, Joel D., and Bert A. Rockman. *In the Web of Politics: Three Decades of the U.S. Federal Executive.* Washington, D.C.: Brookings Institution, 2000.

Ambrose, Stephen E. *Nixon,* vol. 3, *Ruin and Recovery, 1973–1990.* New York: Simon & Schuster, 1987.

Appleby, Paul H. *Policy and Administration.* 1949. Reprint, University [Tuscaloosa]: University of Alabama Press, 1975.

Arnold, Peri E. *Making the Managerial Presidency: Comprehensive Reorganization Planning, 1905–1996.* 2nd ed. Lawrence: University Press of Kansas, 1998.

Balogh, Brian, Joanna Grisinger, and Philip Zelikow. *Making Democracy Work: A Brief History of Twentieth-Century Federal Executive Reorganization.* Charlottesville: Miller Center of Public Affairs, University of Virginia, 2002.

Berg, Clifford L. "Lapse of Reorganization Authority." *PAR* 35, no. 2 (March–April 1975): 195–99.

Brands, H. W. *Traitor to His Class: The Privileged Life and Radical Presidency of Franklin Delano Roosevelt.* New York: Doubleday, 2008.

Byrnes, James F. *All in One Lifetime.* New York: Harper & Brothers, 1958.

Carter, Jimmy. *Why Not the Best? The First Fifty Years.* 1975. Reprint, Fayetteville: University of Arkansas Press, 1996.

Carter, Luther J. "Earl L. Butz, Counselor for Natural Resources: President's Choice a Surprise for Environmentalists." *Science* 179, no. 4071 (January 26, 1973): 358–59.

Crockett, David A. *Running against the Grain: How Opposition Presidents Win the White House.* College Station: Texas A&M University Press, 2008.

Cronin, Thomas E. "The Swelling of the Presidency." *Saturday Review of the Society* 1, no. 1 (January 20, 1973): 30–36.

Dean, Alan L. "General Propositions of Organizational Design." In *Federal Reorganization: What Have We Learned?* edited by Peter Szanton. Chatham, N.J.: Chatham House, 1981.

———. "Organization and Management of Federal Departments." In *Making Government Manageable: Executive Organization and Management in the Twenty-first Century,* edited by Thomas H. Stanton and Benjamin Ginsberg. Baltimore: Johns Hopkins University Press, 2004.

Dean, John W., III. *Blind Ambition: The White House Years.* New York: Simon and Schuster, 1976.

Dyke, Richard W., and Francis X. Gannon. *Chet Holifield: Master Legislator and Nuclear Statesman.* Lanham, Md.: University Press of America, 1996.

Ehrlichman, John. *Witness to Power: The Nixon Years.* New York: Simon and Schuster, 1982.

Emmerich, Herbert. *Essays on Federal Reorganization.* University [Tuscaloosa]: University of Alabama Press, 1950.

———. *Federal Organization and Administrative Management.* University [Tuscaloosa]: University of Alabama Press, 1971.

Ervin, Sam J., Jr. *The Whole Truth: The Watergate Conspiracy.* New York: Random House, 1980.

Fesler, James W., et al. *Industrial Mobilization for War: History of the War Production Board and Predecessor Agencies, 1940–1945,* vol. 1, *Program and Administration.* 1947. Reprint, New York: Greenwood, 1969.

Fisher, Louis. *The Politics of Executive Privilege.* Durham, N.C.: Carolina Academic Press, 2004.

Fox, Douglas M. "The President's Proposals for Executive Reorganization: A Critique." *PAR* 33, no. 5 (September–October 1973): 401–406.

———, et al. "A Mini-Symposium: President Nixon's Proposals for Executive Reorganization." *PAR* 34, no. 5 (September–October 1974): 487–95.

Haig, Alexander M., Jr. *Inner Circles: How America Changed the World; A Memoir.* New York: Warner, 1992.

Haldeman, H. R. *The Ends of Power.* New York: Times Books, 1978.

———. *The Haldeman Diaries: Inside the Nixon White House.* New York: G. P. Putnam's Sons, 1994.

Hart, John. "Executive Reorganization in the USA and the Growth of Presidential Power." *Public Administration* 52, no. 2 (June 1974): 179–91.

Heale, M. J. *Twentieth-Century America: Politics and Power in the United States, 1900–2000.* London: Arnold, 2004.

Hess, Stephen. *Organizing the Presidency.* 3rd ed. Washington, D.C.: Brookings Institution, 2002.

Hoff, Joan. *Nixon Reconsidered.* New York: Basic Books, 1994.

Klein, Herbert G. *Making It Perfectly Clear.* Garden City, N.Y.: Doubleday, 1980.

Kutler, Stanley I., ed. *Abuse of Power: The New Nixon Tapes.* New York: Free Press, 1997.

———. *The Wars of Watergate: The Last Crisis of Richard Nixon.* New York: Knopf, 1990.

Lee, Mordecai. "President Nixon Sees a 'Cover Up': Public Relations in Federal Agencies." *Public Relations Review* 23, no. 4 (winter 1997): 301–25.

———. *The First Presidential Communications Agency: FDR's Office of Government Reports.* Albany: State University of New York Press, 2005.

Lewis, David E. "Revisiting the Administrative Presidency: Policy, Patronage, and Agency Competence." *PSQ* 39, no. 1 (2009): 60–73.

Light, Paul C. *The President's Agenda: Domestic Policy Choice from Kennedy to Clinton.* 3rd ed. Baltimore: Johns Hopkins University Press, 1999.

———. *Thickening Government: Federal Hierarchy and the Diffusion of Accountability.* Washington, D.C.: Brookings Institution and Governance Institute, 1995.

Lowi, Theodore J. *The Personal President: Power Invested, Promise Unfulfilled.* Ithaca, N.Y.: Cornell University Press, 1985.

Malek, Frederic V. *Washington's Hidden Tragedy: The Failure to Make Government Work.* New York: Free Press, 1978.

Mason, Robert. *Richard Nixon and the Quest for a New Majority.* Chapel Hill: University of North Carolina Press, 2004.

Mazmanian, Daniel A., and Mordecai Lee. "Tradition Be Damned! The Army Corps of Engineers Is Changing." *PAR* 35, no. 2 (March–April 1975): 166–72.

Meier, Kenneth J., and John Bohte. "Span of Control and Public Organizations: Implementing Luther Gulick's Research Design." *PAR* 63, no. 1 (January–February 2003): 61–70.

Meyer, Kenneth R. *With the Stroke of a Pen: Executive Orders and Presidential Power.* Princeton, N.J.: Princeton University Press, 2001.

Milkis, Sidney M. "Remaking Government Institutions in the 1970s: Participatory Democracy and the Triumph of Administrative Politics." *Journal of Policy History* 10 (spring 1998): 51–74.

Moe, Ronald C. *Administrative Renewal: Reorganization Commissions in the Twentieth Century.* Lanham, Md.: University Press of America, 2003.

———. "The Domestic Council in Perspective." *Bureaucrat* 5, no. 3 (October 1976): 251–72.

Moe, Terry M. "The Politicized Presidency." In *The New Direction in American Politics,* edited by John E. Chubb and Paul E. Peterson. Washington, D.C.: Brookings Institution, 1985.

Mosher, Frederick C., et al. *Watergate: Implications for Responsible Government.* New York: Basic Books, 1974.

Nathan, Richard P. *The Administrative Presidency.* New York: John Wiley, 1983.

———. *The Plot That Failed: Nixon and the Administrative Presidency.* New York: John Wiley, 1975.

Newbold, Stephanie P., and Larry D. Terry. "The President's Committee on Administrative Management: The Untold Story and the Federalist Connection." *Administration & Society* 38, no. 5 (November 2006): 523–55.

Newland, Chester A. "MBO Prospects and Challenges in the Federal Government: Conclusion." *Bureaucrat* 2, no. 4 (winter 1974): 421–26.

Nixon, Richard M. *Public Papers of the Presidents of the United States: 1969.* Washington, D.C.: GPO, 1971.

———. *Public Papers of the Presidents of the United States: 1970.* Washington, D.C.: GPO, 1971.

———. *Public Papers of the Presidents of the United States: 1971.* Washington, D.C.: GPO, 1972.

———. *Public Papers of the Presidents of the United States: 1972.* Washington, D.C.: GPO, 1974.

———. *Public Papers of the Presidents of the United States: 1973.* Washington, D.C.: GPO, 1975.

———. *RN: The Memoirs of Richard Nixon, with a New Introduction.* 1978. Reprint, New York: Simon & Schuster, 1990.

Patterson, Bradley H., Jr. *The White House Staff: Inside the West Wing and Beyond.* Washington, D.C.: Brookings Institution, 2000.

Perlstein, Rick. *Nixonland: The Rise of a President and the Fracturing of America.* New York: Scribner, 2008.

Pfiffner, James P., ed. *The Managerial Presidency.* 2nd ed. College Station: Texas A&M University Press, 1999.

———. *The President, the Budget, and Congress: Impoundment and the 1974 Budget Act.* Boulder, Colo.: Westview Press, 1979.

———, and Mary Boardman. *Managing the Executive Branch in the 20th Century: Consolidation and Disaggregation.* PAR online monograph series, Foundations of Public Administration. http://www.aspanet.org/scriptcontent/pdfs/FPA-MEB-article.pdf. Accessed July 9, 2009.

Pierson, Paul. *Politics in Time: History, Institutions, and Social Analysis.* Princeton, N.J.: Princeton University Press, 2004.

Pious, Richard M. "Sources of Domestic Policy Initiatives." *Proceedings of the Academy of Political Science* 32, no. 1 (1975): 98–111.

Porter, Roger B. "Economic Advice to the President: From Eisenhower to Reagan." *Political Science Quarterly* 98, no. 3 (autumn 1983): 403–26.

President's Committee on Administrative Management. *Report of the Committee, with Studies of Administrative Management in the Federal Government.* Washington, D.C.: GPO, 1937.

Price, Raymond. *With Nixon.* New York: Viking, 1977.

Reichley, A. James. *Conservatives in an Age of Change: The Nixon and Ford Administrations.* Washington, D.C.: Brookings Institution, 1981.

Relyea, Harold C. "Homeland Security: The Concept and the Presidential Coordination Office—First Assessment." *PSQ* 32, no. 2 (June 2002): 397–411.

———. "Organizing for Homeland Security." *PSQ* 33, no. 3 (September 2003): 602–24.

Robertson, David. *Sly and Able: A Political Biography of James F. Byrnes.* New York: Norton, 1994.

Rose, Richard. "Implementation and Evaporation: The Record of MBO." *PAR* 37, no. 1 (January–February 1977): 64–71.

Rozell, Mark J. *Executive Privilege: Presidential Power, Secrecy, and Accountability.* 2nd ed. Lawrence: University Press of Kansas, 2002.

Rudalevige, Andrew. *Managing the President's Program: Presidential Leadership and Legislative Policy Formulation.* Princeton, N.J.: Princeton University Press, 2002.

———. *The New Imperial Presidency: Renewing Presidential Power after Watergate.* Ann Arbor: University of Michigan Press, 2005.

Safire, William. *Before the Fall: An Inside View of the Pre-Watergate White House.* Garden City, NY: Doubleday, 1975.

Schell, Jonathan. *The Time of Illusion.* New York: Knopf, 1976.

Schick, Allen. "The Coordination Option." In *Federal Reorganization: What Have We Learned?* edited by Peter Szanton. Chatham, N.J.: Chatham House, 1981.

Seidman, Harold. *Politics, Position, and Power: The Dynamics of Federal Organization.* 5th ed. New York: Oxford University Press, 1998.

Seyb, Ronald P. "Reform as Affirmation: Jimmy Carter's Executive Branch Reorganization Effort." *PSQ* 31, no. 1 (March 2001): 104–20.

Shani, Moshe. "U.S. Federal Government Reorganization: Executive Branch Structure and Central Domestic Policy-Making Staff." *Public Administration* 52, no. 2 (June 1974): 193–208.

Shultz, George P., and Kenneth W. Dam. *Economic Policy beyond the Headlines.* 2nd ed. Chicago: University of Chicago Press, 1998.

Small, Melvin. *The Presidency of Richard Nixon.* Lawrence: University Press of Kansas, 1999.

Somers, Herman Miles. *Presidential Agency: OWMR, The Office of War Mobilization and Reconversion.* 1950. Reprint, New York: Greenwood, 1969.

Stenberg, Carl W. "Some Comments on Reorganizing the Federal Executive Branch." *Bureaucrat* 1, no. 1 (spring 1972): 59–63.

Tubbesing, Carl D. "Predicting the Present: Realigning Elections and Redistributive Policies." *Polity* 7, no. 4 (summer 1975): 478–503.

United States. Office of Management and Budget. *Papers Relating to the President's Departmental Reorganization Program: A Reference Compilation; March 1971.* Washington, D.C.: OMB, 1971.

————. *Papers Relating to the President's Departmental Reorganization Program: A Reference Compilation; Revised, February 1972*. Washington, D.C.: OMB, 1972.

Warber, Adam L. *Executive Orders and the Modern Presidency: Legislating from the Oval Office*. Boulder, Colo.: Lynne Rienner, 2006.

Warshaw, Shirley Anne. *Powersharing: White House–Cabinet Relations in the Modern Presidency*. Albany: State University of New York Press, 1996.

Weinberger, Caspar W. *In the Arena: A Memoir of the 20th Century*. Washington, D.C.: Regnery, 2001.

Weinberger, Jane. *As Ever: A Selection of Letters from the Voluminous Correspondence of Jane Weinberger, 1970–1990*. Mount Desert, Me.: Windswept House, 1991.

West, William F. *Controlling the Bureaucracy: Institutional Constraints in Theory and Practice*. Armonk, N.Y.: M. E. Sharpe, 1995.

Whitaker, John C. *Striking a Balance: Environment and Natural Resources Policy in the Nixon-Ford Years*. Washington, D.C.: American Enterprise Institute for Public Policy Research, 1976.

Wildavsky, Aaron. *The Politics of the Budgetary Process*. 2nd ed. Boston: Little, Brown, 1974.

————. *The Politics of the Budgetary Process*. 3rd ed. Boston: Little, Brown, 1979.

INTERVIEWS

All interviews were conducted by the author by telephone unless otherwise indicated Titles reflect positions interviewees held in spring 1973.

Cavanaugh, James H. Domestic Council Associate Director for Human Resources. March 2, 2007.

Dean, John W., III. Legal Counsel, White House. February 13, 2007.

Fairbanks, Richard W., III. Domestic Council Associate Director for Natural Resources. February 6, 2007.

Lynn, James T. Counselor to the President for Community Development. March 23, 2007.

Mead, Dana G. Domestic Council Associate Director for Community Development. June 1, 2007.

Parker, Douglas M. Assistant Director, Office of the Counsellor for Community Development. August 17, 2006.

Schleede, Glenn R. Assistant Director, Office of the Counsellor for Natural Resources. E-mail interview, December 12–13, 2006.

Taft, Julia Vadala. Deputy Director for Health, Office of the Counsellor for Human Resources. August 9, 2006.

Taft, William H., IV. Executive Assistant to the Counsellor for Human Resources. August 14, 2006.

Whitaker, John C., Undersecretary of Interior. February 16, 2007.

INDEX

*Citations in **bold** are to photos.*
All agencies, bureaus, commissions, councils, departments, and offices have free-standing entries. Some subagencies or programs are free standing; others are listed under their respective free-standing entries.

ABC, 182
ACTION, 108, 116, 127, 128
Advisory Commission on Intergovernmental Relations, 116
Agnew, Spiro, 55, 119; as chair of Office of Intergovernmental Relations, 41; and resignation, 251n40; as vice chair of DC, 186
Alaska Native Claims Settlement Act, 176
Albert, Carl, 55
Alger, Mark, 40; and super-secretary proposal, 43–45, 47
Ambrose, Stephen, 57
Anderson, Jack, 249n1
Anderson, John B., 56, 219n5
Appalachian Regional Commission, 135, 139, 240n21
Armstrong, Anne, 24, 75, 76
Army Corps of Engineers, 2, 159; and NR Committee, 167, 170, 172, 174
Arnold, Peri, 8
Ash Council, 8, 229n87; and Congress, 29; and misrepresentations of, 39, 189; and OMB, 99, 229n87; recommendations of, 2, 12, 28, 31, 218n66; and Schultz, 21; and strengthening the presidency, 211n2 (chap. 1)
Ash, Roy: and Alger, 44–45; as Assistant to the President, 39, 40–41, 58, 76, 103, 198, 221n61; and Butz, 103, 193; and Cole, 67; as critic of counsellor experiment, 39, 102, 187, 189, 200; and the Dean legal document, 47, 49; as director of OMB, 20, 28, 39, 40, 41, 58, 79, 85, 99, 110, 198, 231n113; and disbanding of counsellor experiment, 187, 189; and Ehrlichman, 39, 41, 45, 102, 181, 183; and Flanigan, 28–29; and Haig, 187; and Haldeman, 39, 41, 104; as head of Ash Council, 2; and the House Appropriations subcommittee, 180; and Malek, 99–102, 104–105; and management of executive branch, 99–102, 198 (*see also* management-by-objectives); as one of Big Five, 20, 99; and Nixon, 189; and statutory legislation for reorganization, 39, 41–42; and "two-hatted" responsibilities, 20, 21; and Weinberger, 79, 100–102, 181, 183, 192
assistant(s) to the president, 20–21, 31, 38–39. *See also* Big Five
Associated Press (AP), 117, 118
Atomic Energy Commission (AEC), 159, 165; and Butz, 167, 169, 170, 247n39; and Dixy Lee Ray, 169, 173; and EPA, 169–70; and Nixon reorganization plan, 2; and NR Committee, 170–74; and Schleede, 165

Ball, Neal, xiii
Baltimore Sun, 62, 162
Bellmon, Henry, 141
Bennington (Vt.) Banner, 62
Bernstein, Carl, 70
Better Communities Act (BCA), 143–44, 145, 154
Big Five, 19; Ash, 20, 39, 99, 181; Ehrlichman, 20, 41, 148, 181; Haldeman, 20; Kissinger, 20, 51; Shultz, 20, 21, 51. *See also* assistant(s) to the president

Bohte, John, 13

Bonneville Power Administration, 174

Bowen, Otis R., 234n40

Bradley Patterson H., 22

Brennan, Peter J., 34; before a congressional committee, 74; and Weinberger, 94, 103, 122, 123, 227n64

Brinegar, Claude, 147, 242n57; confirmation hearing of, 73–74; and DCD bill, 146; as second class secretary, 201

Broder, David, 118

Brookings Institution, xi, xii

Brownlow Committee, xi, 8; and the Nixon reorganization plan, 57; rationale of, 199; and reorganization plan, 10, 11, 14, 99

Buchanan, Pat, 188–89

Budget and Accounting Act, 98

Bureaus: Employment Compensation, 108; Land Management, 174; Mines, 176; Outdoor Recreation, 174; Reclamation, 172, 174; Sport Fisheries & Wildlife, 174; Budget, 21, 98–99, 204 (see also Office of Management and Budget); Standards, 108

Burns, Arthur, 23, 75

Bush, George W., 9; administration of, 203, 207, 212n12, 214n41, 234n43

Butz, Earl, 5, 242n57; administrative appointment of, 75; and the AEC, 169–70, 173; and CEQ, 160–61; and confirmation of, 69, 75; and counsellor duties, 167–70; and counsellor-to-counsellor relationships, 96–97, 103; and disbanding of counsellor experiment, 190, 191, 193–94; and Ehrlichman, 75, 79, 159–60, 222n5; and Fairbanks, 164–65, 166, 171, 177–78; and energy policy, 159, 168, 169; and Interior, 62, 156, 161–62, 166, 168–69; and the DC, 157, 177–79; and loss of status, 161–63; and loyalty oath, 58, 156; and the MBO project, 104–105; and meetings with Nixon, 36, 80, **81**, 86, 88–89, 156; and

NR Committee activities (see Natural Resources Committee); and the OMB, 157; oversight areas of, 51–52; in policy coordination role, 168–69, 171–73, 175, 177, 179; and public face of reorganization, 85–86, **87**, 159–60, 167–68; qualifications of, 133, 206; reporting policies of, 103, 175–77; 245n19; and self-definition of his counsellor role, 25–26, 97, 157–58, 159, 166–67, 170, 178; two-hatted role of, 33; as USDA Secretary, 58, 69, 75, 167; and Watergate, 184–85; and Weinberger, 51, 97, 170, 171, 175, 193; and Whitaker, 172–73

Buzhardt, Fred, Jr., 188

Byrd, Robert, 62, 69

Byrne, William Matthew, Jr., 183

Byrnes, James: as director of war mobilization, 202, 204; as FDR appointee, 202, 254n9; as a prototype counsellor, 202–205, 207; and Somers, 253n8; and Truman, 254n14

Cabinet: and the counsellor experiment, 83–84; and hierarchical status of, 9, 20, 38, 49, 131, 162, 187; meeting of May 10 (1973), 5–6, 188–91, 251n35; members of appointed as counsellors, xi, 5, 20; and Nixon reorganization of, 2, 5, 6, 9, 27–31, 33–36, 55, 57, 109; post-Nixon reorganization of, 9; strengthening of, 8, 16, 18–19, 29–30, 37, 60

Campbell, Phil, Jr., 147, 173

Carlucci, Frank, 93

Carter, Jimmy, 9, 10, 196

Cavanaugh, James, 83, 94; and the HR subcommittees, 131–32; and Taft, 122, 130, 237n81; and Weinberger, 122, 129, 130, 132, 226n49

CBS, 182

Chamber of Commerce, 182

Christian Science Monitor, 23

Civil Service Commission, 126, 235n62

Clark, Dick, 141–42

Clean Air Act, 169, 173

Clinton, Bill, 9, 212n12

Coastal Zone Management Act, 176

Colby, William, 188

Cole, Kenneth: and CDC, 148, 155; and the CHR, 115, 131; at the DC, 41, 42, 49–50, 83–84, 94, 95, 177, 191, 226n48; and Ehrlichman, 50, 78, 84, 130, 177; and Haig, 194; and Lyng, 222n5; and Nixon, 183; and NR Committee, 162, 166; and Weinberger, 129–30, 185, 192, 237nn80, 81, 252n41

Collier, Calvin (Cal): at CDC, 135, 146, 150, 153, 243n67; and the DCD bill, 145; as director of CDC, 138–139, 146, 150–51, 153, 154; and the disbanding of counsellor experiment, 193, 239n20, 252n48; and Lynn, 137–38, 150, 193; and Mead, 153–54

Collier, Harold, 137

Colson, Charles, 34

Commerce Department. See Department of Commerce

Commission on Economy and Efficiency, 8, 11

Committee on Human Resources (CHR), 115–32; and the DCD, 140; Health Subcommittee, 125–26, 131, 185; Human Development Subcommittee, 127; Income Security Subcommittee, 126–27; kick-off meeting of, 181; and the name issue, 130–31; and national health insurance, 201; as prototype for counsellor program, 198; scope of, 108–109, 138–39; 109–13; and subcommittee schedules, 234n51; and the welfare reform task force, 126

Committee to Reelect the President, 70, 90

Community Action Programs (OEO), 108, 135

Community Development Committee

(CDC); and the BCA, 143–44; and the DC, 152–55; kick-off meeting of, 147–49, 183; and Lynn confirmation, 72; organizing of, 137–39; as prototype for counsellor program, 155; reports to the counsellor of, 151–51; and Rural Development Subcommittee (Senate), 141–43; Rural Development Working Group, 98, 150, 155; scope of, 134–37; staff of, 239n20; subcommittees of, 149–51, 243n67. See also Department of Community Development

Comprehensive Employment and Training Act (CETA), 123

Congressional Directory (1973), 75, 221n61

Connolly, John, 188

Cost of Living Council, 125, 175, 235n56

Council of Economic Advisors: and the CHR, 116, 125, 236n70; to Eisenhower, 207; and NR Committee, 172

Council on Economic Policy, 20

Council on Environmental Quality (CEQ), 159; and Interior, 172; and NR Committee, 160–61, 170, 173–75, 249n60

Council on Human Resources, 113, 130, 170. See also Committee on Human Resources

Council on International Economic Policy, 28

counselor. See counsellor experiment

counsellor experiment: assessment of (political goals, 197–98 /management goals, 199–200 /organizational structure, 200–202 /successes, 149, 155, 169, 170, 178, 206–208); choice of personnel for, 33, 36–37; as a concept, 30–36, 47–50; and confirmation confusion, 69–76; and conflicts in the executive branch, 73–75, 83–84; creating the structure, 38–47; criticism of, 13, 15, 17, 42, 61–62, 83, 155, 200, 209, 220n43; duties and responsibili

counsellor experiment (*cont.*)
ties of, 40, 43–44, 50–53, 90–91; as
exemplars, 24–26; historical overview
of, 19–24; implementation of, 77–82;
legal status of, 15, 19–20, 38–39, 85,
180, 187, 224n21; role of counsellor,
63–68 (line vs. staff management
functions, 23, 32–33, 57, 84, 85, 209,
214n38 /policy vs. management
functions, 99, 100); terminology, 23,
73, 168, 212n7; and "two-hatted"
administrators, 20, 22–23, 41, 205,
206, 207; unveiling of, 54–60. *See also
individual counsellors by name.*
Crider, Bobbie J., 243n67
Crockett, David, 212n14
Cronin, Thomas, 16

Dean, Alan, 13, 19
Dean, John, 158; and Ervin, 46–47; and
the executive order, 38, 63–64 firing
of, 250n19; and the HR counsellor,
108; and legal documents for the
counsellor experiment, 38–39, 47–50,
224n21; and the NR counsellor,
158–59; and reorganization plans, 32,
41, 61; and "Role of the Counsellors"
memo, 63, 64, 68; and Watergate, 28,
32, 89, 183
Democratic National Committee, 70
Democratic Party, 18–19
Dent, Frederick B., 147, 242n57
Department of Agriculture (USDA), 2,
3; Agriculture Research Service, 108,
158 (Soil and Water Conservation
Division, 158); and Butz, 36, 58, 62
(*see also* Butz, Earl); and CDC, 148,
134, 150; and CHR, 40, 125–29; in the
counsellor experiment, 5, 51–52, 96,
108, 158; and the DCD bill, 145; and
DNR, 3, 80, 141 (*see also* Department
of Natural Resources); Economic Research Service, 108 (Natural Resources Economics Division, 158); Food
and Nutrition Service, 108; and food

stamps for strikers, 94; and Lynn, 134;
and NR Committee, 105, 170–71,
172; and pesticide standards, 123; and
rural development, 141
Department of Commerce, 2, 25; and
Brinegar confirmation, 74; and
CDC, 135, 139, 142, 147, 148, 150;
and CHR, 40, 125, 128, 129, 135; in
the counsellor experiment, 51–52,
108, 163; and EDA, 139; and Lynn,
133, 137, 151; National Bureau of
Standards, 108; NOAA, 159 (*see also*
National Oceanic and Atmospheric
Administration); and NR Committee,
172; reorganization of, 11; and rural
development, 142
Department of Community Develop-
ment (DCD), 42, 57, 241n48; bill
to create, 3, 50, 140, 144–46, 238n,
241n47; and rural development,
141–42
Department of Defense (DOD): and
CHR, 124–25, 131; and Schlesinger,
188; and Weinberger, 37. *See also*
Army Corps of Engineers; U.S. Army
Department of Education, 9
Department of Energy, 9, 253n59
Department of Energy and Natural Re-
sources (DENR), xii, 173, 194, 219n22
Department of Health, Education, and
Welfare (HEW), 2, 5, 9, 126, 235n56;
and CDC, 51, 135, 138, 150; and
CHR, 109, 114, 115, 117, 126–28; in
the counsellor experiment, 40, 44,
108, 192; and Department of Human
Resources, 117; Finch at, 23; and NR
Committee, 150; Richardson at, 37,
124; Weinberger at, 33, 70–71, 109,
112, 113, 119, 181, 215n27, 224n21,
252nn42, 47
Department of Health and Human
Services, 9
Department of Homeland Security, 9,
203, 207, 212n12. *See also* Office of
Homeland Security

Department of Housing and Urban Development (HUD) 2; and CDC, 40, 134–35, 150; and CHR, 40, 51, 108, 126, 236n70; in the counsellor experiment, 51, 72, 108, 139–40; creation of, 135; and the DCD bill, 145–46; and disbanding of counsellor experiment, 193; and executive reorganization, 62, 135; hierarchical status of, 34; and housing policy, 72, 73, 96, 108, 149–50; and impoundment, 73; and Lynn, 5, 33, 51, 58, 69, 72, 134, 145 (*see also* Lynn, James); Nixon's vision of, 34, 36–37, 80, 85, 241n50; and rural development, 142, 149

Department of Human Resources (DHR), 110, 112, 117, 118

Department of the Interior, 164, 168; and Butz, 62, 166 (*see also* Butz, Earl); and CEQ, 172; and CHR, 40, 51, 127, 128, 160–61; and coal reserves, 168; in the counsellor experiment 2, 32, 108 158; and energy issues, 160–61; hierarchical status of, 83, 130, 156, 161–63; and Indian affairs, 115 (*see also* Indian affairs); and NR Committee, 51, 166, 170–72, 174–76

Department of Justice, 32

Department of Labor, 2; and Brennan confirmation, 74; Bureau of Employee's Compensation, 108; and the CHR, 40, 51, 126–28; in the counsellor experiment, 97, 108; Employment Service Women's Bureau, 108; Manpower Administration, 108; and manpower revenue sharing, 121–23; reorganization of, 11; and strikers, 94; and Weinberger's reporting forms, 103

Department of Natural Resources (DNR), 3, 50, 80, 141, 161, 162

Department of Transportation (DOT), 2; and BCA bill, 144; and CDC, 51, 147, 150, 201; in the counsellor experiment, 51, 134, 148, 163; and the DCD bill, 146; Federal Aviation Administration, 138; and Lynn, 134, 135, 144; and NR Committee, 158, 170, 174

Department of the Treasury, 40, 99, 127, 172. *See also* Shultz, George

Department of Veterans Affairs, 9. *See also* Veterans Administration

DiBona, Charles, 159–60, 173

District of Columbia (municipal government), 135, 153

Domestic Council (DC): Agnew at, 186; and CDC, 134, 147–48, 152–55; and CHR, 115, 192; Cole at, 41, 49, 78, 83–84, 129, 177; and Congress, 71, 180; and disbanding of counsellor experiment, 191, 192, 194–95, 237n79; establishment of, 211n2 (chap. 1); Fairbanks at, 160, 162–63, 164–66, 170, 172, 177–79; and the MBO project, 104; and NR Committee, 157, 164, 171, 177–79, 194; in Nixon's first term, 16–17, 120; and OMB, 65, 100, 104, 180; and relationship to the counsellor experiment, 42, 44, 56, 58, 68, 97, 104, 115, 129–32, 164, 180, 185, 209, 237n79; and role in the reorganization plan, 37, 41, 49–50, 56, 84, 180, 211n2 (chap. 1); staff reduction of, 42, 56, 58, 129, 148, 164, 177, 202,; and working relationship with counsellors, 78–79, 164, 180; and Weinberger turf war, 95, 129–32, 186; Whitaker at, 164

Doonesbury (comic strip), 87

drug czar, 40, 108; and CHR, 125, 128. *See also* Special Action Office for Drug Abuse Prevention

Economic Development Administration (EDA), 135, 154; and CDC, 150; elimination of, 139, 240n21

Economic Research Service, 108, 134, 158

Economy Act, 10

Ehrlichman, John: and the Ash proposals 39–42, 45, 49–50; as Assistant to the

Ehrlichman, John (*cont.*)
President, 57, 103, 148, 181; and Butz, 159–60, 178, 222n5, 250n20; and the CHR, 115; counsellors reporting to, 22, 43, 46, 50, 52, 84, 91, 148, 177; and Dean, 32; and the Dean legal packet, 47, 49; and decentralization of decision-making, 16, 60; and the DC, 44, 120, 129–31, 152, 155, 177; as domestic policy advisor, 20, 58, 251n31; as intermediary, 87, 91, 115; and loyalty oath, 58, 156; managing the counsellor experiment, 78–80, 97, 102, 148, 168, 181–86; and the media, 60, 62–63, 86, 88, 182; and meetings with Nixon, 88, 182, 218n1; and the NR Committee, 158; and official/ legal status of counsellors, 39, 41, 64, 75–76, 78, 162, 224n21; and preparation of counsellors, 49, 88; and the relationship between Congress and the president, 18–19, 56; and reorganization vision, 5, 6, 31–37, 41–45, 92, 105, 164, 168–69, 172, 177, 181, 191, 199–202, 209, 211n2, 215n16; resignation/departure of, 5, 17, 173, 186–87, 188, 213n32, 251n35; and the "Role of the Counsellors" memo, 63–68, 78, 107, 220n40; and size of each counsellor's staff, 42, 44, 100, 155; and the unveiling of counsellor plan, 49–50, 55–60, 61; and the Watergate affair, 32, 102, 182–83, 249n11; and Weinberger, 43–45, 78–81, 88, 90, 109, 115, 181, 186, 222n4, 229n98, 241n46, 250n20. *See also* counsellor experiment
Eisenhower, Dwight: administration of, 8, 133, 196, 207; and reorganization, 10, 11
Eisenhower Building. *See* Old Executive Office Building (OEOB)
Electoral College, 27
Elliot, Roland, 95, 228n71
Ellsberg, Daniel, 183

Emmerich, Herbert, 14
Environmental Protection Agency (EPA), 159; and AEC, 169, 247n39; and Butz, 167, 168; and Clean Air Act, 169–70, 173; and HRC, 123; and NR Committee, 97, 170, 174–75, 249n60
Equal Employment Opportunity Commission (EEOC), 108, 110, 127, 128
Ervin, Sam J., Jr.: and impoundment, 145, 146, 217n54; and reorganization, 47, 217n55; as Senate Government Operations Committee chair, 46–47, 218n1; as Senate Watergate Committee chair, 46–47, 199
Erwin, William (Will) W., 142, 149, 150
Evans, Rowland, 37, 45
Executive Office of the President (EOP): and budget requests for, 180; and the counsellors, 38, 43, 44, 48, 115, 220n40, 224n21; establishment of, 99; during FDR's administration, 204; and NR Committee, 172; and reorganization, 31 85, 99, 211n2 (chap. 1), 241n50; and staff vs. line functions, 57, 85, 209; and staff reduction, 41, 43, 48, 55, 58, 161. *See also* Domestic Council
executive privilege: and appointees, 39; and the counsellor experiment, 56, 70–72, 158, 183–84, 198; historical use of, 69; as Nixon strategy, 4, 184

Fairbanks, Richard (Dick) W., III, 87; and Butz, 159, 164–65, 166, 170, 172, 177–78; and Cole, 166; after counsellor experiment demise, 194; at the DC, 194; and draft presidential message, 160; and Ehrlichman, 183, 249n11; and Morton, 162–63; and NR Committee kick-off event, 162, 166, 171; and role in counsellor experiment, 83, 169–70, 171, 178, 179
Farmers Home Administration, 134, 150, 152, 158
Farrell, Michael J., 224n21

Federal Aviation Administration (FAA), 138

Federal Bureau of Investigation (FBI), 70, 89

Federal Highway Administration, 134

Federal Regional Councils, 152

Federal Register, 38

Federal Reserve Bank, 23

Federal Trade Commission (FTC), 110, 133, 205, 252n48

Fesler, James, 204, 205

Finch, Robert, 23, 75

Fine Arts Commission, 108, 128

Flanigan, Peter, 28; as Assistant to the President, 169; and Cabinet reorganization, 29–30

food stamps, 105; and CHR, 126; for strikers, 93–94, 120, 227n65

Ford, Gerald, 88; administration of, 25, 252n48, 254n15; and reorganization, 10, 196; and revenue sharing, 144; as U.S. Representative, 55

Fri, Robert, 173

Furgurson, Ernest, 62, 83

Garment, Leonard (Len), 93, 193

Gilmour, Robert, 14

Gosden, Craig, 95

Grace Commission, 9

Gray, L. Patrick, 89

Great Depression, 10

Great Society program, 4, 37

Haig, Alexander: as chief of staff, 6, 186, 251n31, 251n35; and Cole, 194, 251n31; and disbanding of counsellor experiment, 187, 189, 191

Haldeman, H. R.: as Assistant to the President, 23, 58; and the Cabinet resignation memo, 28; as chief of staff, 20, 31; as intermediary, 87, 95; and legislative approval for reorganization, 39, 41; and loyalty oath, 156; and the MBO project, 105; and protocol status of counsellors, 75–76, 83, 99,

100, 104, 224n21; on reorganization and Watergate, 17–18; and reorganization proposals, 28, 31, 33–36, 47, 49–50, 77, 181, 187; resignation/departure of, 5, 186, 188, 251n35; and size of each counsellor's staff, 42, 155; and Watergate, 28, 32, 184, 213n32; and Weinberger, 117, 215n12

Hanks, Nancy, 119

Harding, Warren G.: reorganization efforts of, 5, 8, 11

Health Industry Advisory Committee, 185

Heineman Task Force, 2, 8, 11

Herbers, John, 88

Hess, Stephen, 22

Hickel, Walter, 163

Higby, Lawrence, 48

High Seas Conservation Act, 176

Hoff, Joan, 17

Holifield, Chet: and DCD bill, 42, 145, 146, 241n47; and reorganization, 3, 56, 57, 211n3; at the White House breakfast (January 5, 1973), 55

Hoover, Herbert: administration of, 5, 10; as Commerce Secretary, 11; as consultant to presidents, 11; and reorganization, 5, 10–11, 196

Hoover Commission(s), 8

Horton, Frank, 55, 56

Howard, W. Richard, 18–19

Hullin, Tod, 48; and Alger memo, 44; and counsellors' information packet, 63; and MBO implementation, 104; and the president's energy message, 159–60; and talking points for Ehrlichman, 81

Human Resources Committee. *See* Committee on Human Resources (CHR)

Hyde, Floyd H., 146

impoundment (impounding), 4, 18, 123, 198; and confirmation of counsellors, 73, 158; and Ervin, 145, 146, 217n54

Income Security Subcommittee (CHR), 94, 105 126–27, 192

Indian affairs: and CHR, 108, 124, 127, 192; and Interior, 115–116, 128, 163.

Interior Department. *See* Department of the Interior

Internal Revenue Service (IRS), 47

Javits, Jacob, 55, 56, 73

Johnson, Donald E., 90, 226n48

Johnson, Lyndon (LBJ): and HUD, 135; and OEO, 40; reorganization efforts of, 2, 8, 10, 11

Joint Committee on Reorganization, 8

Journal of Housing, 154–55, 185

Justice Department, 32

Keep Commission, 8

Kehrli, Bruce, 48; and clearances, 75–76, 82; and counsellor staff salaries, 42–43, 191, 224n21, 239n20; and office space acquisition, 42, 81–82, 98; and paper handling protocols, 95

Kennedy, Edward (Ted), 72, 221n47

Kennedy, John F., 10

Kissinger, Henry: as Assistant to the President, 23, 51, 58; and Butz, 52; as foreign affairs advisor, 20, 21

Klein, Herbert, xiii, 16

Kleindienst, Richard, 250n19

Krogh, Egil "Bud," Jr., 146, 147, 241n46

Kutler, Stanley, 28

Laird, Melvin, 24, 192

Laitin, Joe, xii, xiii

Larson, John W., 165, 175, 178, 193, 194

Legal Services Corporation, 92–93, 94, 120

Lehrer, Jim, 182

Letson, William, 147

Light, Paul, 214n38

Lindsay, John, 62

Lippman, Theo, Jr., 162

Long, Robert, 173, 174

Los Angeles Times, 1, 162, 185

Lutz, Theodore, 146, 147

Lyng, Richard, 222n5

Lynn, James: administrative appointment of, 75; assessment of his counsellorship, 208–209; and Better Communities Act (BCA), 143–44, 145, 154; and Brinegar, 146, 147, 201; and Butz, 96, 147; and CDC committee, 146–51 (*see also* Community Development Committee); and Collier (Calvin), 137–39, 150, 153, 252n48; and the Commerce Department, 133; confirmation of, 69, 72–76, 137, 183, 198; and congressional hearings, 73, 142, 185; as counsellor for community development, 36, 51, 52, 72, 75–79, 83, 92, 133–55; and Department of Community Development (DCD), 140, 144–46; and disbanding of counsellor system, 187, 190, 191, 193; and executive privilege, 72, 183, 184, 198; and first meeting of CDC, 147–49, 151; as HUD secretary, 33, 58, 62, 75, 140, 145, 151; and MBO project, 104; and Mead, 153, 244n77; and the media, 225n41; and meetings with Nixon, 36–37, 80, **81,** 86, 88–89; and the organizing of his counsellorship, 137–39; and Parker, 145, 147; as presidential coordinator, 25, 136, 147, 150, 152, 155, 157, 200, 201, 209; and public appearances as CD counsellor, 85, 86, **87;** qualifications of, 205–206; reporting policies of, 103, 119, 151–52, 200; and revenue sharing, 140; and rural development, 140, 141–45; and self-definition of his role as counsellor, 25, 97, 135–36, 147, 153, 155, 200, 222n1, 238n5, 239n9; and Weinberger, 96

Magnuson, Warren, 73

Malek, Fred, 47, 185; and the counsellor experiment, 99–102, 105, 181; and the MBO project, 99–100, 104, 230n108, 231n113; and reorganization, 181 management-by-objectives (MBO): and the counsellor experiment, 104–105, 187, 231n113; and the MBO project, 99–100, 198, 229n85, 230n108. *See also* Office of Management and Budget (OMB); and management-by-objectives

manpower revenue sharing, 143, 234n40; administrative implementation of, 122, 123, 192, 198; and CHR, 121, 122, 127, 192

Mansfield, Harvey, 13

Mansfield, Mike, 3, 55

Marine Mammal Commission, 176

Mason, Robert, 22

Mayo, Robert, 24

Mazmanian, Dan, xii, xiii

McConahey, Stephen: and blueprint for CHR, 110–12, 113; and disbanding of counsellor experiment, 252n47; and the Human Development Subcommittee, 127–28; and inter-counsellor staff contacts, 84, 98; and manpower revenue sharing, 121–22; in proactive role, 105, 126, 226n46, 231n110; and staff meetings, 119

McCord, James, xi

McGovern, George, 27

Mead, Dana G., 155, 222–23n7; and CDC staff, 153–54; and Lynn, 83, 152, 153, 244n77

Meet the Press (NBC news program), 62, 86, **87,** 117

Meier, Kenneth, 13

Michel, Peter A., 138, 153, 239n20

Milkis, Sidney, 14, 22

Minnick, Walter, 31, 32, 44

Mitchell, John, 183

Model Cities program, 34, 37

Moe, Ronald, 16–17

Moe, Terry, 16, 22

Morton, Rogers, 115, 163, 164, 168; hierarchical status of, 83, 161–62, 166

Moynihan, Daniel Patrick, 23, 127, 136

National Atmospheric and Space Administration (NASA), 2

Nathan, Richard, xv, 12–13, 15, 196

National Academy of Public Administration (NAPA), 199, 200, 209

National Association of Housing and Redevelopment Officials, 154

National Bureau of Standards, 108

National Cancer Institute, 108, 236n70

National Capital Housing Authority, 135

National Capital Planning Commission, 135

National Coal Association, 168

National Endowment for the Arts, 119, 127, 128

National Endowment for the Humanities, 127, 128, 129

National Foundation for the Arts and Humanities, 40, 108

National Governors Association, 85

National Health Insurance Task Force, 126, 132

National Industrial Pollution Control Council, 168

National Institute for Occupational Safety, and Health (HEW), 40, 108

National Journal, 82, 108, 119, 122, 167, 233n34

National League of Cities, 182

National Oceanic and Atmospheric Administration (NOAA), 52; and NR Committee, 158, 167, 170–71, 174; and priority monitoring, 176. *See also* Department of Commerce: NOAA

National Park Service, 174

National Performance Review, 9

National Science Foundation, 2

National Security Council, 20, 21

Natural Resources Committee (NR Committee), 169; and the DC, 171, 177–78; establishment of 170–73; and issues affecting, 171–72; meetings of, 185; organization of, 166–69, 173; policy areas of, 172–73; proposed subcommittees of, 173–75 (*see also*

Natural Resources Committee (*cont.*)
Timber Supply Task Force); and
reporting to counsellor Butz, 175–77.
See also Butz, Earl

New Deal, 4

New York Times, 23; and the Agnew appointment to DC, 186; and articles
by Herbers, 88; and the Legal Services
Corporation bill, 93; and Lynn, 144,
225n41; and Nixon reorganization, 1,
30, 62; and "supersecretaries" (supercrats), 46, 61, 186; and Weinberger,
118, 185, 225n41

New Yorker, 18

Newland, Chester A., 231n113

Newsweek, 45, 182

Nixon, Richard: and administrative
reorganization plan, 5, 14, 15, 19–20,
33, 47, 48, 52, 55, 61, 69–70, 162, 187,
196, 198, 199–200, 205; and anti-PR
efforts, xi, xii; and appointment of
loyalists, 4, 153, 156; and Ash, 198;
and asserting executive privilege, 4,
39, 56, 69–70, 184; and bipartisan
congressional briefing on reorganization, 54–58, 61, 64–65, 86; and
bureaucracy as enemy, 4, 5, 7, 15–18,
27–28, 37, 45–46, 61, 64, 67, 157; and
confrontation, 79, 161; and control, 4;
DENR proposal of, 173, 194, 253n59;
and domestic policy, 87–88, 96, 181;
and executive action, 30, 61; and firing Dean, 250n19; and foreign policy,
23, 87, 88; and governing by veto, 4,
88–90, 93, 123, 167–68, 198; and his
goal of reorganization, 15, 37, 64–65,
85, 121, 197–98, 199, 200; and impoundment, 4, 18, 73, 123, 158, 198,
217n54; and Kleindienst, 250n19; and
marginalizing Congress, 168, 198–99,
233n24; and media leaks, 33–34, 37;
and meetings with the counsellors,
79–80, **81**; New Federalism, 121, 143;
and reorganization of EOP, 211n2
(chap.1), 241n50 (*see also* Executive

Office of the President); and revenue
sharing (*see* manpower revenue sharing: administrative implementation
of); and secrecy, 33–34, 63, 76, 107;
State of the Union address(es) of,
2, 116, 121, 140, 143, 148, 152; and
super-department reorganization,
xi, 5–6, 220n43 (*see also* super-secretaries); and the budget proposal for
FY1974, 4, 85, 161; and the Cabinet,
83, 161, 188, 209; and the executive
order, 10, 19, 38, 41, 48, 61, 63–64, 76,
219n22; and the MBO project, 105
(*see also* management-by-objectives);
and the OMB, 4 (*see* Office of Management and Budget); and Watergate,
96, 181, 182–84, 186–87;

Novak, Robert, 37, 45

Office for Emergency Management
(OEM), 204

Office of Consumer Affairs, 108, 125, 128

Office of Economic Opportunity (OEO)
(War on Poverty agency) (in EOP),
24, 40; and CDC, 51, 135; and CHR,
40, 51, 108, 125, 127, 135; in the
counsellor experiment, 2, 128; and
legal services, 92–93; and Rumsfeld,
24

Office of Economic Stabilization (OES),
204

Office of Emergency Preparedness
(EOP), 58, 85, 134, 147, 241n50

Office of Executive Management, 35, 100,
229n87

Office of Homeland Security (OHS)
(White House), 203, 207. *See also*
Department of Homeland Security

Office of Intergovernmental Relations, 41

Office of Management and Budget
(OMB), xii: and anti-PR effort, xii,
under Ash, 20, 28, 39, 40, 41, 58, 79,
110; and BOB, 99; and Butz, 166;
and CHR, 125; creation of, 99, 221n2
(chap. 1); and confirmation of direc-

tors, 20, 56, 221n44; and commitment to reorganization plan, 77; and
the DC, 95, 180; and the DCD bill,
145, 146; and disbanding of counsellor experiment, 187; and first-term
reorganization proposals, 31, 39–40,
110, 218n66; hierarchical status of (in
counsellor experiment), 38, 43, 45;
under Lynn, 208–209; and managing
the executive branch, 99–100; and
manpower revenue sharing, 121–22;
and the MBO project, 104–105, 198
(*see also* management-by-objectives);
and NR Committee, 165, 173, 175;
renaming of, 35; and relationship to
the counsellors, 43, 65–67, 98–103,
121–22, 142, 153, 157, 180, 181, 185,
187; under Shultz, 56, 207; under
Weinberger director, 25, 40, 43, 56, 71,
78, 109–110, 112, 133, 222n4, 227n66;
and the Weinberger power struggle,
125, 127, 131, 181, 192. *See also* Bureaus: Budget
Office of Personnel Management, 235n62
Office of Pipeline Safety, 170, 174
Office of Saline Water, 174
Office of the Special Trade Representative, 172
Office of War Mobilization (OWM), 204
Office of War Mobilization and Reconversion (OWMR), 204, 205
Old Executive Office Building (OEOB),
xiii; allocation of space in, 82, 191;
Butz's office in, 97, 160, 167, 171, 175,
193; counsellor events in, 162–63;
entry passes to, 224n21; Fairbanks's
office in, 87; and location of counsellors, 38, 58, 98, 164; Lynn's office
in, 73, 137, 150, 193; Mead's office
in, 153; Mess hall, 82; and Nixon
"hideaway" office, 29, 79, 82; OMB
directors offices in, 222n4; as status
symbol, 42, 148, 175, 205; and Weinberger's office in, 108–109, 119, 124
O'Neill, Paul, 102, 122, 234n43

Parker, David, 83–84, 98
Parker, Douglas M., 193, 239n20; at
CDC, 148, 153–54; and CDC kick-
off meeting, 147–48; and the rural
development portfolio, 138, 142,
145–46, 155
Peace Corps, 116
Pentagon, 37
Pentagon Papers, 183
Percy, Charles, 55, 56
Phillips, Howard, 93
Pious, Richard, 19
Plowshare program, 159
Porter, Roger B., 206, 254n15
Price, Ray, 23, 49, 217n63
Price Task Force, 8
Proxmire, William, 72, 73, 193
Public Health Service, 126
public library construction grants, 108,
135
Purdue University, 133

Railroad Retirement Board, 2, 40, 108,
126, 128
Raoul-Duval, Michael: at CDC, 153, 154,
239n20; and CDC kick-off meeting,
148; at DC, 194; and the DCD bill,
146; and transportation issues, 138,
243n67
Ray, Dixy Lee, 169, 173
Reagan, Ronald: and Lyng, 222n5;
reorganization efforts of, 9, 10–11,
31, 196; and super-secretaries, 2
15n12
Reichley, A. James, 19, 216n34
Relyea, Harold, 203, 207–208
reorganization: congressional patterns
of, 10–12; and Nixon's first term,
2–4; and Nixon's second term, 5–7;
review of, 15–19; pre- and post-
Nixon patterns of, 12–15; pre- and
post-counsellor experiment, 196–97;
presidential patterns of, 7–9; public
responses to, 17, 18, 62, 85–86.
(*See also* super-secretaries)

Reorganization Act(s): and the *Chedda* decision, 11; and congressional consent, 5, 46; expiration of, 6; history of, 10–12, 196–97, 212n12

Republican National Convention, 4

revenue sharing (special), 120–23, 127, 140. *See also* Better Communities Act

Ribicoff, Abraham; and the DCD bill, 145; and opposition to counsellor reorganization, 61–62, 69, 219n22, 249n3

Richardson, Elliot, 37, 124–25, 131, 130, 188

Ridge, Tom, 203, 207–208

Risher, Eugene, 60

Rodriguez, Justine Farr, 113; as Deputy Director for Income Maintenance, 113, 119, 128; and Income Security Subcommittee, 94, 112, 126

Rogers, William, 21, 34

Romney, George, 36

Roosevelt, Franklin: and administrative powers 20; and Brownlow Committee, 8, 10, 57, 99; and establishment of EOP, 99; and the executive order, 38, 203, 204; managerial style of, 203–204; reorganization efforts of, 8, 10, 11, 14

Roosevelt, Theodore, 8, 11

Rosenthal, Jack, 1

Ross, Norman (Norm), 165, 170, 178, 194, 245n19

Ruckelshaus, William, 164, 173

Rudalevige, Andrew, 22

Rumsfeld, Donald, 24, 214n41

Rural Community Development Administration, 145

Rural Development Act, 139, 141, 149, 152

Rural Development Service, 134, 152

Rural Development Working Group. *See* Community Development Committee (CDC): Rural Development Working Group

Rural Electrification Administration, 89, 134, 152

Rural Telephone Bank, 134

Safire, William, xiii, 83

Schleede, Glenn: and Butz, 168, 169, 193; and the DC, 194; in NR Committee, 159, 165, 178

Schlesinger, James, 165, 188

Scott, Hugh, 45, 55

Secret Service, xiii

Seidman, Harold, 22

Senior Opportunities and Services (OEO), 135

Shani, Moshe, 22

Shultz, George, 46: and access to the president, 22; as Assistant to the President, 41, 58, 76, 103, 221n61; and confirmation, 20, 56; in counsellor structure, 22, 46, 51, 52, 58; after disbanding of counsellor experiment, 213n32; and the MBO effort, 104; as one of Big Five, 21; performance of, 203, 206–207; reporting to, 103; and self-definition of role, 21; as spokesperson on energy, 160; as treasury secretary, 40; two-hatted role of, 20, 23, 41

Simon, William, 160

Sirica, John, 79

Small, Melvin, 22

Small Business Administration (SBA), 2, 51, 135

Social Security Administration, 126

Soil Conservation Service, 158, 174

Somers, Herman Miles, 203, 205–208, 253n8

Soviet Union, 37

Special Action Office for Drug Abuse Prevention, 40, 108. *See also* drug czar

Spivak, Lawrence, 63, 86, **87,** 117

Strelow, Roger, 165

super-secretaries. *See individual counsellors (super-secretaries) by name. See also* counsellor experiment

Taft, Julia Vadala. *See* Vadala (Taft), Julia

Taft, William Howard, 8, 11

Taft, William (Will) H., IV: and Cavanaugh, 122, 130, 237n81; and CDC, 98; at CHR, 94, 110–12, 119, 229n98; later career of, 252n42; and McConahey, 110–112, 122, 128; and Vadala, 252n42; and Weinberger, 110, 114, 120, 227n64

Task Force on Welfare Reform, 117, 126

Tennessee Valley Authority (TVA), 159, 167; and NR Committee, 170–71, 174, 249n60

Thurmond, Strom, 140

Timber Supply Task Force, 175

Time (magazine), 93

Timmons, William, 84, 93

Toth, Robert, 1

Tower, John, 73

Train, Russell, 160–61, 163, 173

Trent, Darrell M., 147

Truman, Harry, 3, 8, 10, 11, 196, 254n42

Tubbesing, Carl, 22

United Press International (UPI), 58–59, 60

Urban Mass Transit Administration, (UMTA), 135, 149

U.S. Army, 159, 186.

U.S. Conference of Mayors, 182

U.S. Forest Service: and coal reserves, 168; and lumber/timber pricing, 172; and NR Committee, 158, 174

U.S. Geological Survey, 174, 193

U.S. House of Representatives: Appropriations Subcommittee, 129, 166, 180; Committee on Government Reform, 212n12; and the DCD bill, 144; Government Operations Committee, 3, 42, 55, 211n2 (chap. 1), 253n59; Judiciary Committee, 199; and the Legal Services Corporation bill, 93; and Nixon, 107; and reorganization of committees, 40

U.S. News & World Report, 45, 117, 182, 186

U.S. Senate: Agriculture and Forestry Committee, Rural Development Subcommittee, 136, 141; and CDC bill, 3, 50; Committee on Banking, Housing, and Urban Affairs, 72; Committee on Commerce, 73; Committee on Finance, 70–71; Committee on Labor and Public Welfare, 71, 72, 74; and confirmations, 20, 27, 67–70, 73–75, 163, 165, 198, 209, 221n44 (of Lynn, 72–73, 183, of Weinberger, 70–72, 183); and executive privilege, 56; Government Operations Committee, 3, 46, 145, 217n55, 218n1, Subcommittee on Reorganization, Research, and International Organizations, 55, 61–62, 253n59; and reactions to the counsellor proposal, 61–62; and reorganization of committees of, 40; Watergate Committee, xi, 46–47, 89, 95, 102, 199, *see also* Watergate

U.S. Supreme Court, 11, 254n9

Vadala (Taft), Julia, 113, 229n98; and abolition of counsellor experiment, 238n91, 252n43; and Cavanaugh, 132; as CHR Deputy Director for Health, 112, 125–26, 131; later career of, 252n42; and Taft, 252n42; and Weinberger, 119, 185, 252n47

Veterans Administration (VA), 9, 108; and CHR, 125–27, 235n56; in the counsellor experiment, 40, 128; and Weinberger, 90. *See also* Department of Veterans Affairs; veterans affairs

veterans affairs, 226n48; in the DHR, 110; and the Human Development Subcommittee, 127; health care benefits of, 125; reduction of costs on, 88, 89, 90; and Weinberger, 89–90, 110, 120, 192. *See also* Department of Veterans Affairs; Veterans Administration

VISTA, 116

Wall Street Journal, 201

War on Poverty, 40

War Production Board (WPB), 204

Warren, Gerald, 143

Washington Evening Star. See *Washington Star*

Washington Post, xi; and the counsellor experiment, 23, 62, 74; and Ehrlichman, 182, 191; on executive reorganization, 46, 61; and Watergate, 70; and Weinberger, 118

Washington Star, 30, 33

Water Resources Council, 2, 174

Watergate, xi, xiii, 118, 228n71; and affect on Nixon's power, 93, 123, 146, 194; and the counsellor experiment, xiii, 17–18, 19, 28, 46–47, 158, 179, 184–87, 249n9; and cover-up, 5, 24, 28, 32, 70, 143, 249n11; Ehrlichman's preoccupation with, 81, 102, 182–83, 227n66, 242n56; Nixon's preoccupation with, 79, 89, 95, 96, 184, 227n66, 250n19. *See also* U.S. Senate: Watergate Committee

Weinberger, Caspar, Jr.: administrative appointment of, 75; and Agnew, 186; and areas of jurisdiction, 108–109, 124–125, 205; and Ash, 79, 100–103, 181, 183, 192; as assistant president, 25, 95, 102, 107, 109, 114, 124, 132, 134, 139, 157, 200, 209; and Brennan, 94, 103, 122, 123, 227n64; and Butz, 51, 97, 170, 171, 175, 193; and Cavanaugh, 122, 129, 130, 132, 226n49; and the CHR committee, 115–116 (*see also* Committee on Human Resources); and Cole, 129–30, 185, 192, 237nn80, 81, 252n41; and coordinative role as counsellor, 71, 108, 205; in the counsellor role, 119–23, 135, 201; and counsellor-to-counsellor relationships, 96–98; and counsellor-to-president reporting, 91–96; and the DC turf war, 95, 129–32, 186; and disbanding of

counsellor experiment, 190, 191–92; and Ehrlichman, 43–45, 78–81, 88, 90, 109, 115, 129, 181, 186, 222n4, 229n98, 241n46, 250n20; and executive privilege, 71, 183, 184, 198; and Haldeman, 117, 215n12; and Hanks, 119; and health policy, 252n47; as HEW secretary, 52, 62, 69, 75, 78, 110, 112–13, 116, 119, 120, 181, 215n27, 224n21, 252nn42, 47; and Human Development Subcommittee, 122, 185; and Kennedy, 221n47; and Legal Services Corporation, 92–93, 120; and Lynn, 96, 139; and manpower revenue sharing, 120–23, 234n40; and the MBO project, 104, 105; and McConahey, 110–14, 121–22, 234n41, 252n47; and meetings with Nixon, 80, **81,** 86, 88–89; and the media, 116–118, 121, 185, 225n41; and O'Neill, 102, 122; and OEOB office, 108–109, 119, 124; as OMB director (*see* Office of Management and Budget; and Weinberger as director, and the Weinberger power struggle); as president's spokesperson for HR, 116–18; and public appearances as HR counsellor, 85, 86, **87;** reporting policies of, 25, 101–103, 111–12, 124, 127–29, 151, 175–76, 181, 183, 187, 200; and Richardson, 124; and roles in Nixon and Reagan administrations, 215–16n27; and self-definition of his role as counsellor, 25, 44, 71, 94–95, 97, 100–101, 107, 108, 109, 112, 120, 126, 132, 200; Senate confirmation of, 69–72, 75, 109, 183, 198; as "super-counsellor," 221n53; ; and super-secretaries, 215n12; and Taft, 110, 114, 120, 227n64; and time devoted to CHR, 119–120; and Vadala, 119, 185, 252n47; and veterans affairs, 89–90, 110, 120, 192; and Watergate, 185, 227n66, 228n71

West, William F., 15–16

Whitaker, John C.: and counsellor experiment, 115; and Fairbanks, 178; and hierarchical status of CHR, 130–31, 162; and Nixon's environmental policies, 88; and NR Committee, 172–73, 175, 176; as undersecretary of Interior, 160, 164, 166, 171

White House (physical structure): East Wing, 204, 254n11; Roosevelt Room, 82, 113, 115, 148; West Wing, 42, 49, 79, 149

White House fellow, 110, 112, 113, 152

White House Health Unit, 82

White House Mess, 82, 171, 193

White House Personnel Office, 164

White House press corps, 45, 58, 116, 121, 167, 182

White House Press Office, 151

White House Press Room, 3, 143

White House Protocol Office, 75

White, Margita, xiii

White, Robert M., 173, 176–77

Widnall, William, 56, 57

Wildavsky, Aaron, 13

Williams, Harrison, 74

Wilson, Rufus, 226n46

Witcover, Jules, 182

Woodward, Bob, 70

Wounded Knee protest, 127

Ziegler, Ron, 40–41, 143, 194; and May 10 (1973) press conference, 189–91, 251n36; and media leaks, 34

Other Books in the Joseph V. Hughes Jr. and Holly O. Hughes Series on the Presidency and Leadership

The Politics of Shared Power: Congress and the Executive, Louis Fisher

Shaping and Signaling Presidential Policy: The National Security Decision Making of Eisenhower and Kennedy, Meena Bose

Games Advisors Play: Foreign Policy in the Nixon and Carter Administrations, Jean A. Garrison

The Managerial Presidency, Second Edition, James P. Pfiffner

Good Advice: Information and Policy Making in the White House, Daniel E. Ponder

Congressional Abdication on War and Spending, Louis Fisher

Vicious Cycle: Presidential Decision Making in the American Political Economy, Constantine J. Spiliotes

Presidents and the People: The Partisan Story of Going Public, Mel Laracey

The Opposition Presidency: Leadership and the Constraints of History, David A. Crockett

The Presidency, Congress, and Divided Government: A Postwar Assessment, Richard S. Conley

The White House World: Transitions, Organization, and Office Operations, edited by Martha Joynt Kumar and Terry Sullivan

Between Law and Politics: The Solicitor General and the Structuring of Race, Gender, and Reproductive Rights Litigation, Richard L. Pacelle Jr.

The Presidency and Women: Promise, Performance, and Illusion, Janet M. Martin

Out of Touch: The Presidency and Public Opinion, Michael J. Towle

Power and Prudence: The Presidency of George H. W. Bush, Ryan J. Barilleaux and Mark J. Rozell

The Character Factor: How We Judge America's Presidents, James P. Pfiffner

The Nerve Center: Lessons in Governing from the White House Chiefs of Staff, edited by Terry Sullivan; foreword by James A. Baker III

Nixon's Business: Authority and Power in Presidential Politics, Nigel Bowles

Saving the Reagan Presidency: Trust Is the Coin of the Realm, David M. Abshire

Policy by Other Means: Alternative Adoption by Presidents, Steven A. Shull

Institutionalizing Congress and the Presidency: The U.S. Bureau of Efficiency, 1916–1933, Mordecai Lee

Scripted for Change: The Institutionalization of the American Presidency, Victoria A. Farrar-Myers

The American Campaign: U.S. Presidential Campaigns and the National Vote, Second Edition, James E. Campbell

Running against the Grain: How Opposition Presidents Win the White House, David A. Crockett

Intelligence and National Security Policymaking on Iraq: British and American Perspectives, edited by James P. Pfiffner and Mark Phythian

Honest Broker? The National Security Advisor and Presidential Decision Making, John P. Burke

The Leadership of George Bush: An Insider's View of the Forty-first President, Roman Popadiuk

Bridging the Constitutional Divide: Inside the White House Office of Legislative Affairs,
  edited by Russell L. Riley
The Unitary Executive and the Modern Presidency, edited by Ryan J. Barilleaux and
  Christopher S. Kelley
The Provisional Pulpit: Modern Conditional Presidential Leadership of Public Opinion,
  Brandon Rottinghaus
White House Politics and the Environment: Franklin D. Roosevelt to George W. Bush,
  Byron W. Daynes and Glen Sussman

DATE DUE

SEP 1 2 2011	